PHILIP PLISSON'S & CELTIC COASTLINES

TEXT BY PATRICK MAHÉ

WITH 102 COLOUR PHOTOGRAPHS

CONTENTS

Barvas
Stornoway
Outer Hebrides
South Uist
Little Minch
Glenfinnan
Iona
SCOTLAND
Edinburgh
Lindisfarne
North Channel
Stranraer
Croagh Patrick
IRELAND
Belfast
ISLE OF MAN
Dun Aengus
Aran Islands
Clonmacnoise
Hill of Tara
Dublin
Irish Sea
GREAT BRITAIN
Anglesey
Liverpool
Glendalough
Llanfairfechan
Machynlleth
WALES
ENGLAND
Coed Llathen
Llandovery
Cardiff
London
Glastonbury
Celtic
Sea
CORNWALL
Penzance
Stonehenge
Carn Euny
English Channel
Brest
Collorec
Landévennec
BRITTANY
Paris
Lorient
ATLANTIC
OCEAN
FRANCE
Bay of
Biscay
Key
Celtic cultural region
Historical site
La Coruña
ASTURIAS
GALICIA
Minho
Citânia de Briteiros
SPAIN
Numantia
PORTUGAL

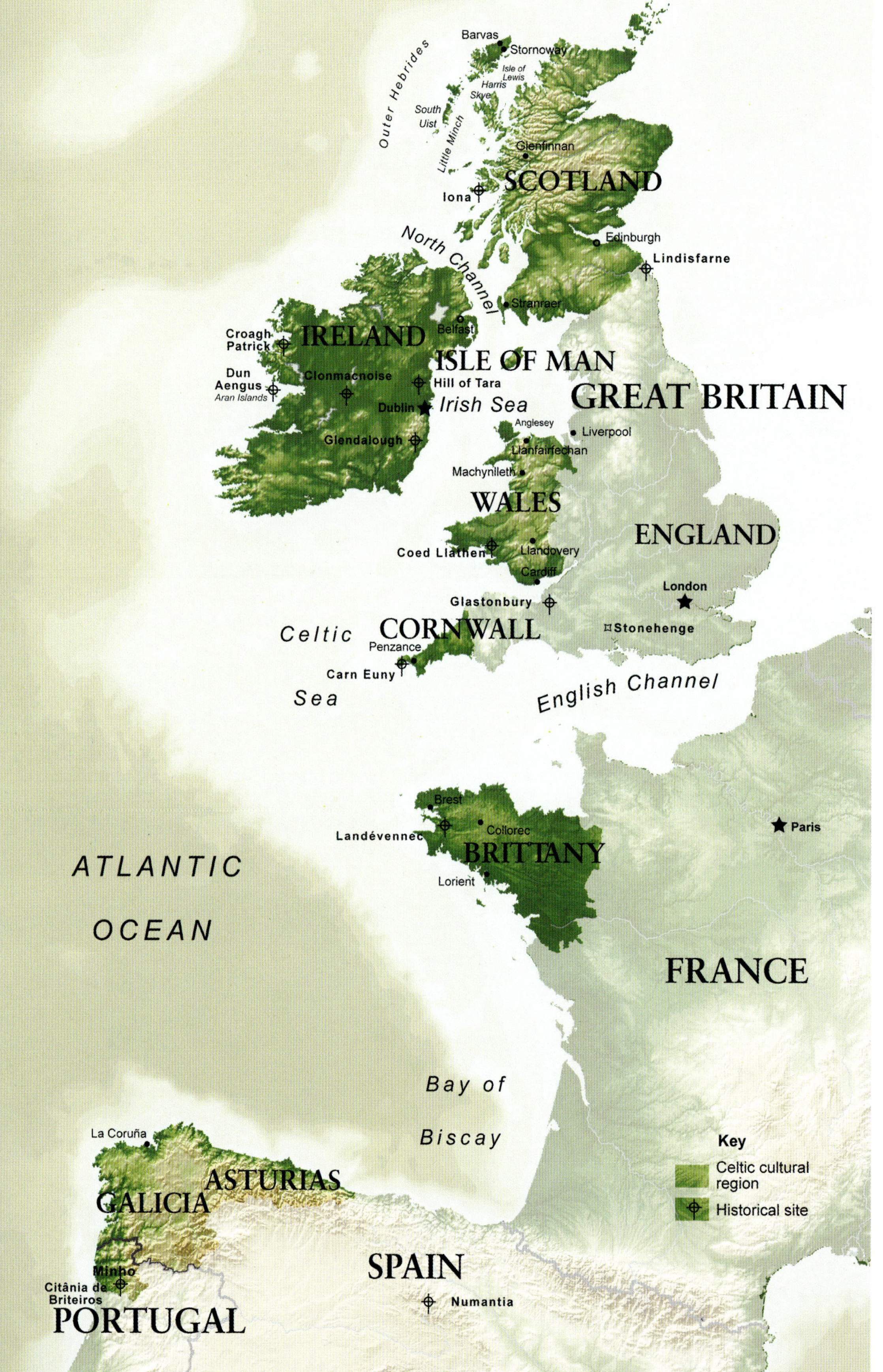

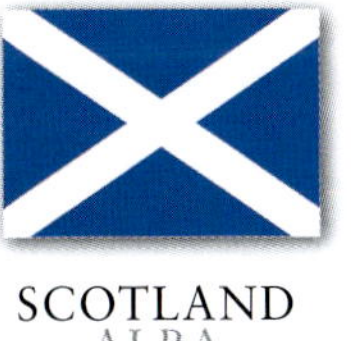

SCOTLAND
ALBA

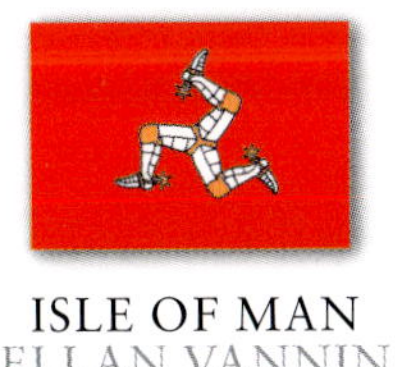

ISLE OF MAN
ELLAN VANNIN

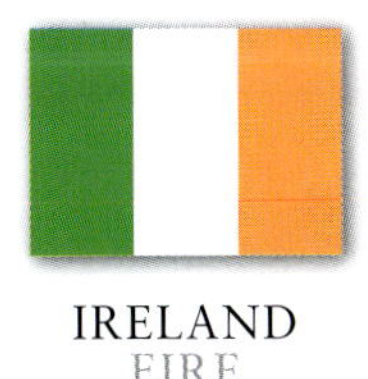

IRELAND
EIRE

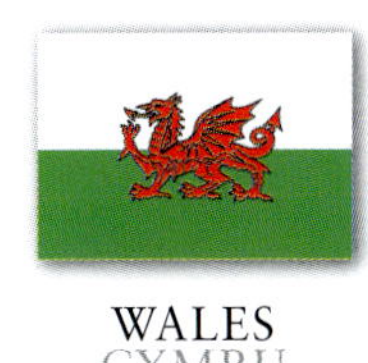

WALES
CYMRU

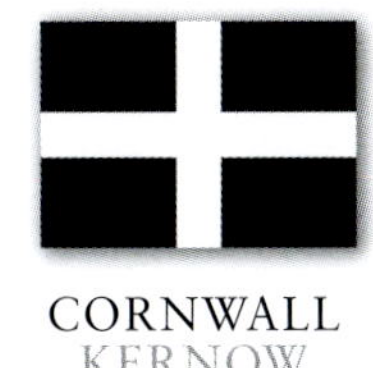

CORNWALL
KERNOW

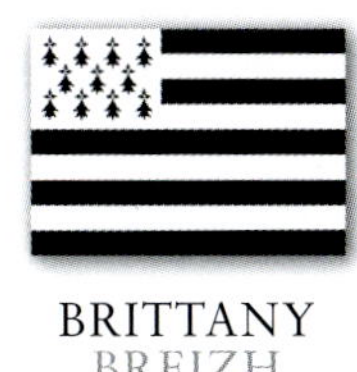

BRITTANY
BREIZH

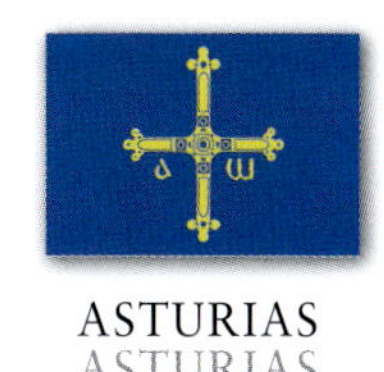

ASTURIAS
ASTURIAS

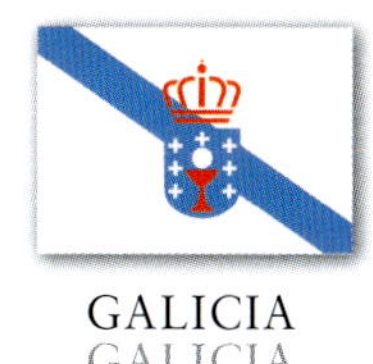

GALICIA
GALICIA

CELTIC SEA · MOR KELTIEK

While the island of Britain managed to repulse the Roman legions and withstand the Viking landings, it was the hordes of Saxons and other Germanic tribes, the Angles and Jutes, who swept down in vast numbers on the South West. Wales, the mountains of Cornwall, part of Devon and the stretch of the Cumberland coast leading to faraway Scotland formed the areas of British resistance. Arthur, the king of a thousand legends, continues to haunt both shores of the Breton Sea, *Mor Breizh*, symbolizing, from the remains of the walls of Caerleon facing the Irish Sea, the immortal hero of a mythical reunification.

In the face of the Saxon invasion, whole clans, later followed by saints and monks, found refuge across the sea. For two centuries, wave upon wave settled in Armorica (the 'land of the sea'), which became present-day Brittany. For fifteen centuries, very strong physical and spiritual links have remained between the peoples on the two shores of the English Channel, known as *La Manche* to the French.

Great Britain and Brittany continue their fraternal festivities in the *Gorsedd* (assemblies of bards), gathering solemnly both sides of the Channel, or in the modern artistic setting of contemporary Pan-Celtic festivals. With neighbouring languages and a common musical heritage, the children of Galicia and Asturias, carried in years gone by on the capricious currents of emigration to the far-off lands of the Iberian peninsula, are now intoxicated with the martial blast of the Scottish and Irish bagpipes and the Breton bands. They all march to the beat of the same drum at popular gatherings, whose staging in the full light of day suggests a dream of reconquest.

Always ready to vent its anger, from feats of arms to heroic surrenders, from glorious celebrations to funeral laments, the wind of History makes the scattered Celts the riders of a marine apocalypse. So many refugees and exiles have crossed the seas, transforming the oceans (*Mor Braz*) into the Celtic sea, *Mor keltiek*.

The six Celtic nations: Brittany, Wales, Cornwall, the Isle of Man, Scotland and Ireland – *'C'hwec'h Bro eun ene'* (Six Nations, One Soul) – plus Galicia and Asturias, have swarmed over the continent, risking the perils of the sea to find their own havens and common roots. Virtues that have faded elsewhere are celebrated here with a single heart and heroes rising from the same root are brought back to life.

This age-old dance of the Celtic peoples, scattered across the seas, calls to us. Where does the Celtic world begin? Each triskelion marks a possible answer.

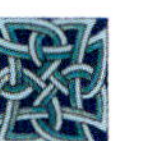

Where does the Celtic world begin?

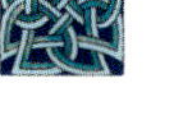

Does it begin in a packed pub in Dublin, where the pounding rhythm of the *bodhran* (a drum struck with a beater) accompanies a round of red ale, where the harp marks the label on a bottle of Guinness the colour of the River Liffey – and where a violin bow brushes against the amber wave of a whiskey from where the souls of the truculent soldier-writer Brendan Behan and all the vanished bards wander? *'Slainte!' 'Yech'ed mat!'*

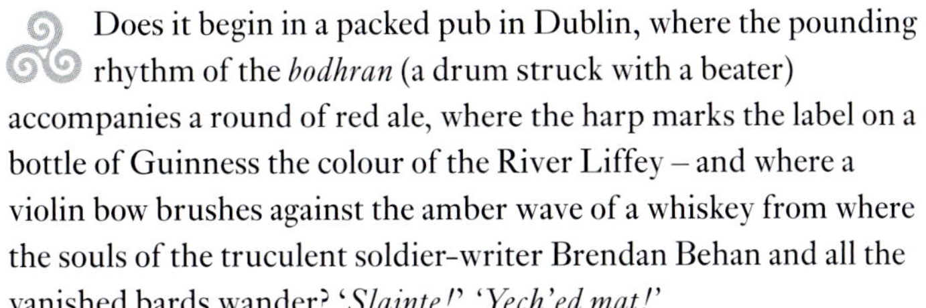

At the Millennium Stadium in Cardiff, where the rugby fans shout themselves hoarse, singing *Hen Wlad Fy Nhadau (Land of My Fathers)* from the first scrum of this sacred event?

In Parkhead in Glasgow, renamed 'Paradise' by fans of Celtic FC, swathed in green scarves embossed with shamrocks and proclaiming in a militant chorus the *Soldier's Song* in the faces of the Bluenoses, their hereditary enemies of Rangers with their allegiance to the British throne and the loyalist lodges of Ulster?

In the peat bogs of Mayo, Sligo, Donegal or Connemara, where Cromwell's rabble of soldiers uttered the cutting epitaph: 'A country where there is not wood enough to hang a man, nor earth enough to bury him'? Nevertheless they still managed to find trees with branches strong enough to use to hang a noose around the necks of travelling musicians, itinerant bards, bagpipe players and clandestine harpists accused of playing seditious tunes.

In the Irish requiem of Ballinamuck, at the end of a failed uprising against the ancient occupier, in the dungeon of Wolfe Tone whose name acted as a talisman for Irish Republicans two hundred years ago? Inspired by the American insurgents driving out the English from the New World in 1796, did this barrister and activist dream two years later of looking down from the masts of the ships of freedom that left Brittany to the sound of Christmas carols and were forced to lie in Bantry Bay due to bad winds? Or in Bonnie Prince Charlie's tragic venture when he set off from Roscoff to take back the crown of the Stuarts of Scotland from the English – again and as always?

In the ditches of Derry in the rebellious north of Ireland, or the heroic trenches of Culloden, just outside Inverness? There, five thousand Highlanders, draped in rich tartan plaids in their clan colours and armed with heavy steel claymores, defied the English cavalry led by the Duke of Cumberland to their last breath.

At Ballon, near the forest of Brocéliande in Brittany, the scene of King Nominoë's defeat of the Frankish archers, or in the funeral lament of Saint-Aubin du Cormier – the Bretons' Culloden – mourning the end of the reign of Francis II, the father of Anne of Brittany?

In the green mountains, grey rocks and rushing streams of the Isle of Skye? Covered with purple moors, it remains a repository of Celtic history. When the sun set over Culloden, it was to Skye that the last troops of the lost clans withdrew. On this island where the Gaelic language refuses to yield to English, bagpipe music is called *pìobaireachd* and whisky *uisge beatha*, and the white cockade of those that history defeated still flies.

In the Gaeltacht on the western edge of Ireland, facing America, the bastion of Gaelic language and Gaelic history, clinging to its rocks? The Uilleann pipes have been played here for centuries, with air provided by bellows worked by the elbow; these pipes now play a part in the magical nights of the Lorient Inter-Celtic Festival in Brittany. For thirty-five years, under the banners of the founding Celtic nations – *C'hwec'h Bro eun ene* (Six Nations, One Soul) – this festival has been a place of fervour.

In the coffin ships used for all the forced migrations, overflowing with Scottish exiles to the southern seas after Culloden who have become today those proud All Blacks who moved from the Jacobite oath to the Maori war cry of New Zealand? Or full of Irish emigrants driven out by the great potato famine in the 19th century? When they landed exhausted and without hope, they had to wander the streets and fight on the quays of Boston and New York where the henchmen of the WASPs (White Anglo-Saxon Protestants) waited for them, coshes in hand.

In the flamboyant St Patrick's Day parades of New York and Chicago where millions of the faithful gather in the streets? Or under San Francisco's Golden Gate where, each 17 March, *Amazing Grace* is played in memory of Joe Sheridan, a barman and magician despite himself who, one freezing evening in 1947 at Shannon airport, invented the recipe for Irish coffee? In a preheated glass, he poured the required measure of Irish whiskey with the reverence given to communion wine. His stroke of genius was to add strong, boiling hot coffee to the alcohol, sweetened with brown sugar. Joe stirred it all up under the winning eye of the red-haired actress Maureen O'Hara and, in a further divine inspiration, slid some lightly whipped cream over the back of an upturned spoon to complete the smoothness of the drink. He let it rest and drew a shamrock of welcome on the cream floating on the surface like the froth on a pint of draught Guinness.

At Giant's Causeway in Ulster, or in Scotland's Mull of Kintyre? Here is the oldest distillery in the world (1604), on the banks of the river of St Columba, one of the founders of Celtic evangelism. Proclaimed a 'Pilgrim for the love of God' and raised to sainthood by his people but not recognized by Rome, he is one of those noble and modest figures who shaped part of Western Europe's common religious heritage.

Under the shoes of a Breton horse or of an Irish wild pony? Or the tanned hull of a *curragh*, a small, rustic sea-going boat? These once criss-crossed the Hebrides and cut through the waves around the lost island of St Kilda in Scotland. Or in the seas around the Blasket Islands, off Connemara? Emerging from a civilization bathed in whiskey, sea spray and beer as black as peat, a work of art sprang forth from these rocky outcrops in the sea – *The Islander*, the life story of the sailor and farmer Tomás Ó Criomhthain. Many storytellers such as Maurice O'Sullivan came from the Blasket Islands, the 'last parish before America'. Like at St Kilda, from where a handful of survivors – men with full beards and women in black blouses bearing small bundles – were evacuated in 1930 to the Scottish mainland after a thousand years of human existence on the edge of the sea cliffs.

In a poem by Kenneth White, the great Scottish writer who settled in Brittany? Or in the odes of Robert Burns, universally celebrated by the Scots, wherever a kilt is worn or a haggis eaten? In a rustic breathless *gwerz* by Xavier Grall, the open-air bard, or Gille Servat's *La Blanche Hermine*, composed in the overheated hideout of the Breton bar Ti-Jos in Montparnasse, in the song of a return *Back to Breizh* by Alan Stivell, bent over his Celtic harp, as distinguished as the swan *An Alarc'h* by Duke John IV, or in the invigorating *Kan Bale Nevenoe* by the profound Glenmor, with his tender heart and granite-like head?:

'Nevenoe, Nevenoe, Nevenoe *Met en deiz e c'hwezho* *Avel menez Arrez...'*	*'Nominoe, Nominoe, Nominoe* *But soon will blow* *The wind from Monts d'Arrée...'*

Glenmor hails us once again in *O Keltia*:

'O Keltia *Lez-Breizh a zo distro* *Ar mor hag an avel* *Sur a gano* *O Keltia, O Keltia...'*	*'Oh Keltia* *Lez-Breizh has returned* *Sea and wind* *Shall sing* *Oh Keltia, Oh Keltia...'*

Milig Ar Skanv, known as Glenmor, both duke and peasant: *Glen* (earth), *Mor* (sea). It says it all. This is how poetic heritage and all the bardic tales of the strolling minstrel of the mountains with his porcelain blue eyes and wild hair drift and take root. He was born among the ruts (*ar vouilhen*) of Maël-Carhaix and right to the end offered a 'table d'hôte' in his triangle of inland Brittany between Rostrenen, Gronvel, Koskerou and his last home in Mellionnec. Brittany's own 'Rocky Mountains', from Roc'h Trevezel to Roc'h Tredudon: the Breton highlands, worn smooth by millennia flirt with the hills from which rise rocky outcrops as sharp as scythes.

With 'Jean-François de Nantes' (the definitely Breton capital of the Duchy), the lament of Jean Quéméneur (from the Rue de Siam to Recouvrance) or the 'Marins de Groix' (the Sailors of Groix)? Or in the sea shanties of the Belfast or Dublin sailors? Or else in the lament of the Glasgow crews sailing from the River Clyde to all the New Worlds, until the sun set on empires?

In the James Joyce, a pub in Paris, its dream of Ireland based on the original manuscripts of *Ulysses* (1922), the author's masterpiece? There we may bump into strangers or brothers, sharing a drop of Jameson's or Paddy's at the counter, savouring a text by Yeats, and on the second round a line from Beckett as a bonus: 'Are you English?' asked an impudent reporter. 'Quite the contrary,' he answered. That line is the signal for a new round: *Me mes tra!* (Let's do it again!). Glasses are still raised there to the posthumous health of Padraig Pearse, a hero of the bloody Easter Rising of 1916 in Dublin – all this amid commemorative plaques stuck up on the walls between two posters bearing the Celtic cross of the G.A.A. – the Gaelic Athletic Association (Gaelic football and hurling) – and a recording of the TV commentary on Celtic's latest victory over Rangers shown in a continuous loop.

With a whisky in hand? Its history is far from cut and dried. Do you want whisky or whiskey? Scotch or Irish? Kentucky Bourbon or Tennessee Whiskey? Glen (valley) or mhor (sea)? A bar or a pub? Lounge or saloon bar? Rock, folk, blues or country music? Whisky conquered the planet in the wake of the Highland regiments, seventy years after the defeat of Culloden. Even American bourbon owes the founding secrets of its manufacturing process to the ancestral and clandestine *poitín* or *poteen* of the Scotch Irish who landed from Ulster in the 18th century. Each bottle bears its own proud crest and colours.

On the Hill of Tara – royal Tara – in Ireland, or in front of the 'Stone of Destiny', a kind of ancient Grail? By the standing stones of Stenness or Callanish, where the cult of the solstice was celebrated, the Broch of Gurness, the ruins of the monastery on Eynhallow Island – all pearls of Orkney? On the promontories of Skye, the cairns of Ireland, the cromlechs of Brittany, the menhirs of Carnac, or the Gavrinis tumulus in the gulf of Morbihan? In the Breton legend of the vanishing village of Ys, the mourning of King Gradlon and the punishment of Dahut, the 'pagan' princess, marking the end of the ancient civilization as it turned to the teachings of St Winwaloe or Corentin, the Bishop of Quimper? Its mysteries survive in the stones, trees and waters, from the Baie des Trépassés (Bay of the Dead) to the Pointe du Raz and as far as the Aber Wrac'h promontories. From the string of islands in the west of Brittany – Sein, Ouessant and Molène – sometimes on starry nights come bardic dreams, in which the mind's eye sees the glow of the Irish pubs in Boston lighting up the horizon. Never fear, even if the *bag ar noz*, the night boat steered by the Ankou, the reaper of souls, is on the lookout for men stumbling home. Is it in the chaos of Huelgoat – its silver river where the roar of the water covers the cries of the damned? In the druidic forests or the Troménie in Locronan? In the shale hollow of the Val-sans-Retour (Valley of No Return) in the forest of Brocéliande, its 'Fairies' Mirror', fountain of youth, the knights of the Round Table, the megalithic tomb of the Giants or Merlin's rock of eternal rest?

'In misfortune and pain
Duchess Anne became queen
Believing that royalty
Would save her fine duchy
It was not what she wanted
Kaoc'h ki gwenn ha kaoc'h ki du'

Is it in the *Tro Breizh* or pilgrimage of Anne of Brittany defying her husband, the king of France, in 1505, in a tour of Brittany lasting a hundred days in the service of the threatened monarchy – more than a quarter of a century before the act of union of 1532?

Does it lie in the neverending legend of King Arthur, wherever his true origins lay? When he returned from Cornwall, Wales or the Isle of Man, armed with his magical sword Excalibur, King Arthur wished to rest there among the hills of the Scottish lowlads. He chose the summits of the Eildon Hills to gaze over his Celtic kingdom. One researcher, sifting through the Arthurian legends, located another Brocéliande in a place called Brekilien, not far from Carhaix. It seems that Arthur, the magician Merlin – having escaped from his invisible prison – and Vivien, the wily fairy of Barenton fountain in Paimpont, met up there after a battle in the 5th century. On firmer ground, the myth takes us back to the mythical Avalon. From this imagined or imaginary island, the fairy folk gallop across the Celtic nations – Wales, Cornwall, Brittany and their Gaelic cousins – Ireland, Scotland and Isle of Man – glorifying the return of the prodigal king gathering the scattered Celtic people under his crown to the sound of harps.

On Route 66, in the steps of Jack Kerouac, poet, writer and father of the Beat Generation, who went off, alone in his mind, to the threshold of death in search of his Breton roots? His maternal grandmother's name was Le Bris. He set off from New York by sea, and when he arrived in Brest, his *Penn Ar Bed*, the end of the world and of his own life, he devoured all the pages of the phone book, spent a fortune in telephone tokens in vain, and set off again, heavy of misfortune, more of a 'heavenly tramp' than ever, with the wind at his heels towards his transatlantic *bag ar noz* and the Ankou watching out for him.

In the cinema, with *Braveheart* or *Barry Lyndon*, or John Ford's *The Quiet Man* with John Wayne and Maureen O'Hara? Or in the music of the mystical and fantastic Sinead O'Connor choosing a Breton label 'for the cause'? From the Dubliners to the Wolfe Tones, the Chieftains to the Corries, the Pogues to U2 (*Sunday Bloody Sunday*), from Elvis Presley, the great-grandson of exiles from Culloden, reviving *Amazing Grace* in memory of his ancestors, from Dan Ar Braz for *L'Héritage des Celtes* to the pipe bands of Edinburgh or Nova Scotia, from the triumphant *bagadou* (bands) of Brittany – Kevrenn Alre, Bagad Kemper, Lokoal-Mendon, Brest Saint Mark – to the *gaiteros* of Galicia like Carlos Nuñez or the thrilling Susana Seivane, from the dancers of *Riverdance* to the Welsh harpists and choirs, from those who love Irish jigs or Scottish reels, the *ceilidhs* or the *Fest Noz*?

With Gareth Edwards, captain of the Welsh rugby team, refusing to walk out onto the pitch at the Parc des Princes in 1975 if, when the national anthems were to be played, they did not replace 'bloody' *God Save the Queen* with *Land of Our Fathers*? With the Scottish rugby team later imposing its *Flowers of Scotland* in the solemnity of Murrayfield, at the gates of Edinburgh Castle? With Bill Millin playing his bagpipes amongst the hail of bullets when he landed on 6 June 1944? With Sean MacBride, a former chief of staff of the IRA in 1930, who later became Assistant General Secretary of the UN and founded Amnesty International ?

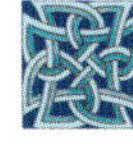

Where does the Celtic world end?

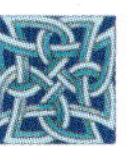

It never ends. It spins endlessly, like a triskelion. Its year begins on 17 March. Amid the excitement and festivity of a worldwide *ceilidh*, St Patrick oversees its rebirth from the mists of the Aran Islands to Queensland, Australia. Night still envelops Cape Cod, below Boston, the capital of the New World Irish when, somewhere beyond the Great Barrier Reef, the day first dawns that will turn into a sleepless night under a banner of Irish green. Green, green, green – the whole world is green. Everywhere, in a breath of solidarity, the same music brings fresh new hope alive in everyone.

AR BED KELTIEK – THE CELTIC WORLD • A WORLD ON WHICH THE SUN NEVER SETS

PATRICK MAHÉ

SCOTLAND·ALBA

At the northernmost tip of Scotland, Orkney and Shetland form a constellation of around a hundred and seventy islands. Only a fifth of this jigsaw puzzle of islands is populated. It is more jagged than the Hebrides, the natural shield for the west coast which is thus protected from storms. Some 20,000 people live in Orkney and some 22,000 in Shetland – weathered by the sea spray and malted like good grain – and all rivals in brotherly Celtic blood.

This is the point where Scotland begins. It is said that these people are descended from 'Ultima Thule', a name that the ancients gave to the remotest, most northerly place they could imagine. Some believe that this means Shetland, tiny vestiges of some engulfed Atlantis, 50 miles from the Scottish mainland. 'Not at all,' retort their neighbours and rivals from Orkney. Facing the breathtaking promontory overhanging the sea, which answers to the name of John O'Groats and whose cliffs gradually turn pink at sunset, is the obelisk of the Old Man of Hoy, a 450-foot needle of rock planted in the sea, higher than the first level of the Eiffel Tower. Gazing out over the immensity of the Atlantic Ocean, this timeless old man keeps watch under the stars. He is the last sentinel of the West, a stony watchman, the last monument of a land seeking a return of sovereignty since it was annexed, three hundred years ago, as a result of the Act of Union of 1707 between England and Scotland.

Scotland's distinctiveness is clear in the complexity and pride of these small island societies. When independence was threatened, they fought in the name of the rebels: Rob Roy, William Wallace, Robert Bruce, and Bonnie Prince Charlie, the last of the Stuarts. Paradoxically, when the British Empire ruled the seas under the Union Jack, the flag which is a synthesis of those of the constituent nations of the 'United Kingdom', many Scots fought in the front line, as if the eternal spirit of the clans justified the continuing pursuit of glory, even for the benefit of a different crown. All that remains of the assaults of these lost soldiers in their richly coloured tartans is the echo of the bagpipes around a world on which the sun never sets. Today there has been a resurgence of the blue and white saltire (the Scottish flag bearing the cross of St Andrew), relegating the Union Jack to the museum of British nostalgia, and the strains of *Flower of Scotland* have now made *God Save the Queen* seem a distinctly foreign anthem.

Noble Scotland – *Alba*, in Gaelic – is captured here in images by Philip Plisson, the master photographer of the sea. The concept was the brainwave of Éric Tabarly, one evening during a great naval parade in Brest in 1996. As a result, from the scattered islands of the far north to the basalt heritage site in the south, near the Mull of Kintyre, Philip trawled along the coast in his 42-foot boat, 'fishing for pictures', camera slung across his shoulder, through ocean mists, between inlets and estuaries, makeshift harbours and rocks swept by the fiercest winds. Scotland, land of the sea. A land in touch with the sea – and sliced across by the Caledonian Canal, which connects the lochs with their dark mysteries. To the west are the Highlands; to the south, the Lowlands. Even back in the days of the Romans, they knew that conquest of this land was impossible.

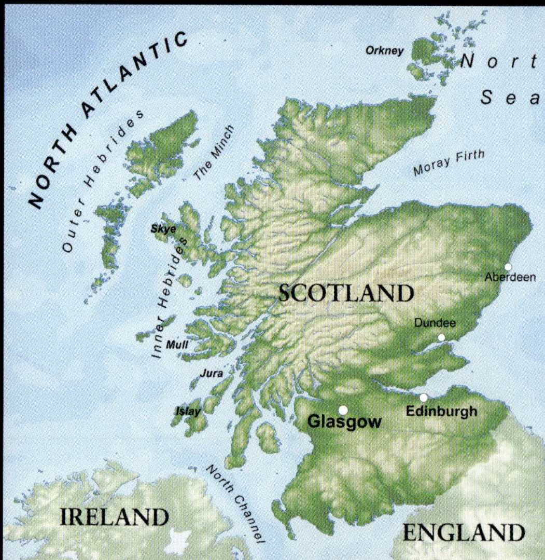

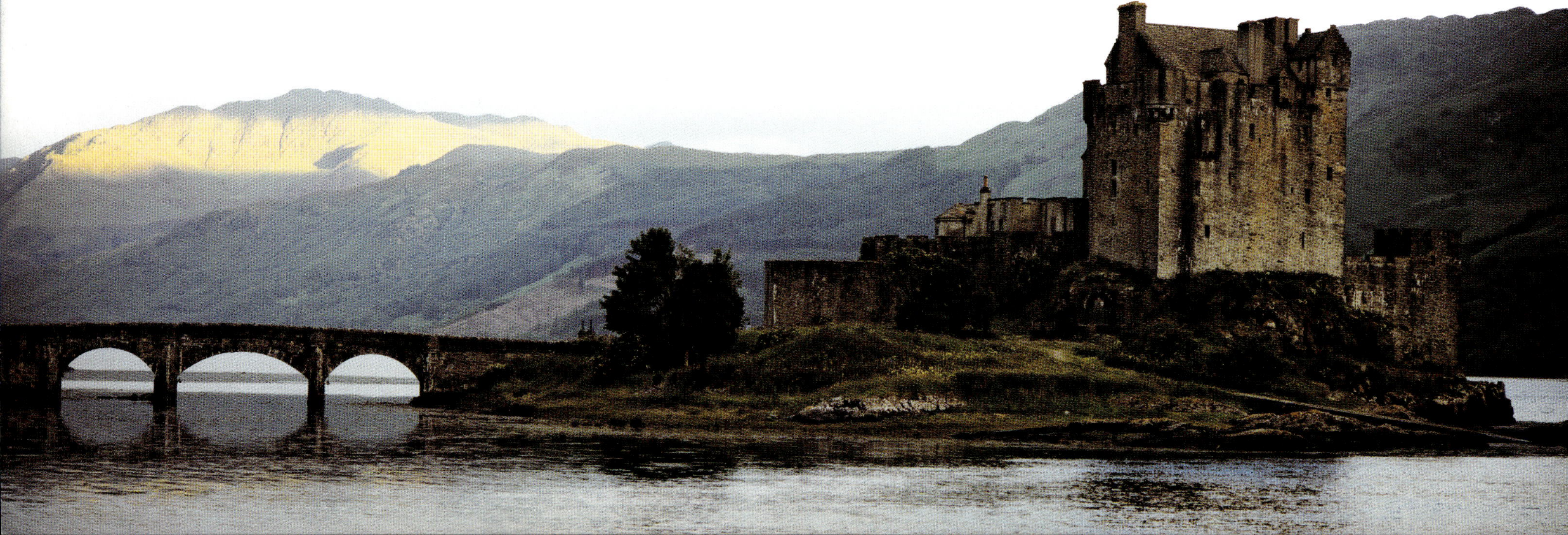

Opposite: Eilean Donan, a symbol of Scottish sovereignty. The first castle was built here in the 13th century, at the meeting point of three lochs, on the main route to the Isle of Skye.

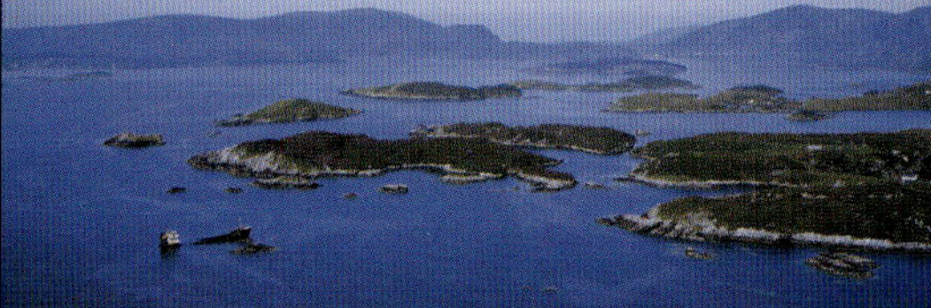

THE PITILESS SEAS
Between Lewis and Harris, twin islands in the Hebrides, battered by the westerly winds, lies the wreck of a cargo ship which had run onto the reef proving that the sea is pitiless.

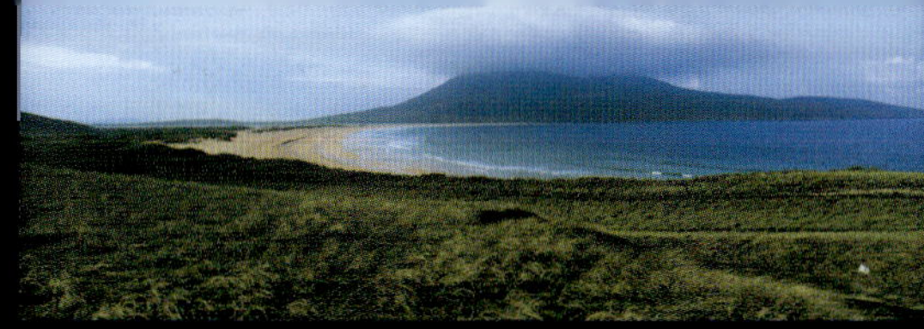

THE WESTERN SHIELD
The view from Harris, with island peaks on the horizon; distant lands, rising from the ocean. Beyond Skye, a hub of Gaelic history, the Hebrides shield Scotland's west coast. The port closest to Harris and Lewis is the fishing town of Ullapool.

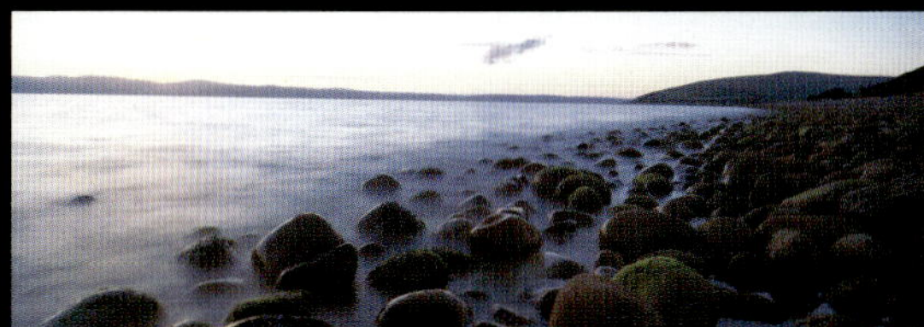

A LAND IN MINIATURE
The Isle of Arran – not to be confused with the similarly named Irish islands of Aran – lies at the mouth of the River Clyde which goes up to Glasgow. The bards declare that this maritime Eden near the Kintyre peninsula in the south-west is 'A miniature Scotland with one hundred kilometres of coastline'.

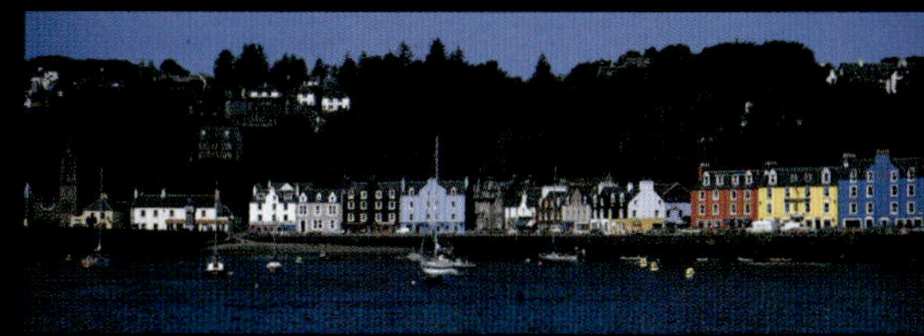

RAINBOW HOUSES
This quay lined with colourful houses and this green hill overlooking the port of Tobermory, in the north-east of the island of Mull, was the last port of call of scientist and explorer Jean-Baptiste Charcot, who went off to conquer the Arctic in 1936, but never returned.

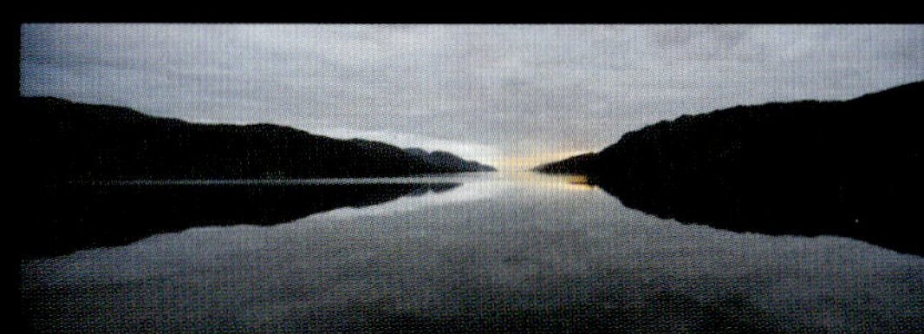

THE MAGIC OF LOCH NESS
The mystery of Loch Ness. Dawn breaks, casting its silver light over the enigma and magic of the Caledonian Canal – from the Roman name of Scotland, Caledonia – lined with conifers planted in the 19th century. It seems as if the legendary monster could loom up at any moment at the foot of Castle Urquhart.

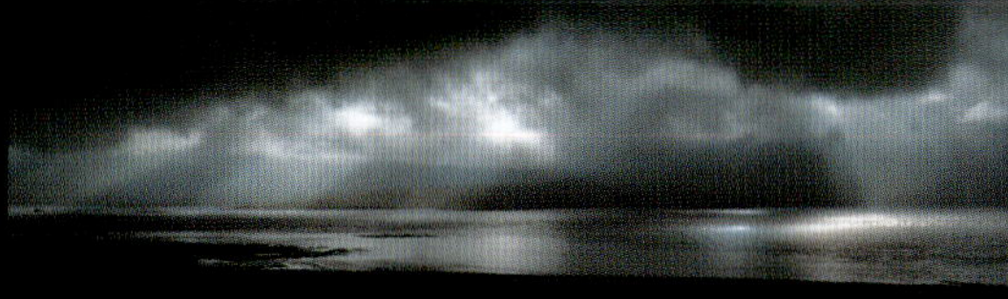

OCEAN HEADLAND
This is the entrance to the natural harbour of Scapa Flow. Beyond it lies the ocean. We are in the far north of Orkney, separated from Shetland by a 12-hour ferry journey from the port of Stromness. Ocean squalls lash the island of Hoy, the last promontory on the western side.

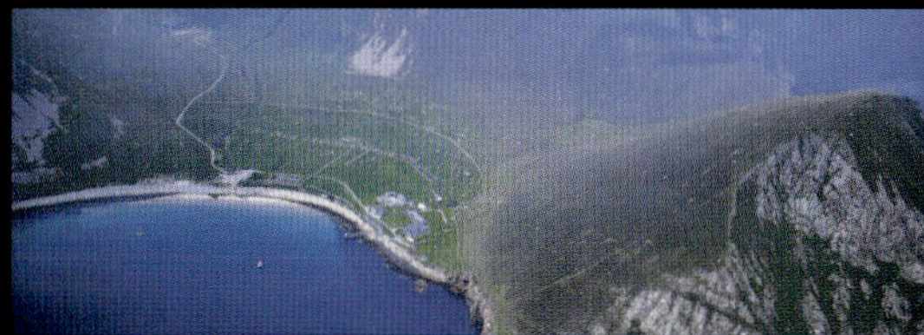

THE ABANDONED ISLAND
The tiny island of St Kilda stands planted like a rocky pyramid in the middle of the sea, some forty miles further west of the Outer Hebrides. The last thirty-seven inhabitants were forcibly evacuated from this harsh, isolated landscape in 1930. Only the ruins of their houses remain.

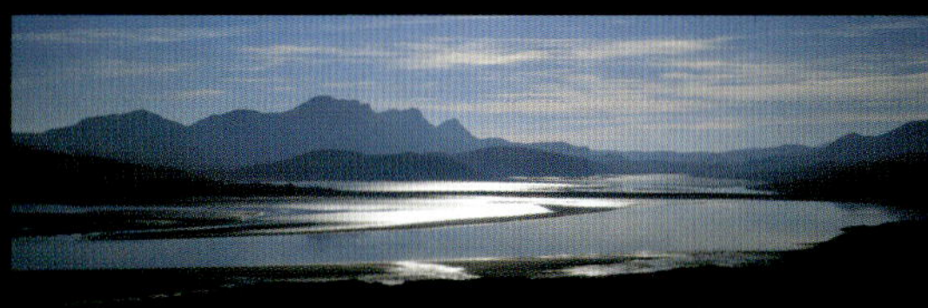

SILVER BEACHES
The sandy beaches sparkle under the sun as it moves, at dawn and at dusk, across the whole length of Tongue Bay, the pearl of the north-east coast, and the roof of the Scottish Highlands, often lacking natural shelters.

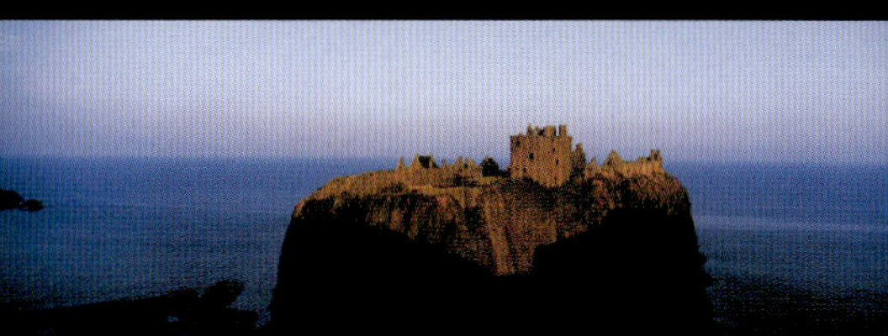

BRAVEHEART
Dunnottar Castle, south of Stonehaven, is to the north-east coast what Eilean Donan Castle is to the west. Built overhanging the sea, the castle was the site of a victory for the Scottish forces, led by William Wallace, over the English in the late 13th century. It remains a symbolically invincible citadel.

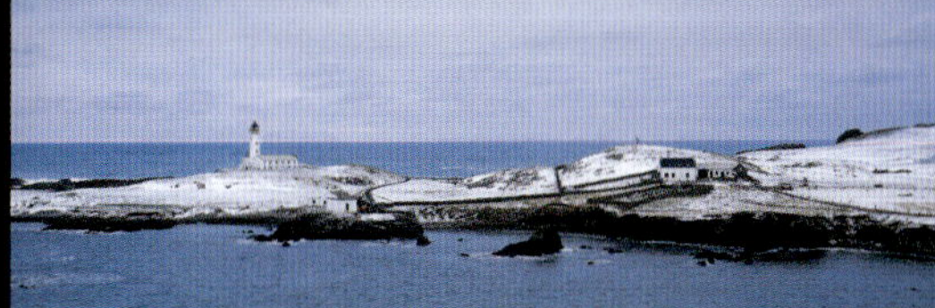

A PRINCESS'S GREETING
Fair Isle lies halfway between Shetland and Orkney. When Philip Plisson flew over the isolated island where twenty families scratch a living, it was being visited by Princess Anne, the patron of the Northern Lighthouse Board, to celebrate the automation of Fair Isle South, the last manned lighthouse in Great Britain.

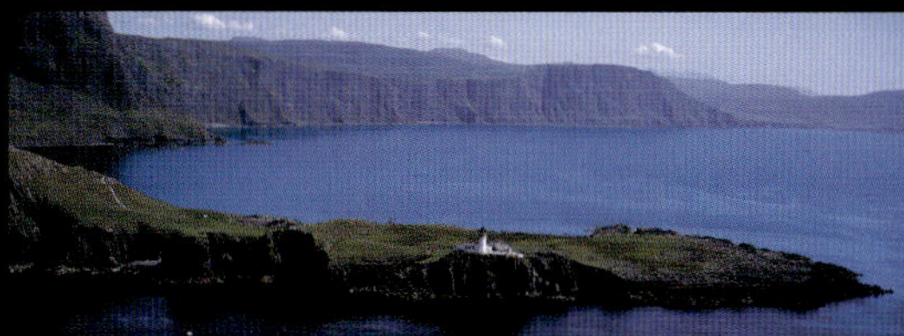

SOVEREIGN ISLE OF SKYE
With Bonnie Prince Charlie's ill-fated campaign, the Isle of Skye saw the end of the Jacobite dream. It is a repository of the Gaelic language and traditions. This is Neist Point, on the western side of the island. The three lighthouse keepers' houses have become B&Bs, half an hour's walk from the foot of the cliffs.

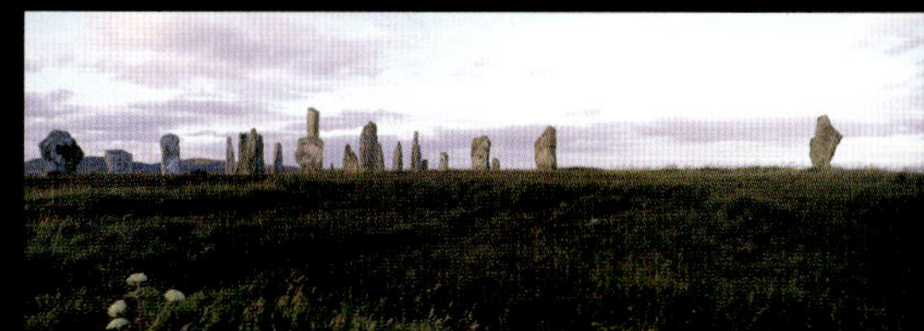

DRUID RITES
Lewis is the sister island of Harris. Facing the vast Atlantic Ocean, the cross-shaped group of standing stones at Callanish (or Calanais) have stood for four thousand years and are thought to have been used for astronomical observations. They are still used for pagan celebrations at the summer solstice (21 June).

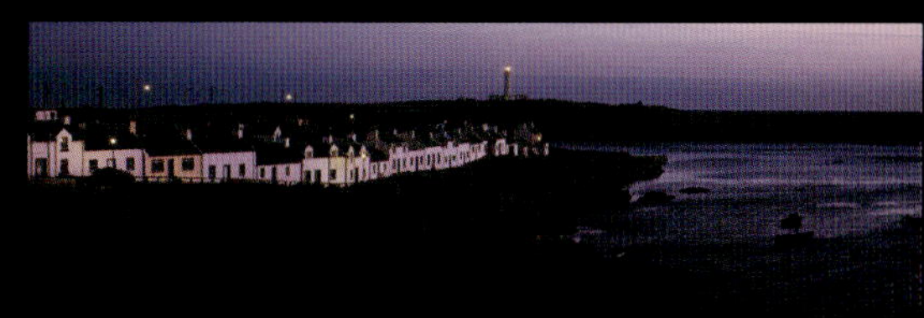

A WARMING WELCOME
Islay (pronounced 'eye-luh') looks across the sea to Ireland and is home to the most peaty whiskies, which may be found in the pubs of Port Ellen and the harbour of Portnahaven. The latter is watched over by the Rinns of Islay lighthouse, not far from the Mull of Kintyre, immortalized by Paul McCartney.

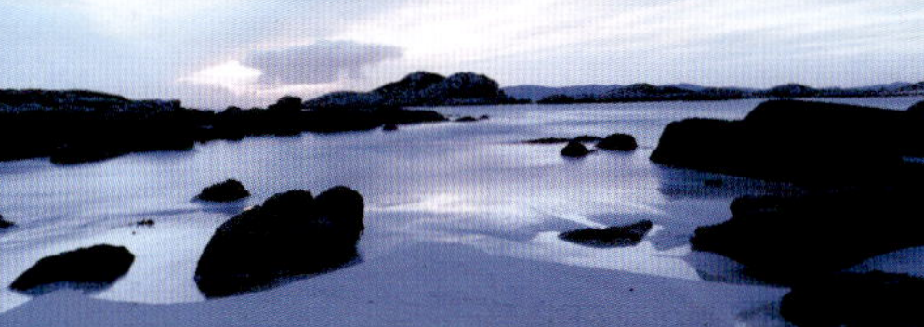

FISHING FOR PICTURES
From loch to loch and estuary to estuary, as here at the mouth of the River Clyde, timeless Scotland is an open invitation to any photographer 'fishing for pictures' to capture the beauty of its natural heritage.

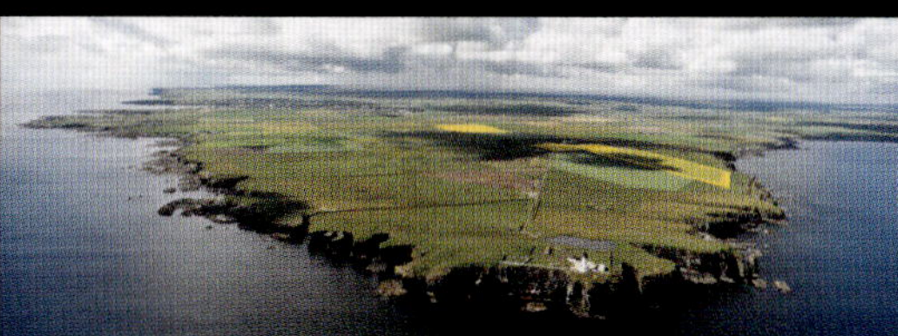

THE PROW OF SCOTLAND
This is Duncansby Head, jutting into the sea, its jagged cliffs forming the north-east prow of Scotland. With Castle Sinclair Girnigoe and the port of John O'Groats, where ferries leave for Orkney, this is a spectacular, vertiginous landscape, matching Cape Wrath at the far north-west corner of the Scottish mainland.

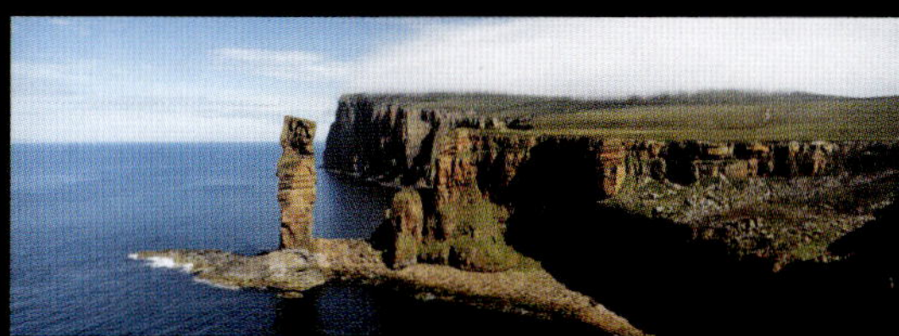

'FINIS TERRAE'
Here is the point where the land comes to an end. This is the Old Man of Hoy – an obelisk of rock, 450 feet high, standing guarc against the vast Atlantic like a sentinel. Hoy is the second largest o the Orkney islands.

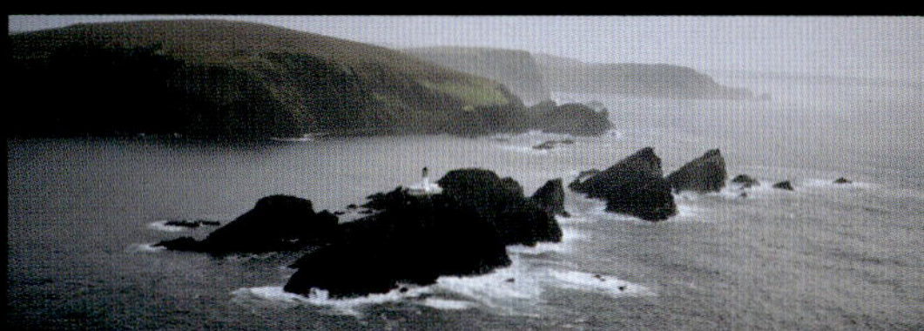

SHETLAND'S END
Just as Land's End is the southernmost point of Great Britain in Cornwall, Muckle Flugga, rising up from a chain of rocky islands, is the northernmost point of Scottish soil, north of Unst in the Shetlands. Its lighthouse, built in 1854 by Thomas Stevenson, has been fully automated since 1995.

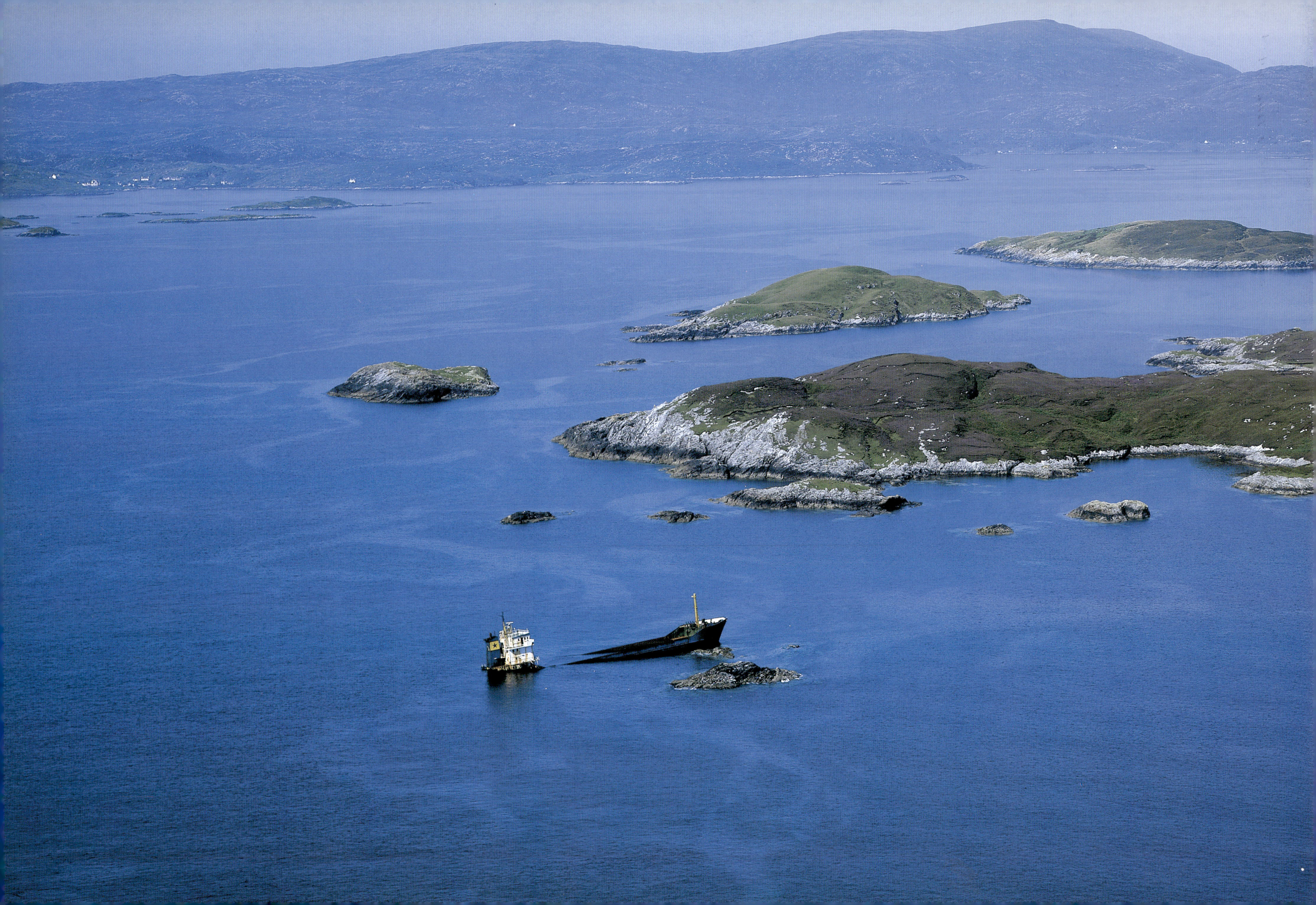

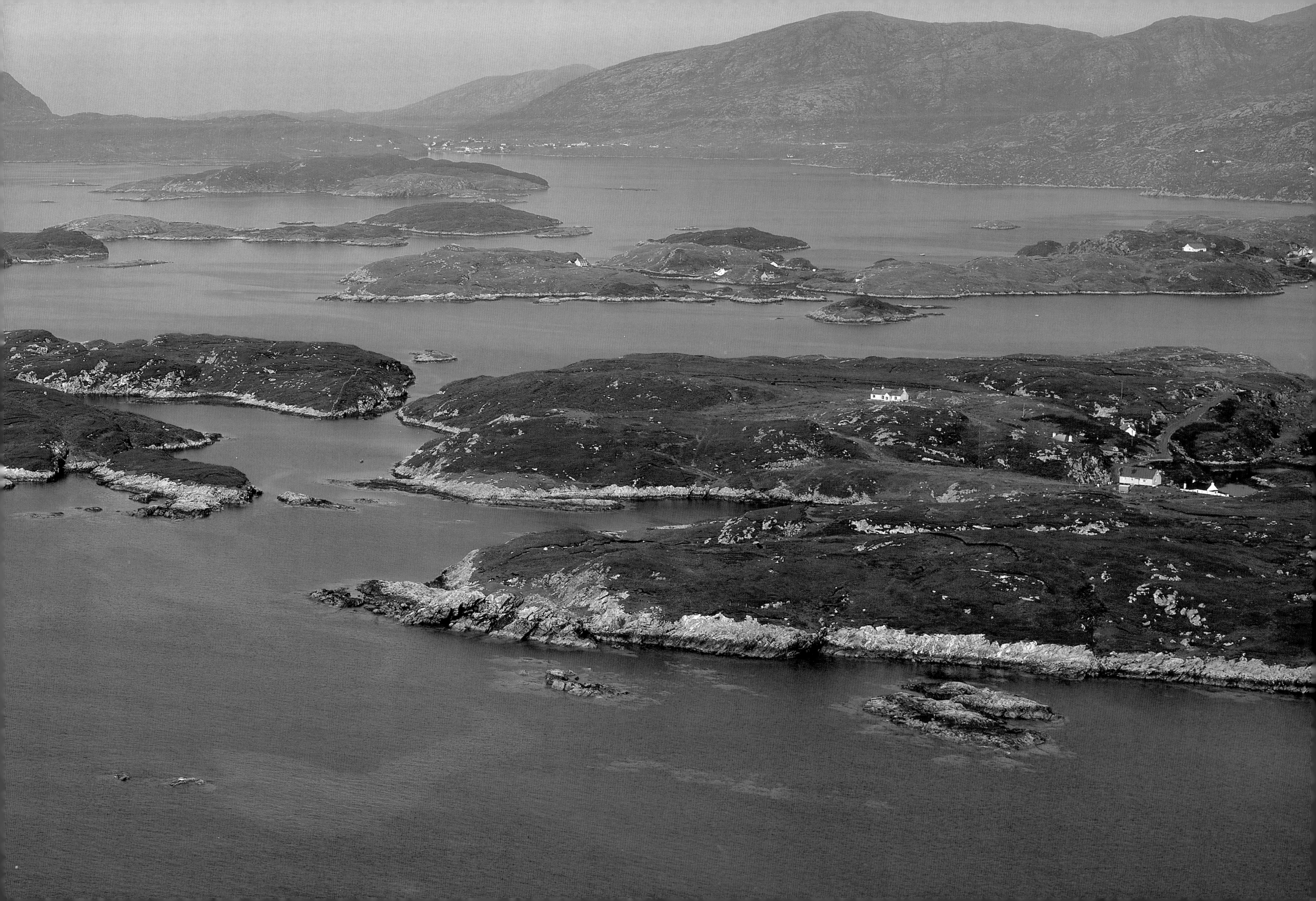

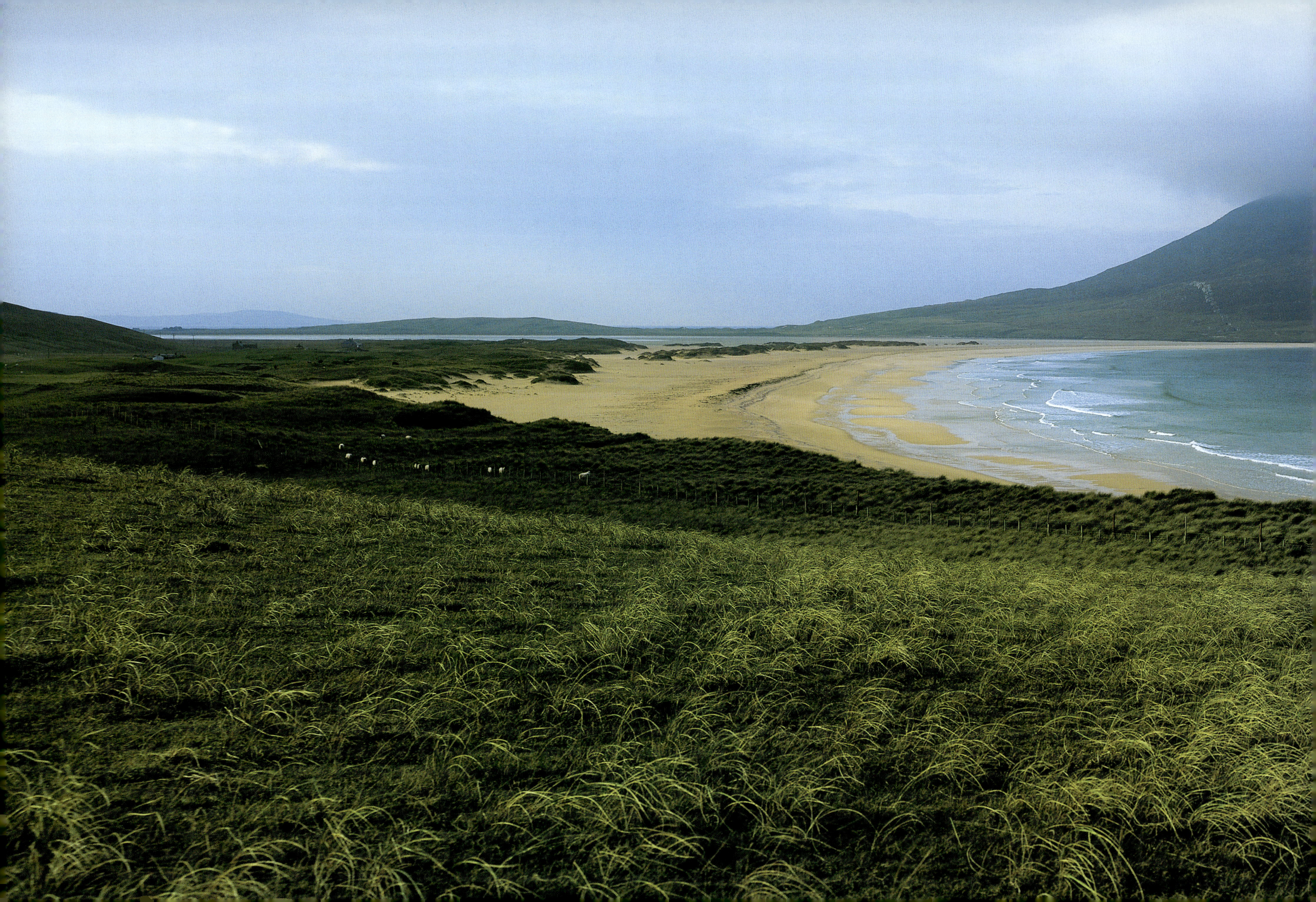

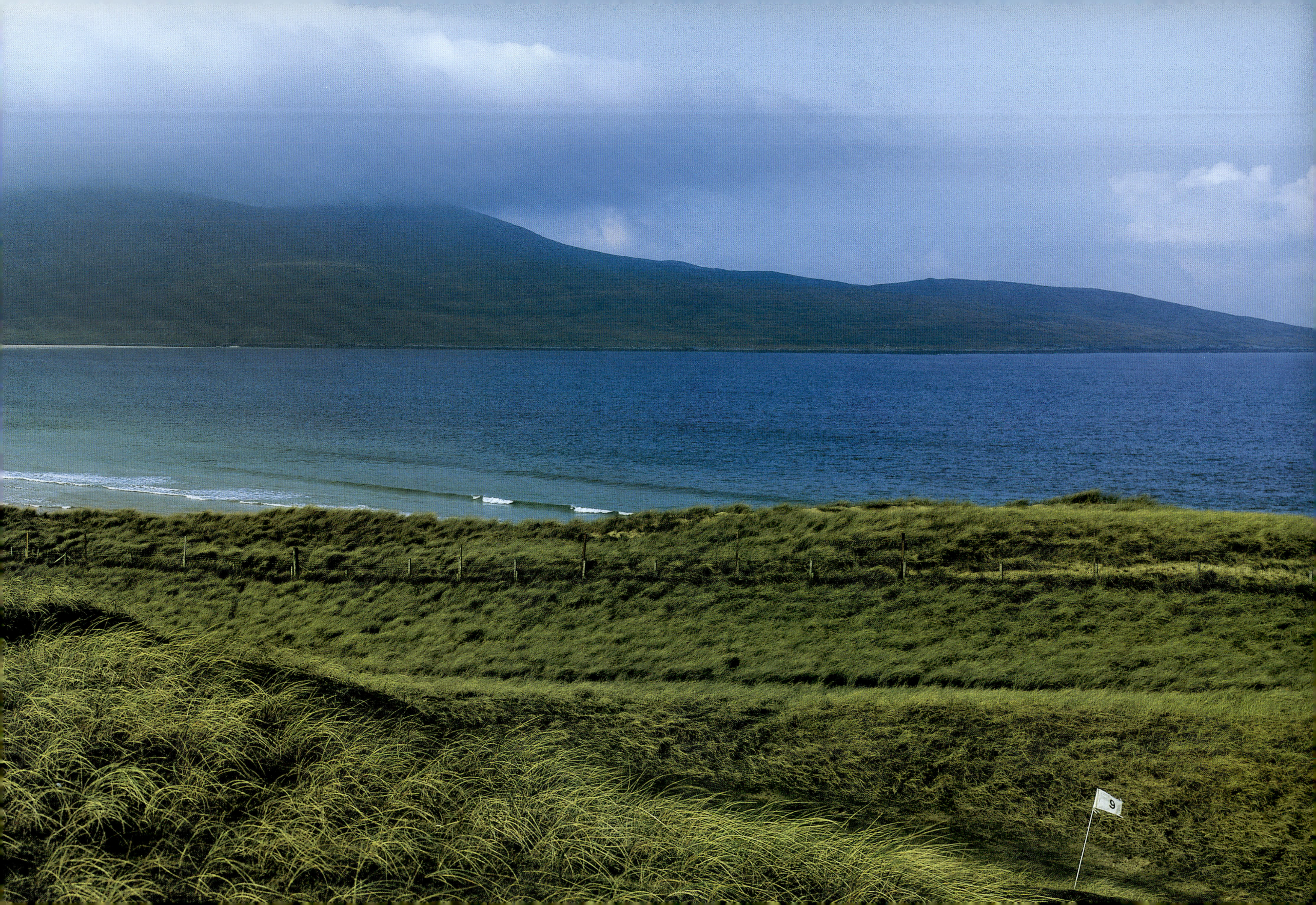

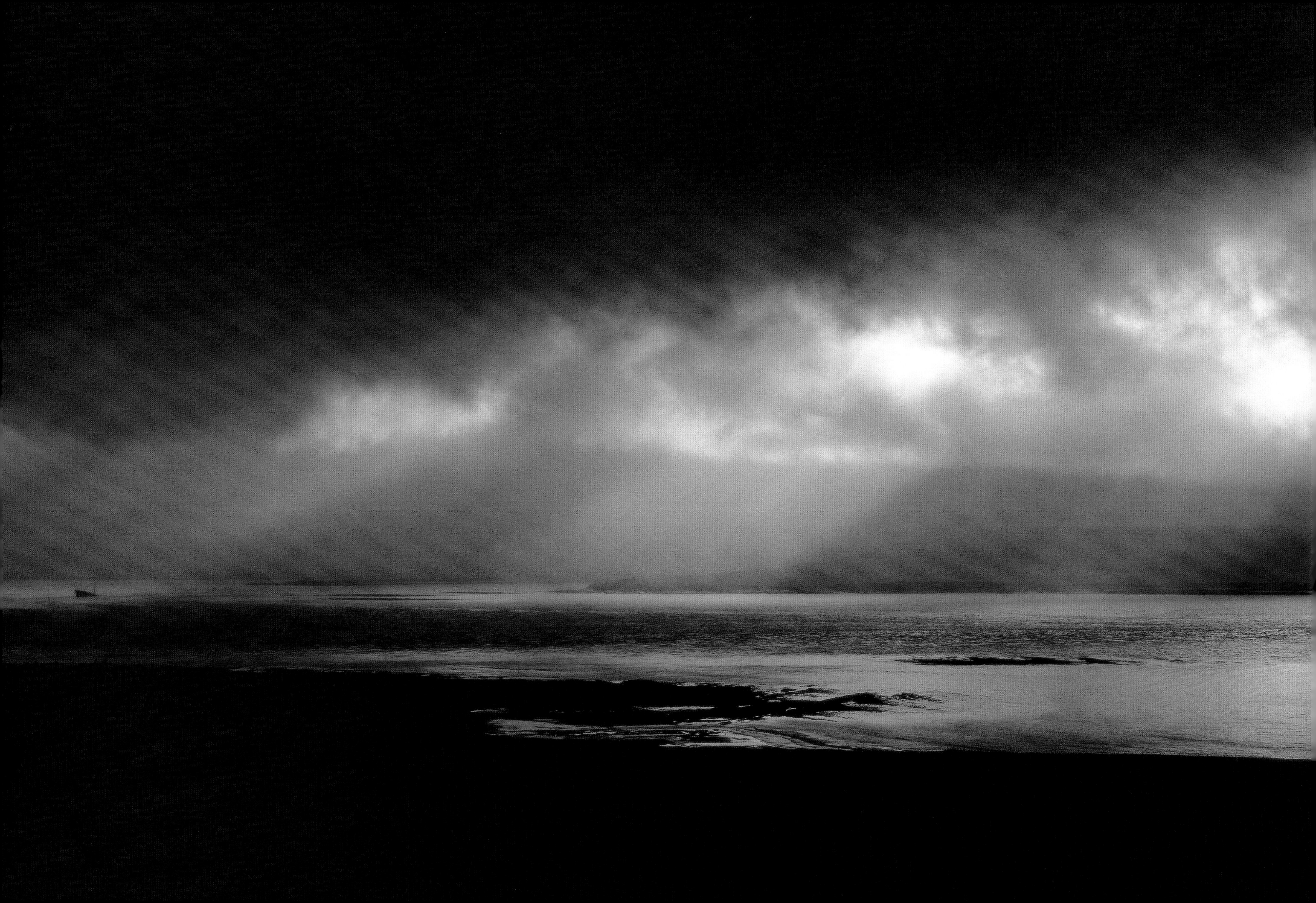

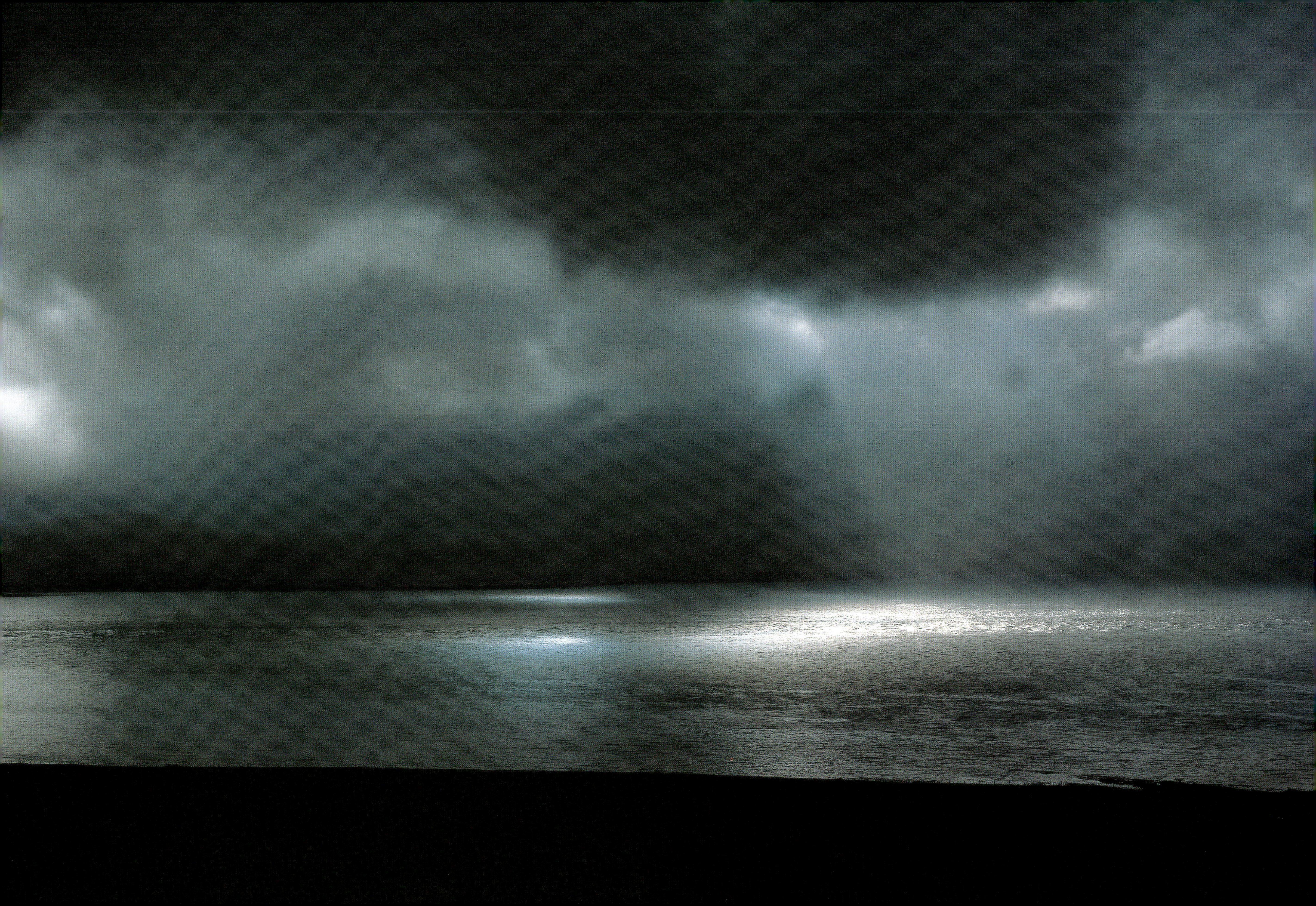

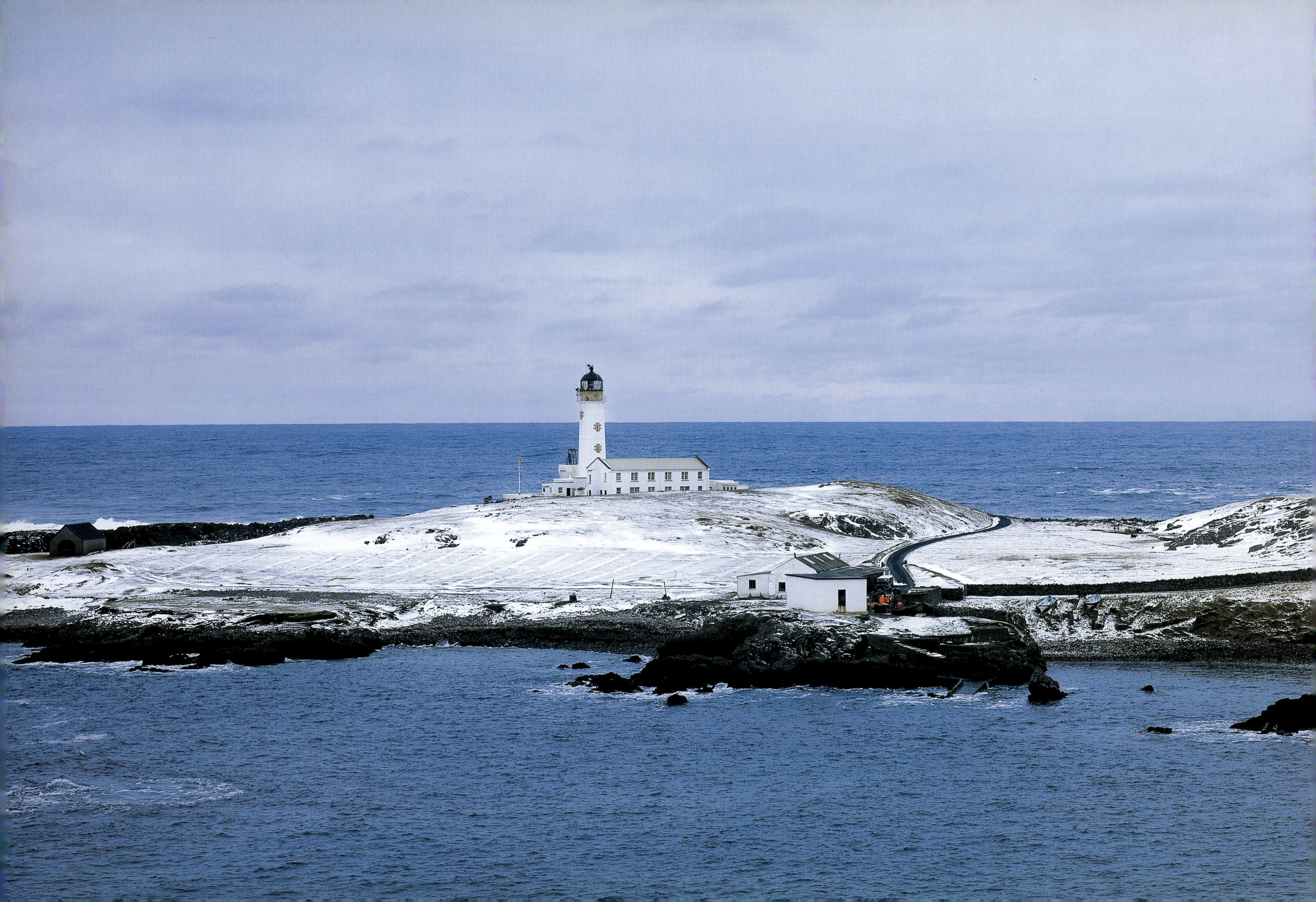

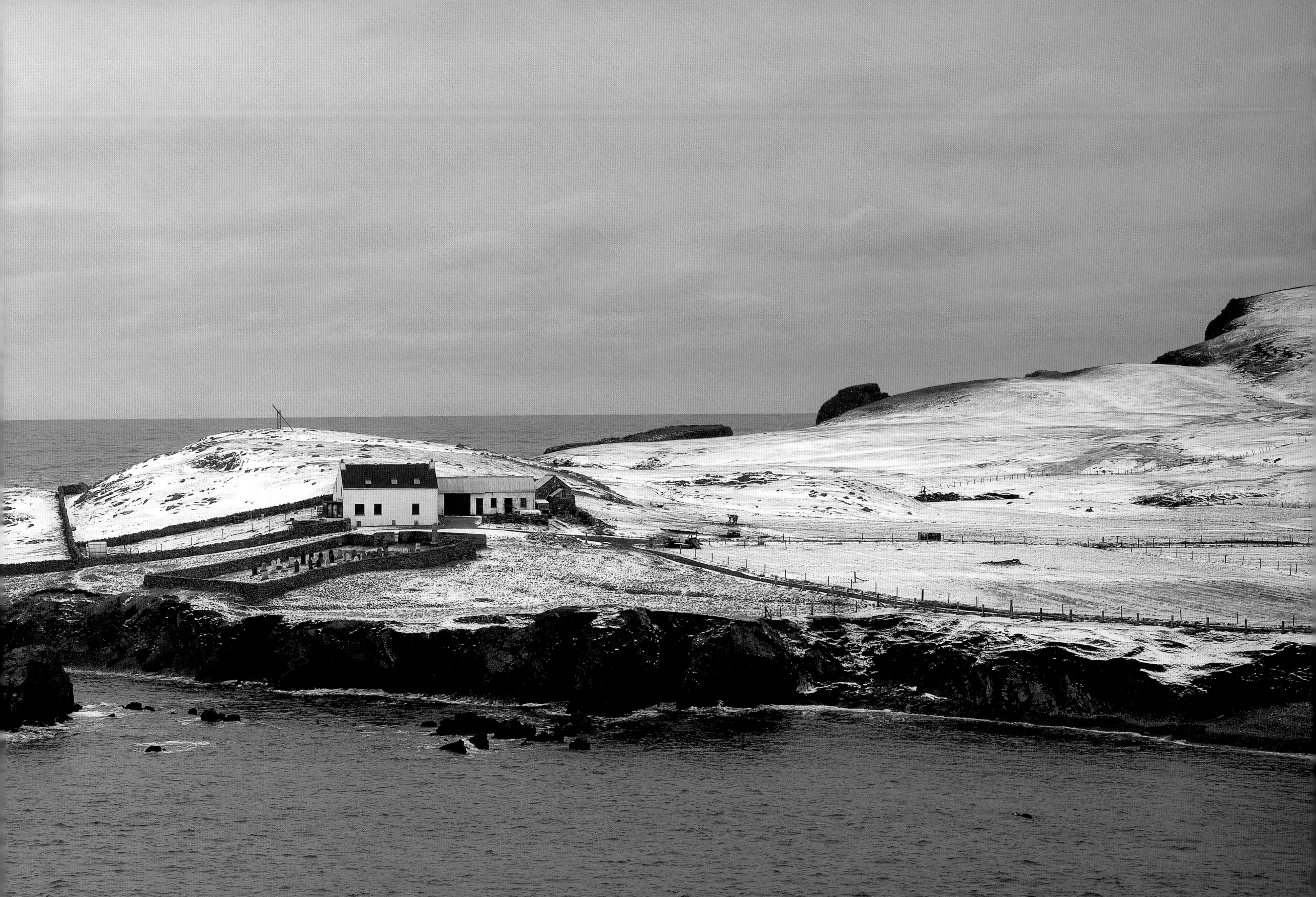

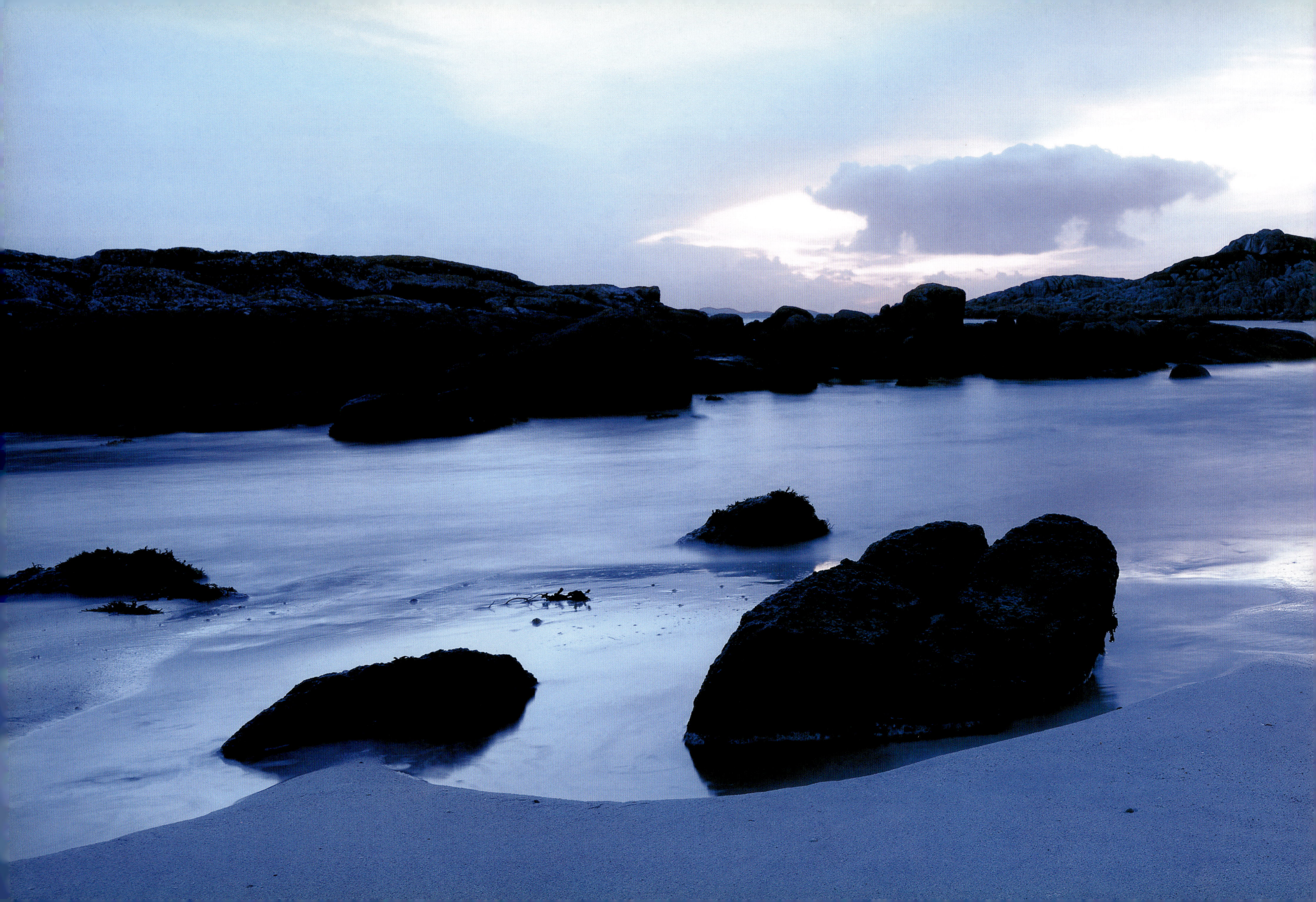

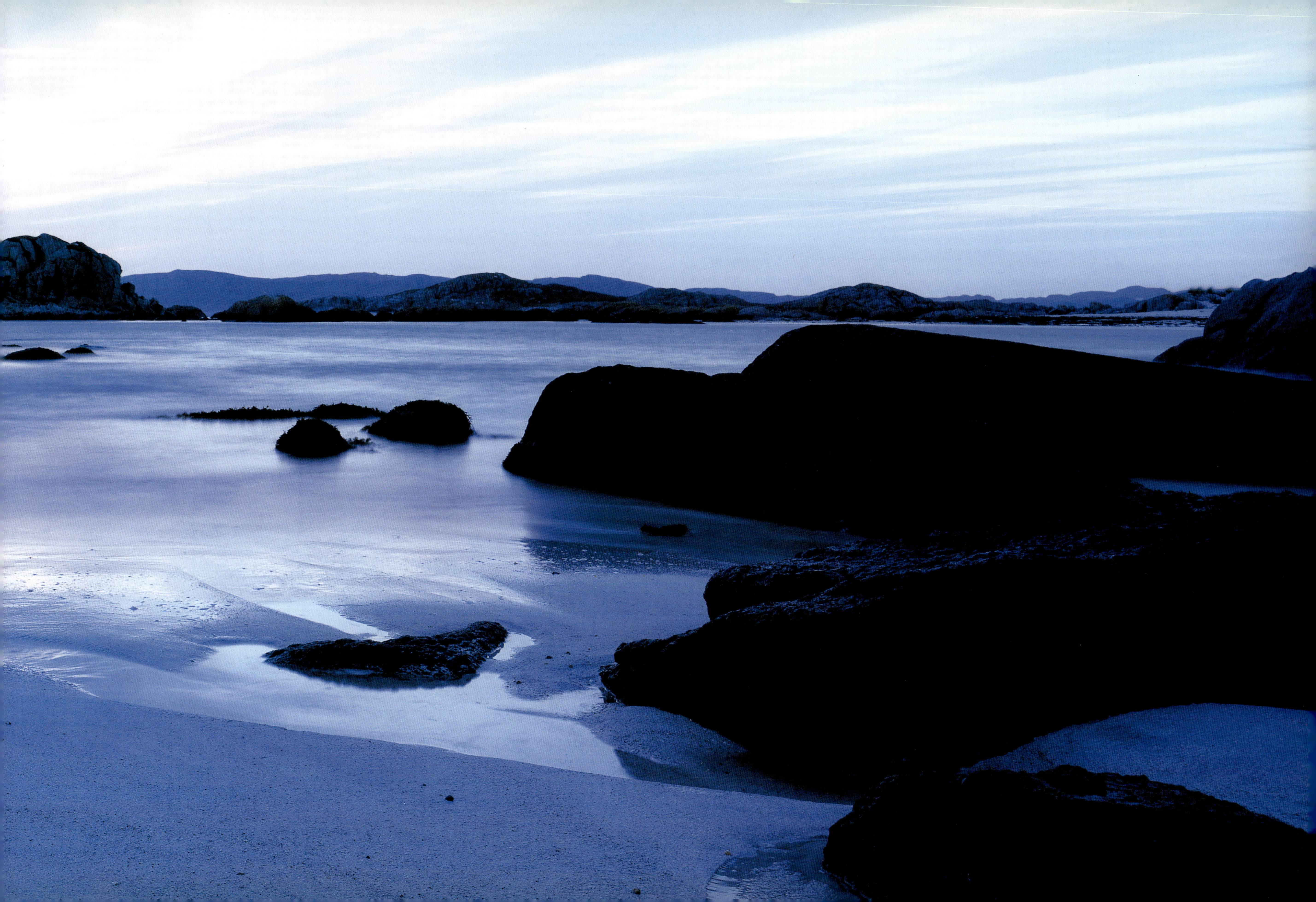

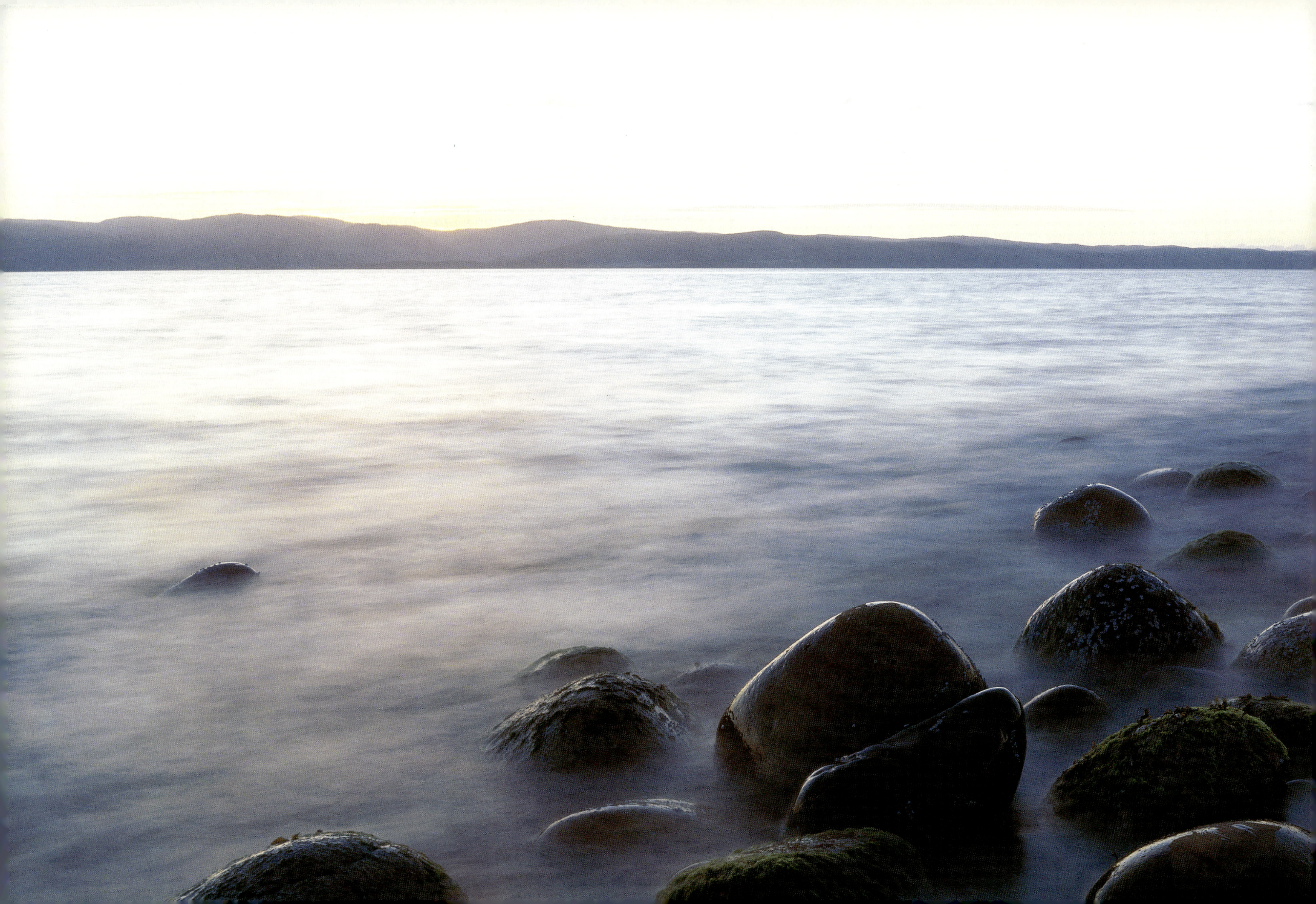

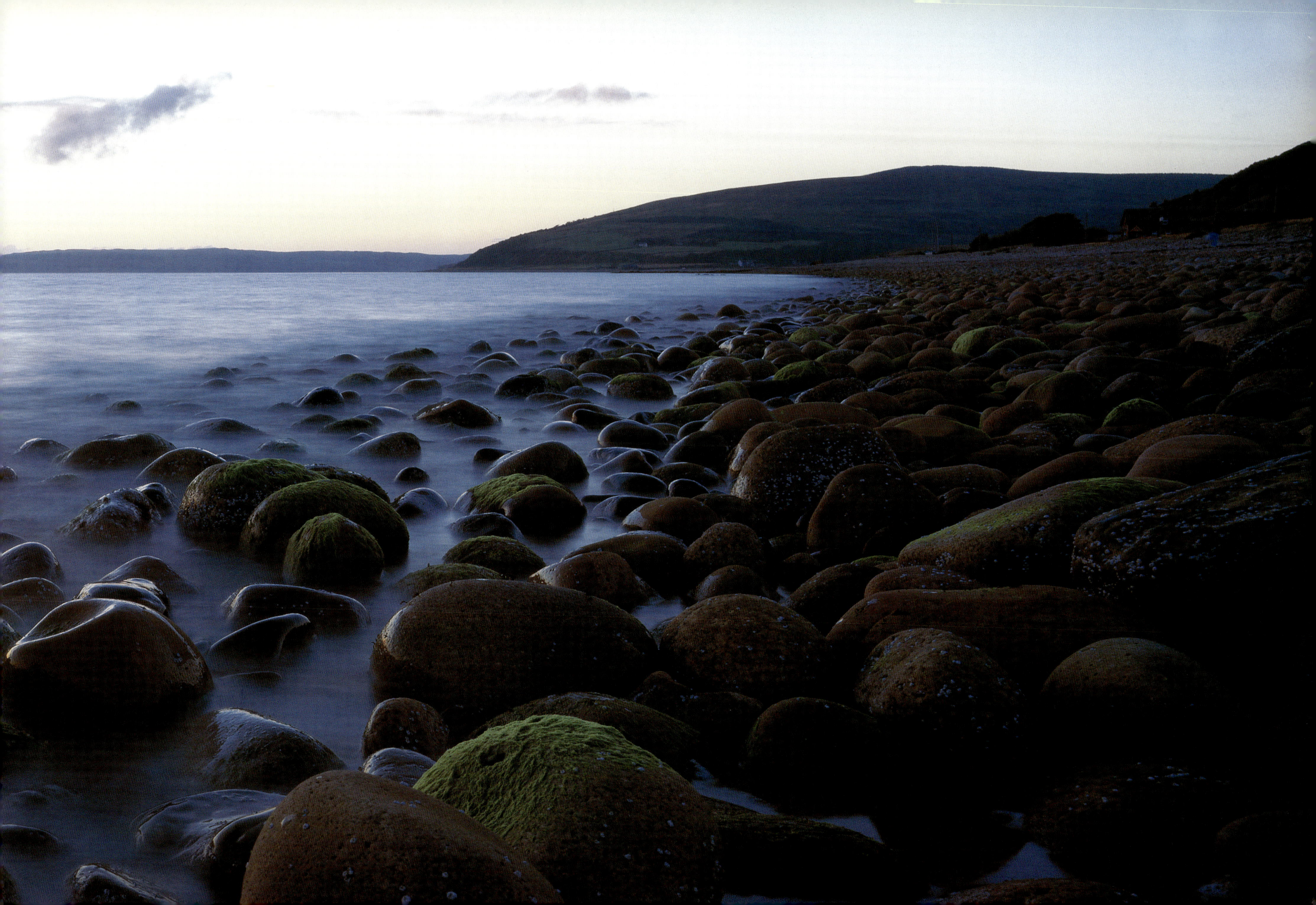

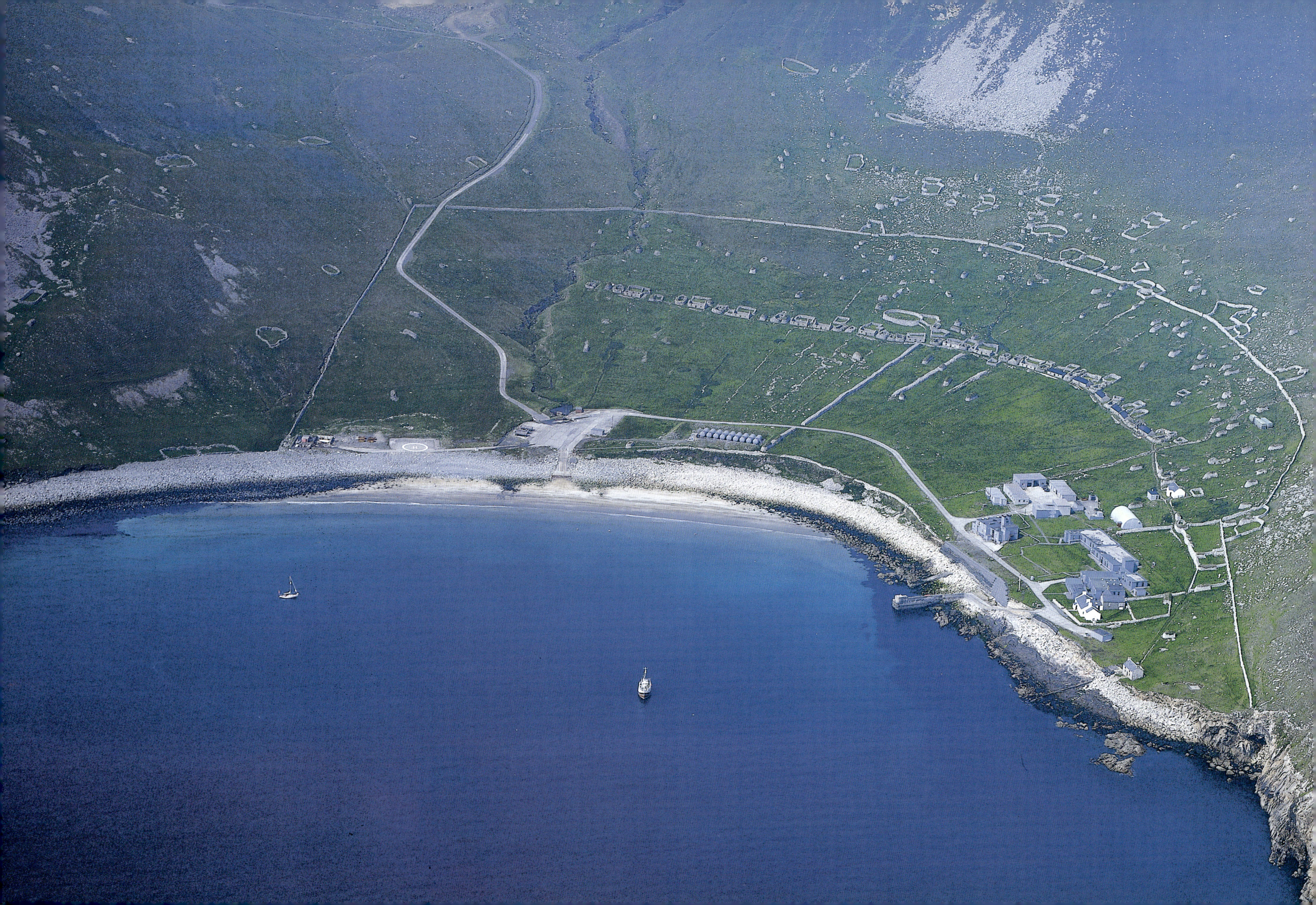

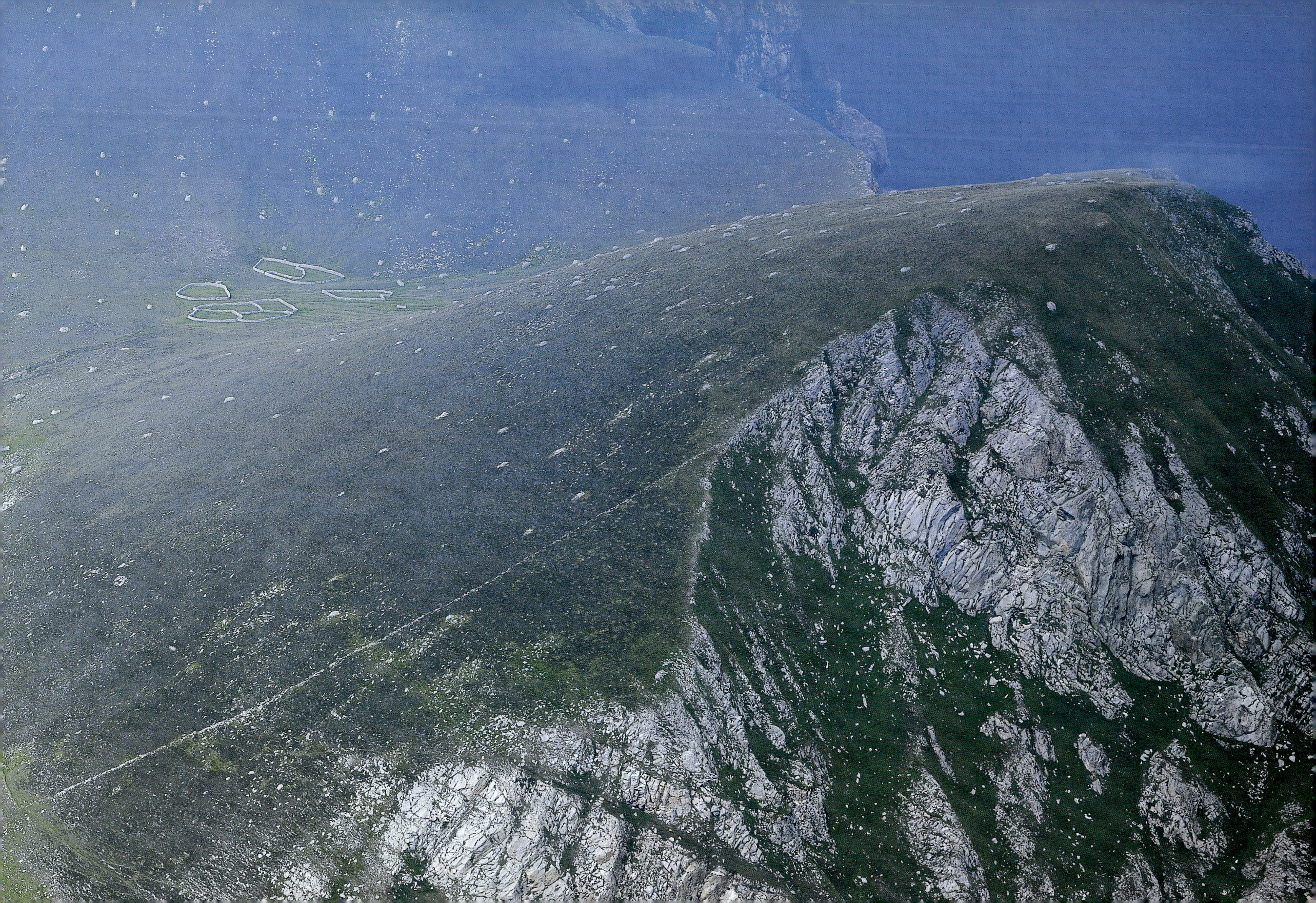

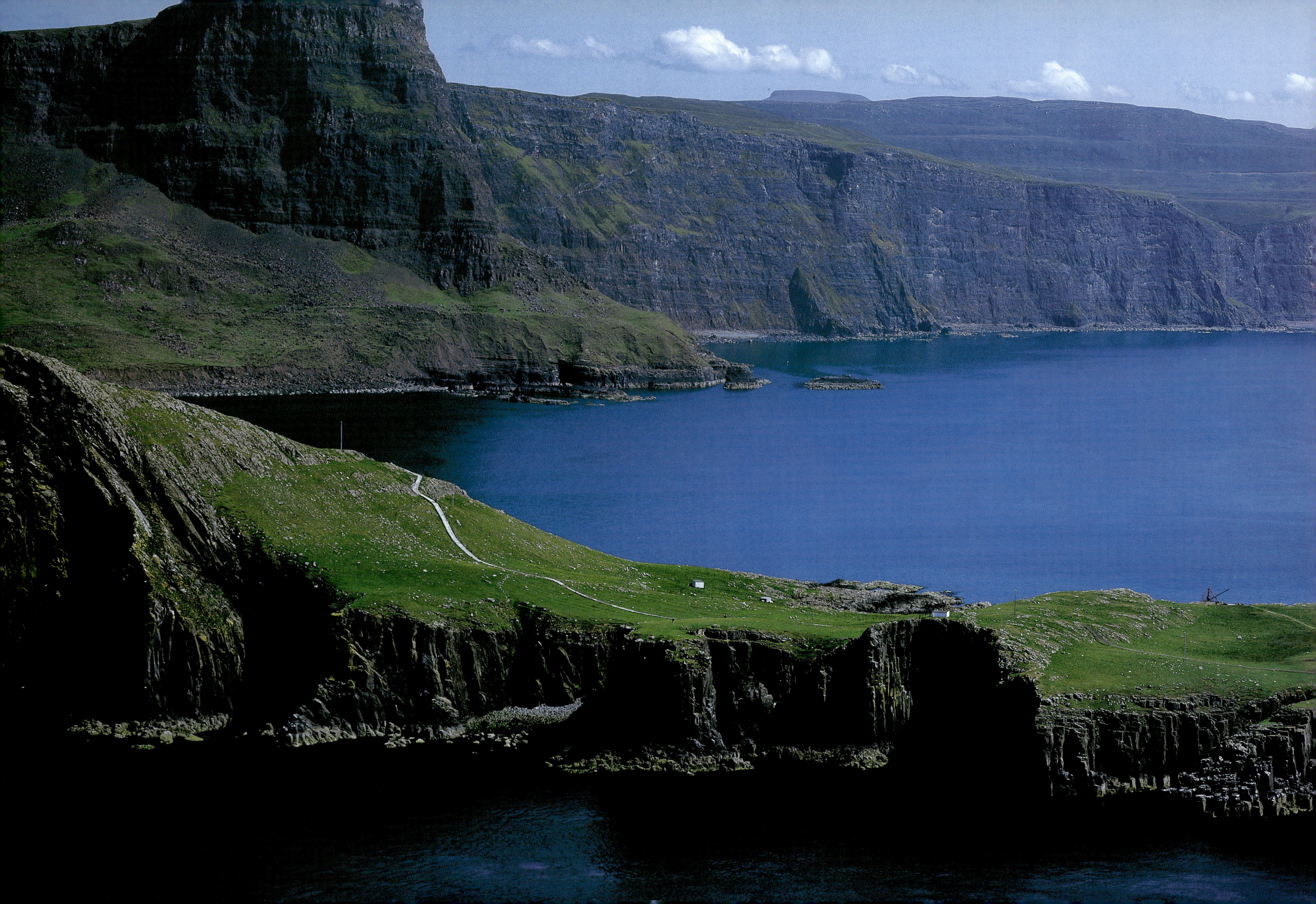

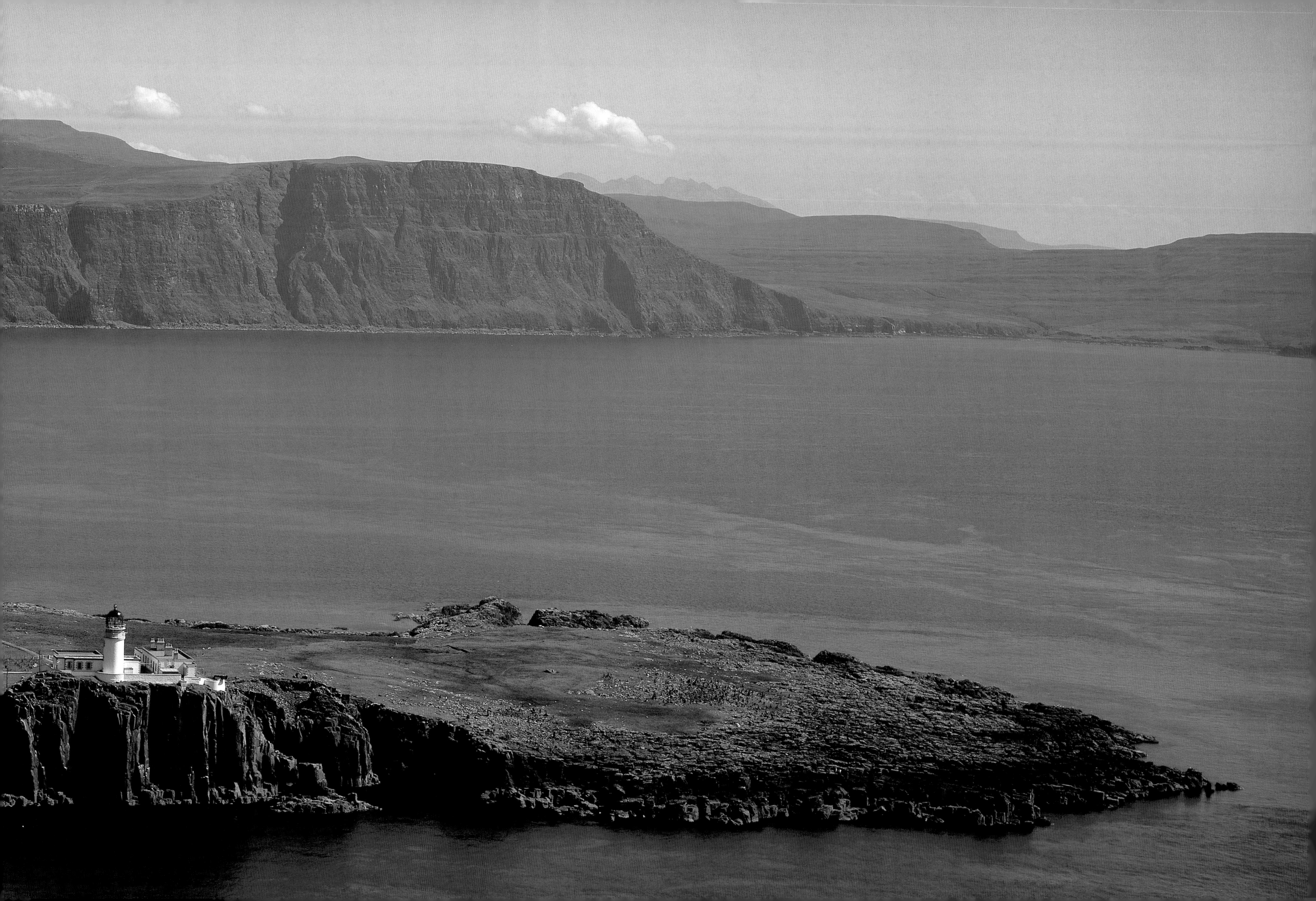

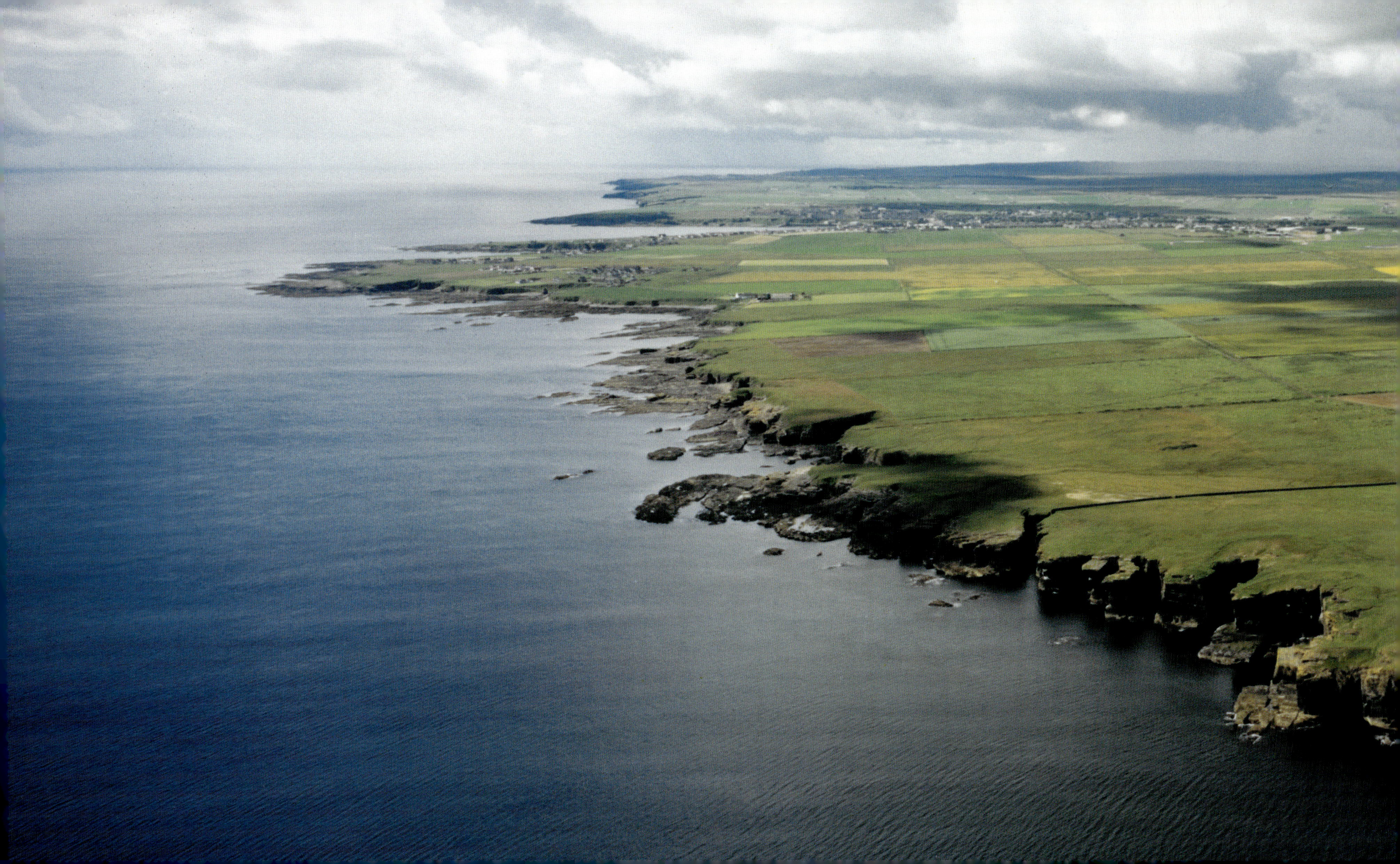

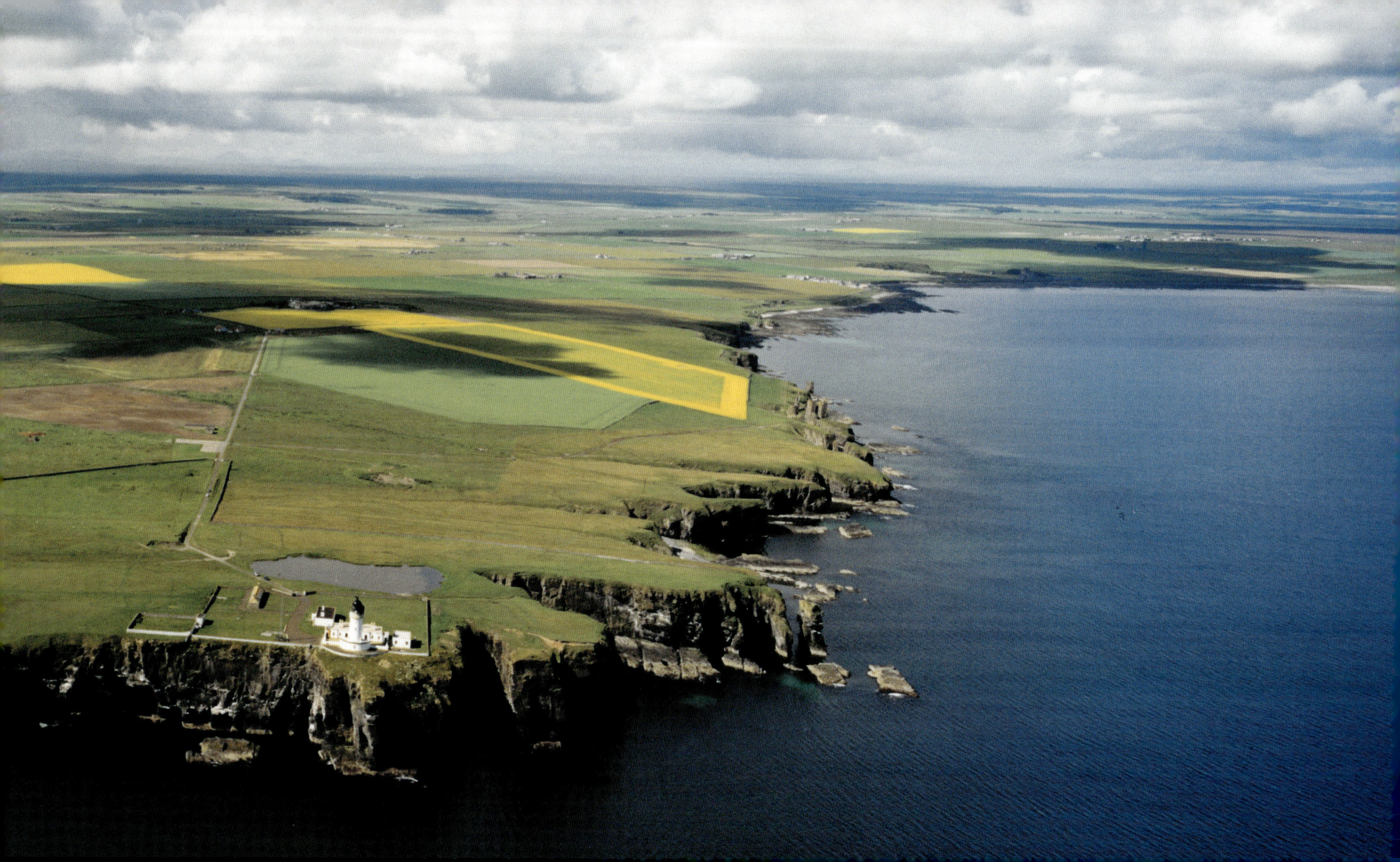

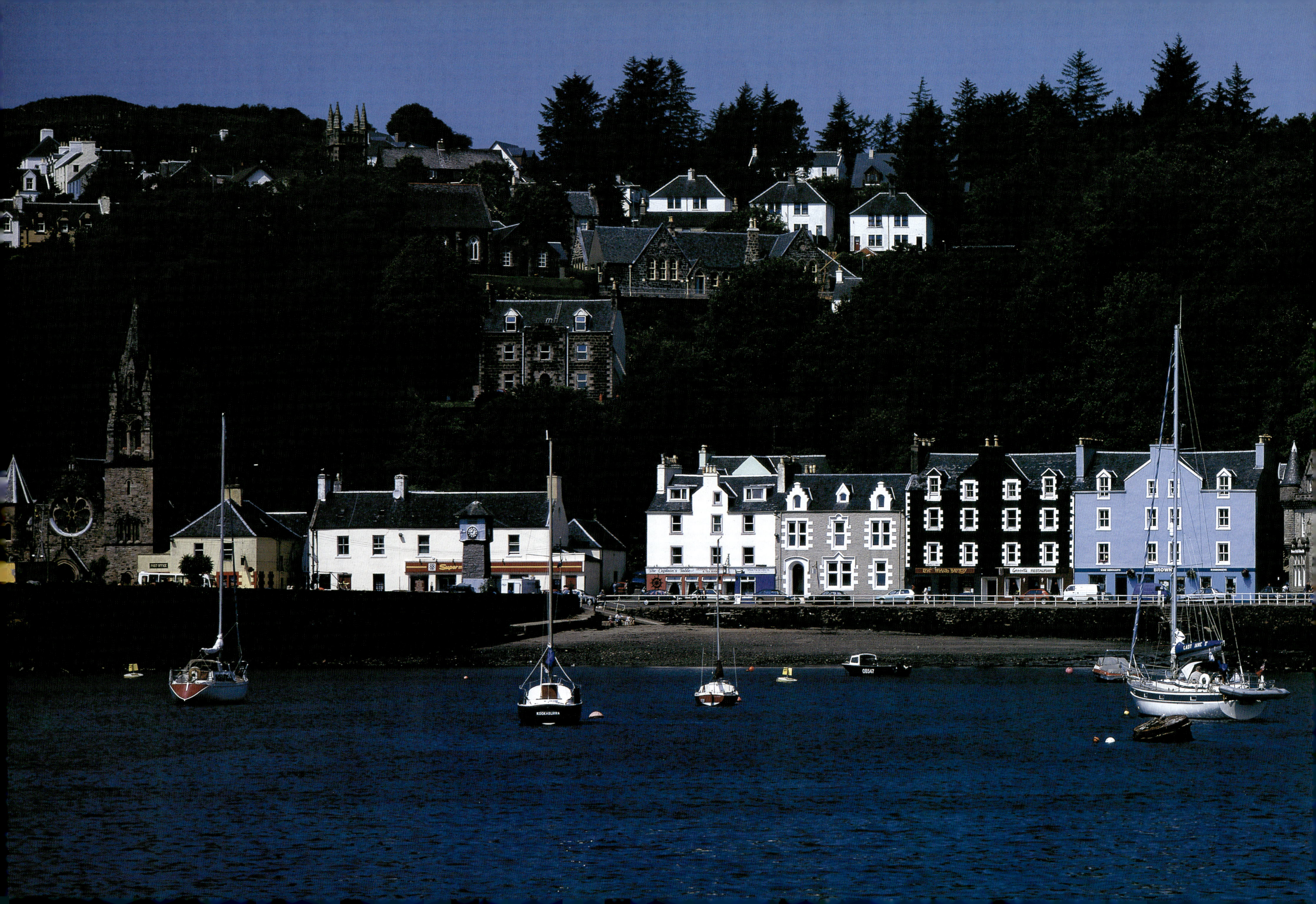

The Captain's Table
RESTAURANT
WINE MERCHANTS
BROWN'S
IRONMONGERS

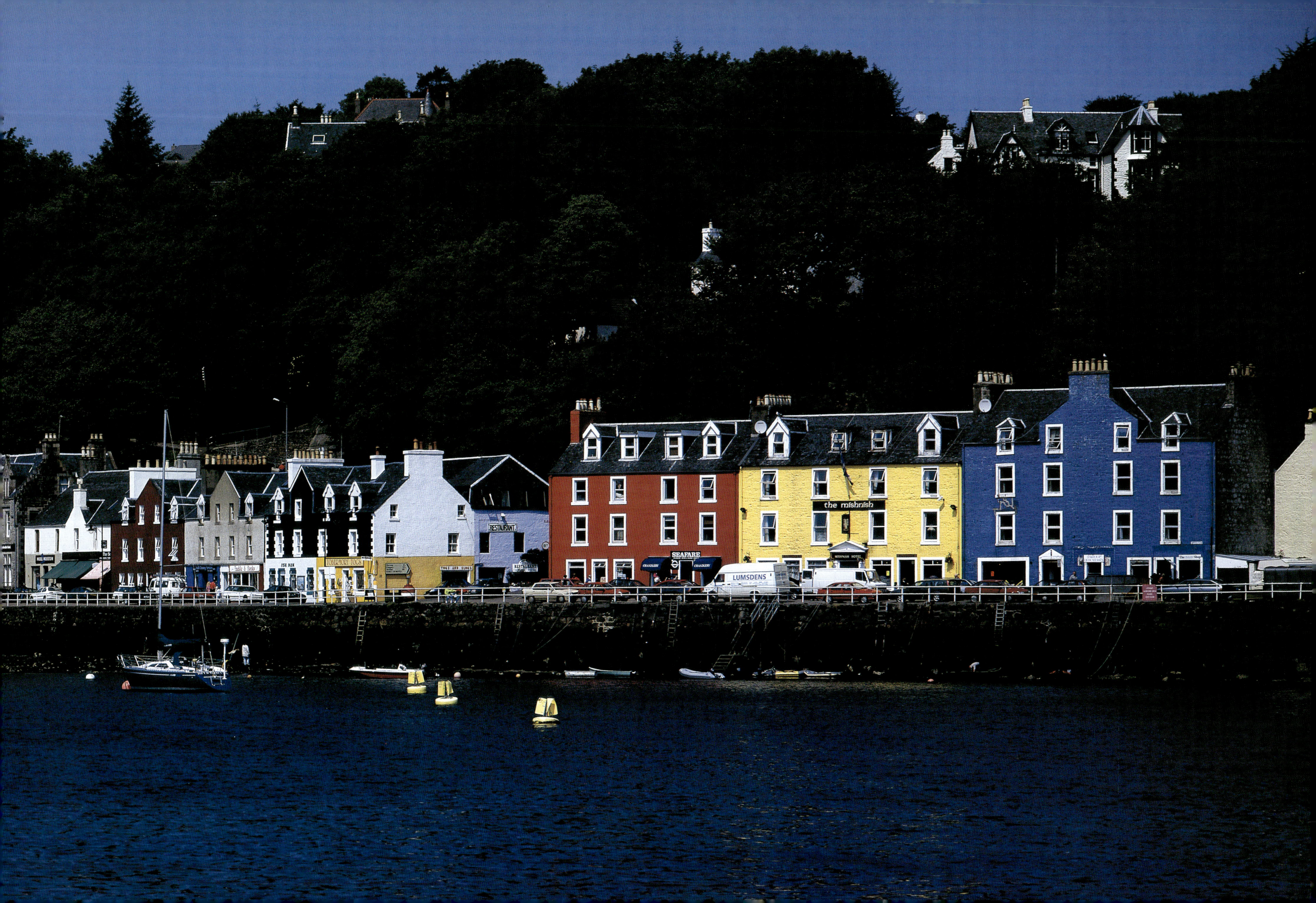
RESTAURANT
SEAFARE
LUMSDENS
the mishnish

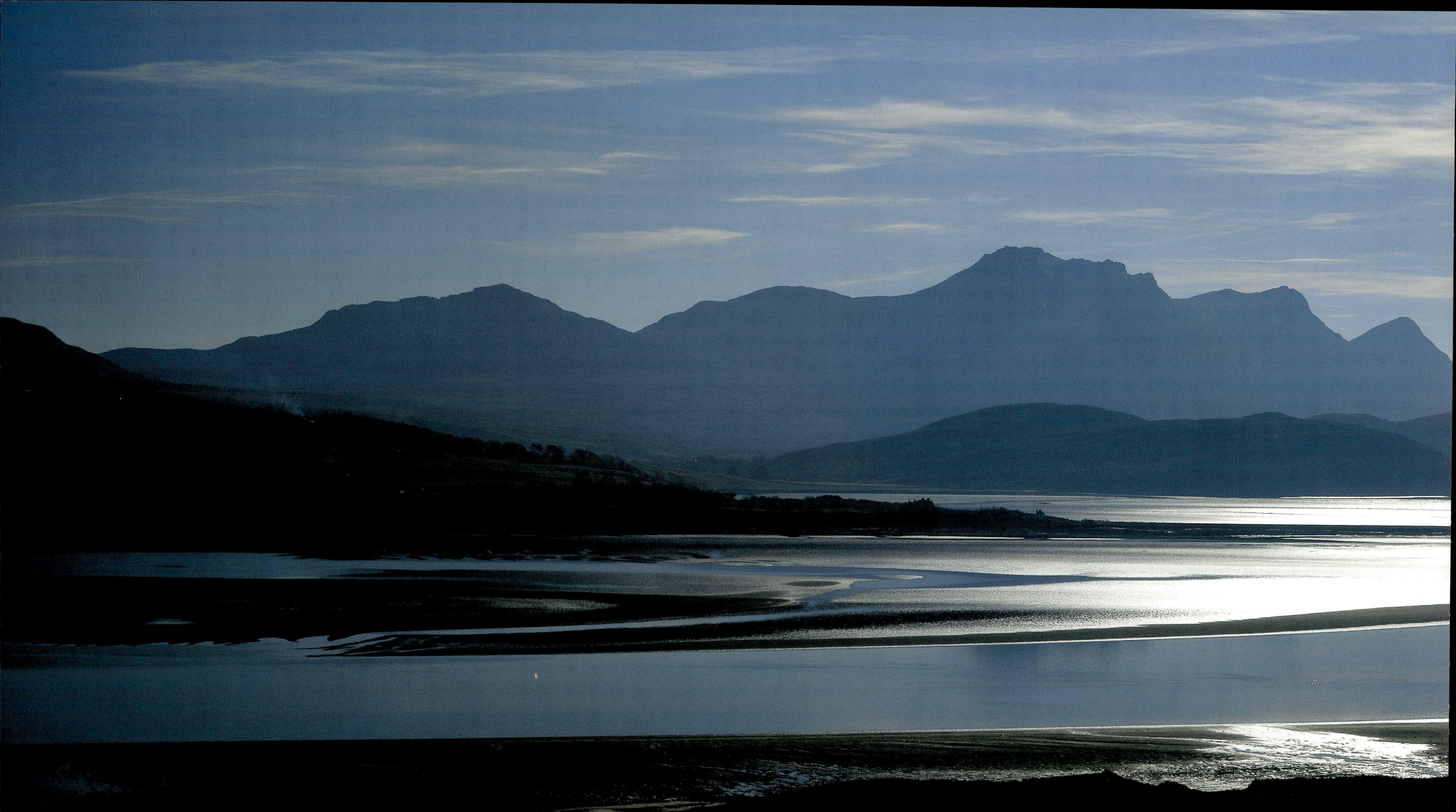

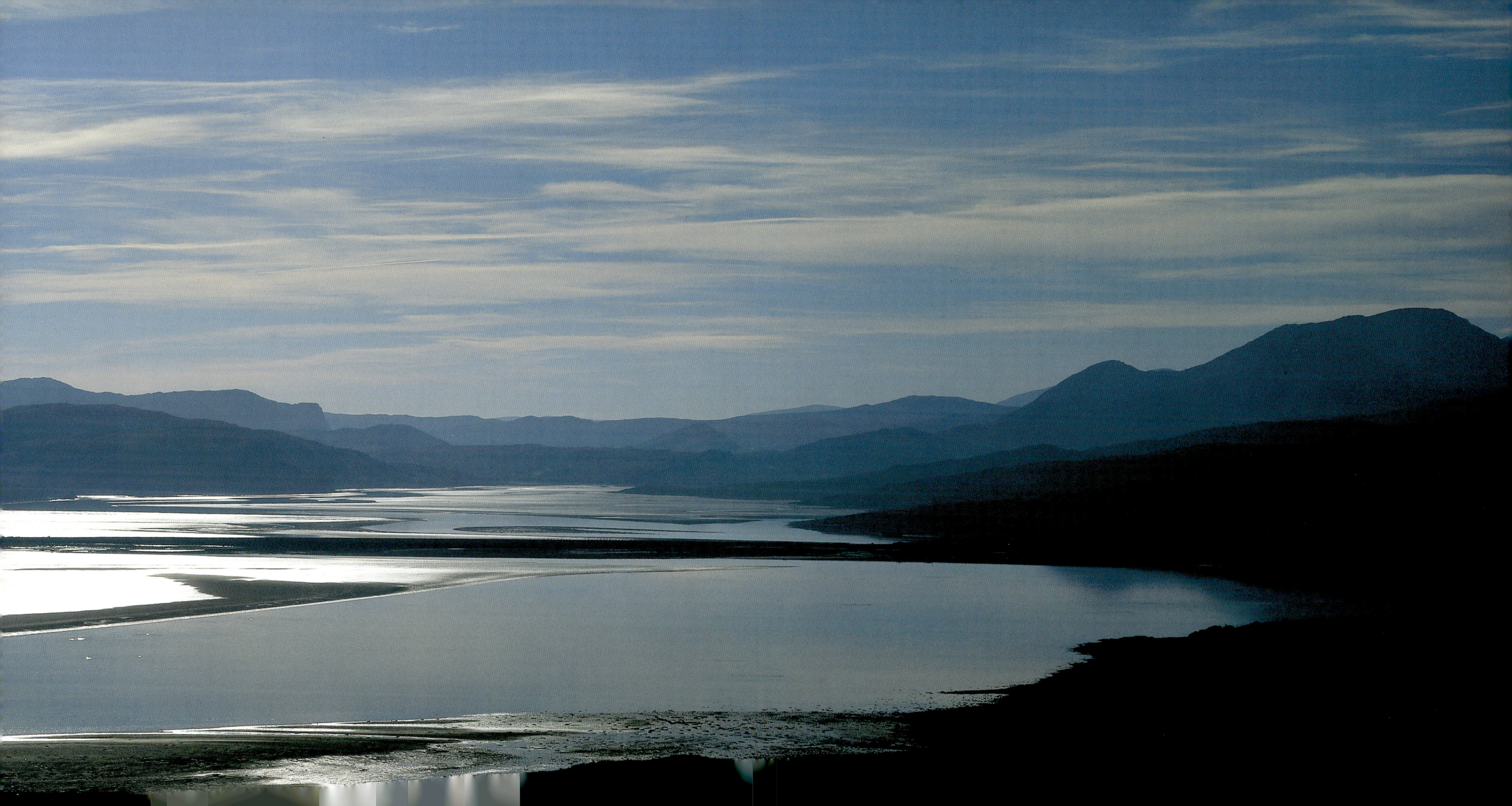

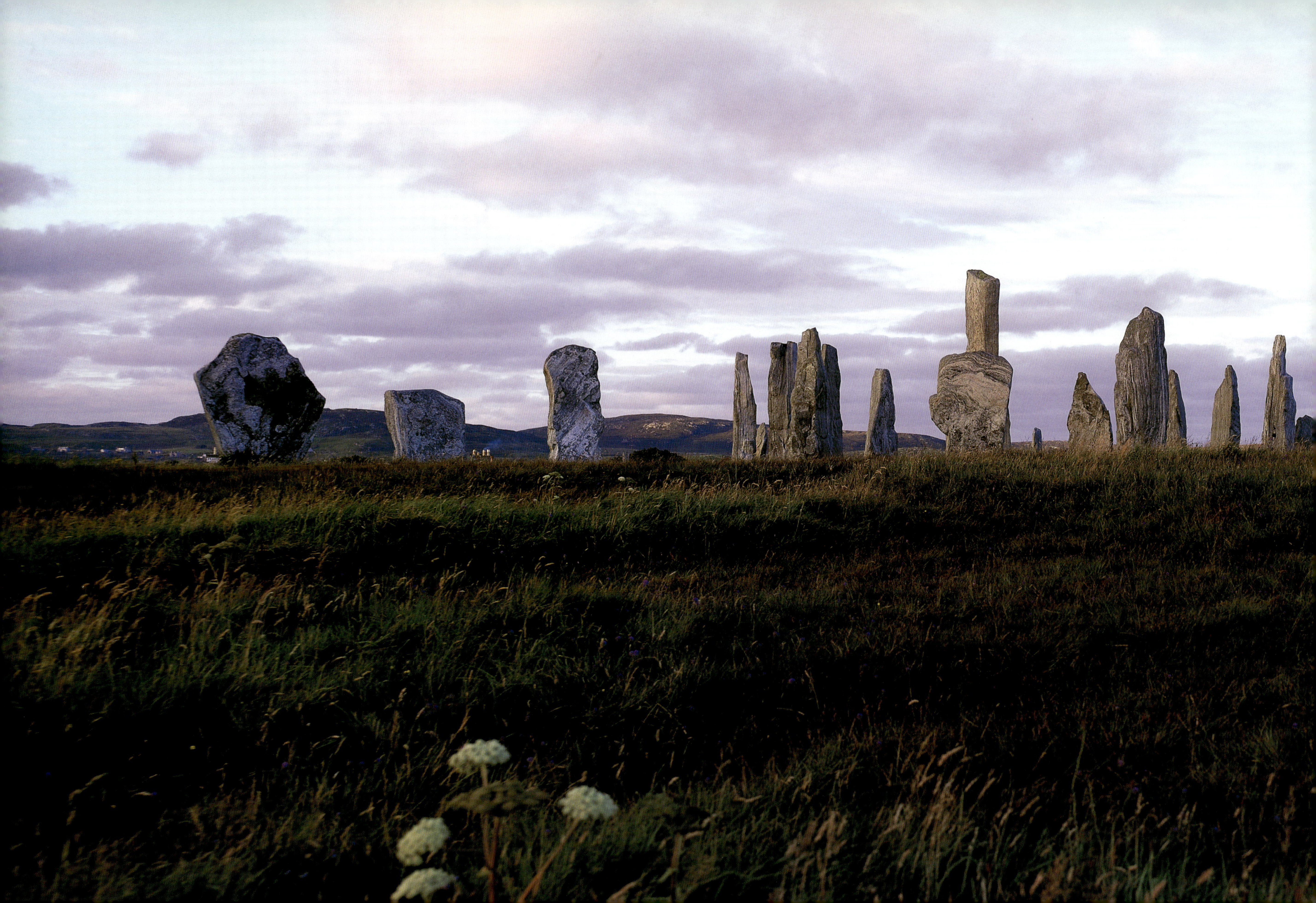

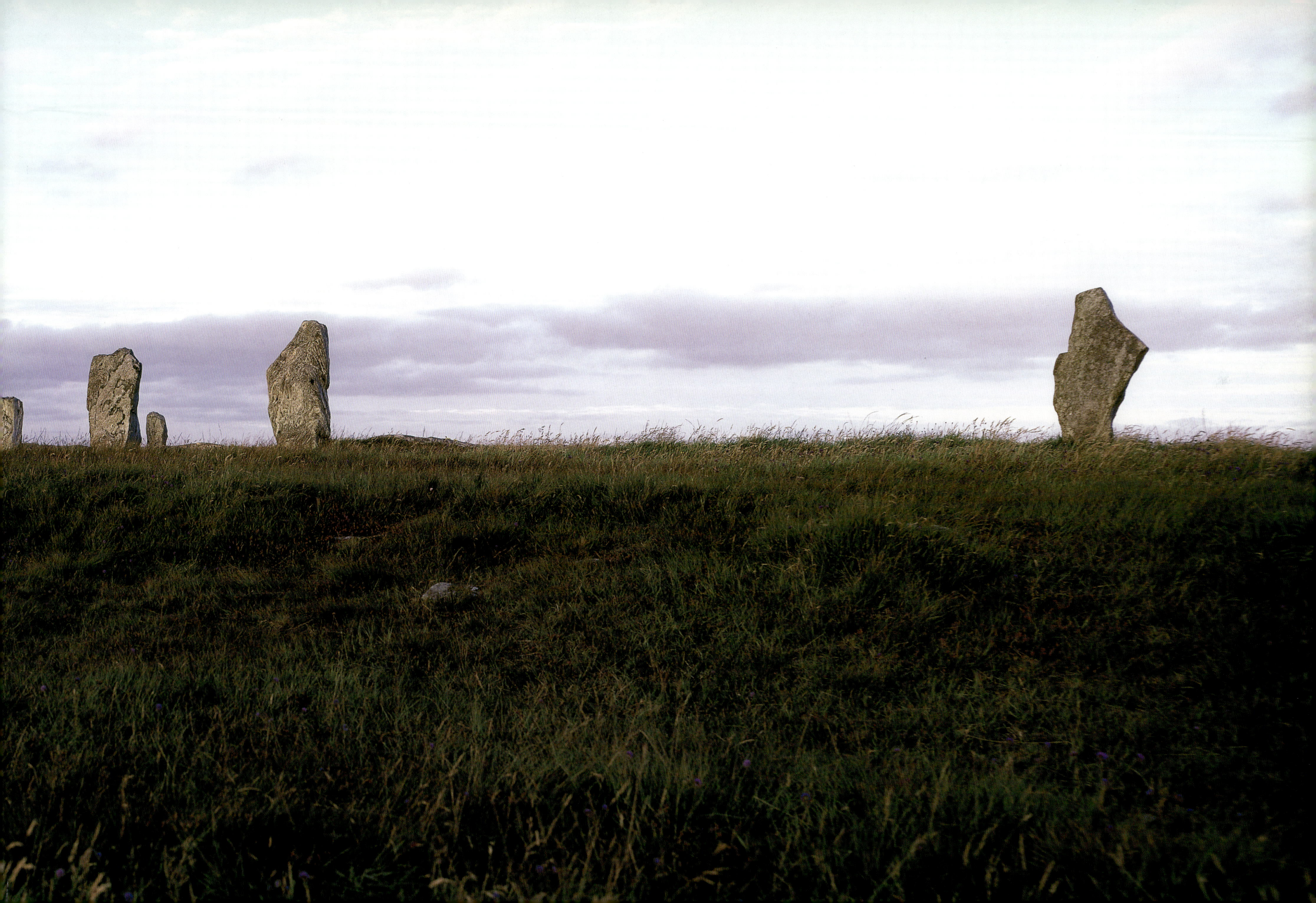

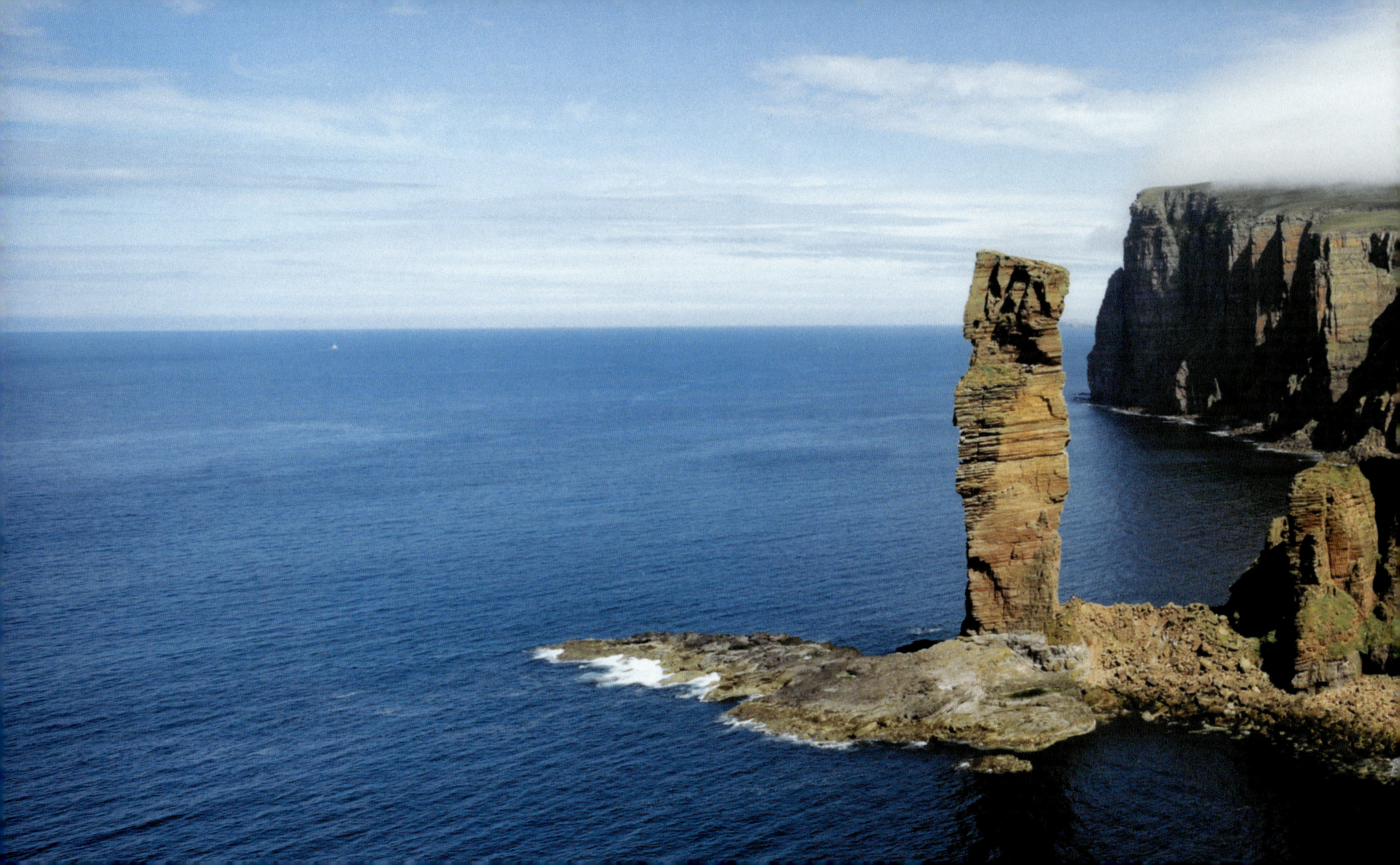

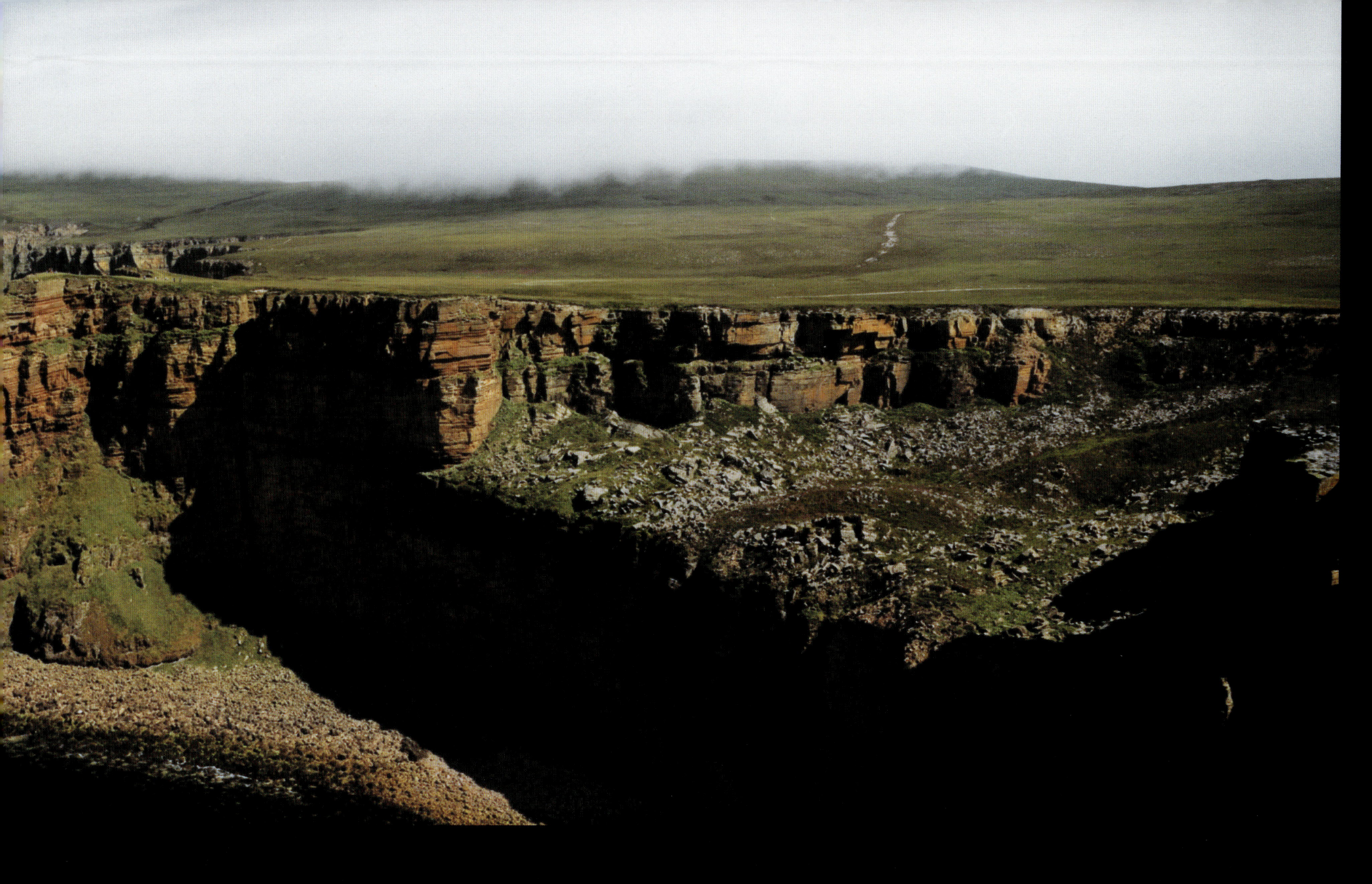

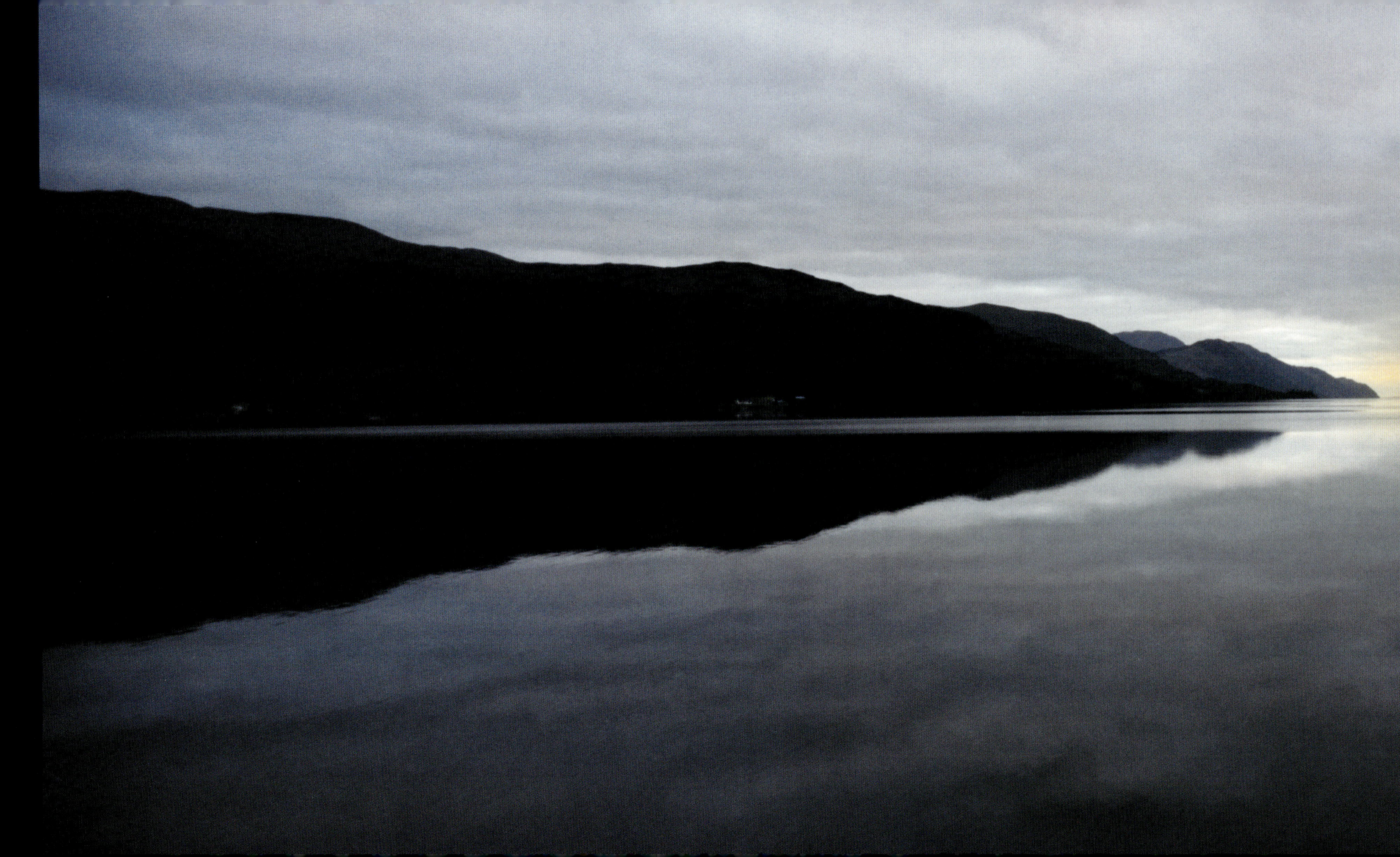

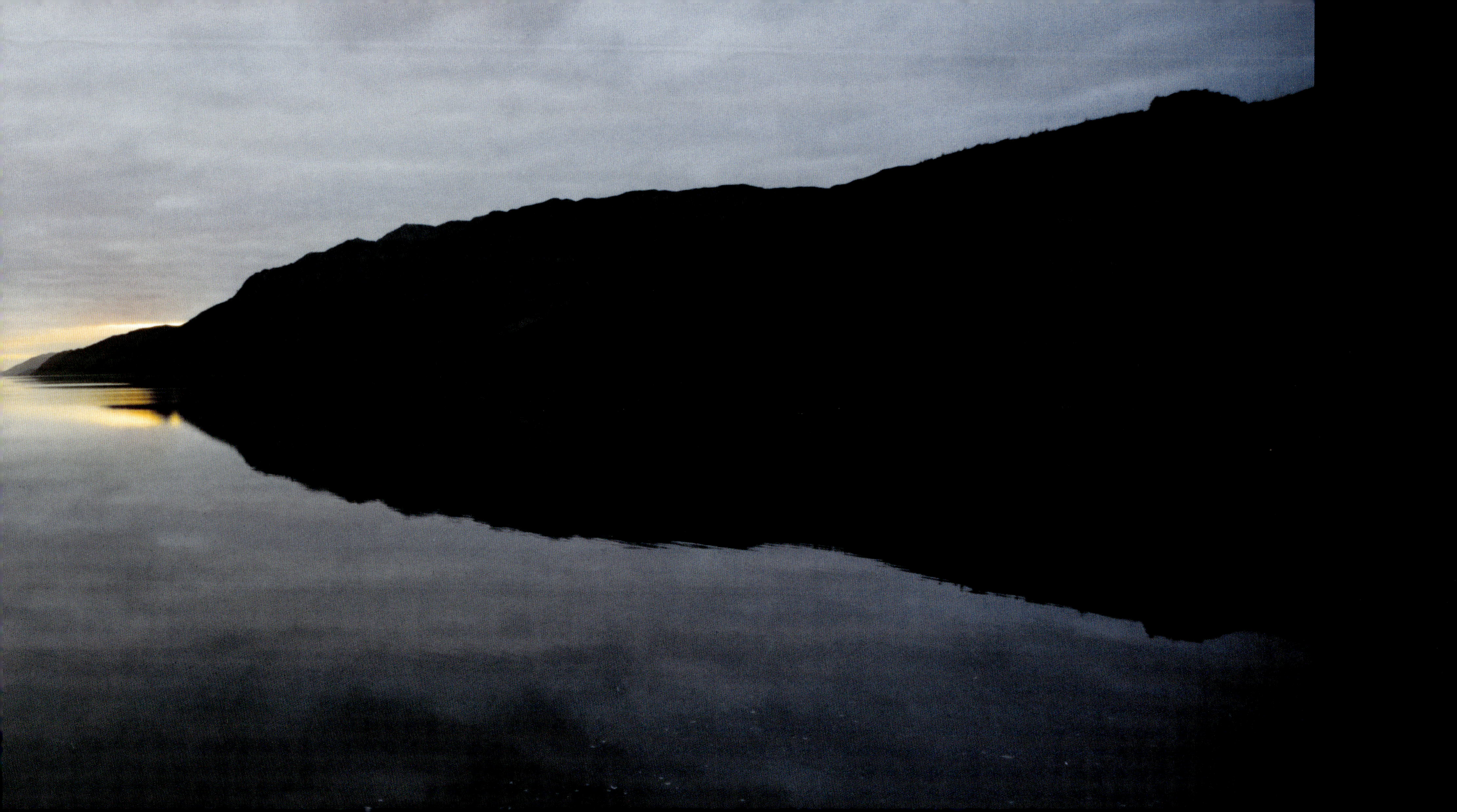

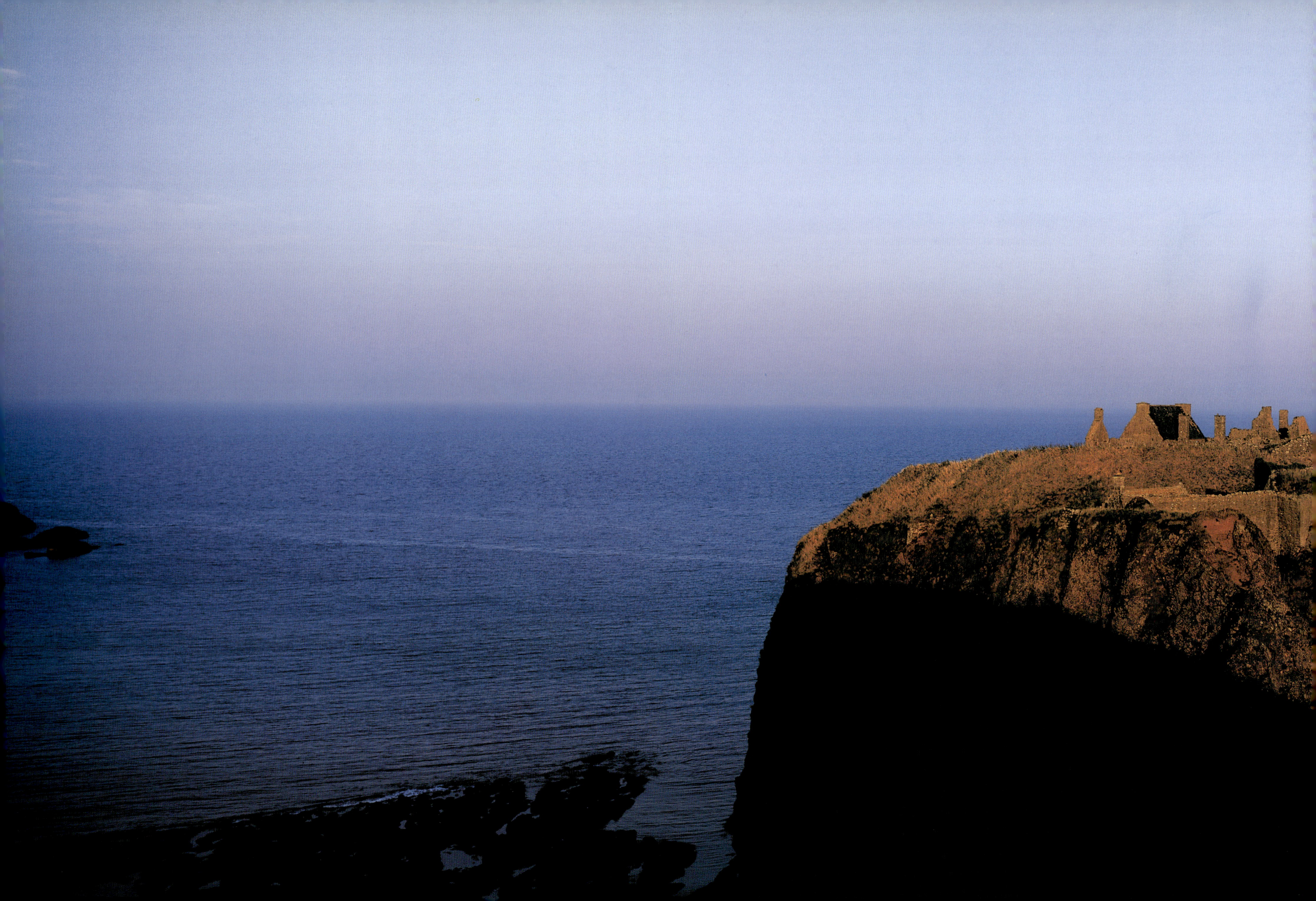

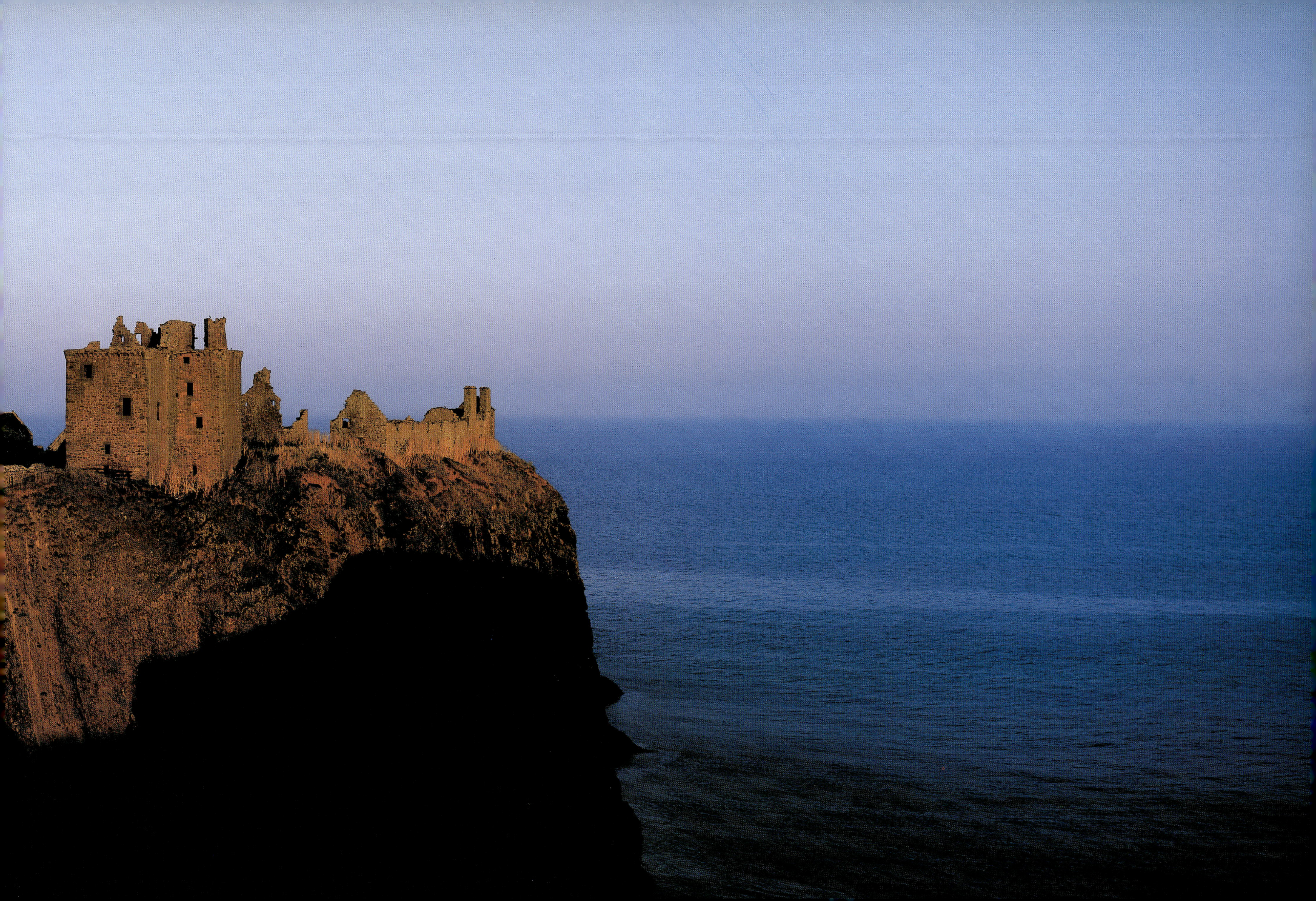

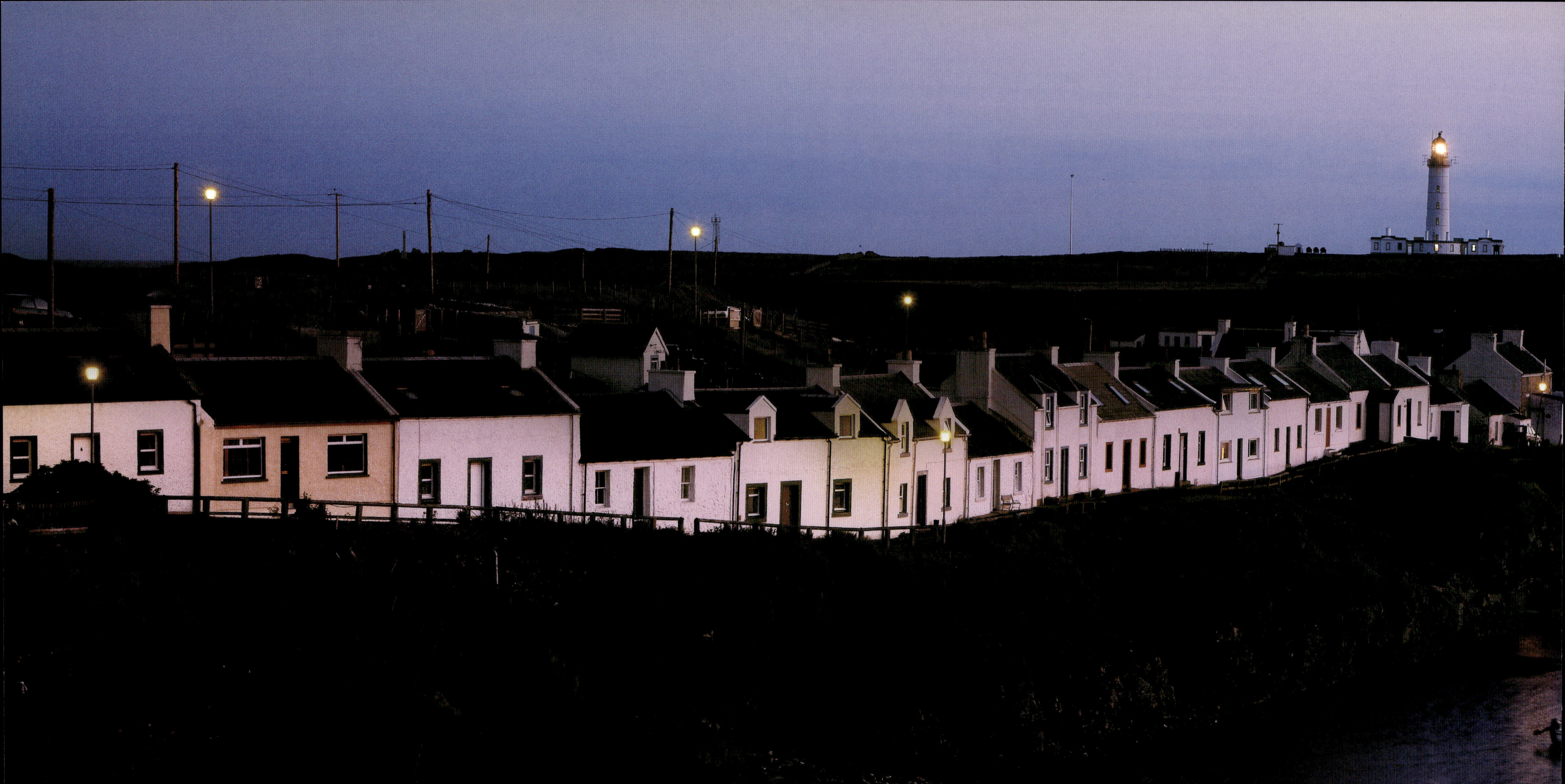

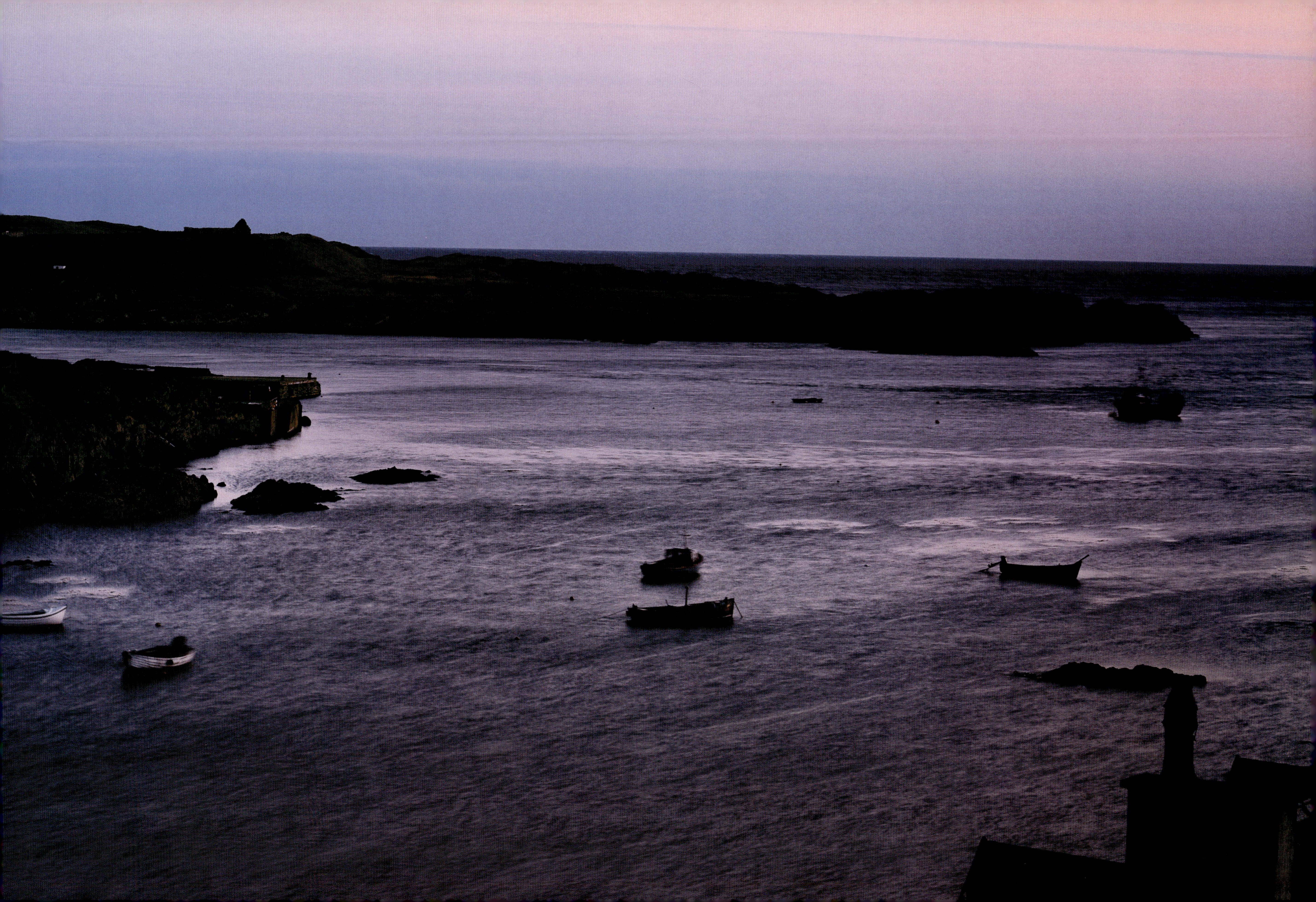

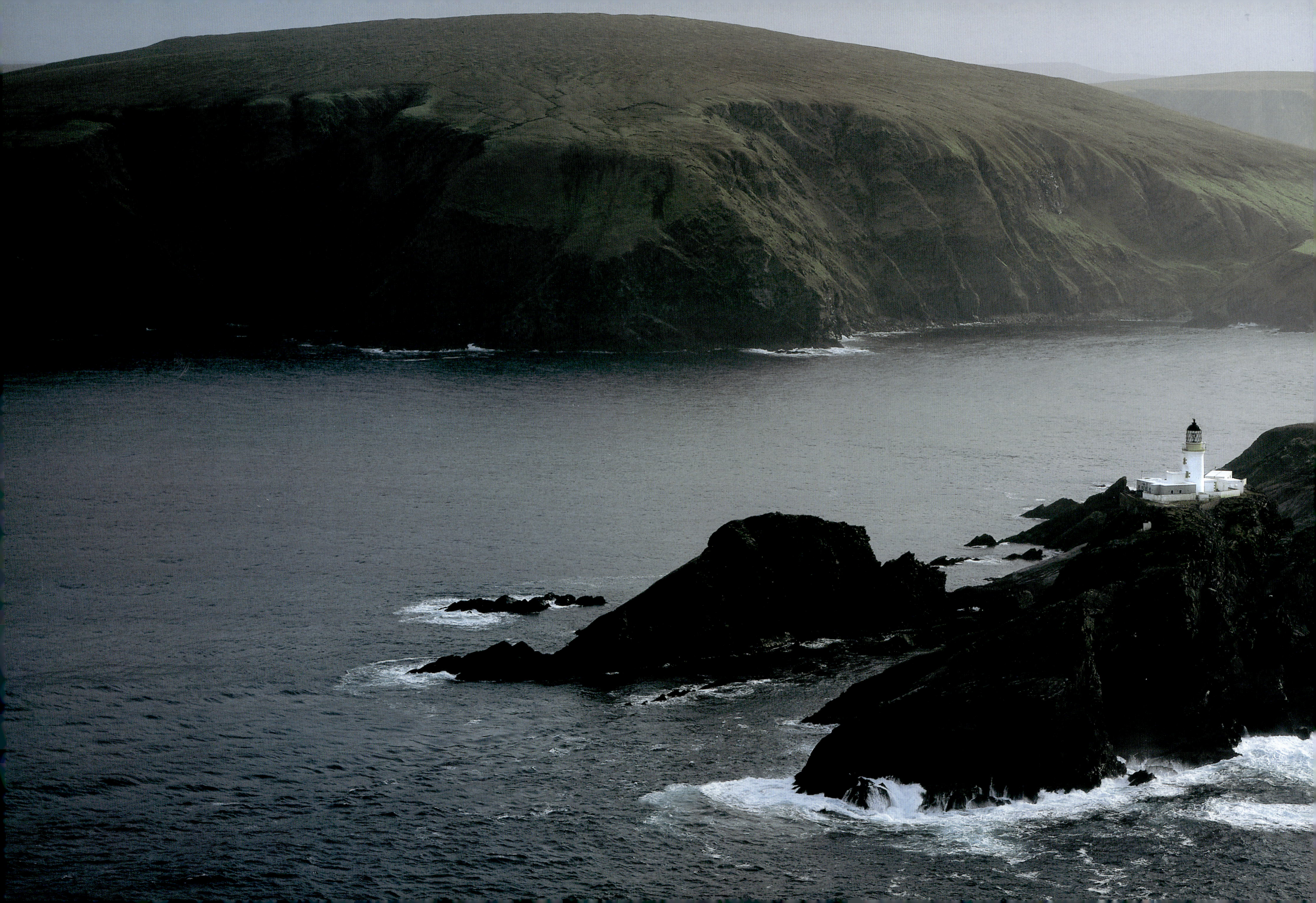

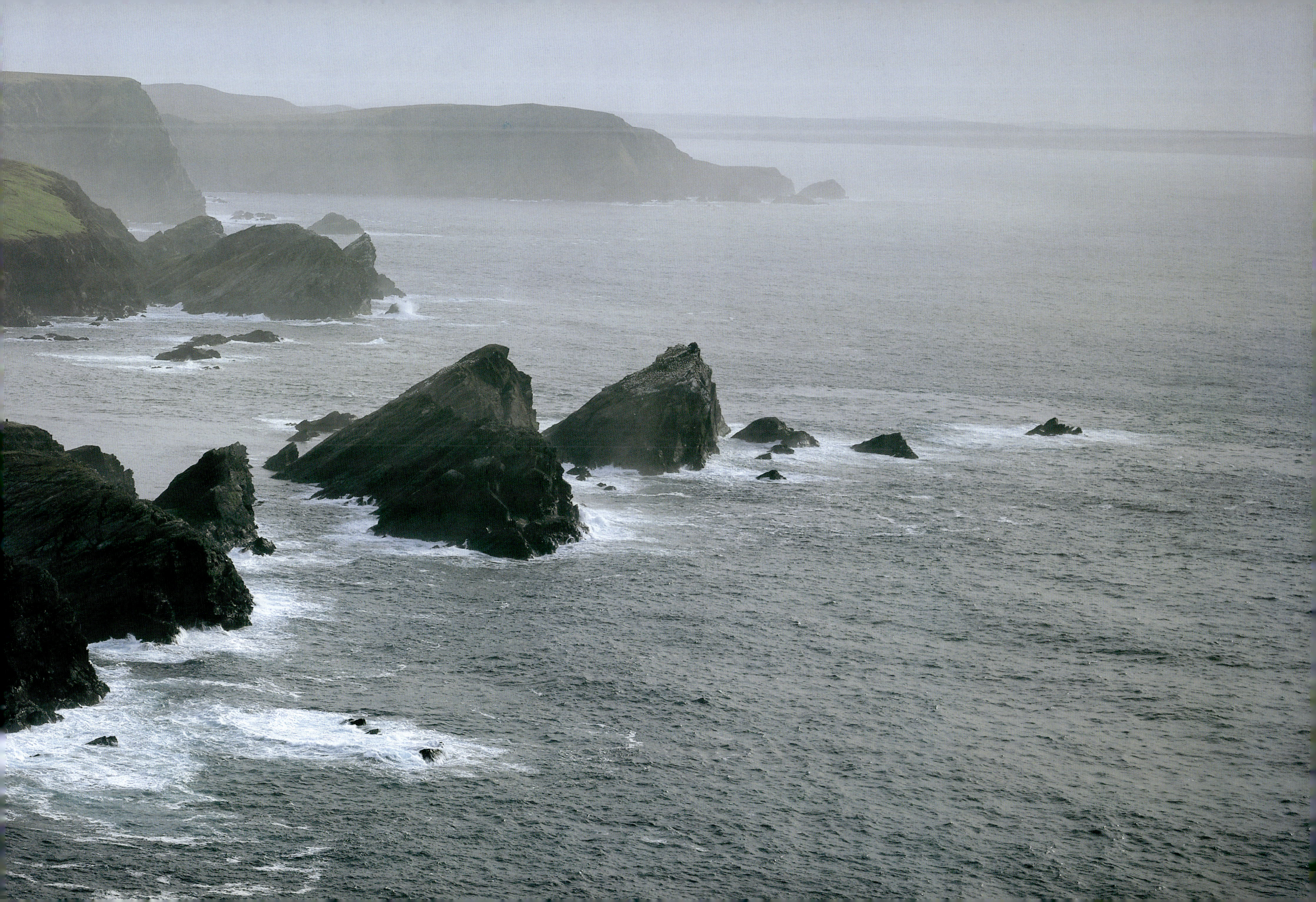

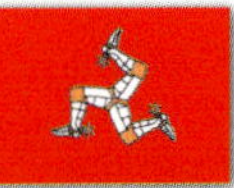

ISLE OF MAN·ELLAN VANNIN

Halfway between the Hill of Tara, where the knights of the high king of Ireland gathered, and the sanctuary of Culloden, where the knell sounded for the clans of Scotland, in the middle of the Irish sea, stands the most unusual island of the Gaelic world: the Isle of Man. It covers no more than 230 square miles and its population consists of some 80,000 people, a third of whom live at the water's edge in the charming seaside town of Douglas (or Doolish, in Manx), halfway along the east coast, where ferries from Belfast and Dublin and Liverpool come to berth.

The island's entire coastline extends for only 70 miles. It begins below the north-facing Point of Ayre lighthouse, at the foot of which is a rich nature reserve. Then you just have to let yourself glide west, from glen to glen and from castle (at Peel, on St Patrick's Isle) to fortress. Port Erin, right at the southern end, means Irish Port. It leads to the Calf of Man, a gently sloping islet from where you can admire the finest sunsets and gaze across the sea to Dublin, Dun Laoghaire and County Wicklow.

On 5 July, the national holiday, Tynwald Hill seems to bristle with a hundred red flames, those of its national flag adorned with the three-legged triskelion, a sign of the rebirth of the seasons through the summer and winter solstices. It has been the symbol of the island since the 12th century.

The Isle of Man has had a tumultuous history. For a long time it was a base for the Vikings who came from Scandinavia to plunder the Celtic and Gaelic lands in the north, and the Breton lands in the south. Later, Scotland fought over it – in vain – with powerful England. Despite the influence of its larger neighbours, the island has been able to maintain its independent character, its ancestral culture and the Manx language (also known as Gaelg).

On this land of gently sloping valleys, which resembles a small corner of Scotland that has moved away to live its life between two twin lands, Man holds fast to its unfettered freedom. Here, in fact, by one of those small miracles of the history of countries and peoples, this island set in the Irish sea established the first parliament in Europe, perhaps in the world, known as the Tynwald. It was founded in at least the 10th century and still thrives today, allowing the island's government to remain separate from the United Kingdom.

This green pebble surrounded by sky blue, culminating in the peak of Snaefell, at 2,000 feet, and where flocks of seals with voracious appetites chase shoals of fish, is a golden grain of sand amid the lands of the European Union. Like its bigger brother, the 'Celtic Tiger' of Ireland, this island of tailless cats and four-horned rams is impossible to tame. Most of its ministers do not belong to any political party and its unwritten constitution perpetuates the values of commitment and honour. This land bathed in the warm currents of the Gulf Stream truly is a paradise – not to mention a tax haven.

Once a year in May and June, the famous Isle of Man TT race turns the island into a paradise for bikers seeking excitement, to the sound of Manx folk music. For everyone, especially sailors, the Isle of Man – with its Celtic crosses, triskelions and Viking cemeteries by the sea – is a real-life treasure island.

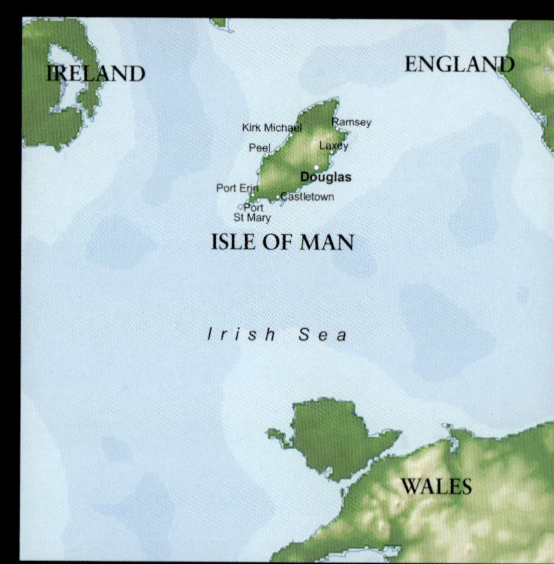

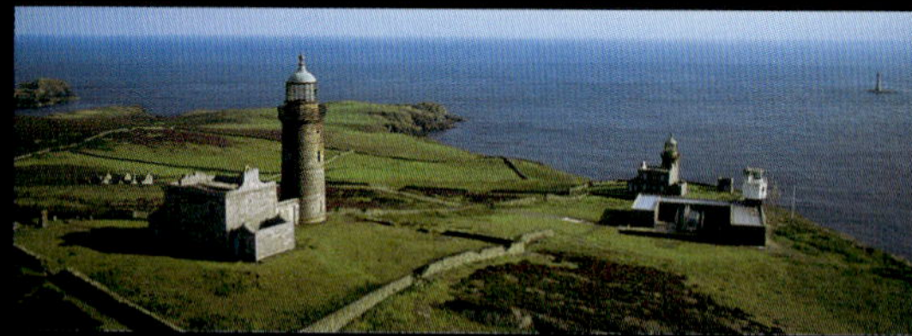

SENTINELS OF LIGHT
The Isle of Man has five lighthouses. In the north, facing Scotland is Point of Ayre; in the east, facing England is Maughold Head, below the town of Ramsey. In the centre below Douglas, the ferry port and capital, stands Douglas Head lighthouse. Then comes Langness and finally Calf of Man, a small island in the south-west.

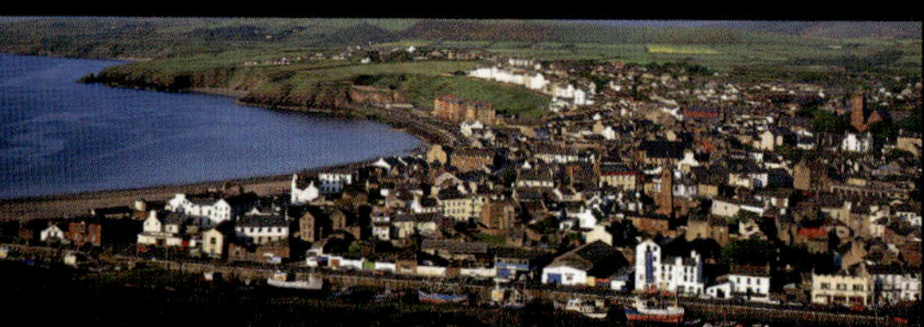

SEASIDE TOWNS
The capital Douglas, the seaside resort of Port Erin and the harbour town of Ramsey are three of the largest population centres. They are seaside towns with a charm from a bygone age, especially Ramsey with the century-old Mooragh Park and its forty acres of gardens, footpaths and lake.

Opposite: Beneath a white cloud of seagulls, Peel Castle stands on St Patrick's Isle and faces the Irish coast.

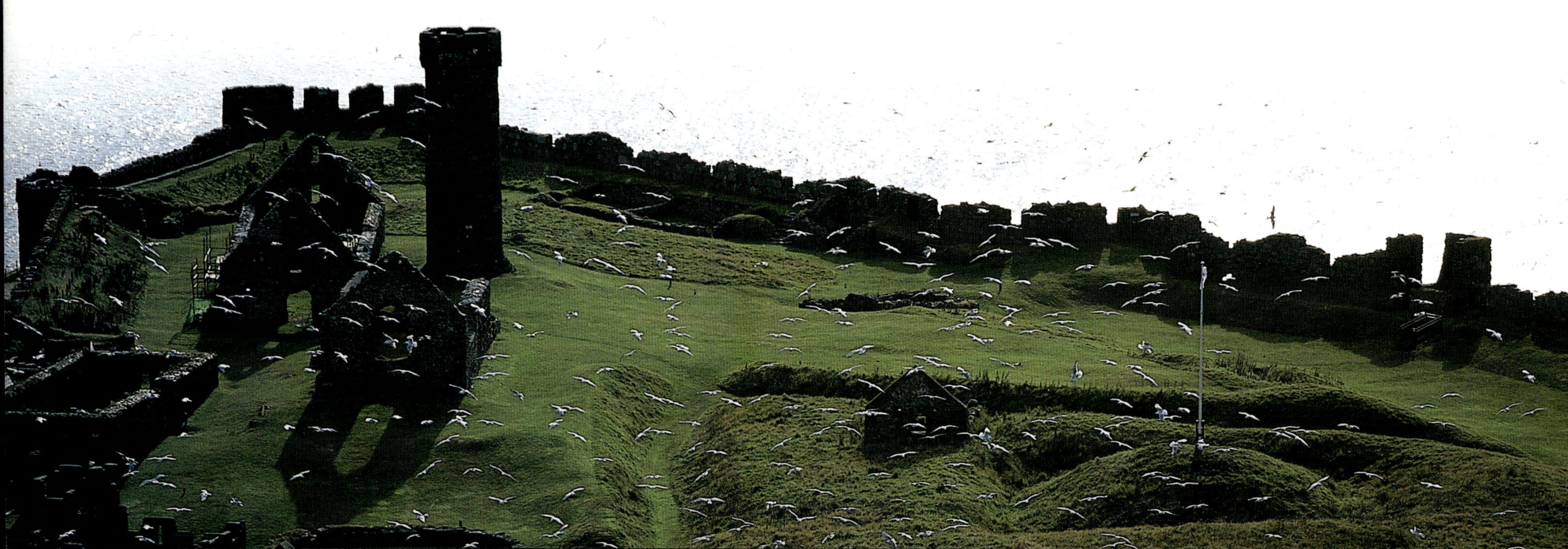

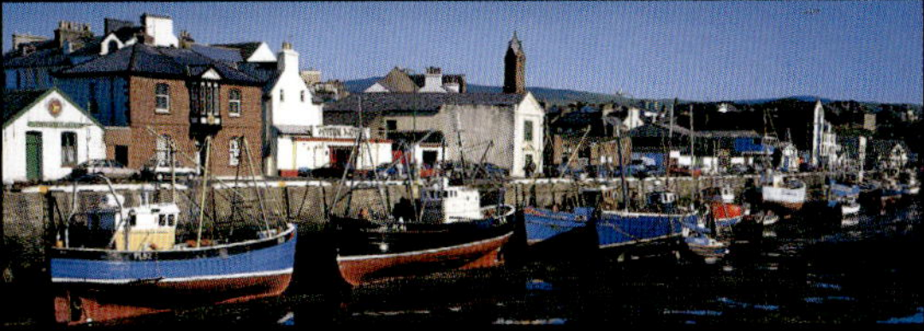

IN THE KINGDOM OF FISH

Kippers, or smoked herring, are a local speciality. On fishmongers' stalls you can see them strung together like golden garlands. The fishing boats unload their fresh catch at around 5 pm, together with their cargo of scallops. The pots are full of lobsters and crabs. These are washed down with ManX Spirit, a clear whisky, and the local beer.

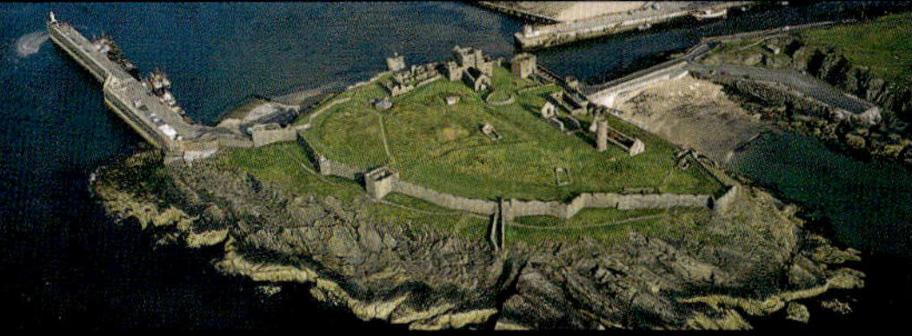

AN ISLAND CITADEL

Celts and Vikings once disputed this patch of land bathed with the warm waters of the Gulf Stream. Since the dawn of time, the Manx people have fought against many would-be conquerors, including the English. Peel Castle, with its crenellated walls, symbolizes the island's tradition of sovereignty. The House of Manannan museum celebrates its spirit of resistance.

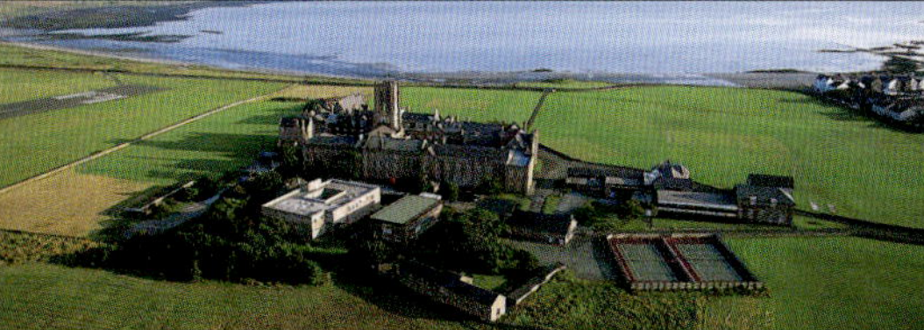

SCHOOL BY THE SEA

King William's College, the jewel of the south, is a famous independent school. It stands by the sea, a few miles outside Port St Mary, a charming village sheltered from the wind at the foot of a hill, and Castletown, famous for the medieval Castle Rushen, the former residence of the Kings and Lords of Mann. At its gate is a famous pub: the Castle Arms.

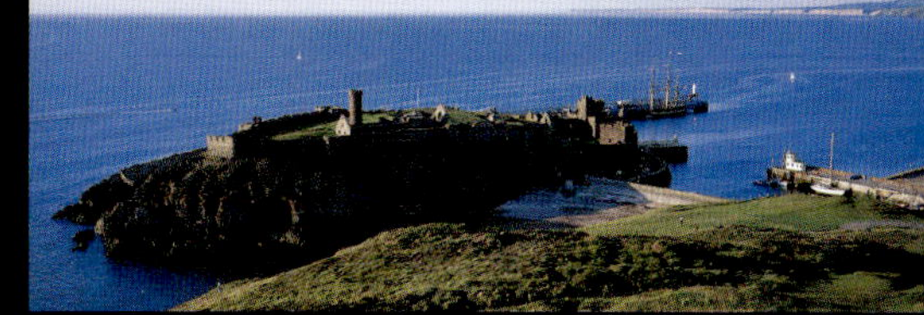

SETTING SUN

At sunset, Peel Castle is tinged with the golden hues of the sky. Peel has earned the nickname of the Sunset City because of the warm red sandstone used to build the castle and cathedral. In days gone by the fishing fleets used to wait for sunset to return to their home port.

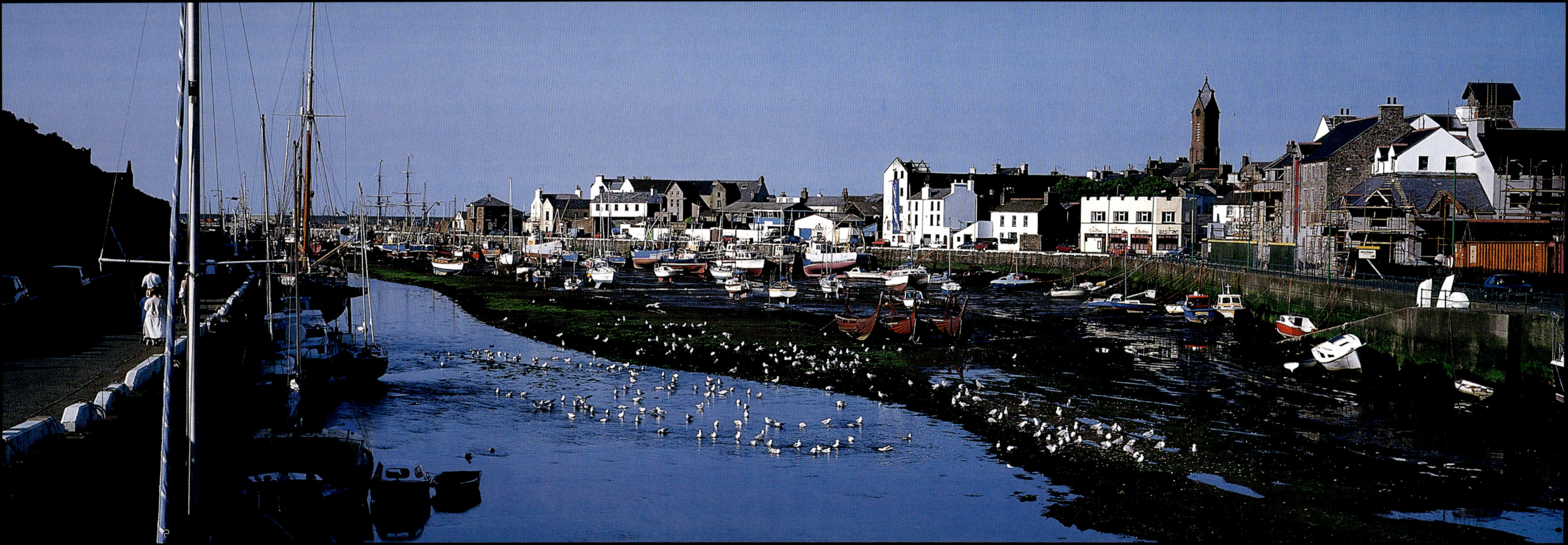

VIKING MEMORIES

Both the Celts and the Vikings have left their mark on the Isle of Man. Visitors can still find Celtic crosses, Nordic cemeteries

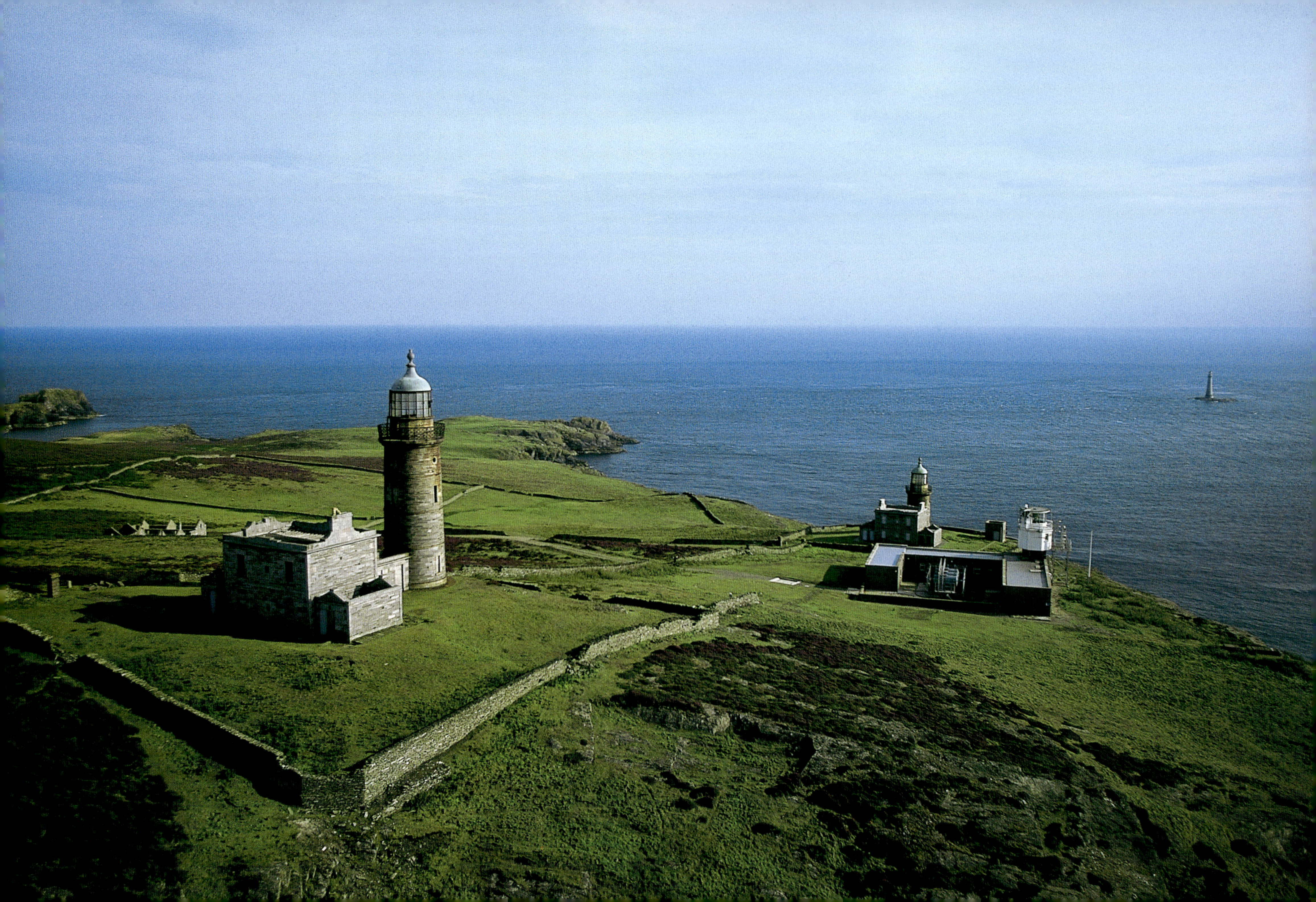

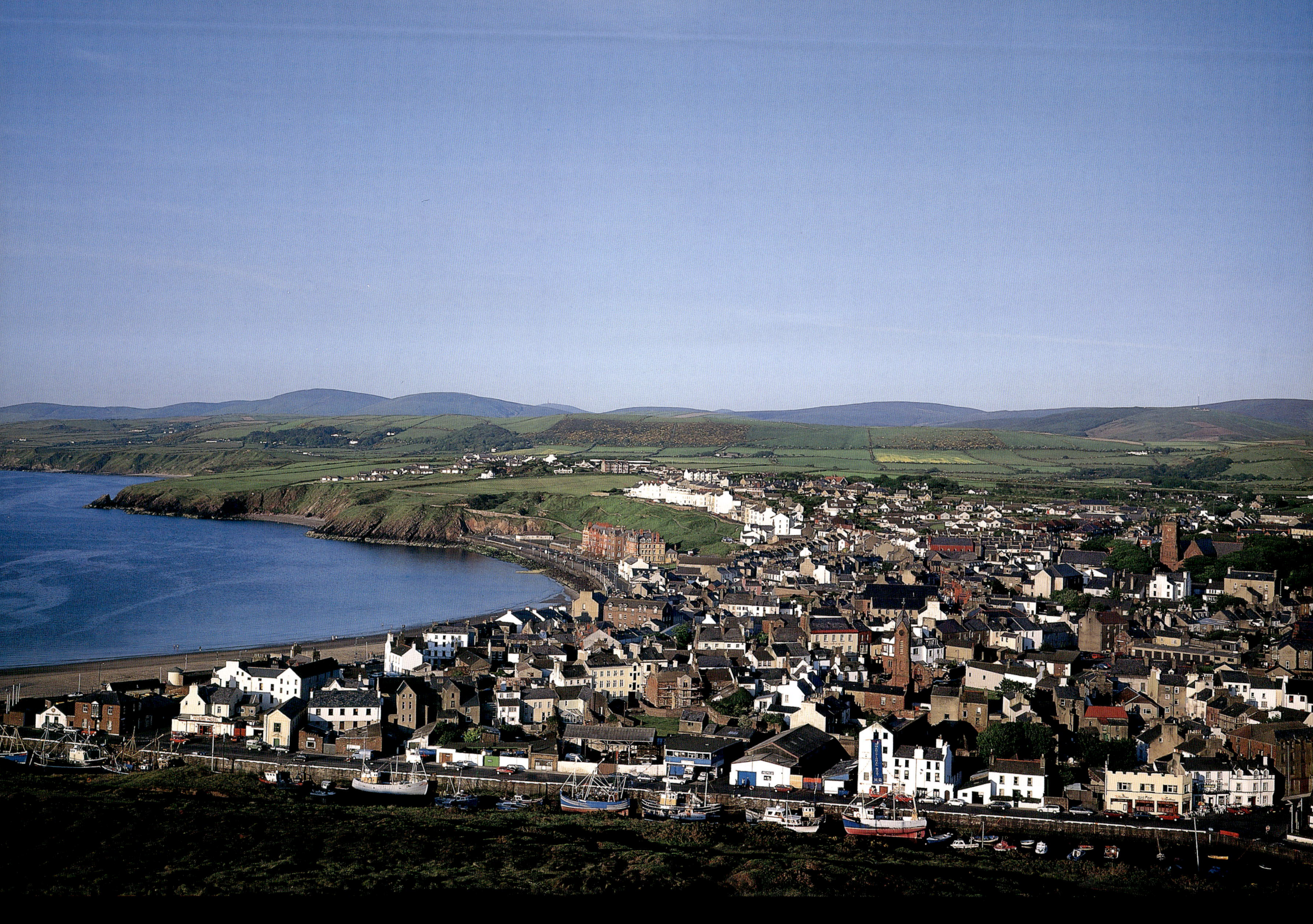

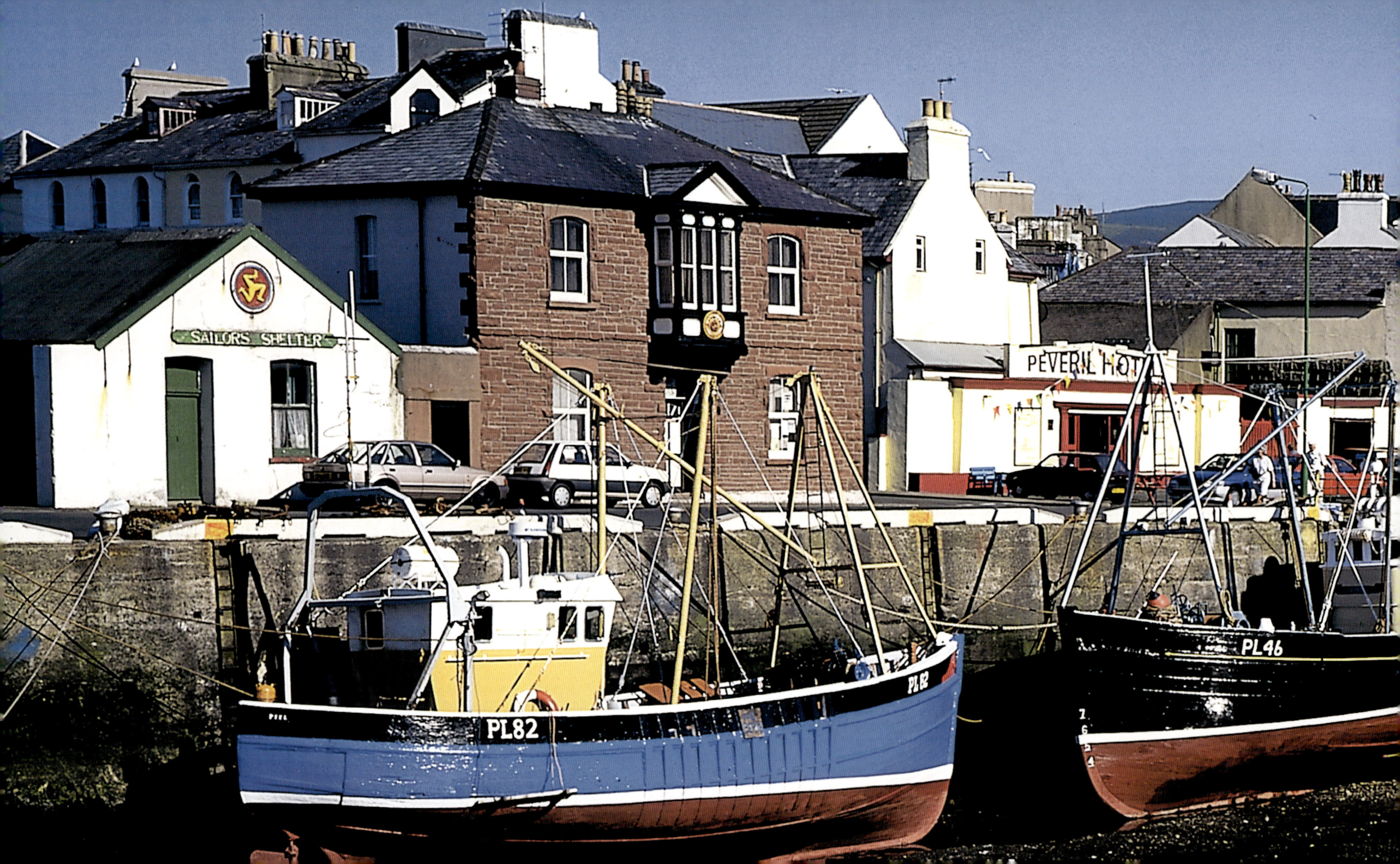
SAILORS SHELTER
PEVERIL HOT
PL82
PL 62
PL46

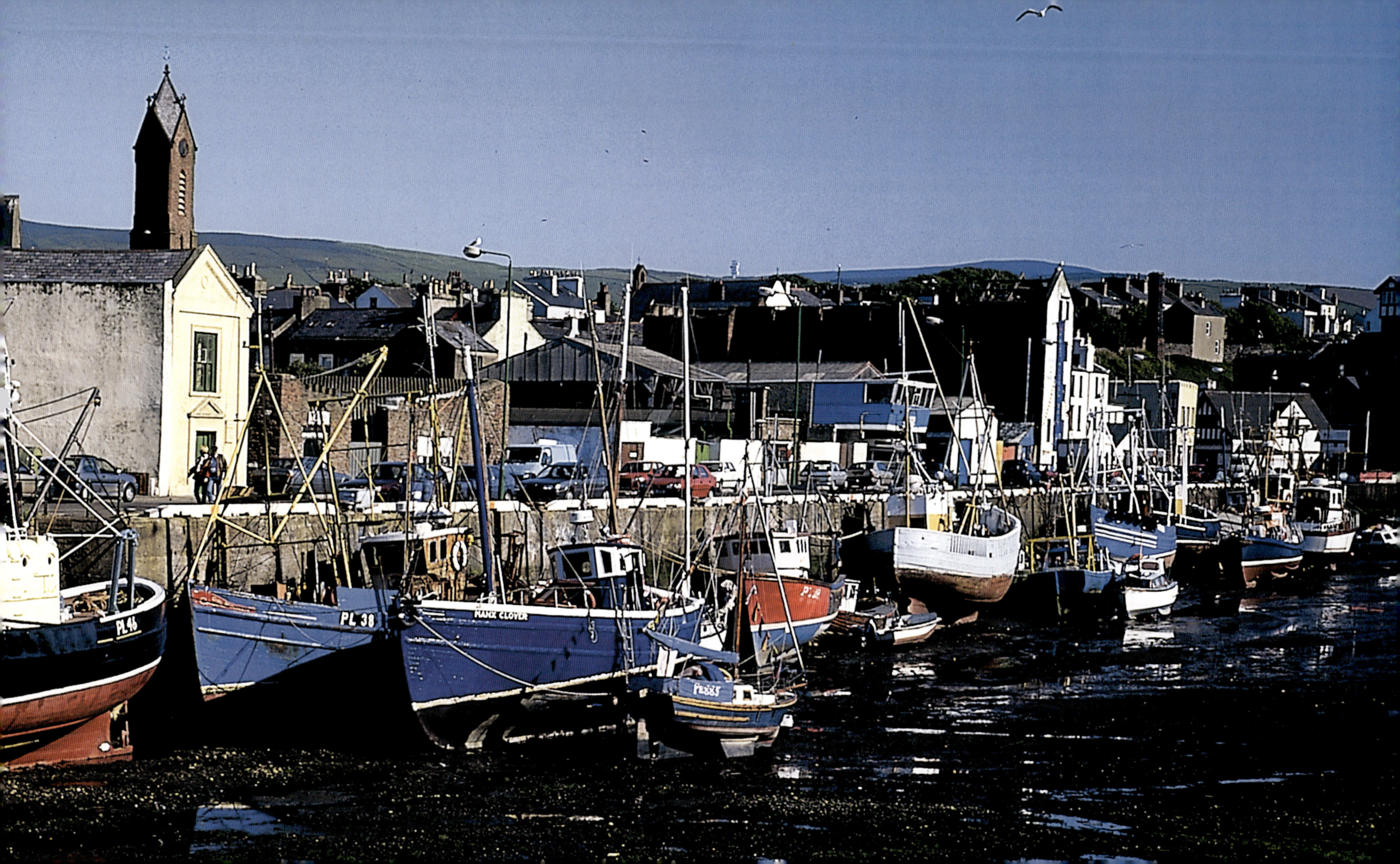
PL46
PL 38
MANX CLOVER

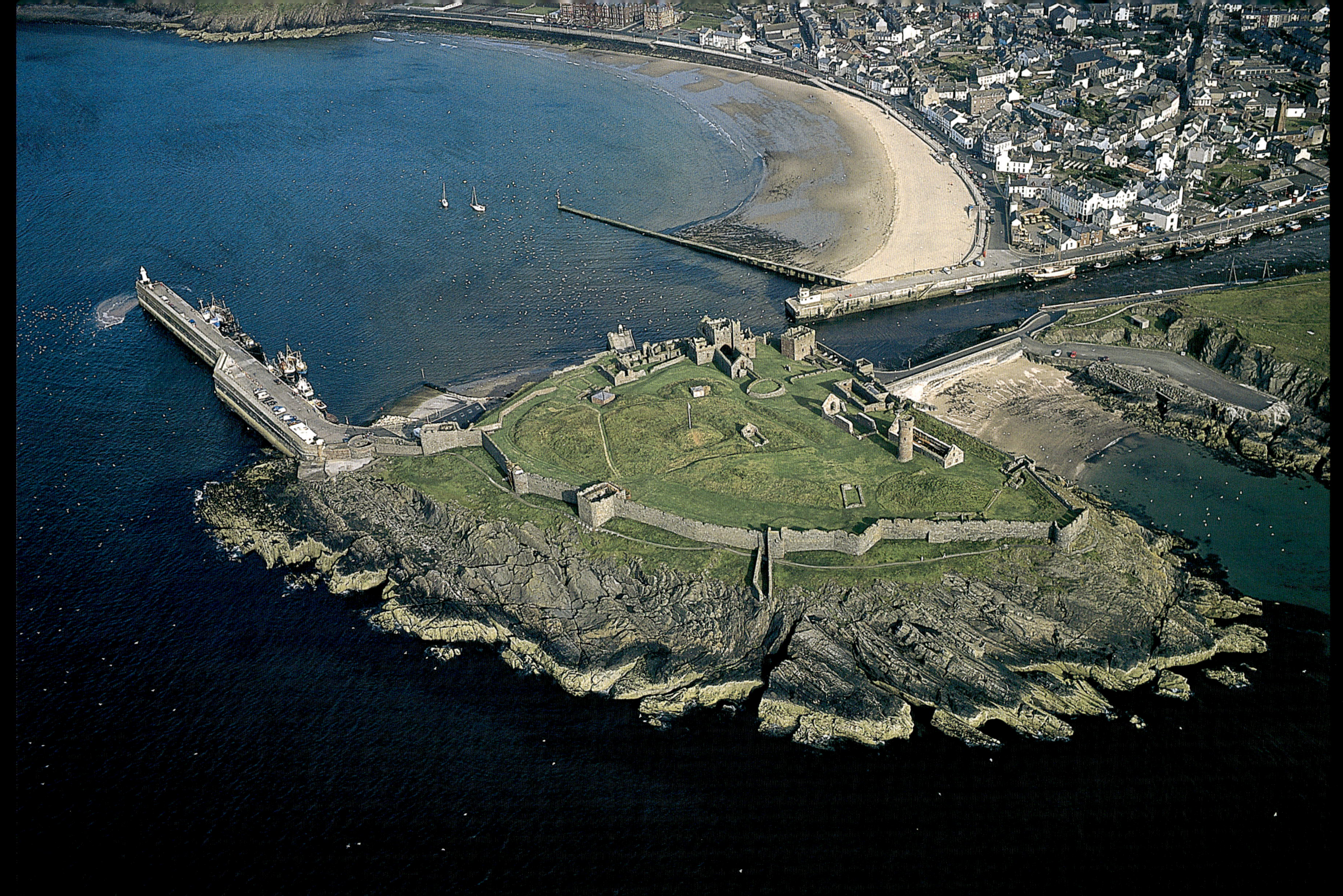

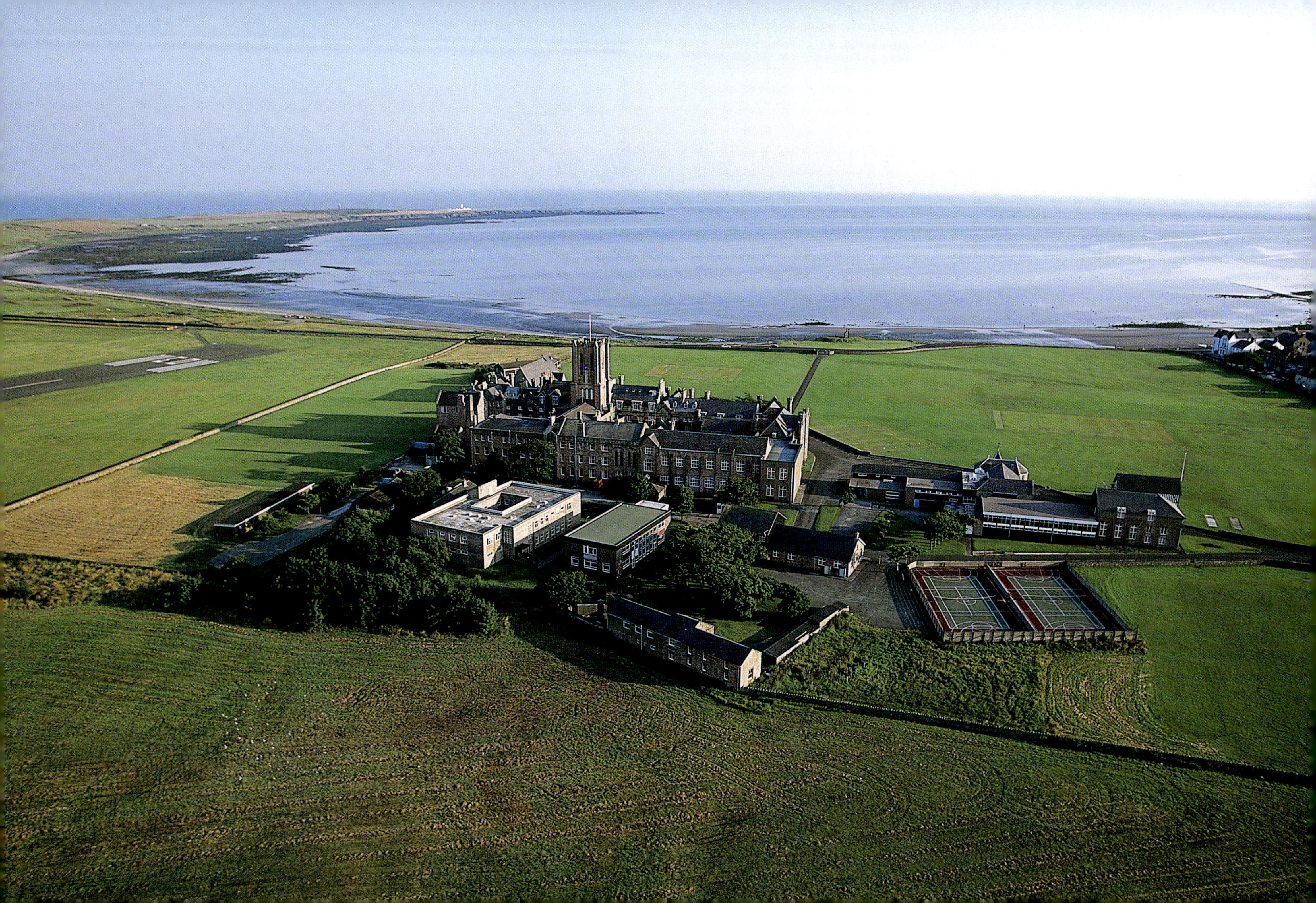

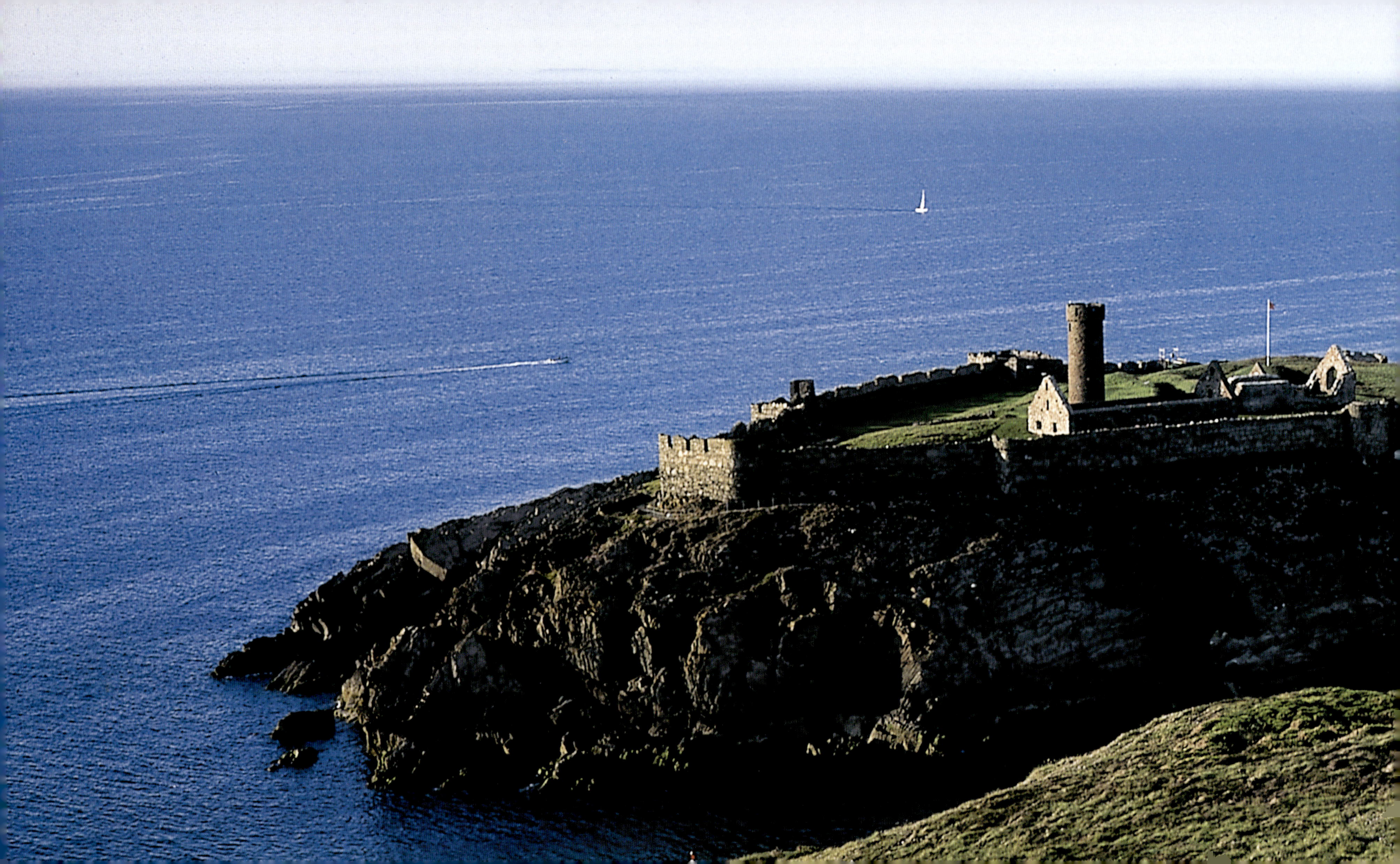

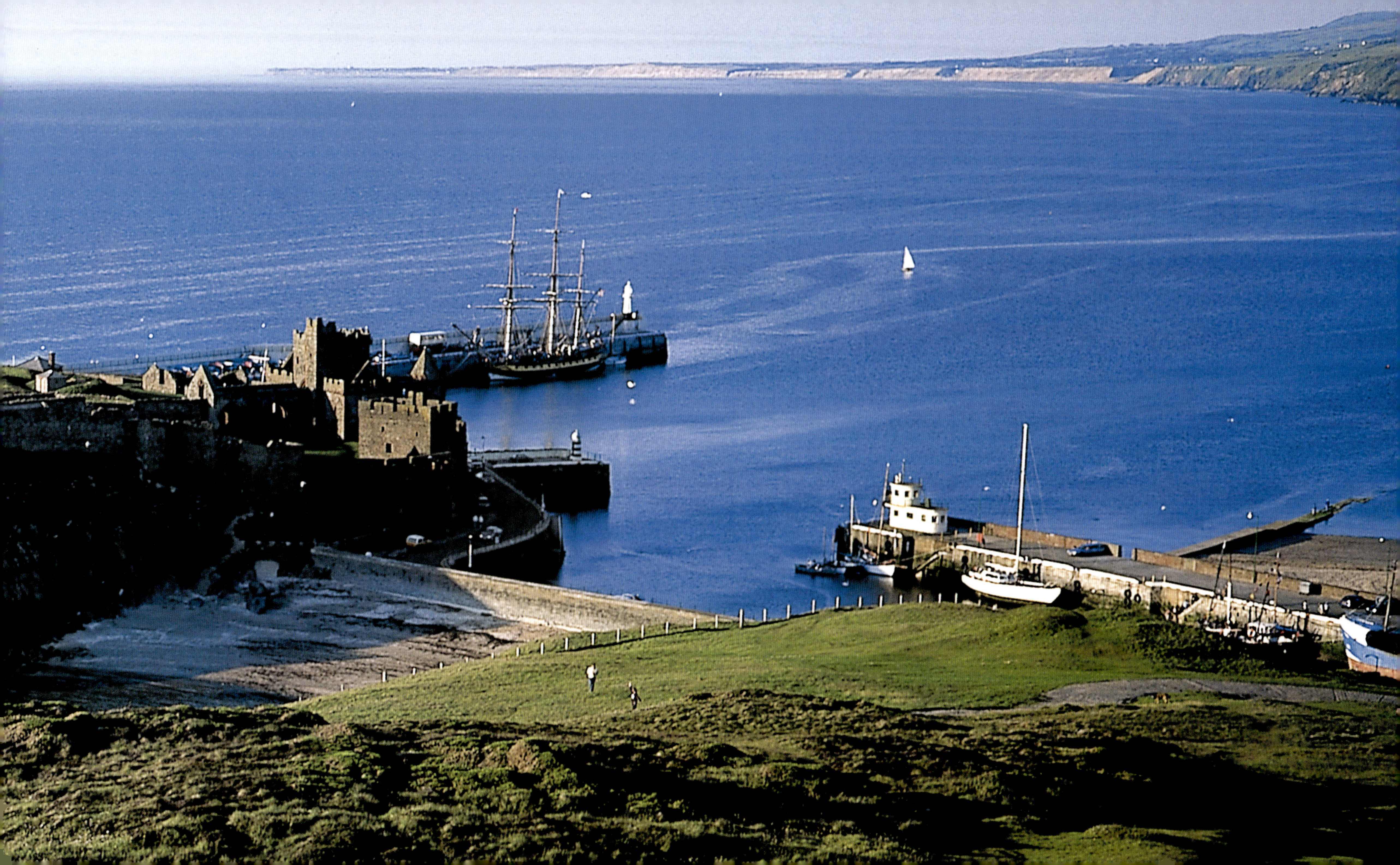

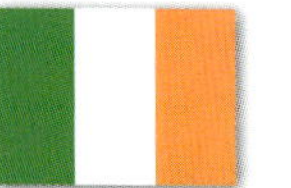

IRELAND·EIRE

From Scotland's Inner Hebrides to Ireland's Giant's Causeway, the spectacular geological sight of 37,000 rocks sculpted through erosion is but a single step – a Giant's step. It was from Ireland that the mythical giant Finn McCool (*Fionn mac Cumhaill* in Gaelic) fought off a challenge by a rival giant from the rocks of Staffa, the neighbouring island with similar submerged columns on Scottish soil. Carried by the dull roar of the waves beating like a drum roll, Finn crossed the waters to battle his foe, accompanied by the rushing of the wind through the pillars of basalt. Today, the Giant's Causeway, the jewel of Ireland, the Emerald Isle, is the pride of the Celtic imagination. Face to the wind, the magic and spells of the legendary heroes of yesteryear are still set to music there. This sea route where Philip Plisson now casts his photographic net is now a World Heritage site. From cliffs to plateaux sliding under the waves, this is the starting point of a tour of Ireland by sea from east to west and north to south. We begin in Ulster, in one of the six counties subject to Great Britain whose unvarying orange colour is still a blot on maps of green Ireland.

Then come the last points of land before America. Donegal, Mayo, Sligo – these counties bewitch us. *'Lig duinn draiocht a churt ort'*, let us cast the die for you. Here the island's legends come alive, and its sovereignty stands proud at the heart of Europe. Under the claws of the Celtic Tiger, with its economy booming at the turn of the millennium, hear the Cliffs of Moher roar. These cliffs rise to 700 feet, rolling away in folds into the endless sea. On the ridge, children appear from nowhere, like leprechauns from the wild moors, telling neverending tales for the tourists.

At the foot of the rocks, out of the caverns and caves wander ceaselessly the ghosts of the Spanish Armada, the fleet of one hundred and thirty vessels sent by Philip II of Spain against Elizabeth I in 1588; its remaining vessels were wrecked in a storm off the Irish coast. Here, the cliffs of Hag's Head rise into the sky; there, Doolin Point bears the scars of the Armada. In the distance lies the Gaeltacht, the region where Gaelic asserts its age-old identity as the majority language.

Then we find ourselves at the Dingle peninsula. At its feet lie the Blasket Islands, home of Tomás Ó Criomhthain, writer, poet, fisherman and farmer. His rural masterpiece *An tOileánach (The Islander)*, a link in the chain between the oral tradition and the written legacy, makes him a figurehead for a culture which seven hundred years of English rule failed to subdue.

To descend into Kerry, with its valleys flecked with sheep, is to see the picture-postcard side of Ireland. Behind Bantry Bay, with its pubs full of whiskey and bardic tales and its giant prawns, where the French fleet came in vain from Brest in December 1796 to help the rebels led by Wolfe Tone, the hero of an unsuccessful independence campaign, you plunge down towards Crookhaven, the last harbour before Mizen Head, the southwesternmost point of County Cork.

It is here that the swells break on Fastnet Rock. In these waters blown by the four winds, a tragic disaster separated French yachtsman Éric Tabarly from the *Pen Duick*. *Kenavo*, Éric. Farewell… A black sail on the Celtic Sea.

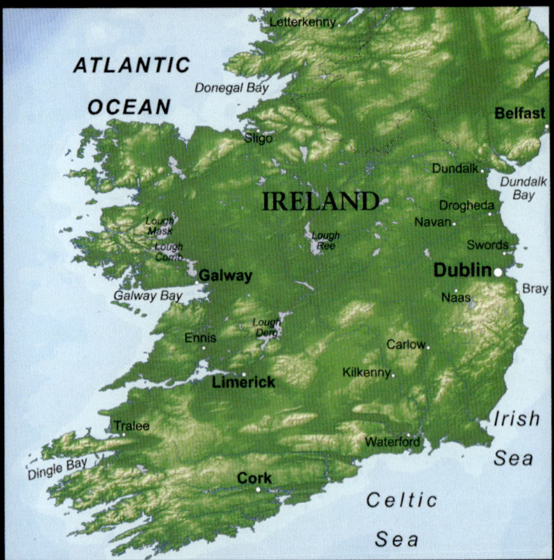

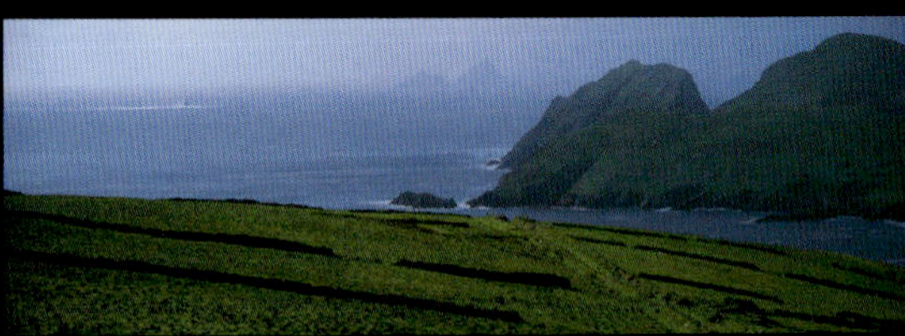

GENTLE KERRY
With the Dingle peninsula and the Blasket Islands, Kerry, in the south-west has beautiful coastal mountains and sheer cliffs. It makes a pleasant destination for tourists, but sailors know its harsher side, especially around the Skellig Islands, just visible on the horizon.

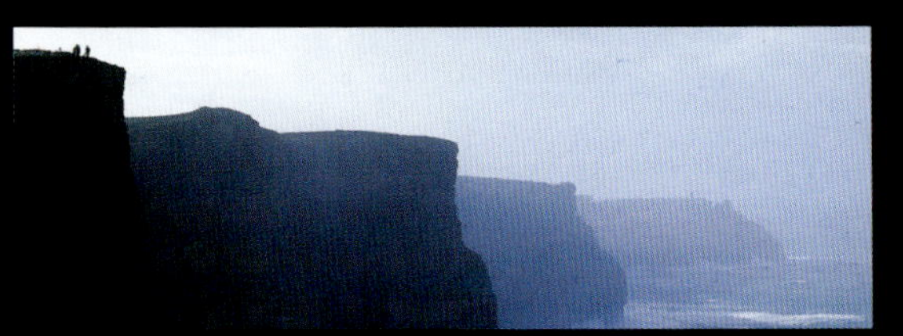

CLIFFS OF MOHER
Like scars written on the rocks, here lies something of a requiem for the 'Invincible Armada' (1588). On the ridge of the Cliffs of Moher which rise to 216 metres, children perpetuate its memory

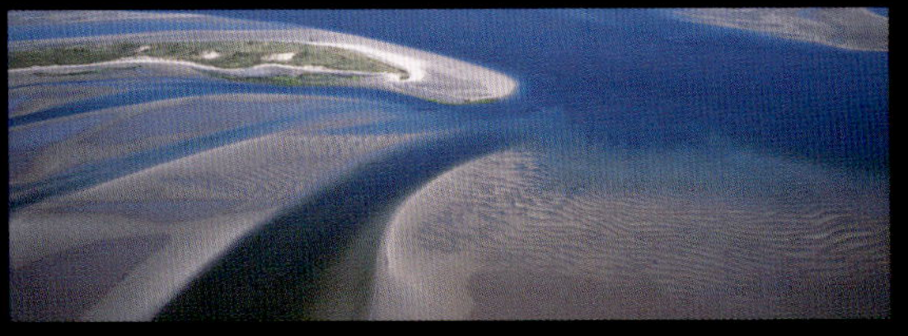

MODERN ART
Like a white gold carpet, the sand emerging at low tide forms a work worthy of a masterpiece of modern art. An ideal shot for the marine painter.

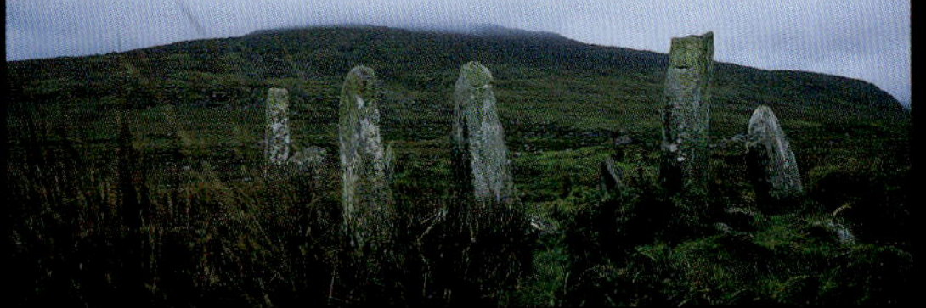

STANDING STONES
Standing stones or menhirs have studded the Celtic lands for centuries. In ancient times they were used as places of worship and ritual, and to celebrate the cycle of the seasons. They are

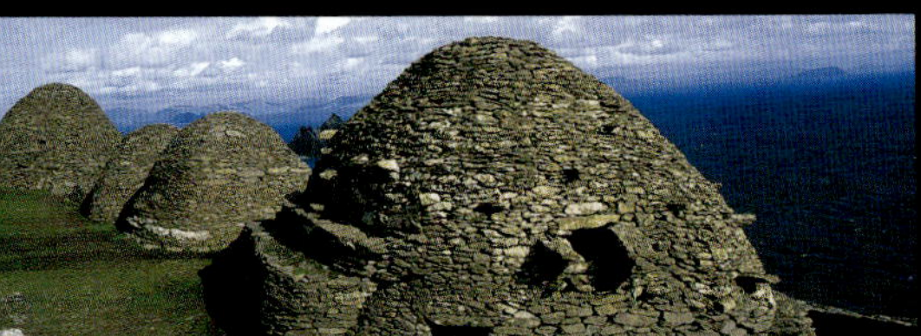

THE MONKS OF ST MICHAEL'S
The stone huts of St Michael's monastery on the island of Great Skellig. Behind lies the mainland and the town of Waterville, with Little Skellig between the two. Monks are believed to have settled

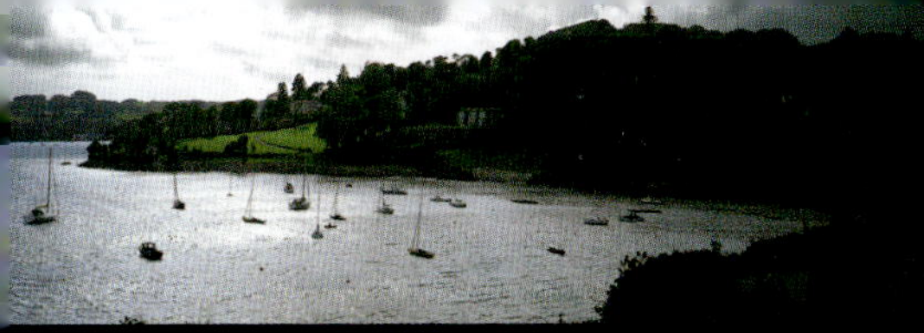

THE HARBOUR OF GLANDORE
South of Cork lies a garden-like stretch of green land. It begins at Kinsale, a popular venue for yachting, and continues as far as the Mizen Head cliffs. In between are harbours that are welcoming in bad weather: Crookhaven, Glandore (above) or Tragumna.

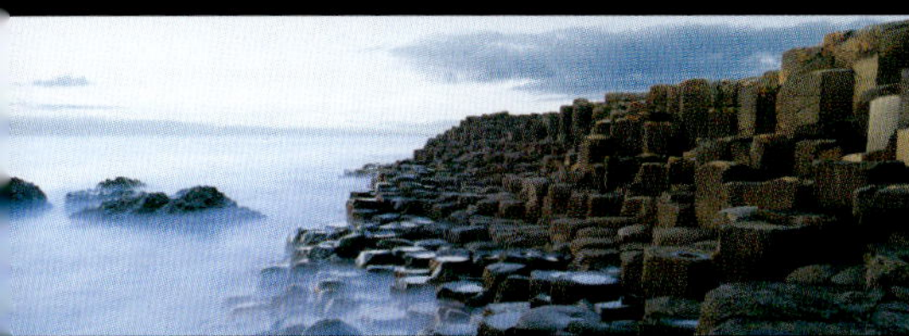

GIANT'S CAUSEWAY
These 37,000 basalt columns sculpted by erosion form the Giant's Causeway. It was from here that Finn McCool, the local hero, crossed the sea to fight a Scottish giant from the island of Staffa. This sea coast, from which the Mull of Kintyre can be glimpsed, is classed as a World Heritage site.

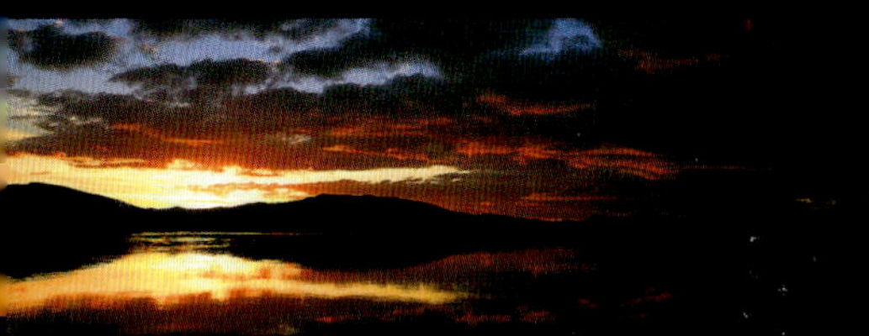

VALENCIA ISLAND
The Skellig Islands are a short distance from Valencia Island. It probably owes its name to the fact that the Spanish berthed here in the 16th century. At sunset, the whole of Kerry is set ablaze.

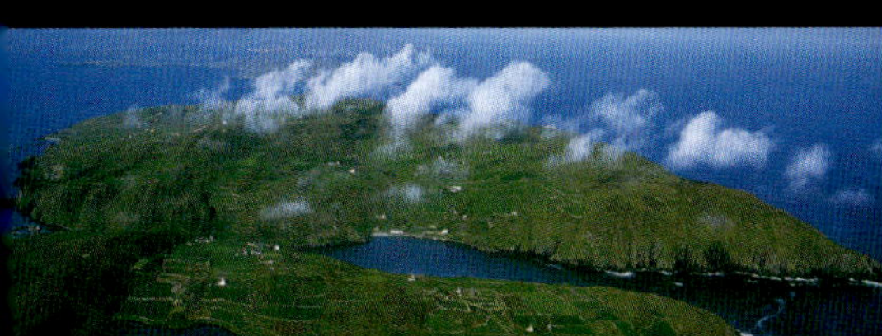

THE ROARING OF THE SEA
This inlet plunges between the steep slopes of Clear Island. It closes the southern end of the archipelago of Long Island Bay. If you rent a fisherman's cottage to admire the view towards Skibbereen and the summits of Sherkin, a few minutes' rowing

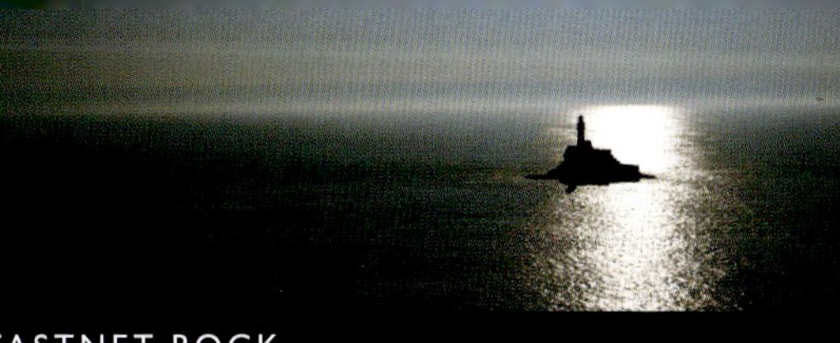

FASTNET ROCK
This pyramid-shaped rock was the last boulder passed by the passengers on the *Titanic* in April 1912. Its Gaelic name is Carrig Aonar – 'lonely rock'. In 1979, fifteen competitors in the famous Fastnet yacht race lost their lives here during a freak storm. The lighthouse is now automated, but the keeper visits once a month.

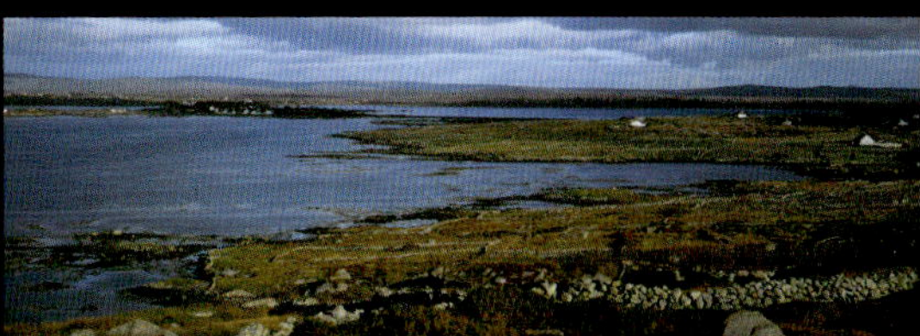

GALWAY BAY
Galway Bay is barred at the horizon by the imposing Inishmore and Inishmaan and their little sister, Inisheer. To starboard, a last gate before the ocean, lies the round island of Gorumna with its lakes like mirrors and its one thousand inhabitants, one of five islands today connected to the mainland by a bridge, and a sanctuary for the Gaelic language.

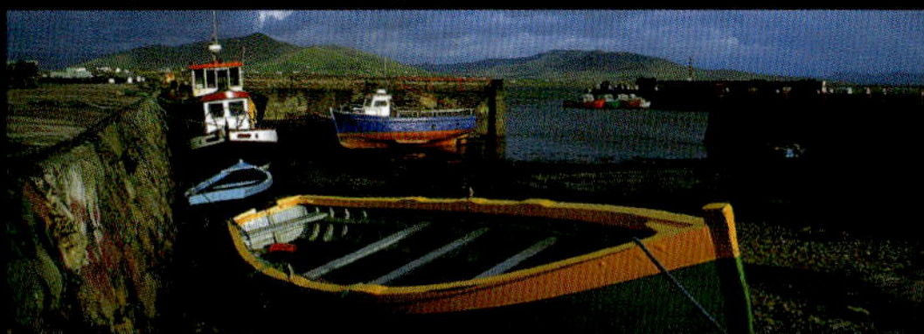

TO THE RHYTHM OF THE TIDES
From Dingle on the west coast to the port of Rossaveel with its backdrop of the Aran Islands, and as far as the east coast ports sheltered from the dominant winds, a whole flotilla of small fishing boats ply their trade.

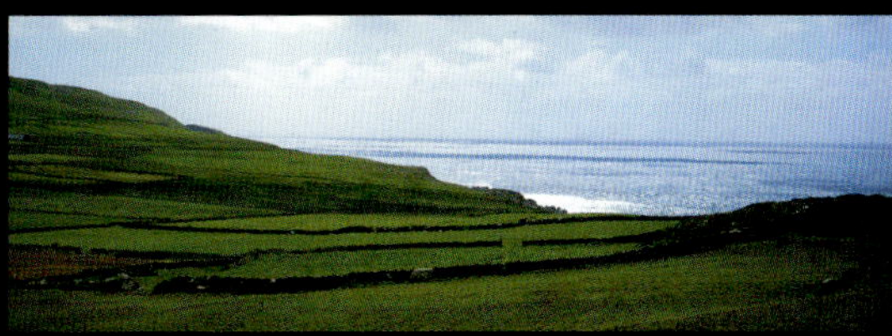

GREAT BLASKET
Off a chain of sheer-cliffed mountains which give the Dingle peninsula its wild beauty, Great Blasket Island, said to look like an enormous beached whale, is full of history, and was home to the poet and fisherman Tomás Ó Criomhthain. Its population was

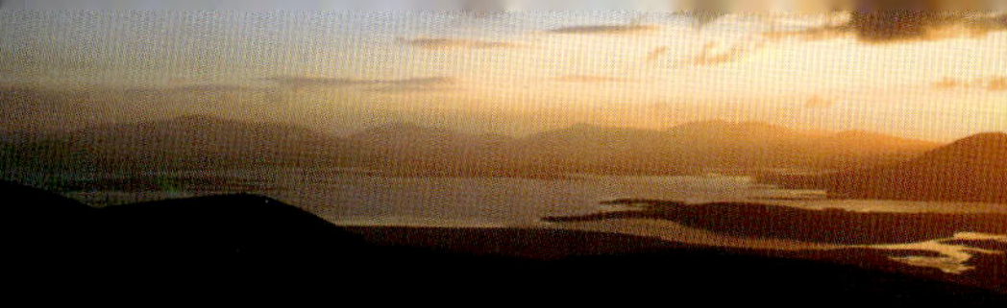

PANORAMIC ACHILL
Achill Island is the largest Irish island (57 square miles) and is flanked by three counties: Mayo, Clare, and Connemara. Here there are Neolithic remains and, on the slopes of the mountain of Slievemore, a deserted village, a lasting memorial to the great potato famine in the 19th century.

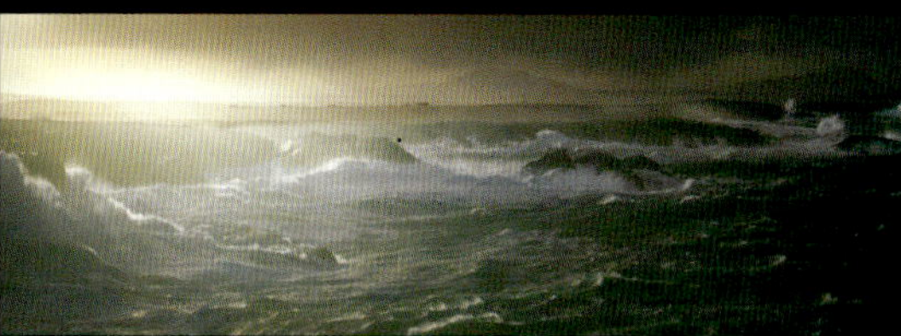

MAYO BLUES
Warning of a fierce gale moving to the north-west. It was in such conditions that the French fleet which left Brittany in 1798 reached the coast of County Mayo to provide support for the Irish insurgents.

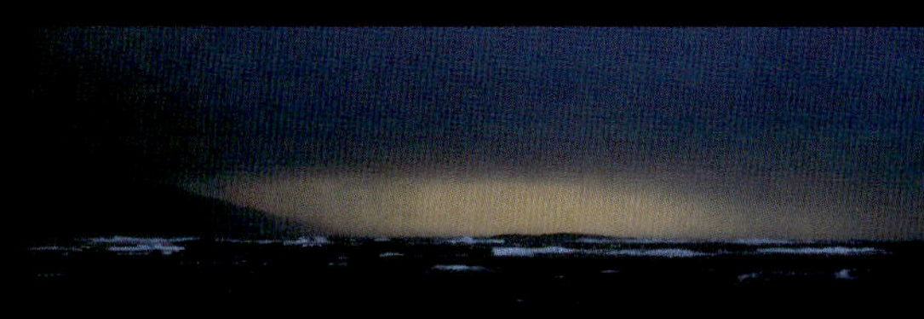

BEWITCHING MULLET
The Mullet peninsula in County Mayo has peat bogs, limestone plains and steep-sided rocks. Stretching from the austere, dark Lough Corrib in the north, to the port of Killarney and Killala Bay, is the Gaeltacht, the land where the Gaelic language is preserved.

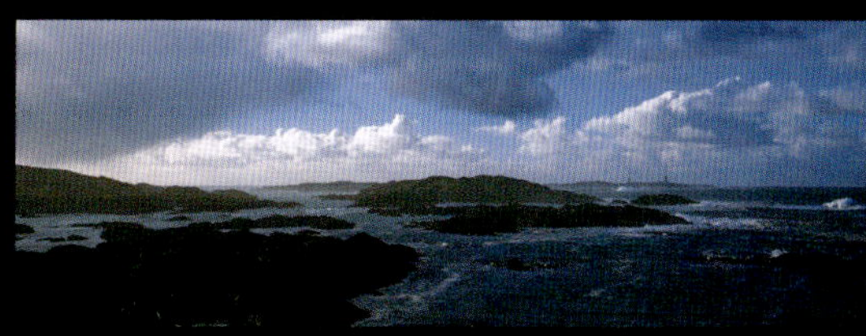

SLYNE HEAD
All around Slyne Head, the most westerly point of Connemara, are small islands, rocks just visible above the water and reefs on which boats can break up even in small storms. On the tiny island of Illaunamid are two lighthouse towers. The road there is

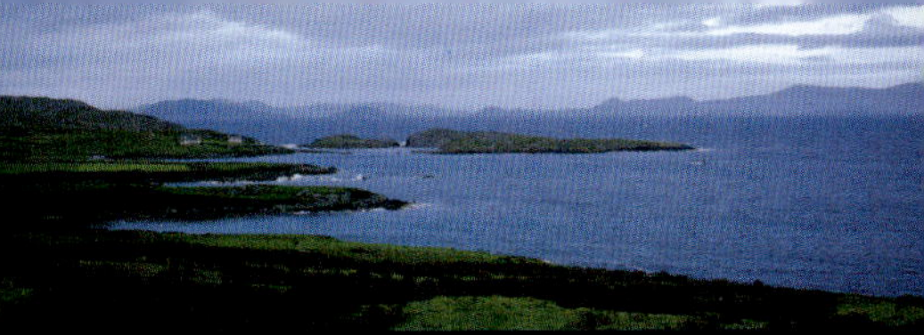

THE CHAOS OF CONNEMARA
The wild and entrancing coast of Connemara, seen from the pretty village of Clifden. Grey rocks form a portcullis to defend the land. It was here that one of Cromwell's officers grumbled: 'There is not wood enough to hang a man, nor earth enough to bury him.' Beyond the village of Roundstone lies a jagged coastline.

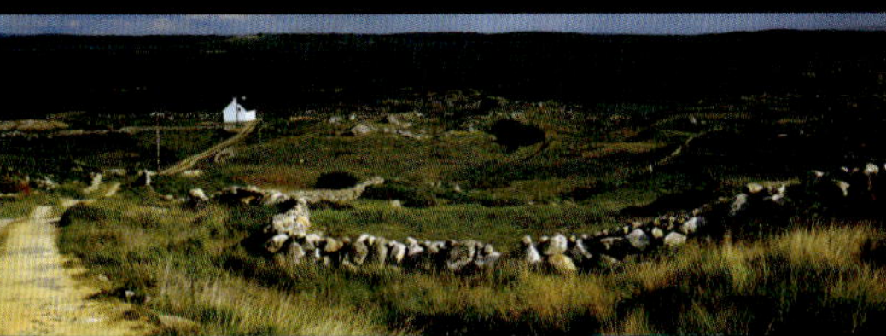

THE STONES OF CARNA
In the far north, beyond Galway and behind Clifden, you pass through this landscape of stones and moorland, rocks and peat. Carna, in the middle of Connemara, is a timeless example of it, despite the flash of a tiny white house sitting on the golden grass reddened like old bronze – a refuge on the road to nowhere.

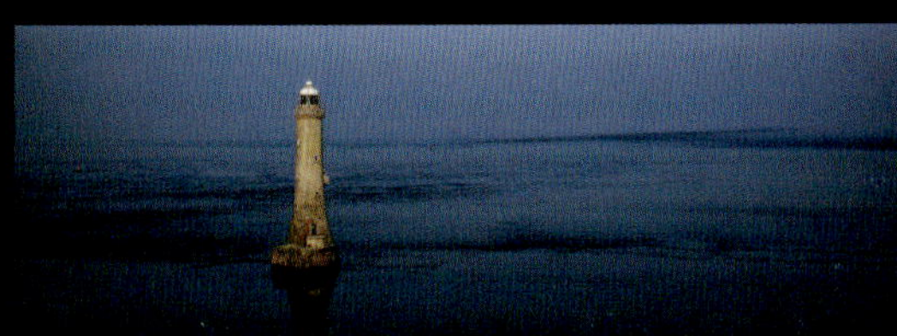

CORK BAY
Inis Sionnach in Gaelic; Haulbowline in English. This lighthouse marks the entrance to Cork Bay, Ireland's southern port of entry. The Irish Navy established its Admiralty here, under its protection. The island has been fortified since 1602. It was handed back to the Irish Free State government in 1923.

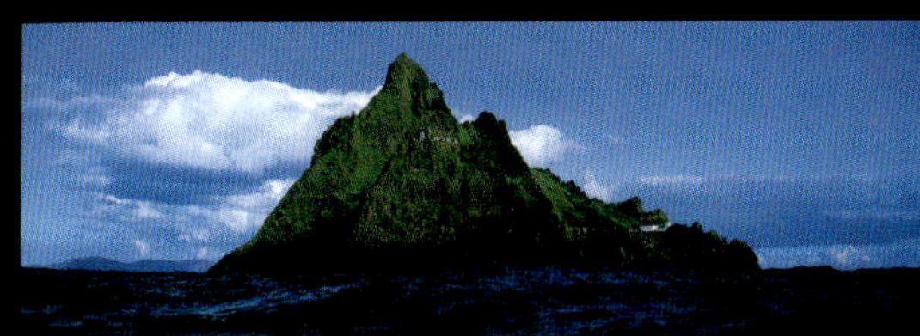

INVINCIBLE SKELLIG
These are the Skellig Islands, off Waterville, a cheerful small Kerry town, wedged between lake and sea. A sheer rock, home to the 6th-century monastery of St Michael – a fortress of faith – Great Skellig rises 700 feet above the water. A zigzagging path leads to its

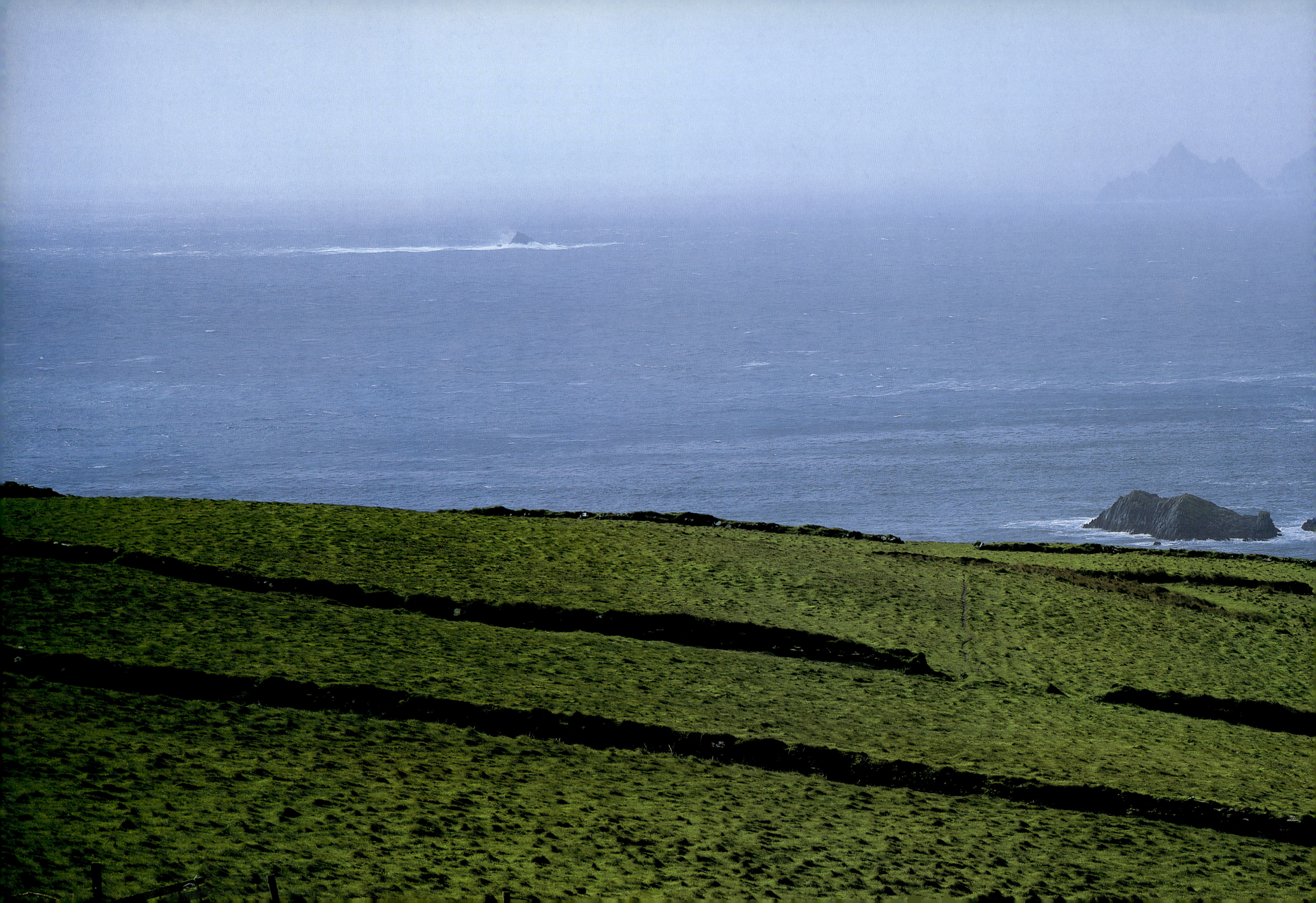

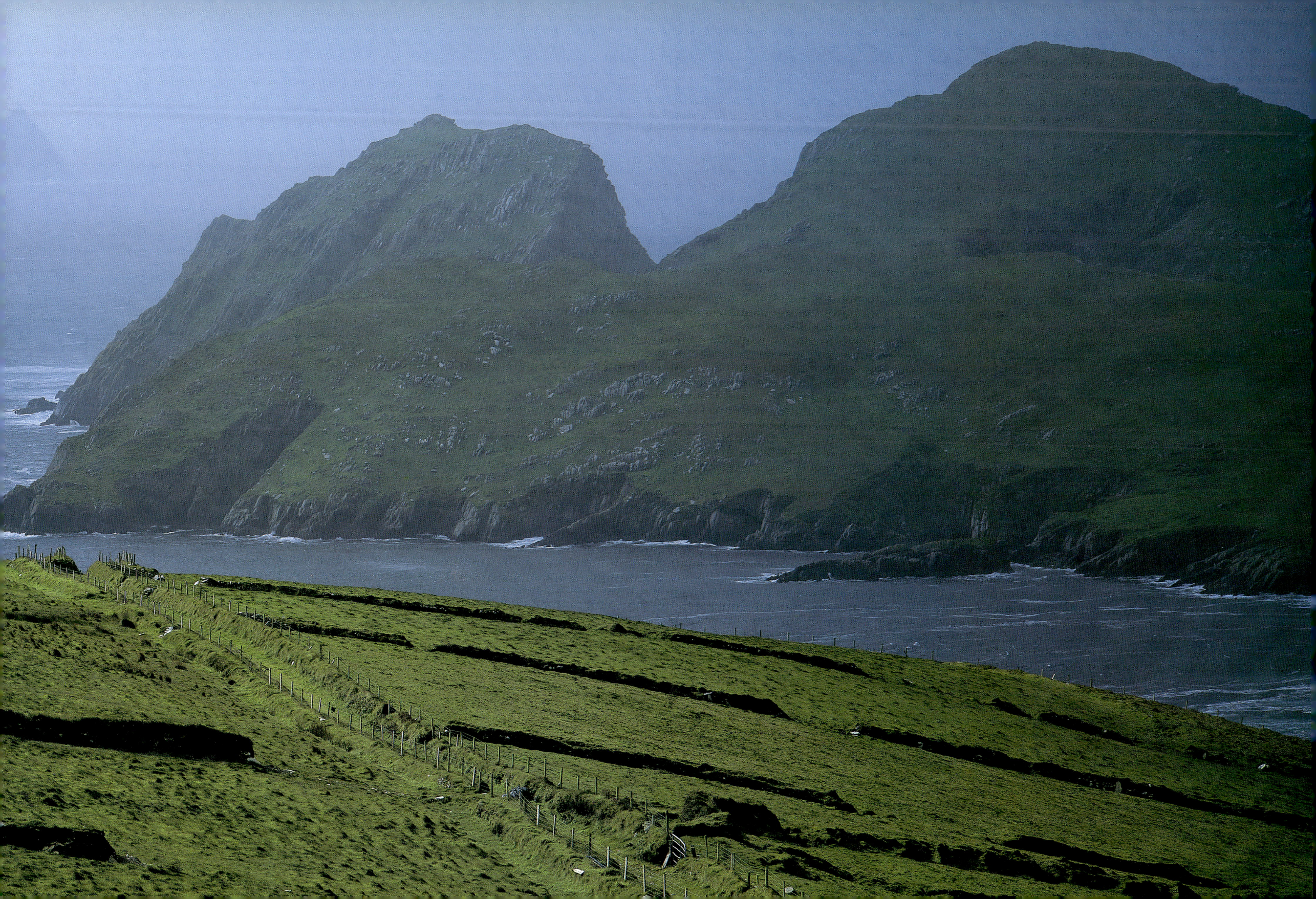

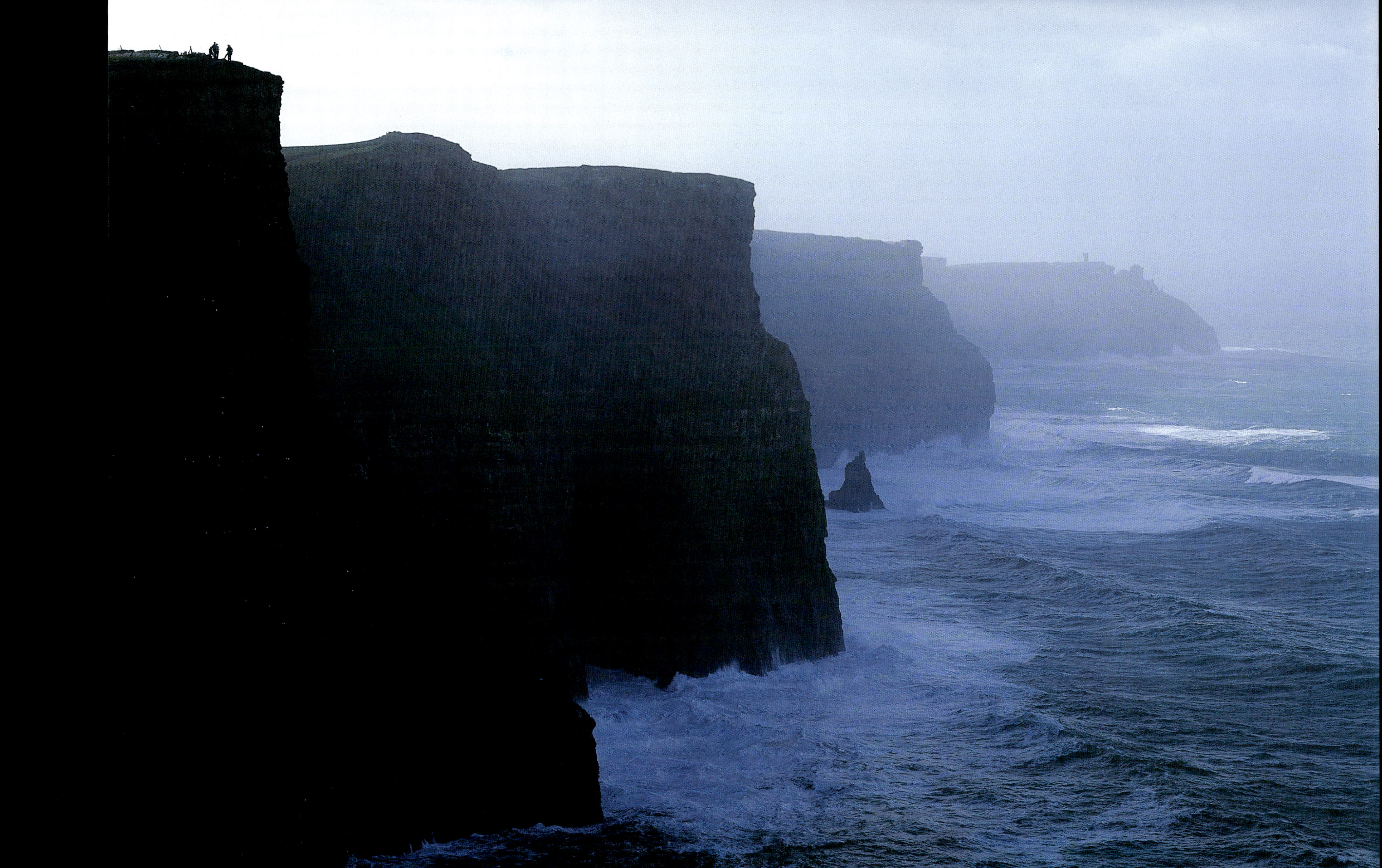

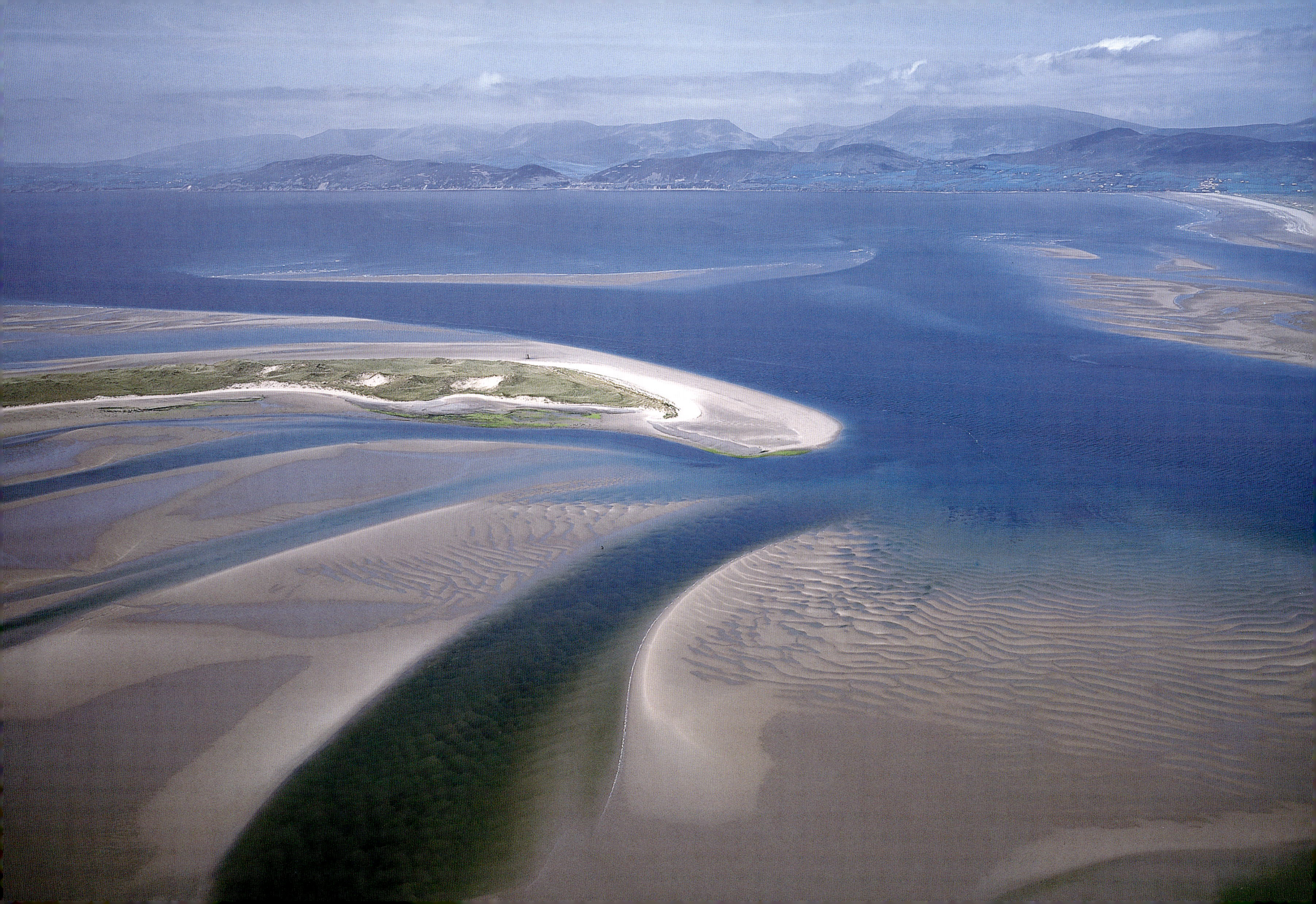

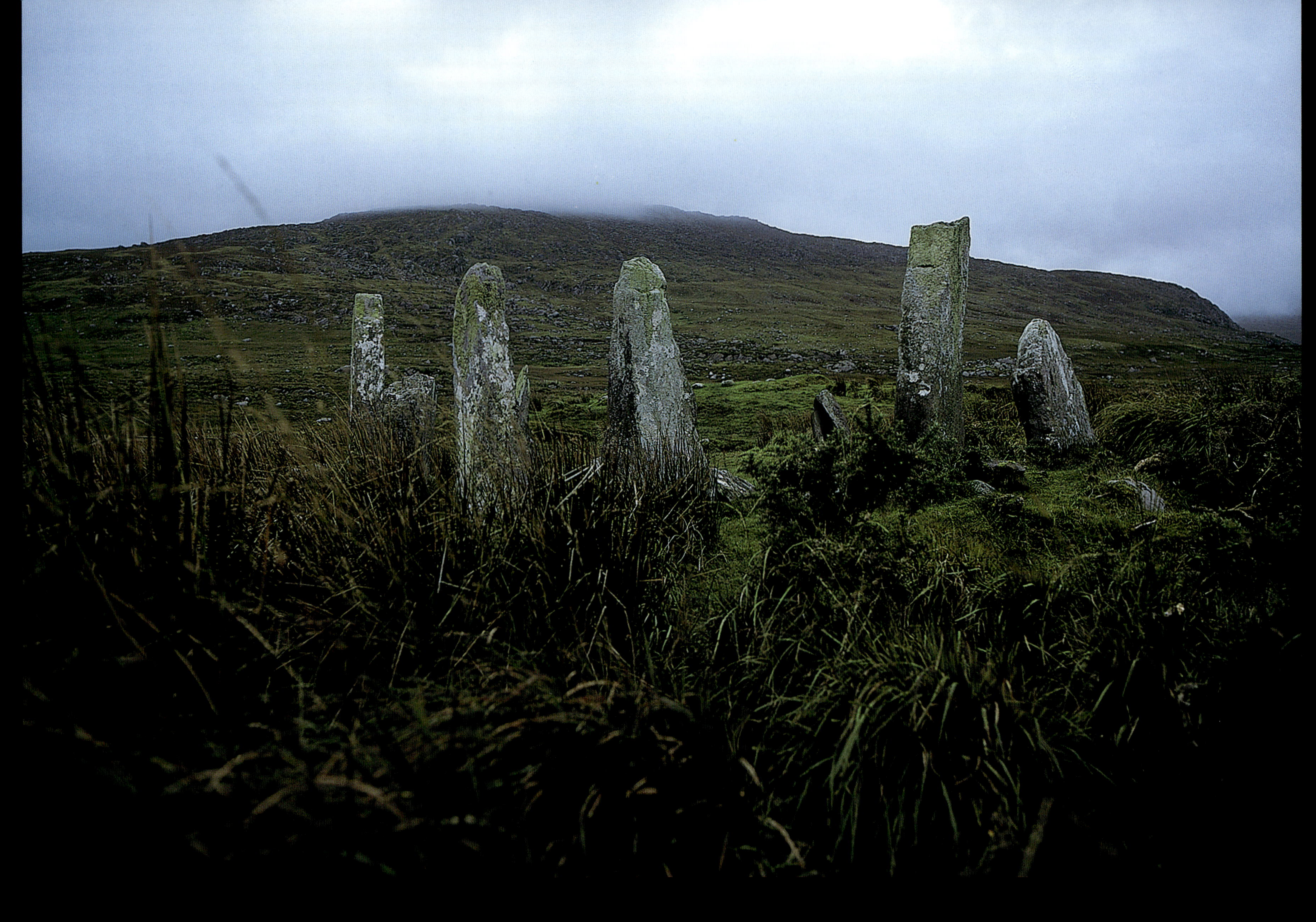

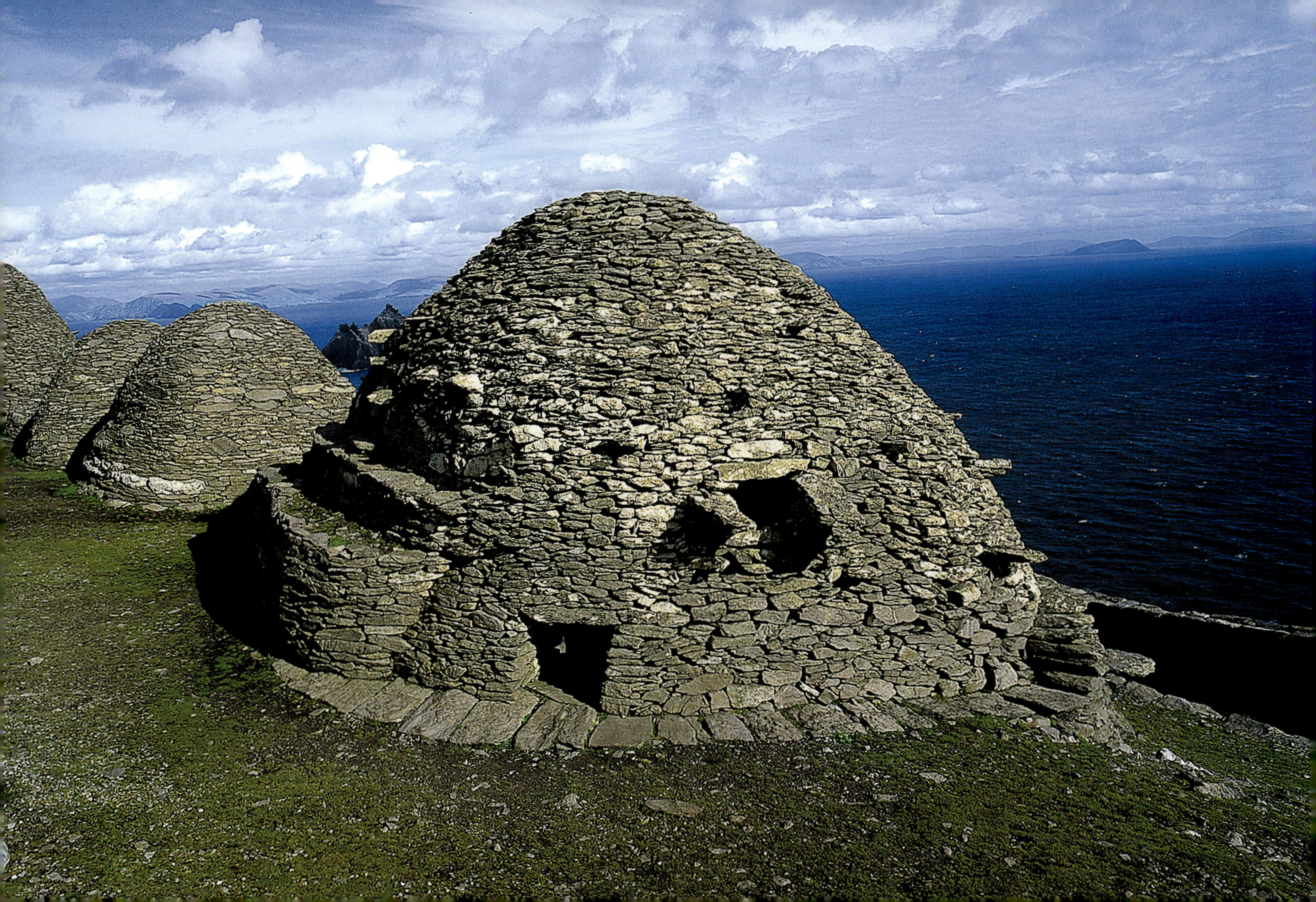

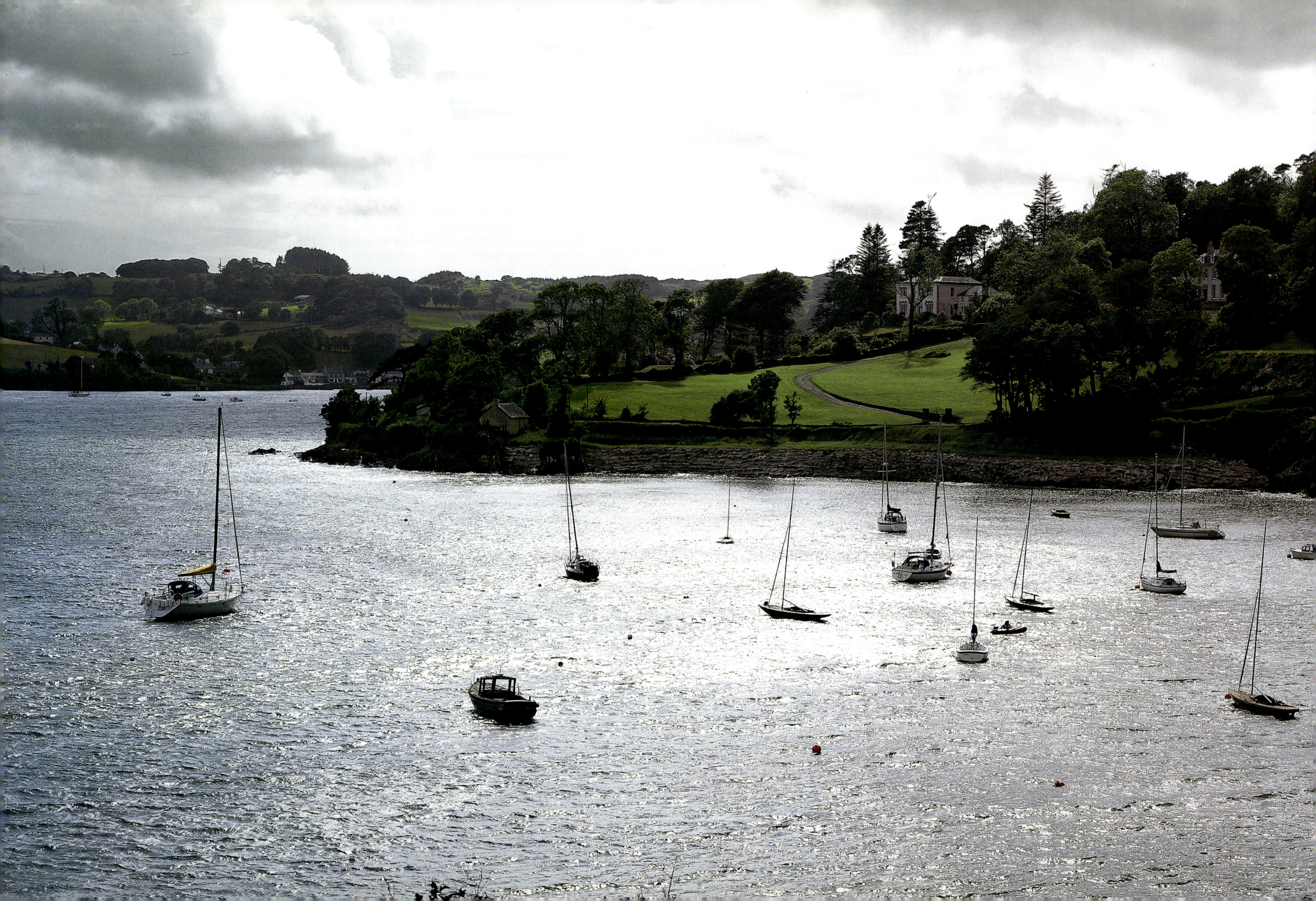

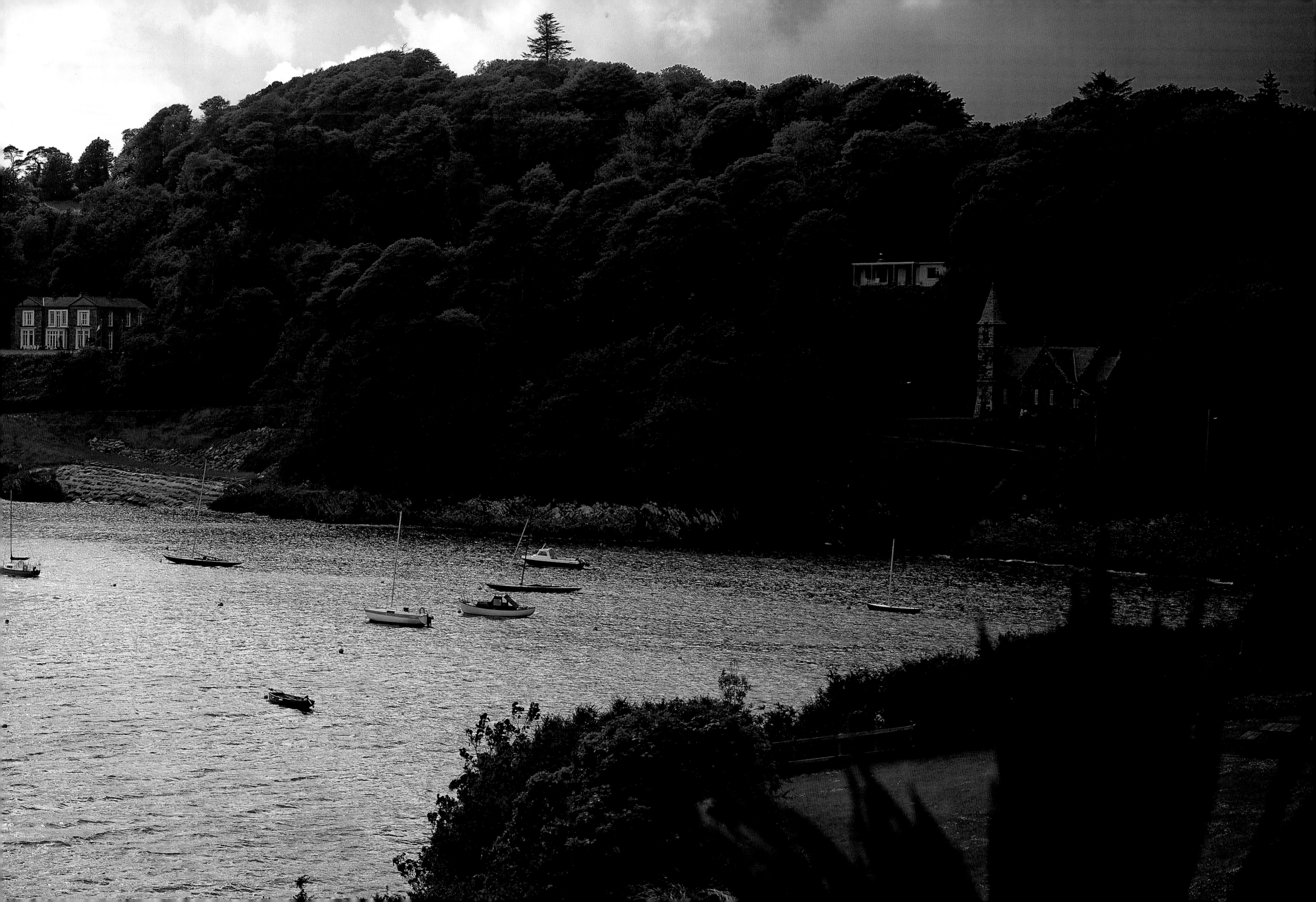

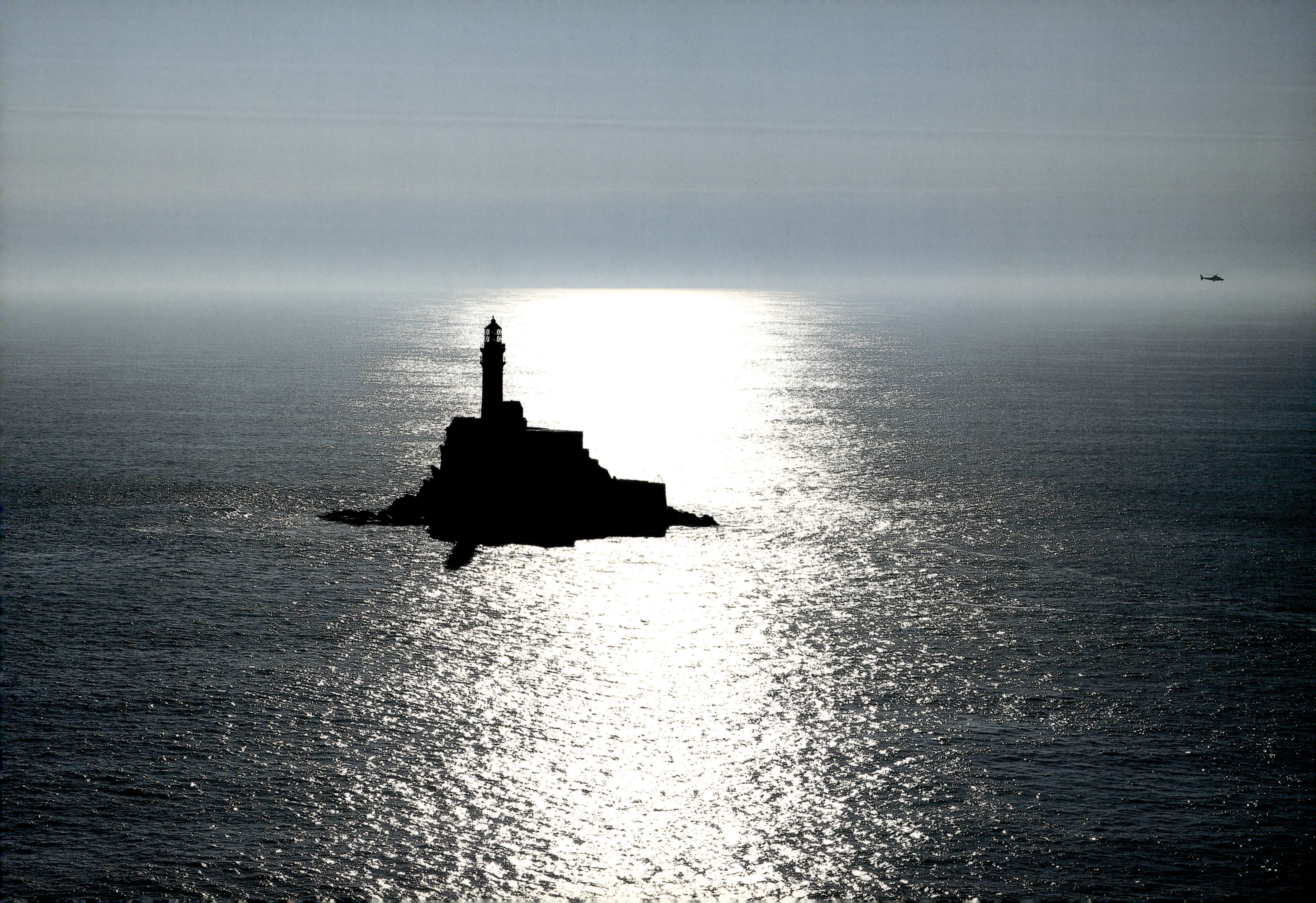

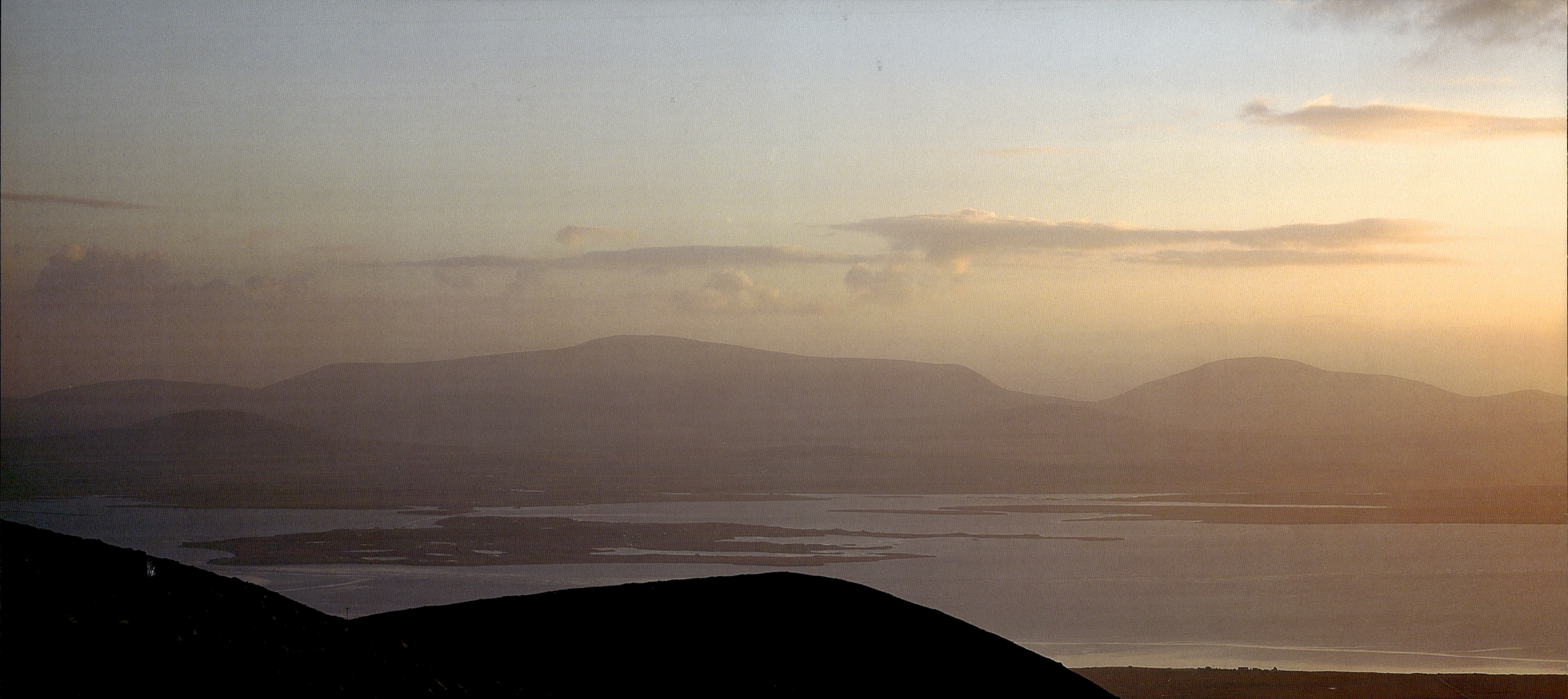

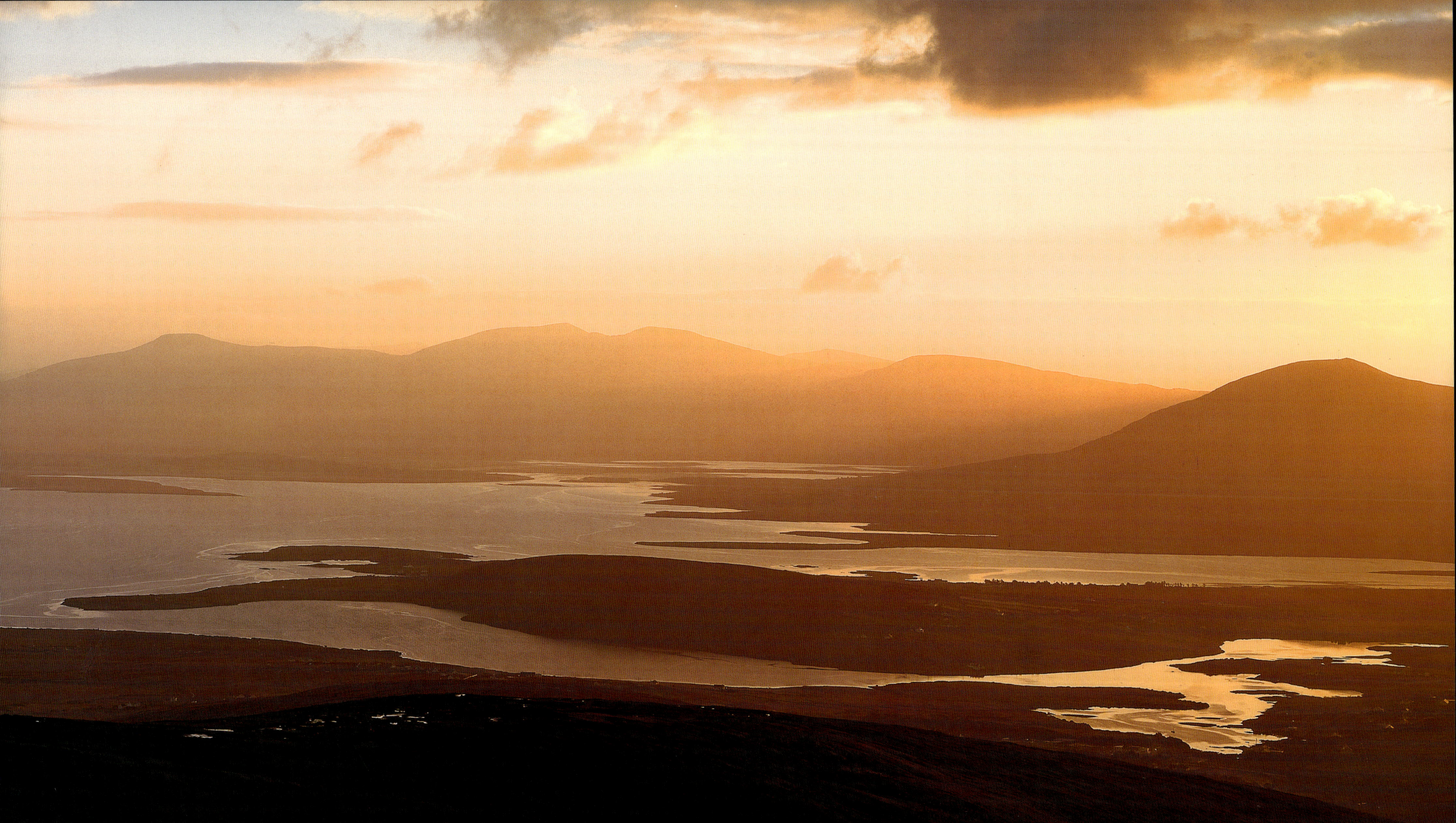

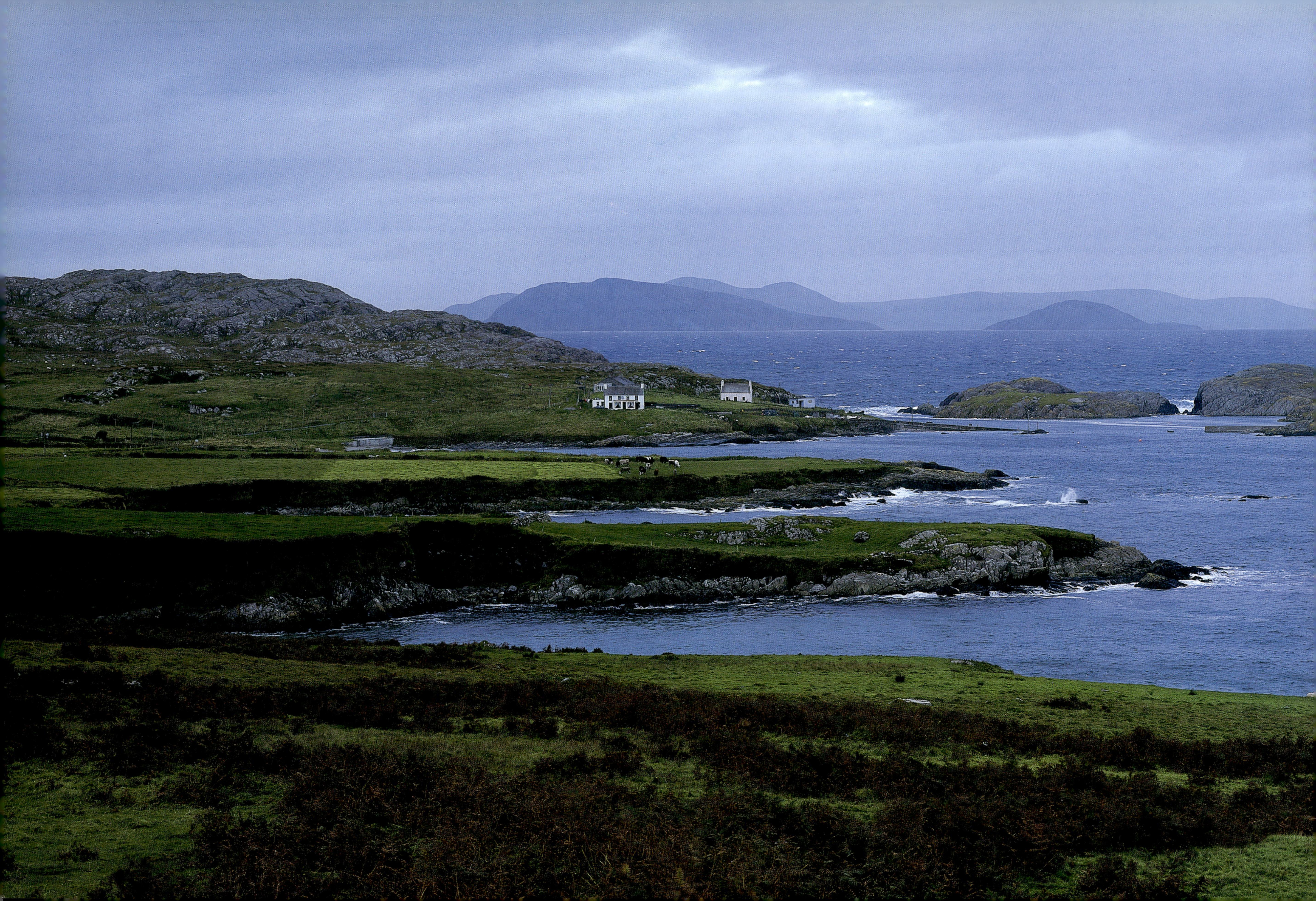

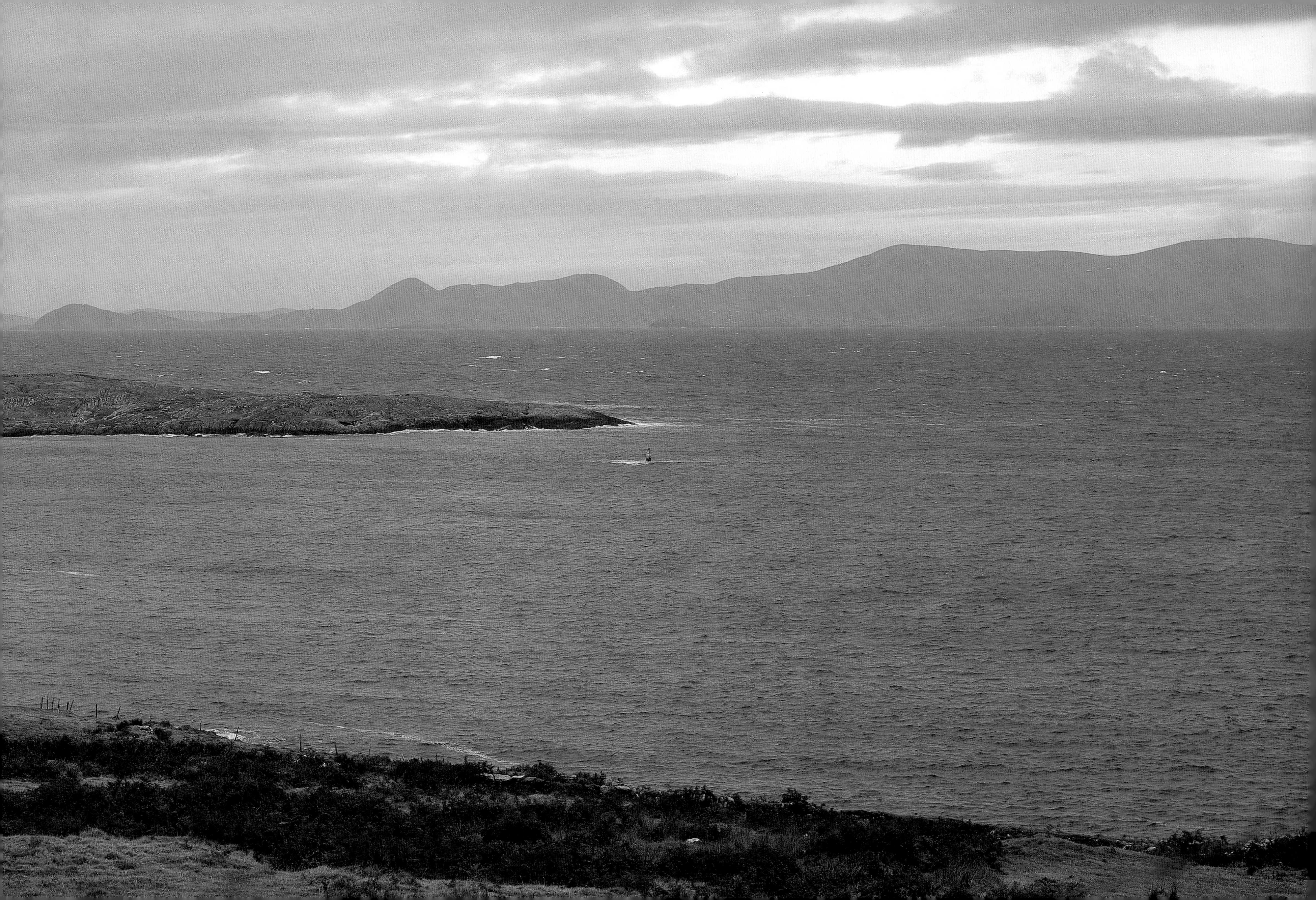

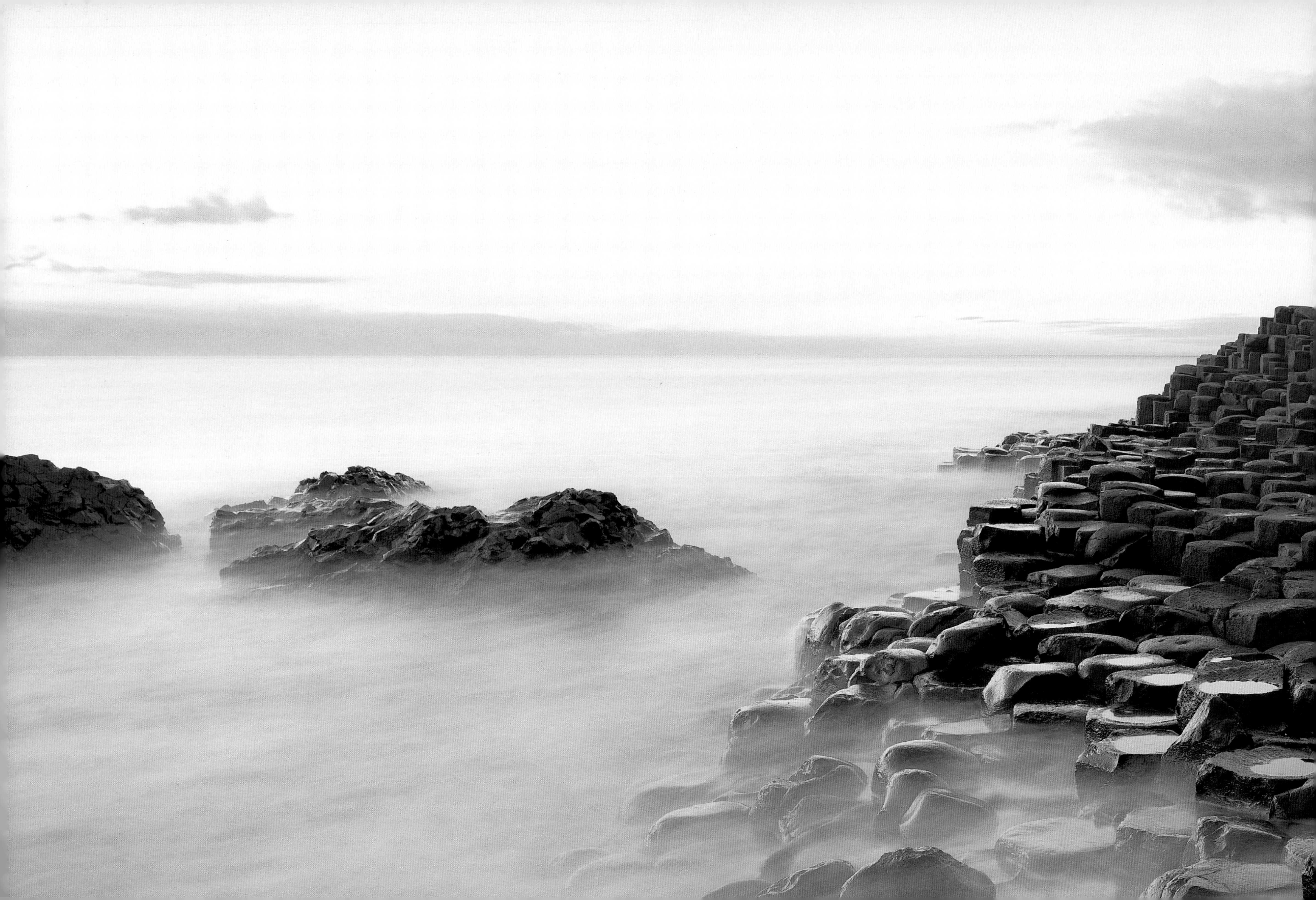

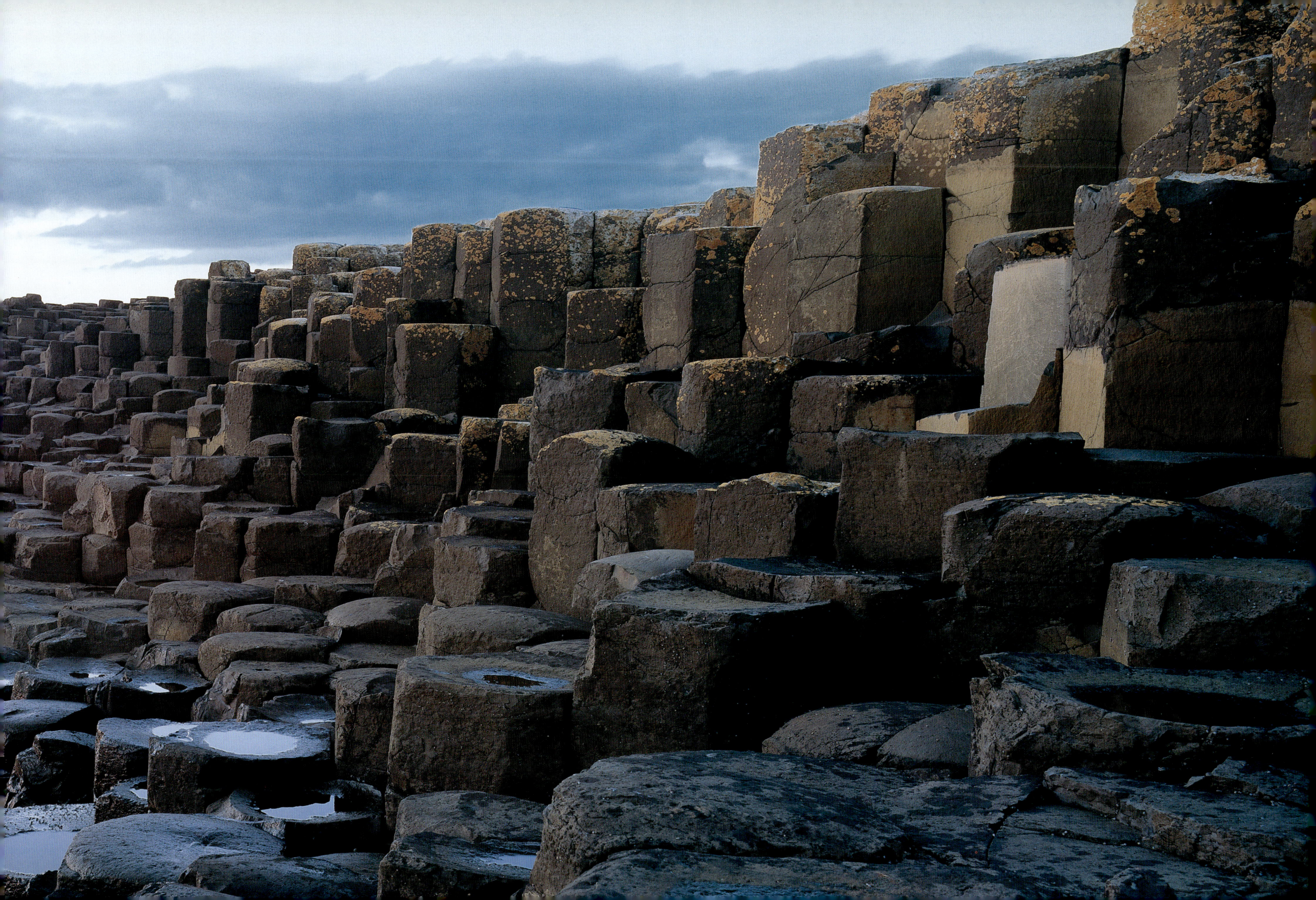

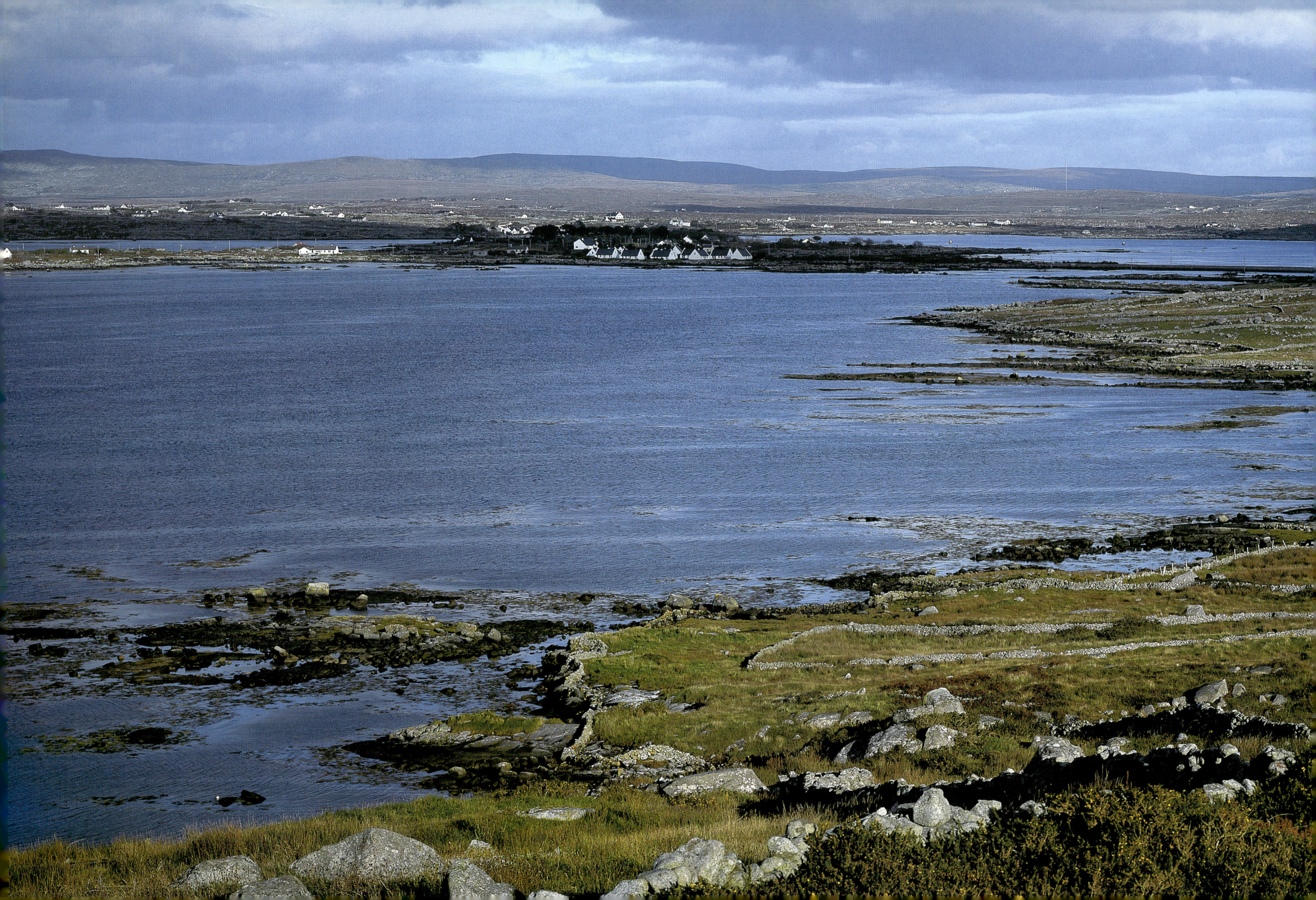

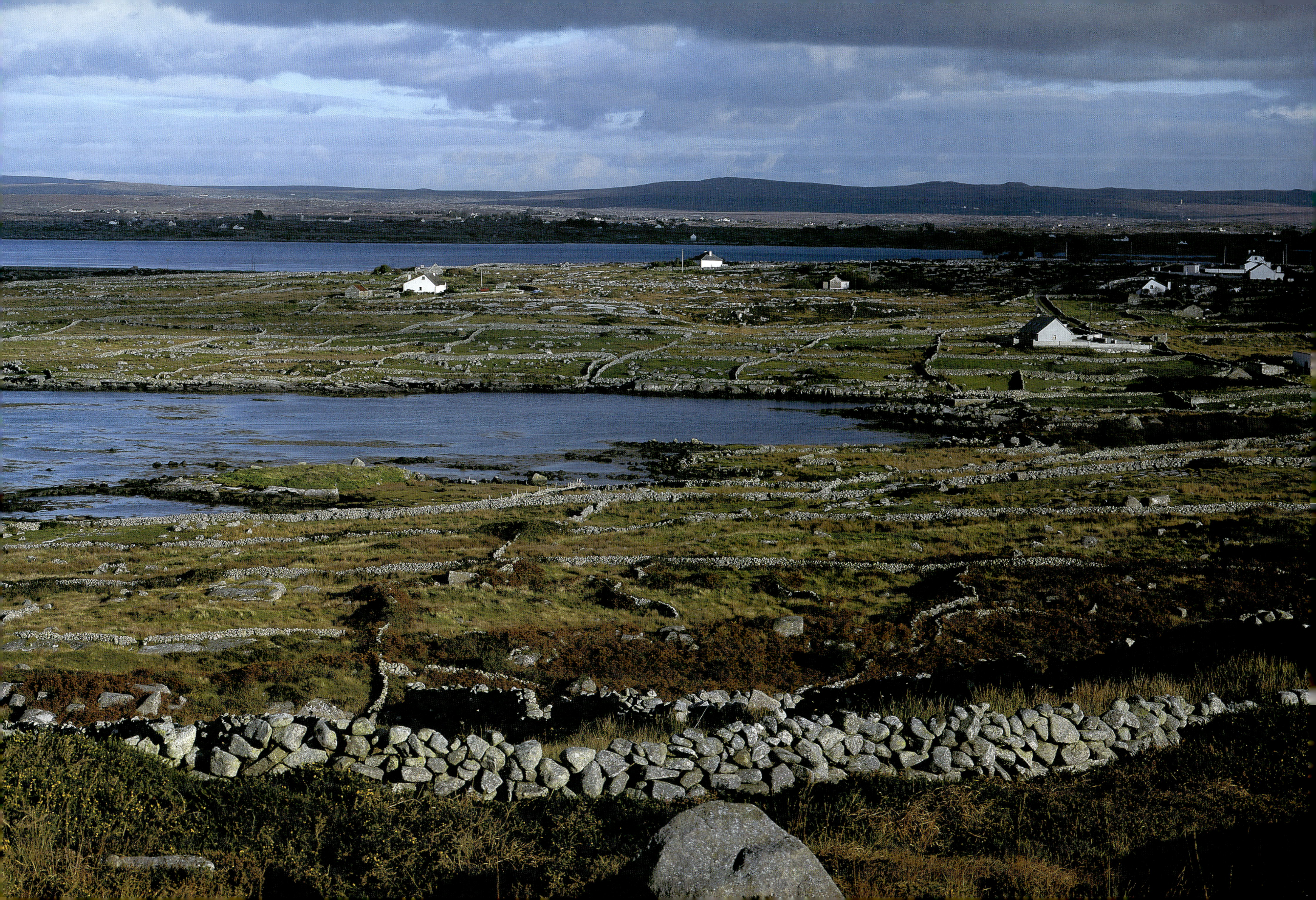

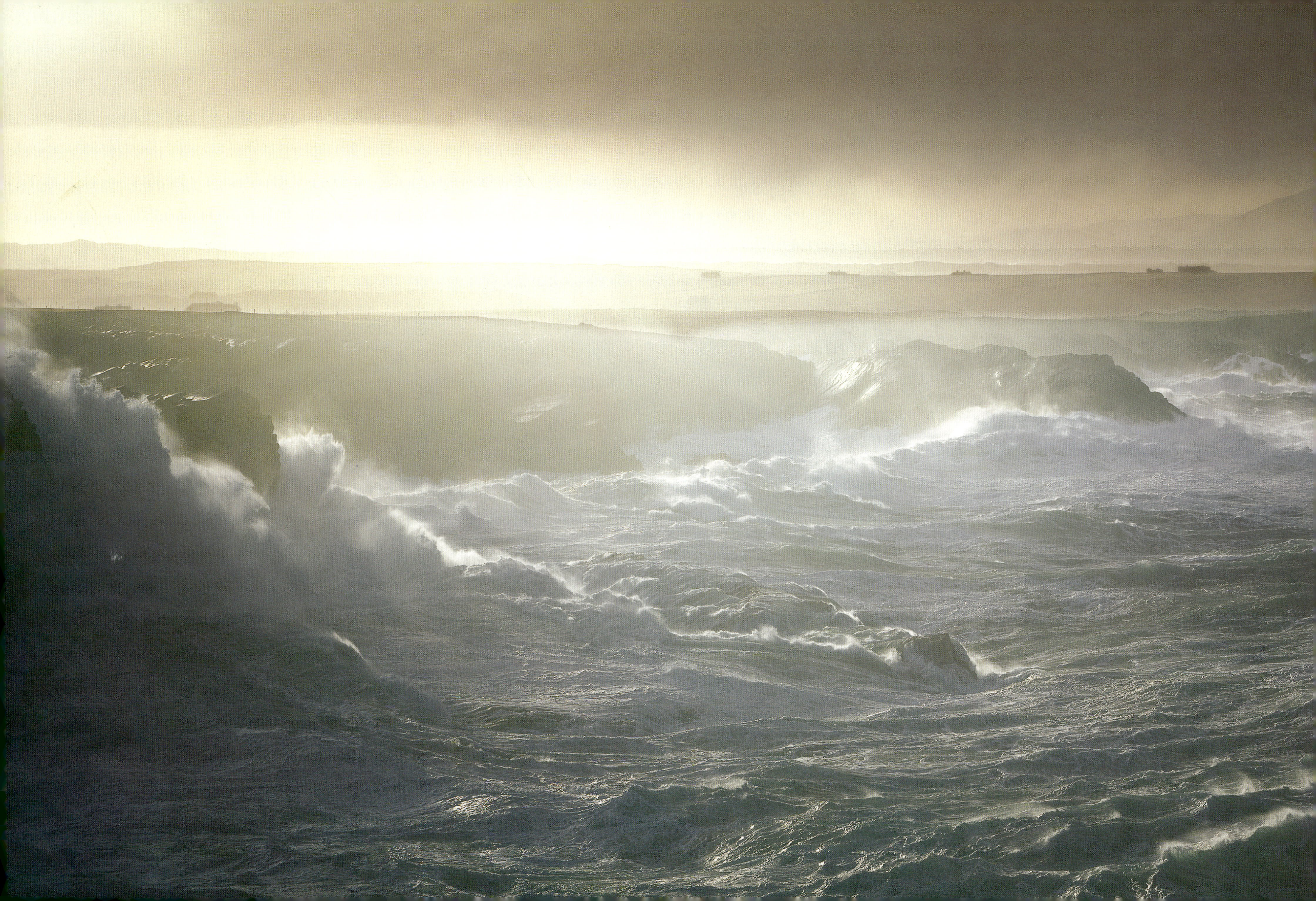

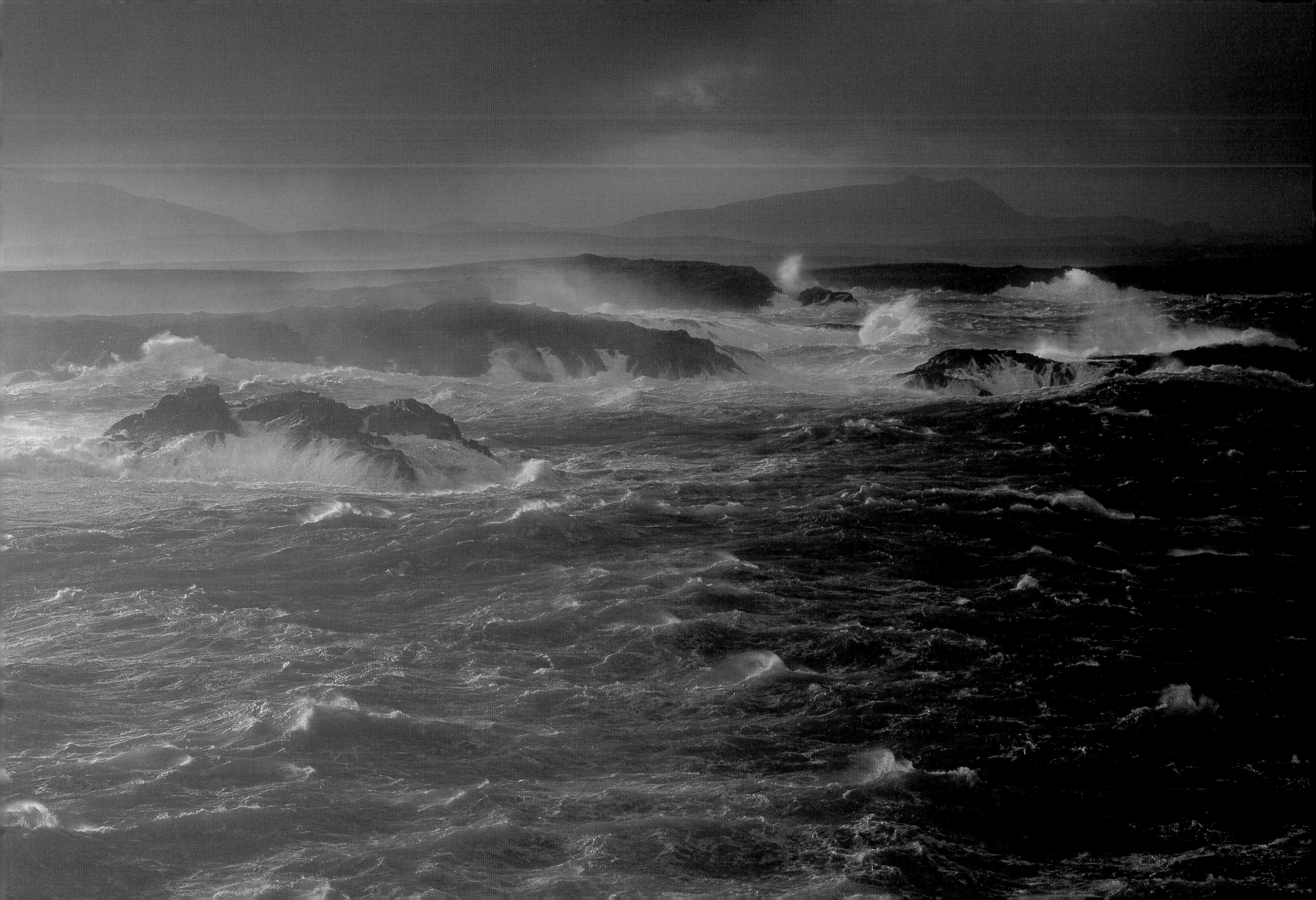

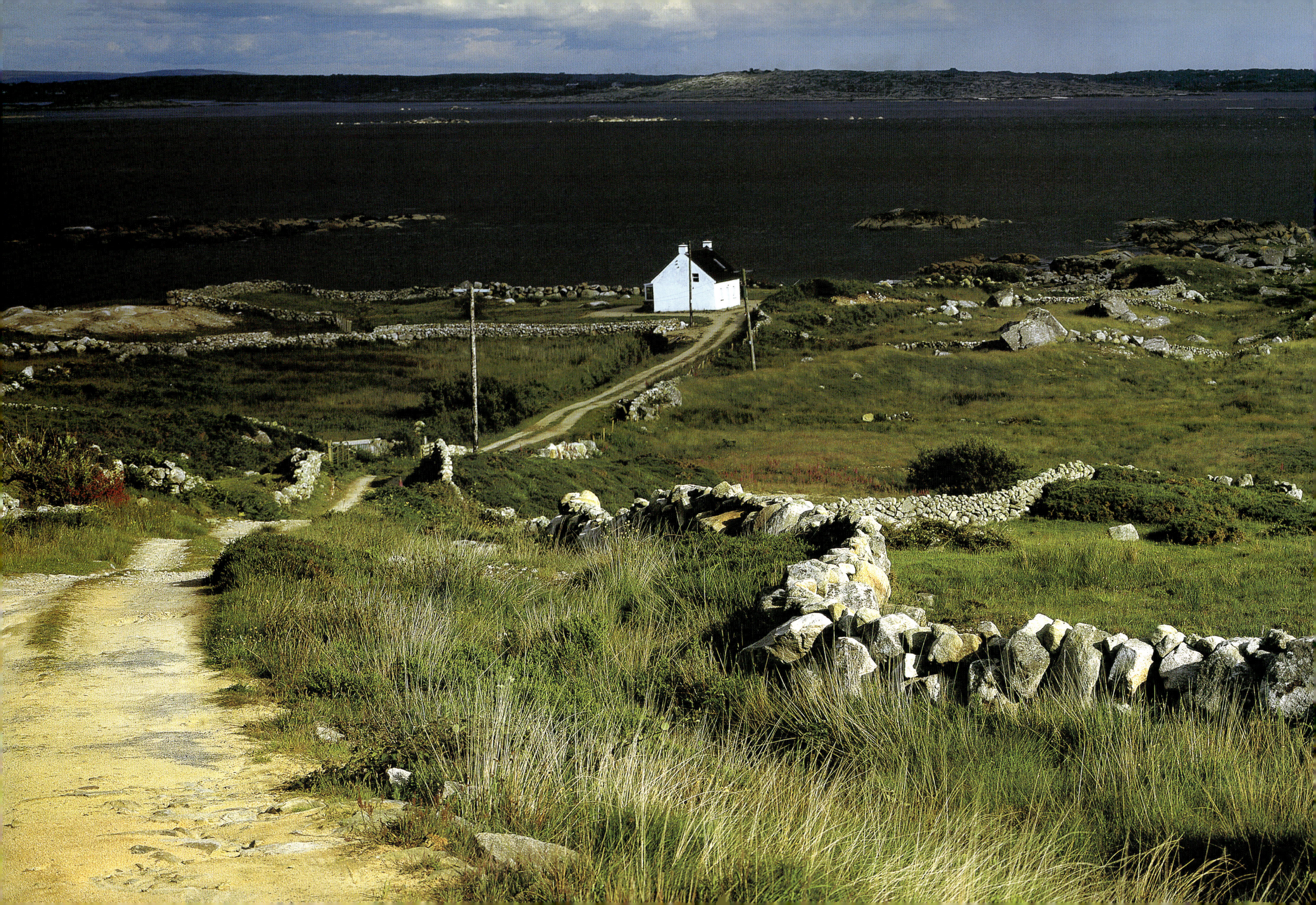

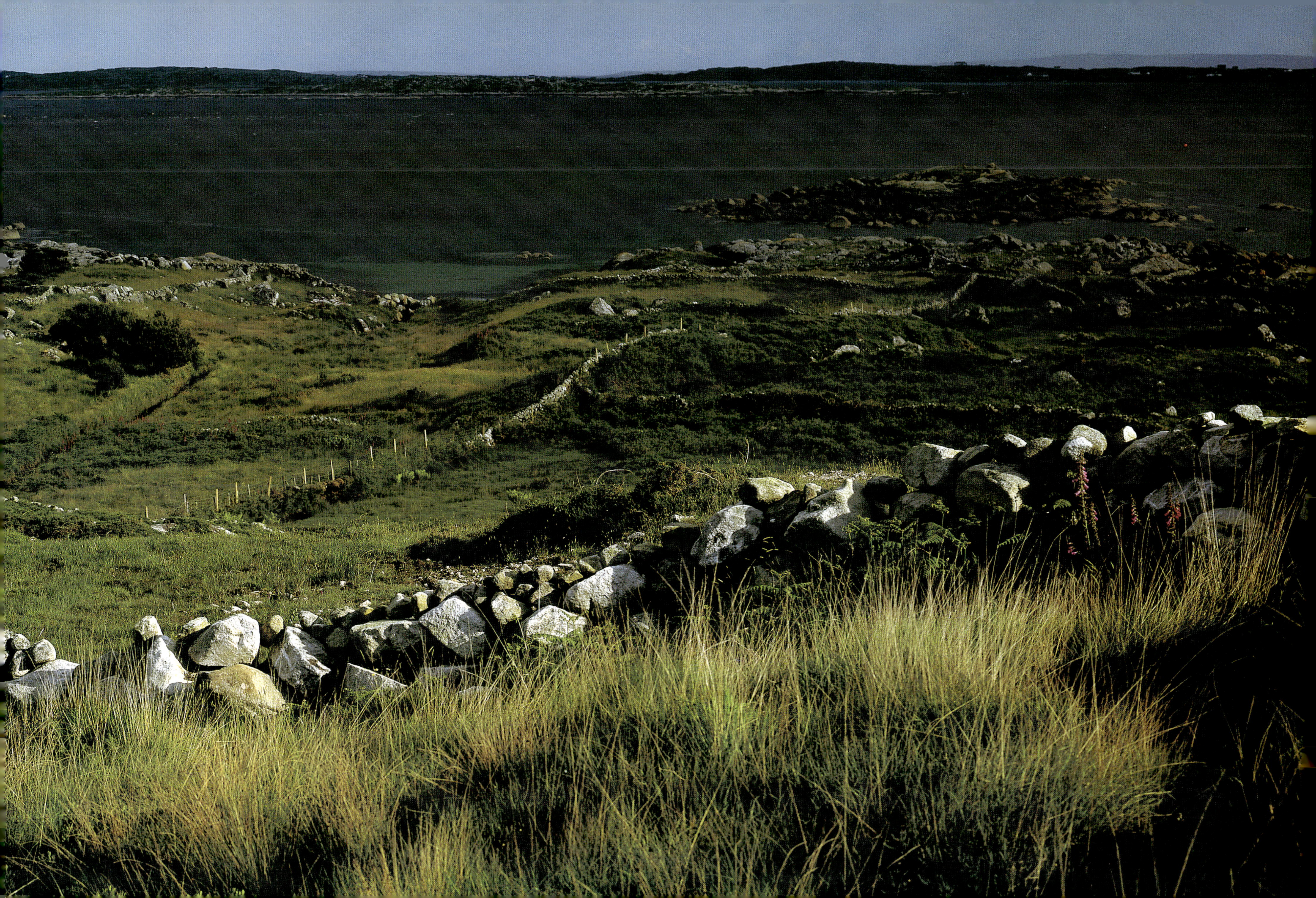

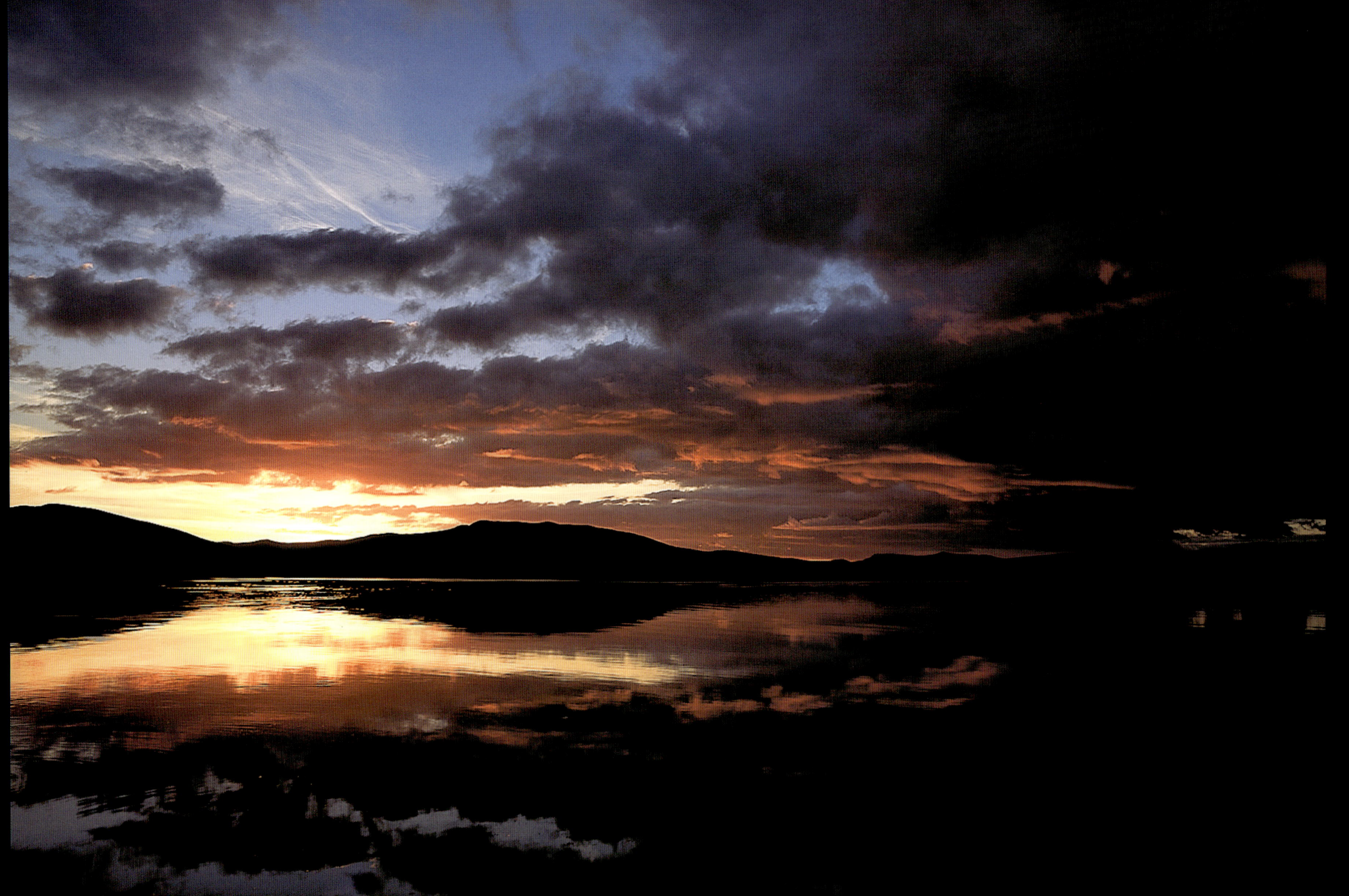

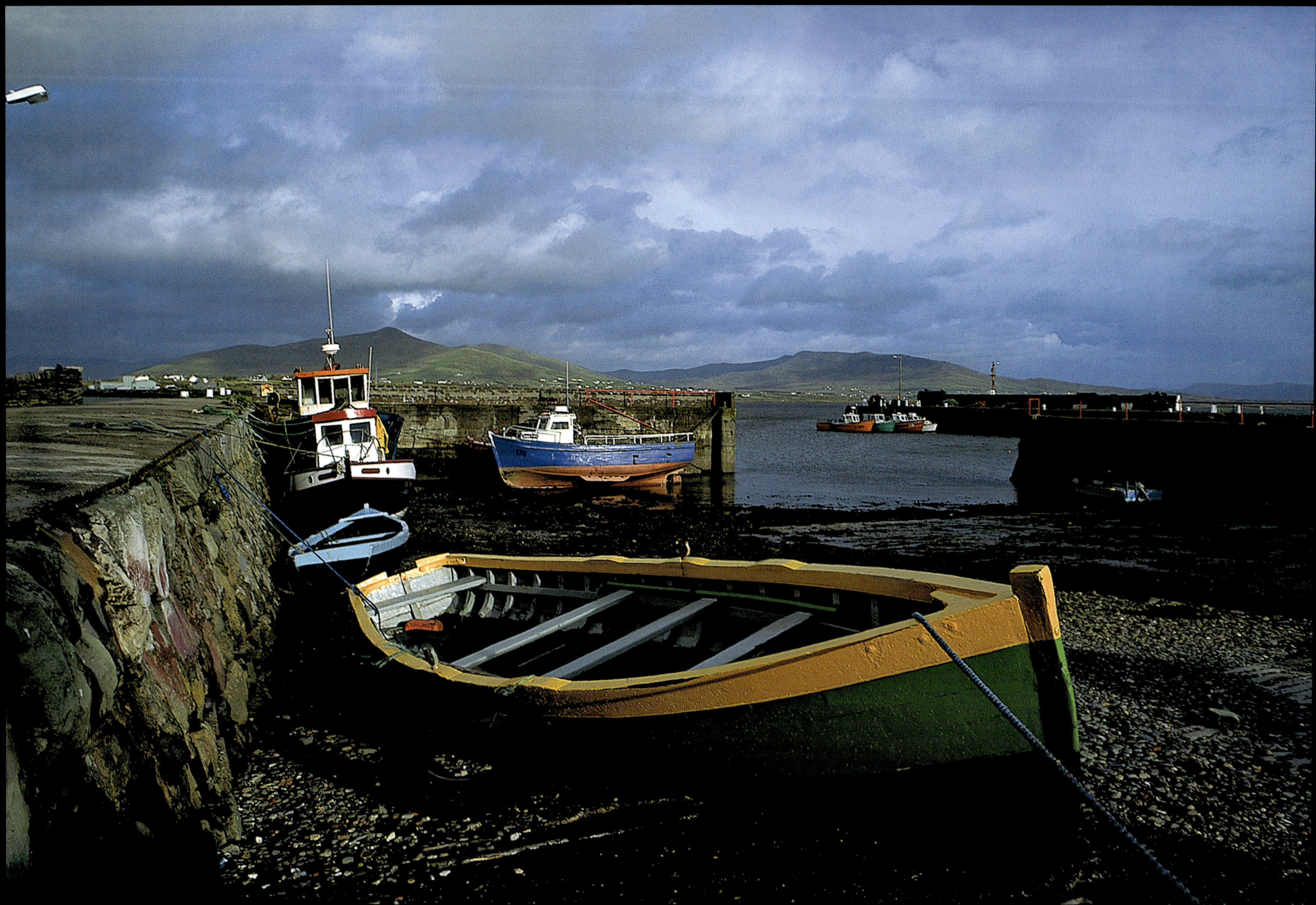

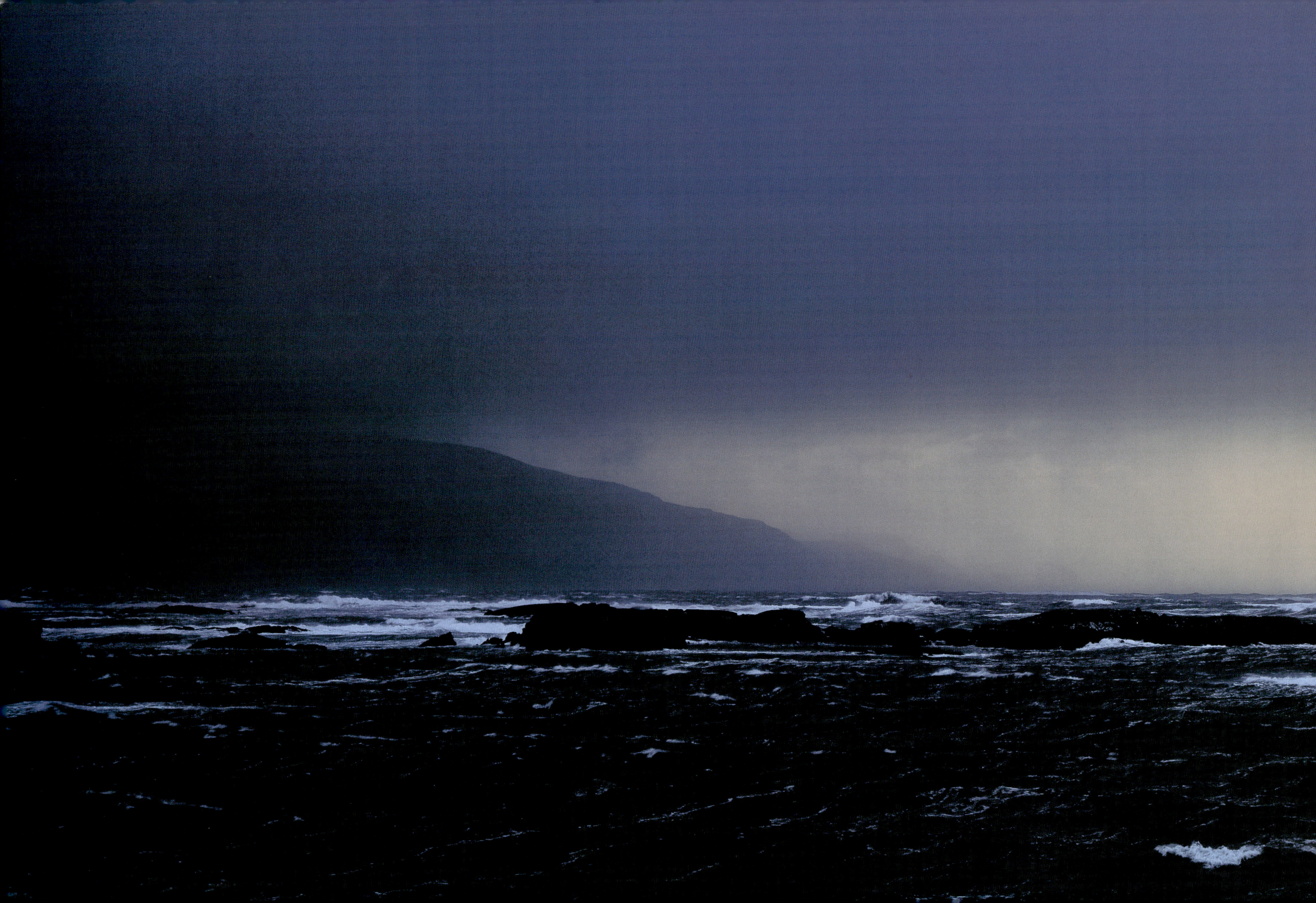

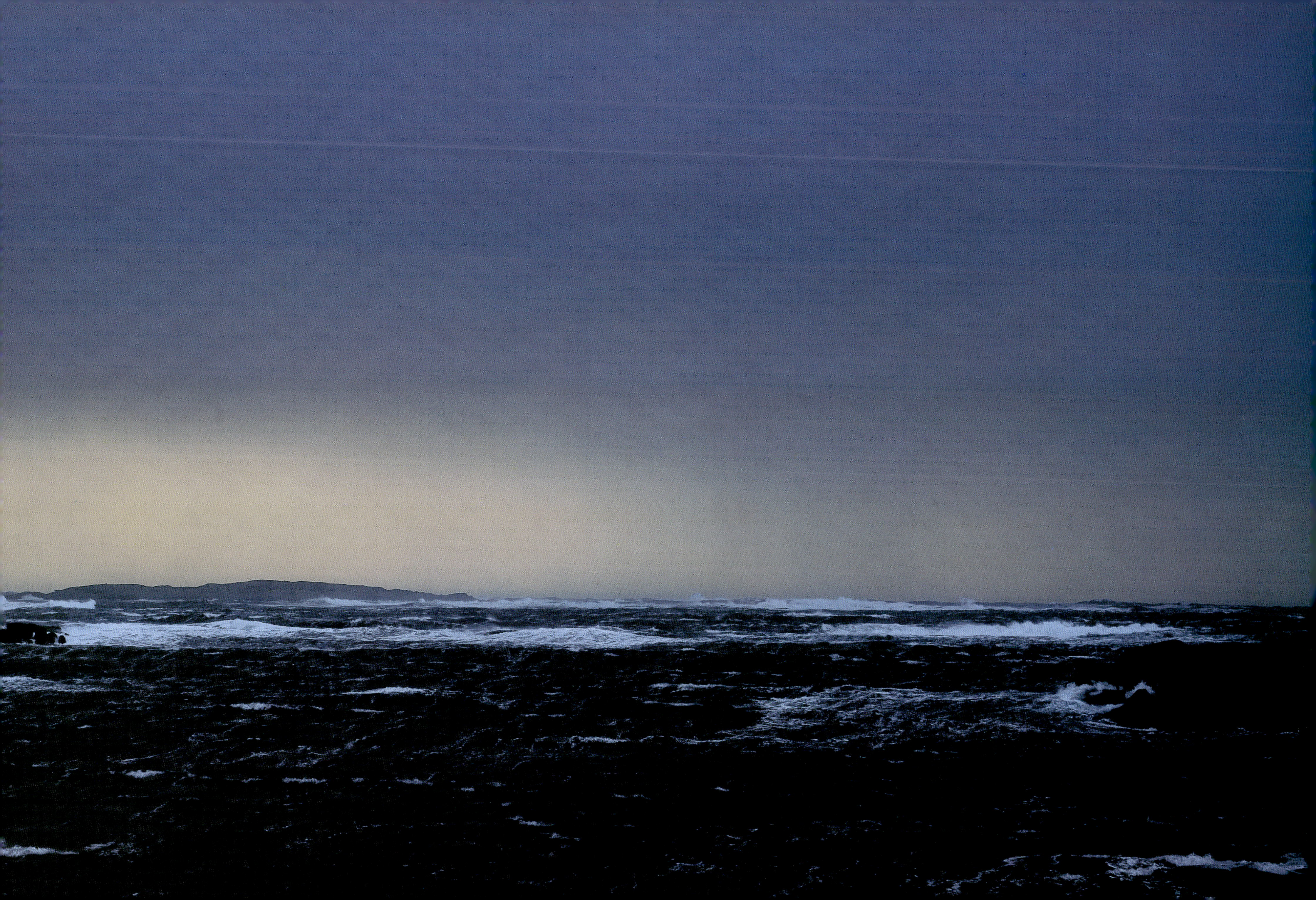

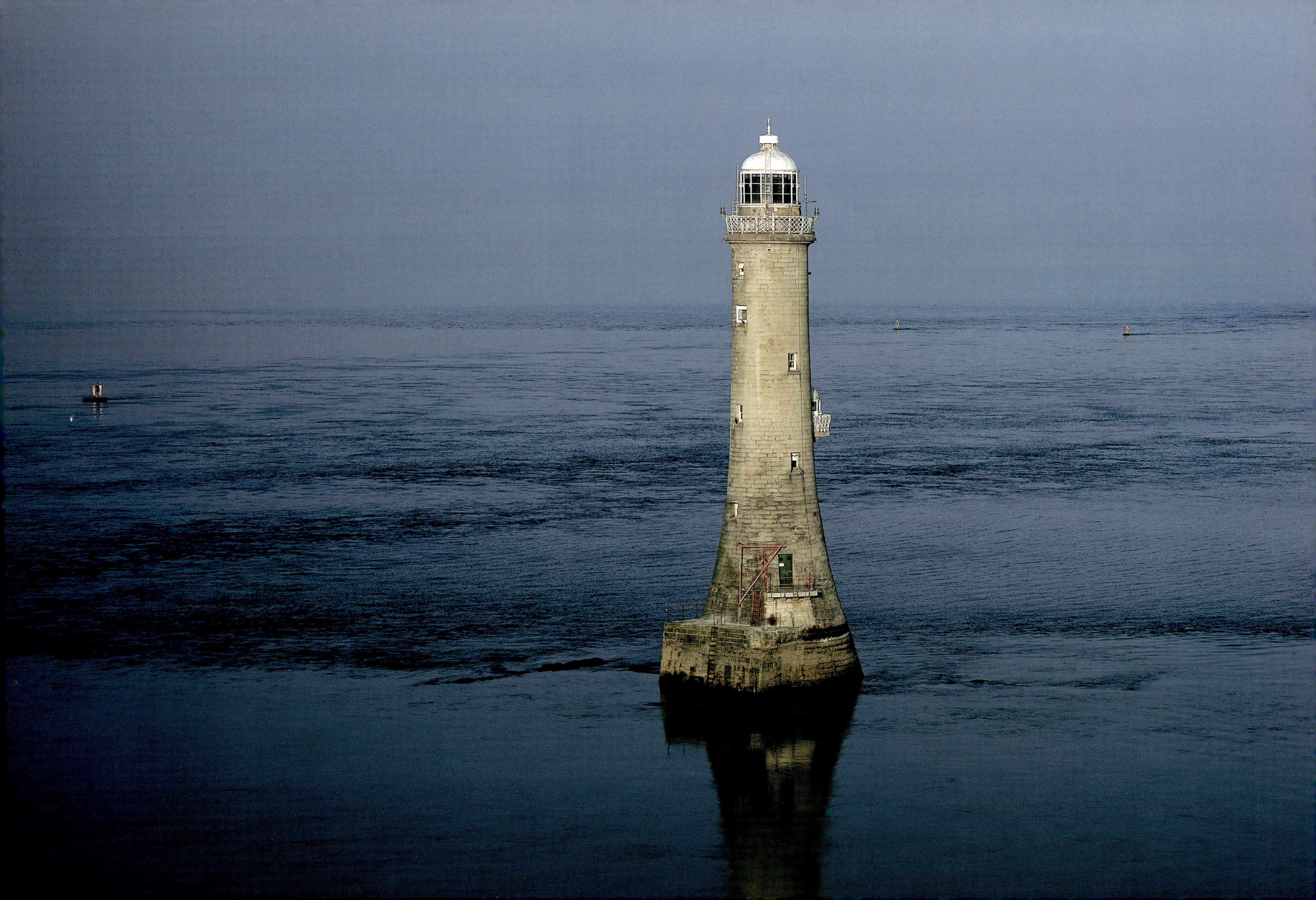

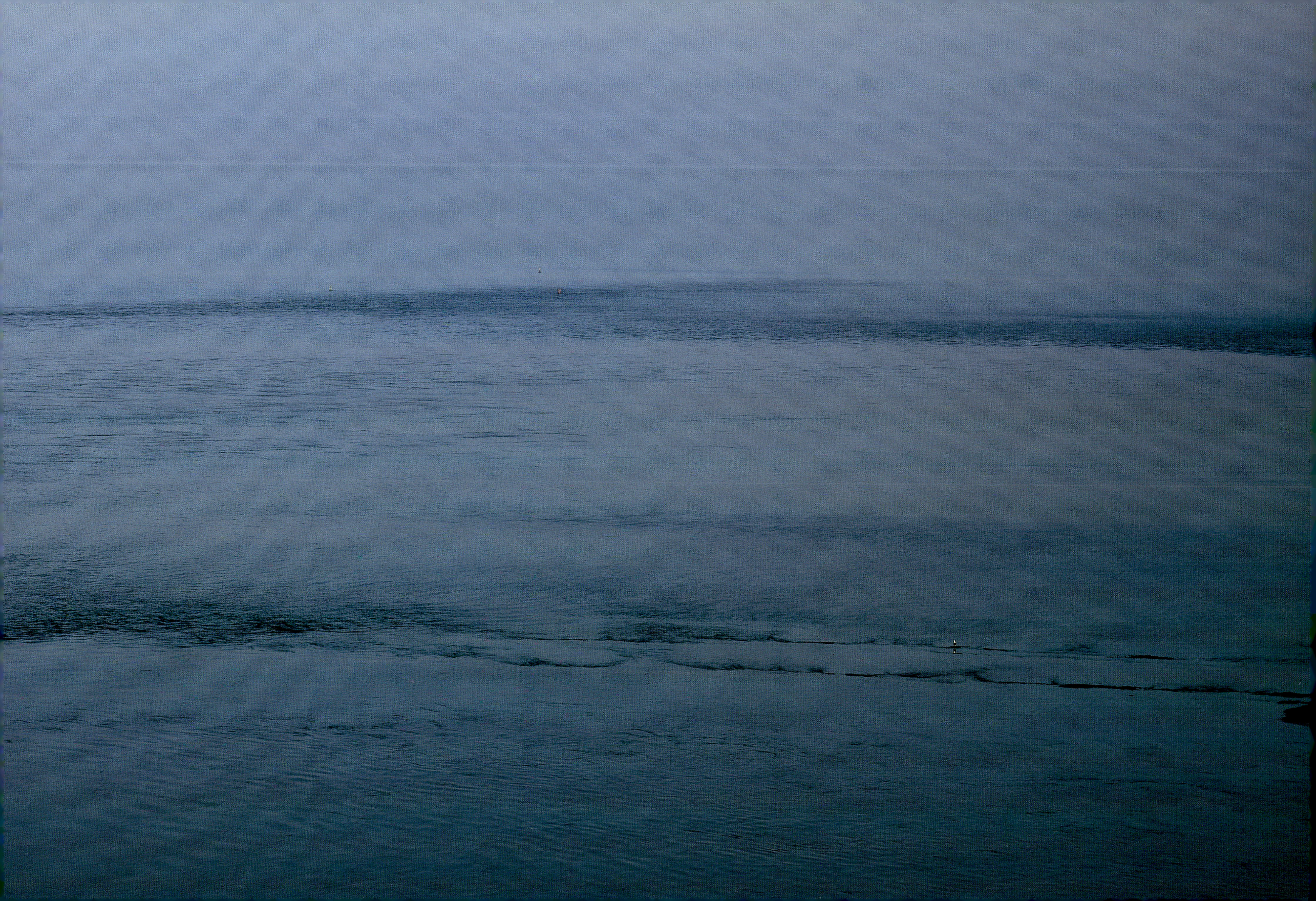

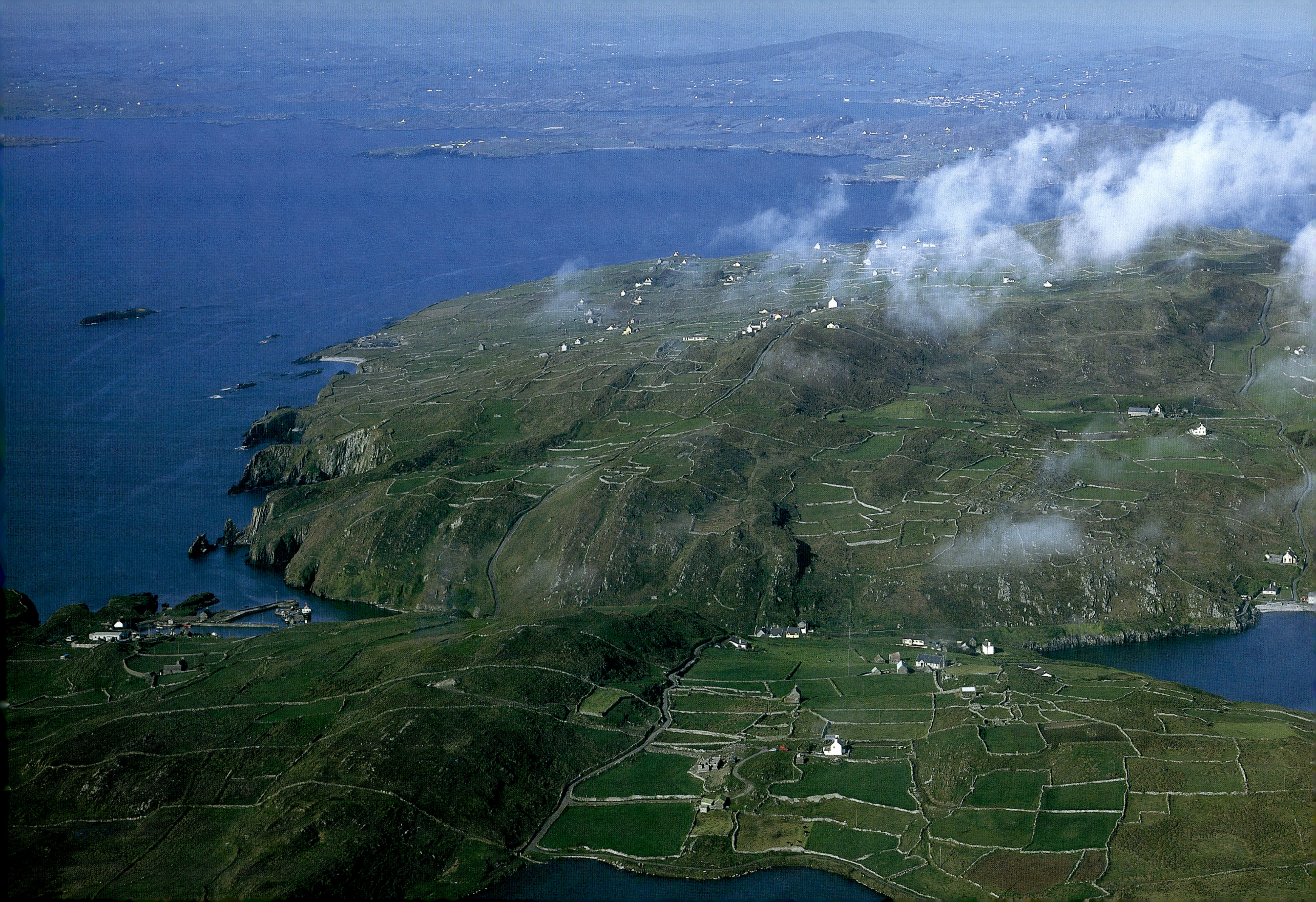

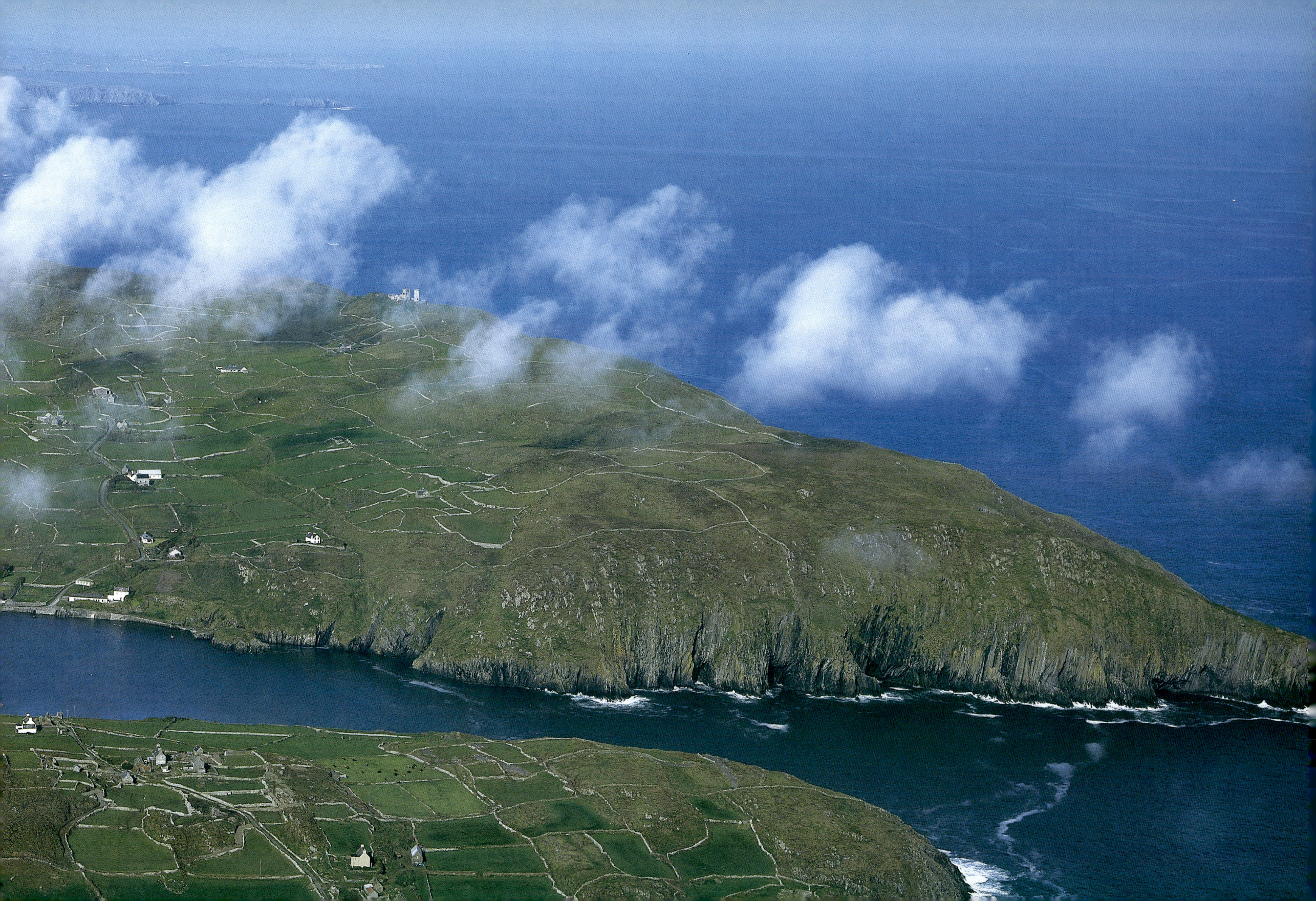

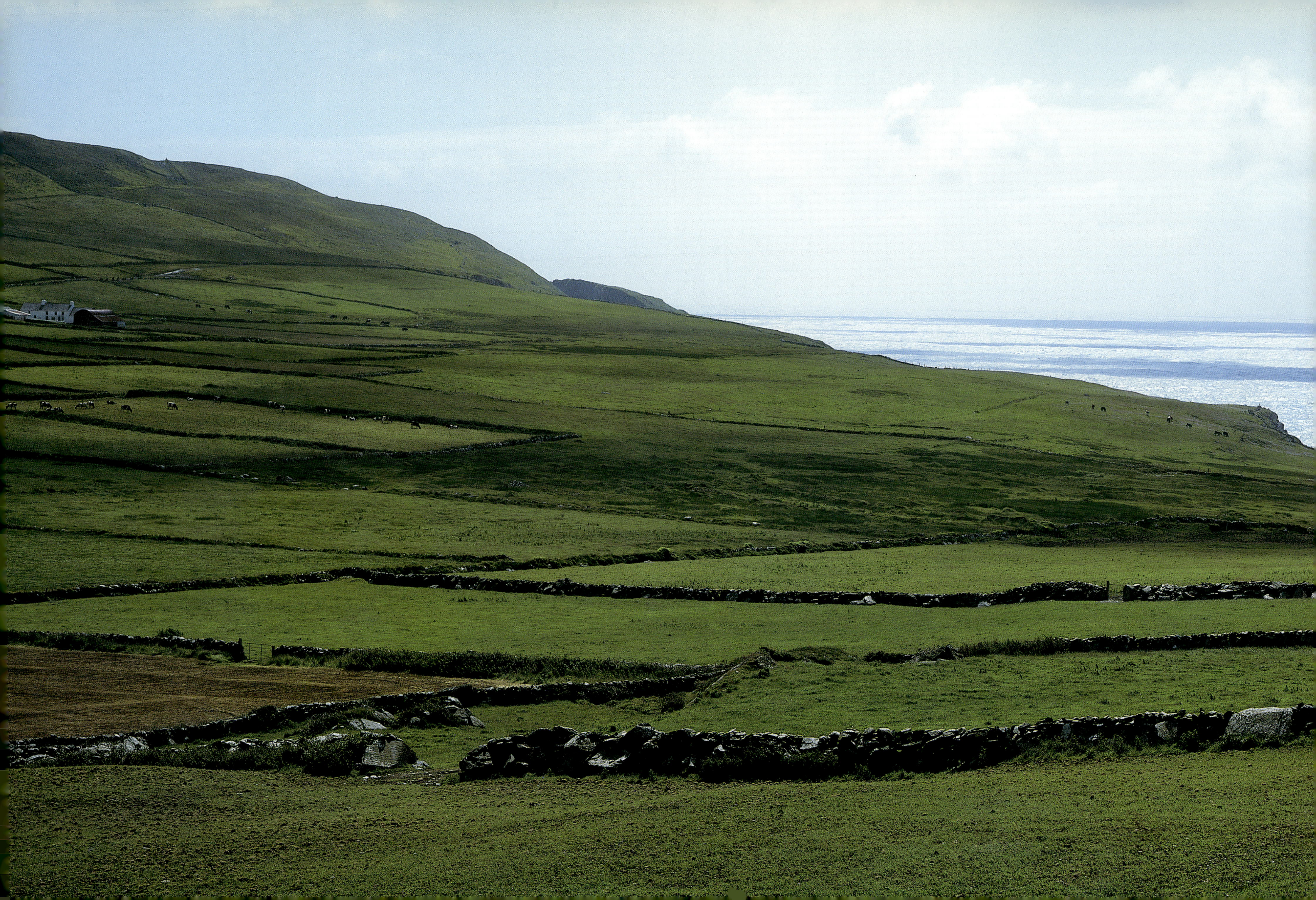

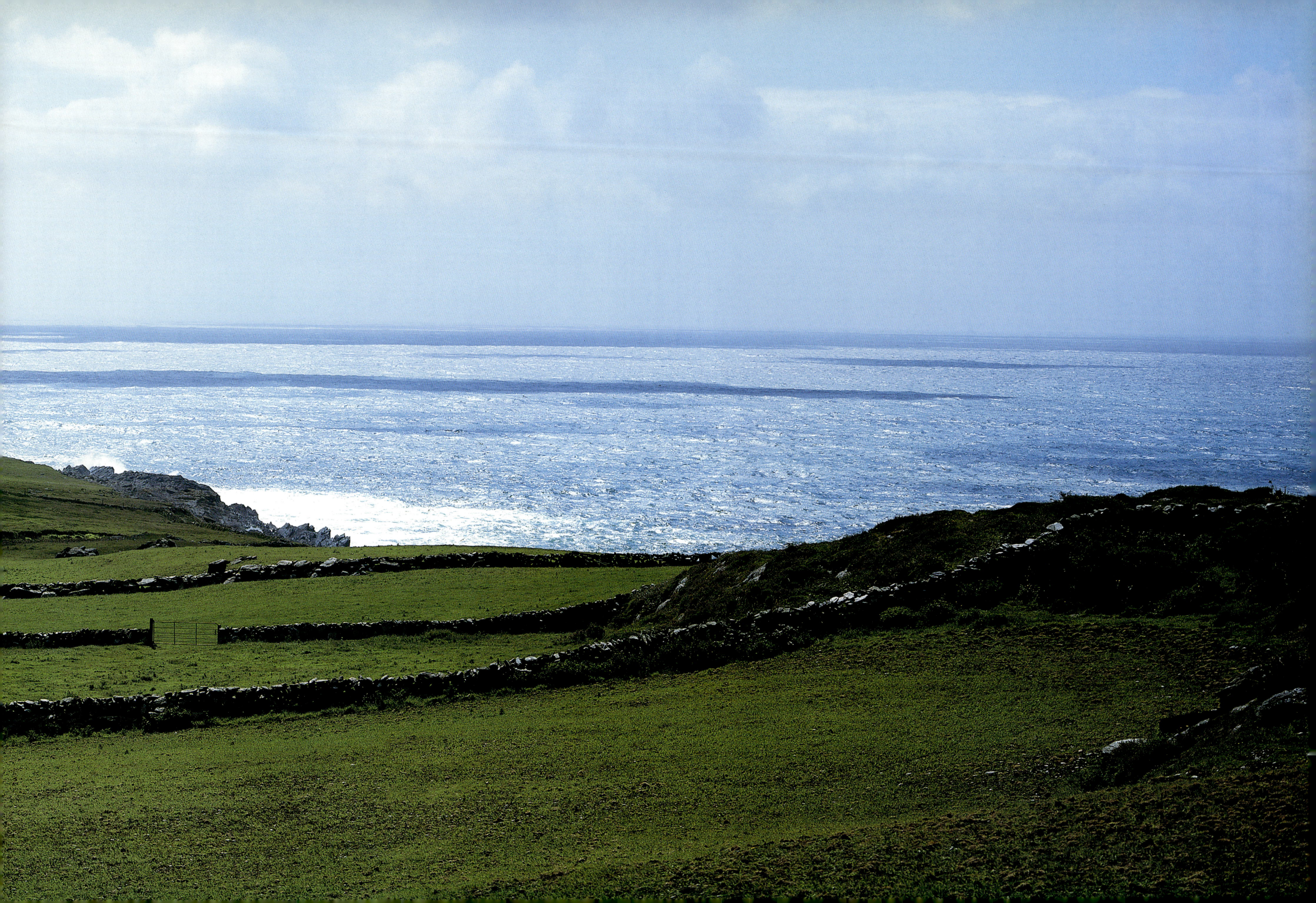

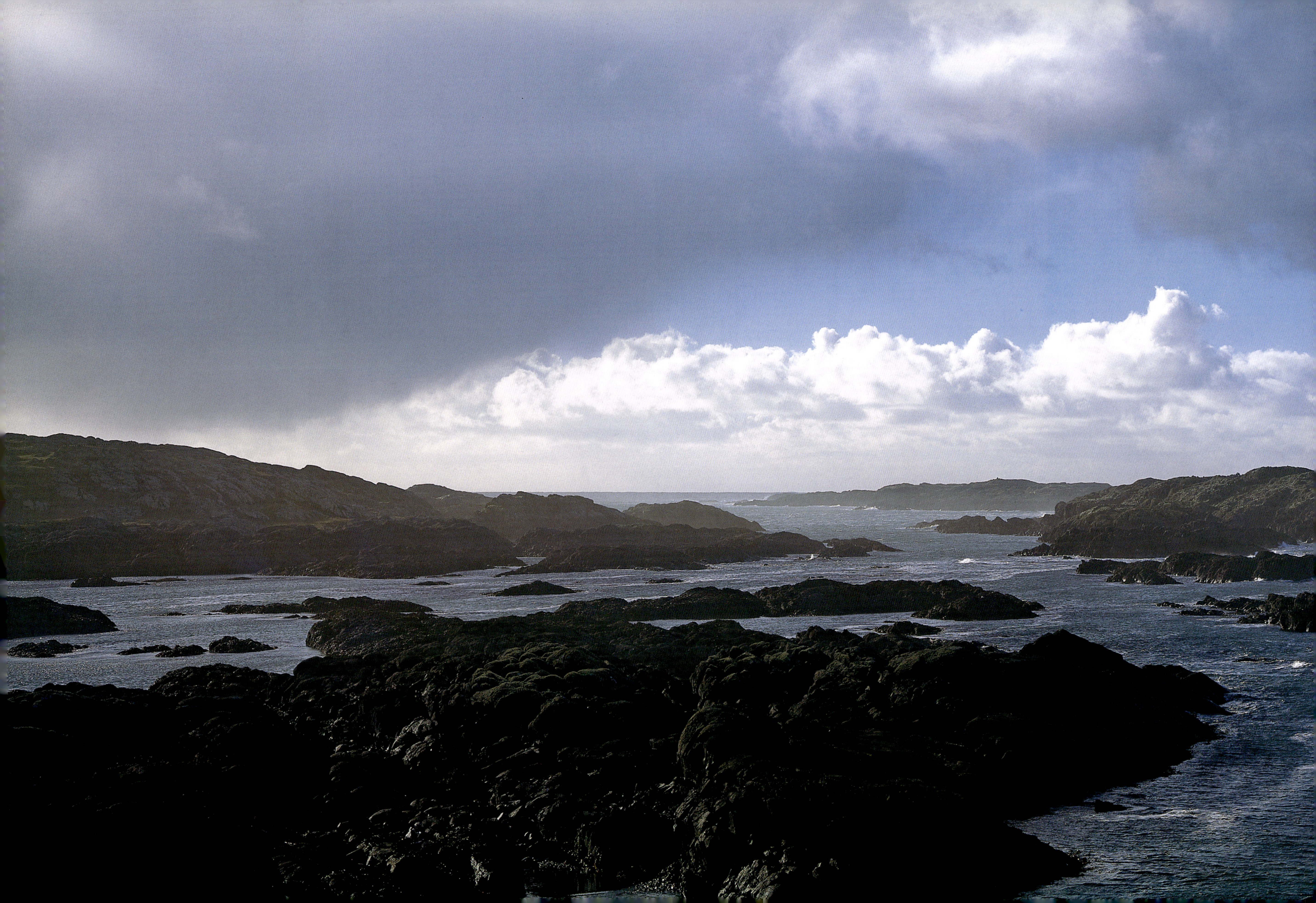

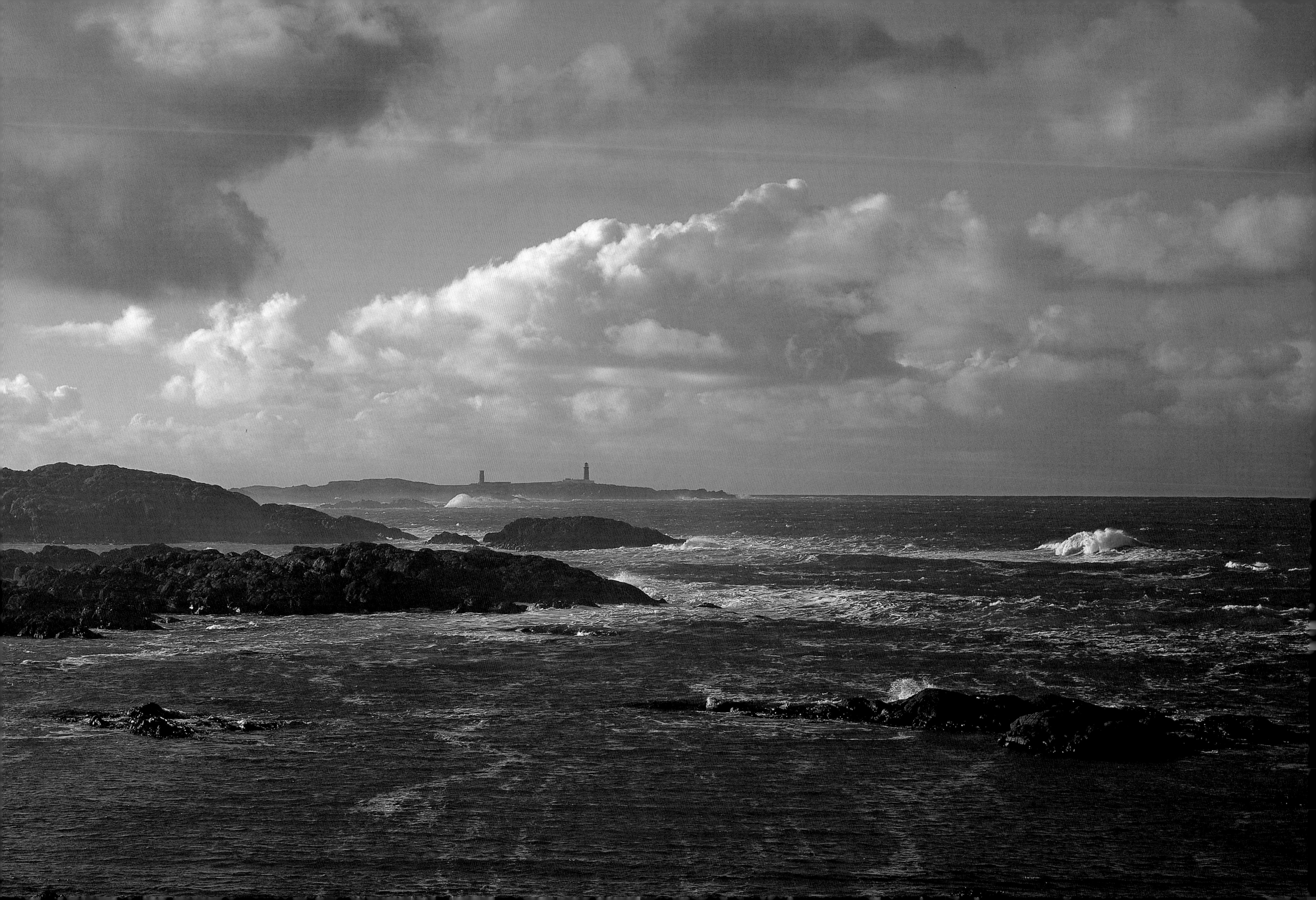

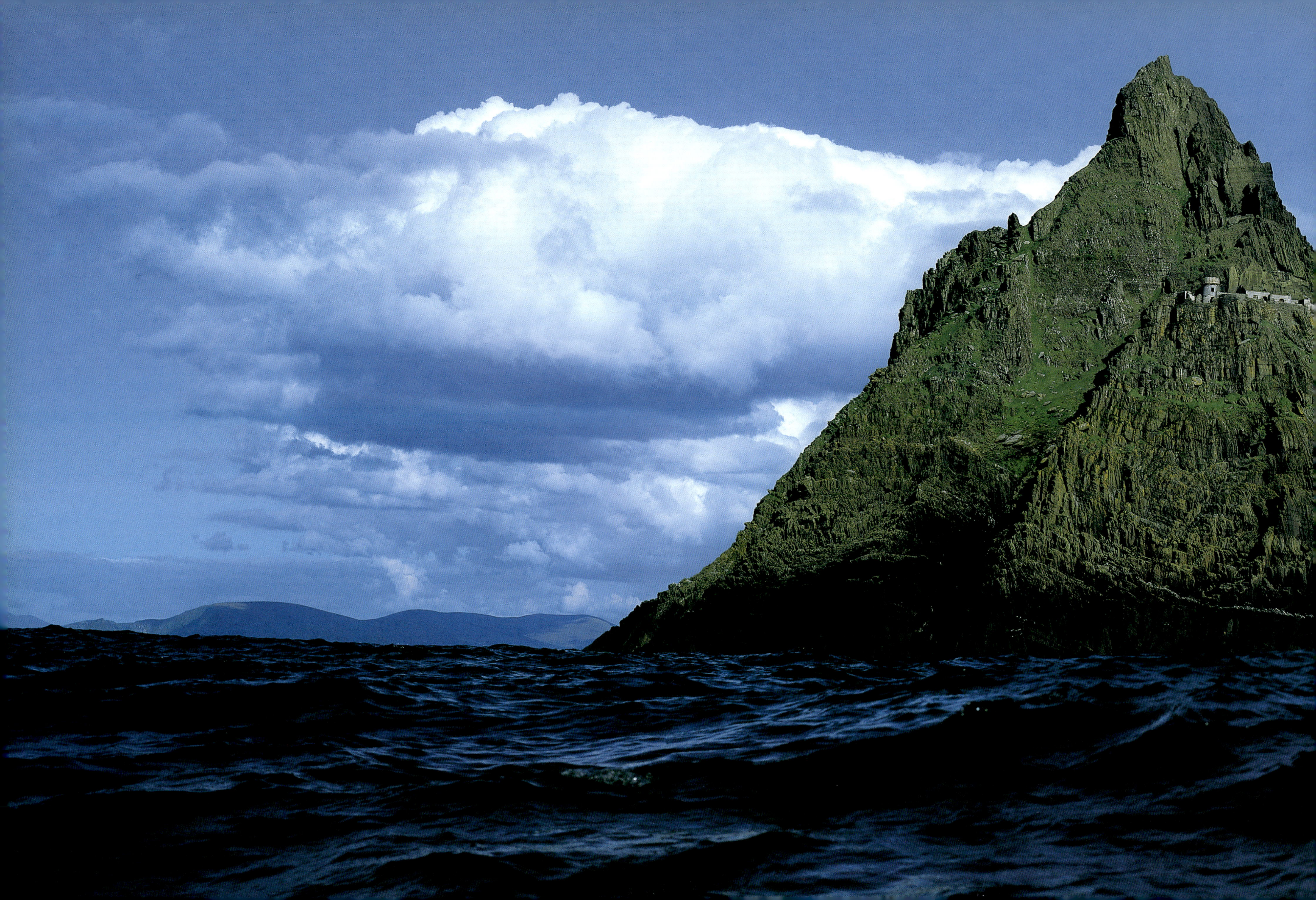

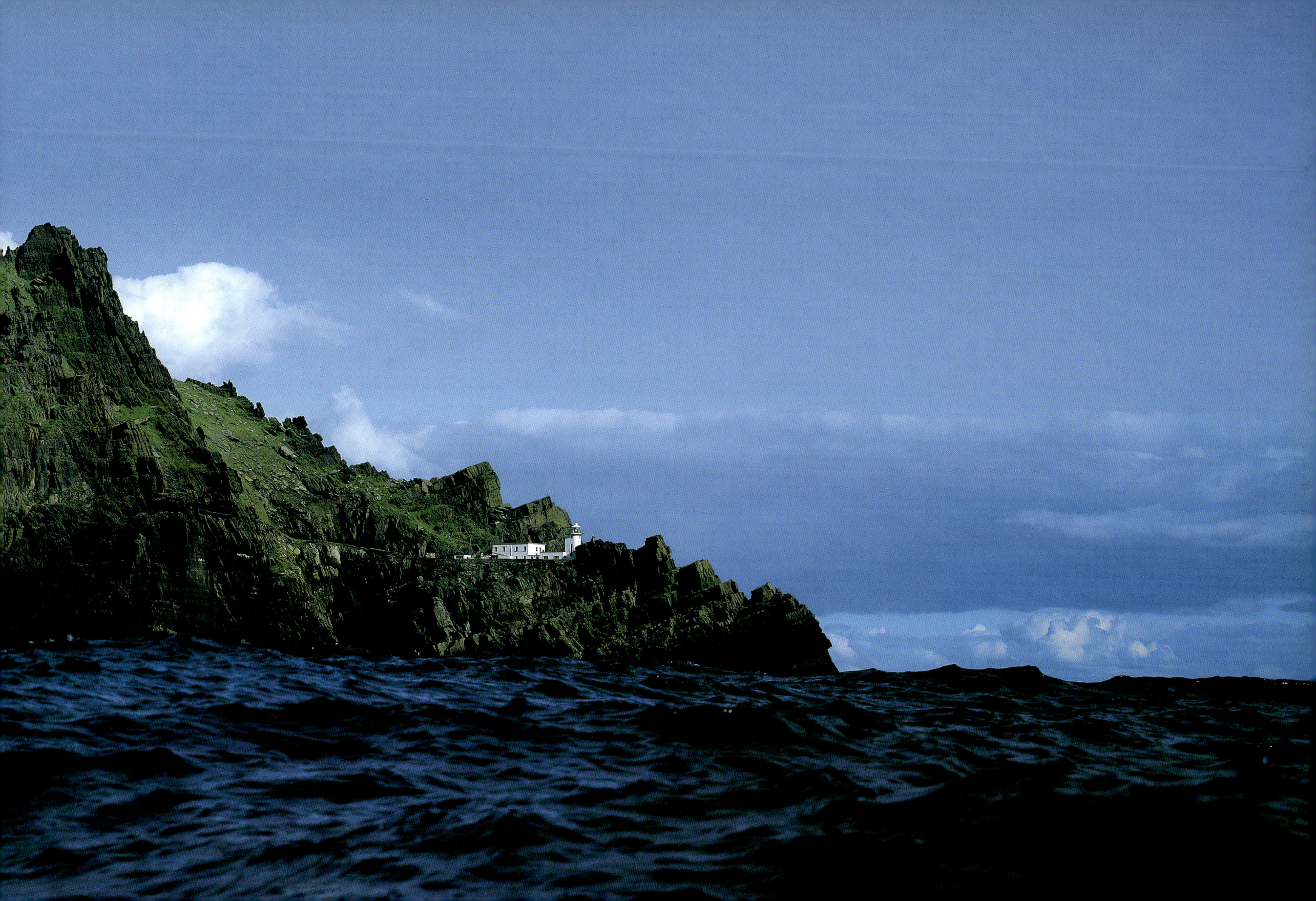

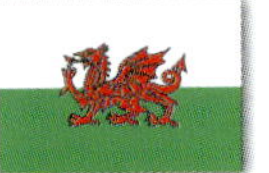

WALES·CYMRU

A LONG SHORELINE, BY THE WATER'S EDGE. The 8,000 square miles of Wales (*Cymru*, in Welsh) lie under the heady blue of the sky. After the Angle and Saxon invasions in the 5th and 6th centuries, the Vikings planted their longboats like swords in the smallest of harbours, marking a new occupation lasting two hundred years. This country was doubly coveted therefore, and its people, like those in neighbouring Cornwall, headed in droves to Armorica – literally *Armor*, the country of the coast – the land which became Brittany.

No Vikings remain in Wales now. As for the Angles of yesteryear, who became the English of today, they have only recently allowed the return of Welsh internal autonomy, after a referendum in 1999, after four hundred years of domination.

You only need to hear the Welsh choirs singing *Hen Wlad Fy Nadhau (Land of My Fathers)* in the red-hot cauldron of the national stadium, surrounded by a sea of waving flags bearing the Welsh dragon during a rugby match between Wales and England, to understand to what extent the warrior spirit of the knights of old survives in the modern world. Dragons are a constant feature on Celtic coats of arms. King Arthur's father, himself a mythical hero in the Celtic lands, bore the name Pendragon, meaning 'dragon's head' or warrior chief.

For a century, the Bretons have shared the Welsh national anthem: they have the same solemn and serious tune, and the same fierce patriotism in the lyrics, but *Land of My Fathers* becomes *Bro Gozh Ma Zadou*, 'The Old Country'.

How many of today's Bretons are yesterday's Welshmen? How many saints, honoured in the *Tro Breizh* pilgrimage (a spiritual tour of the towns of the seven founding saints of Brittany), were children from the small kingdoms and monastic centres of the British Isles, where Wales remains the pearl of the west? More recently, the *Tro Breizh* has expanded to include Wales to ritually honour these Welsh roots. You only need to go along the Étel inlet, in Morbihan, to be dazzled by the islet of Saint-Kado, which Philip Plisson has made into a photographic masterpiece: it is named after St Cadoc, another Welsh emigrant. Setting off from Llancarfan, this Welsh abbot landed by chance at the mouth of the inlet. He then had to brave the devil to build a bridge between the island and the shore. He took a black cat as his companion, in order to thwart the challenge of the evil one 'to take the soul of the first being to cross over'. The small chapel still honours the cult of the adopted Breton under his Welsh colours and arms.

Swansea, Port Talbot, Cardiff and Newport line the Bristol Channel, from where Britons boarded their boats to flee from the Anglo-Saxons. In contrast to the coasts bathed by the Gulf Stream, in the north of Wales lie the highlands of Snowdonia, culminating in the peak of Mount Snowdon (3,560 feet), where the Welsh warriors united their forces to face the invaders. Three million inhabitants and a large Welsh diaspora who sailed away to seek their fortune in the New World now uphold the land of their fathers beyond the seas.

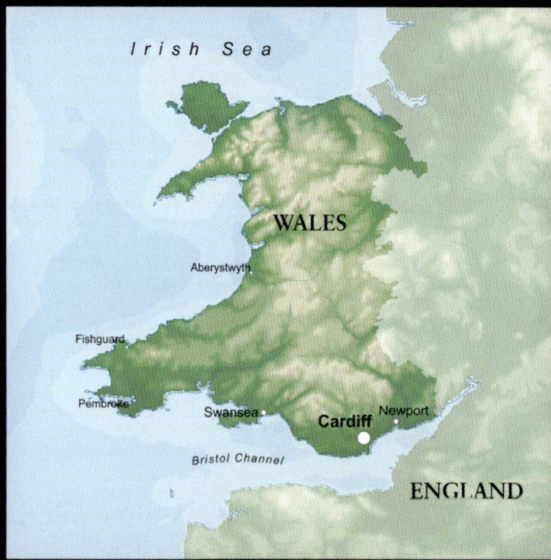

Below: Sheep Island is well-named. At the entrance to Milford Haven, near Angle Bay to the south, the Welsh salt meadow sheep wander and graze.

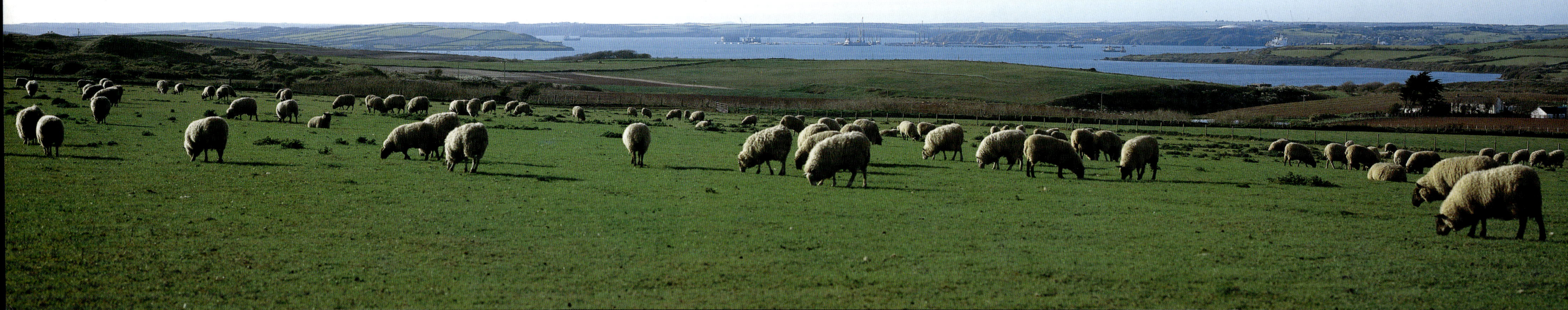

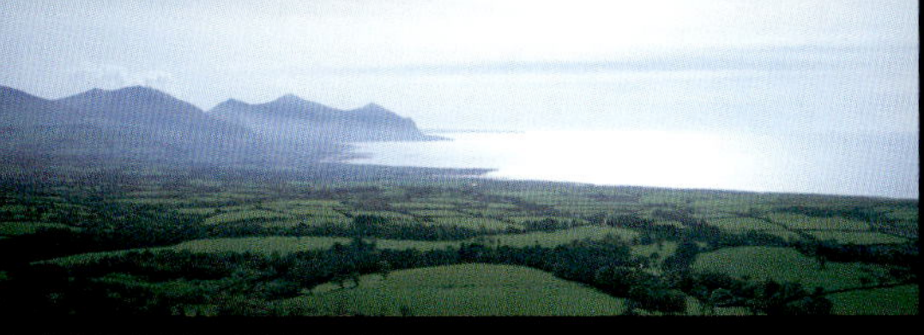

A RECORD-BREAKER
Llanfairpwllgwyngyllgogerychwyrndrobwllllantysiliogogogoch! The island of Anglesey (*Ynys Môn*, in Welsh) is home to the famous village with the longest name in the world. Between the coast of Caernarfon Bay and the green mountains of Snowdonia, its inhabitants make do with the shortened version Llanfair.

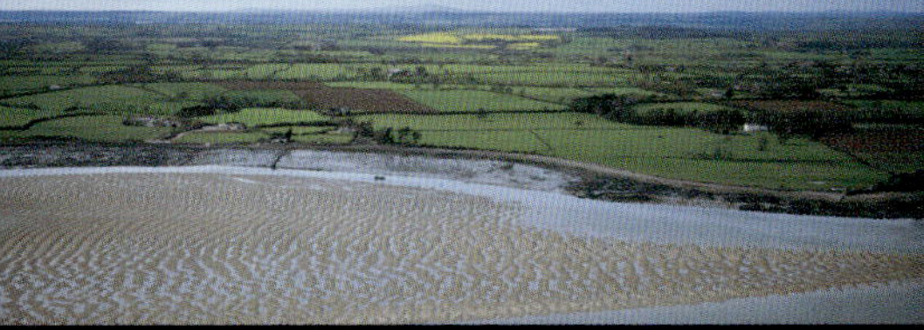

'MAM CYMRU'
The narrow channel of the Menai Strait separates Anglesey, known to medieval chroniclers as *Mam Cymru* (Mother of Wales), from the Welsh mainland. It is crossed by two bridges: the Menai Suspension Bridge and the Britannia Bridge. From the other side of the island, ferries cross Holyhead Bay, en route to Ireland.

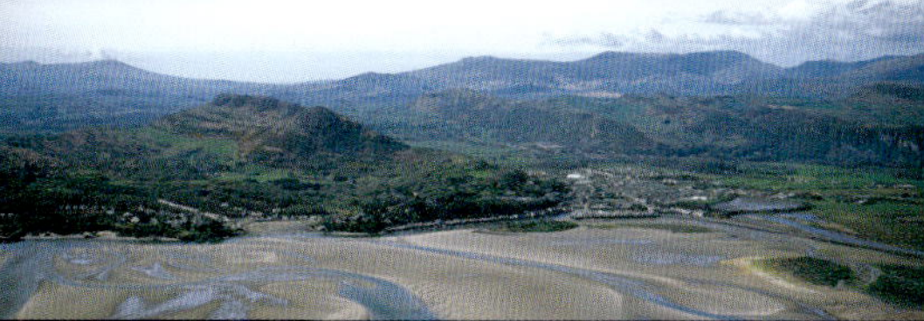

'LAN Y MOR'
On the west coast, the Lleyn peninsula plunges down to the Irish Sea. Tremadog Bay is a tourist hotspot whose long beaches between 'Lan y Mor' (land and sea) are a great tourist attraction. Just offshore are the two small islands of St Tudwal.

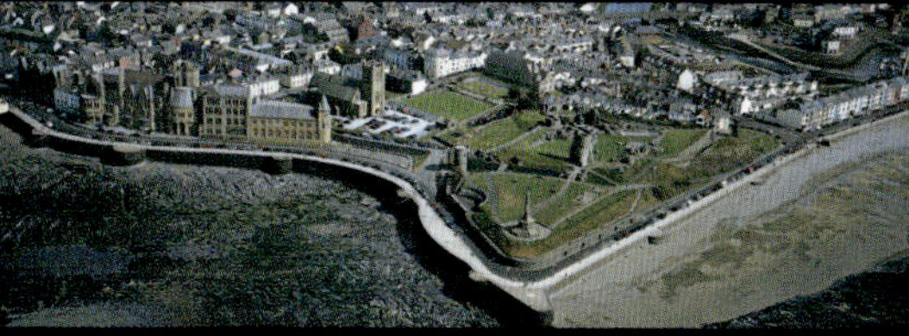

CITADEL TOWN
Here the Welsh dragon flew proudly for centuries. Dating from well before the fortifications of Aberystwyth Castle (12th century) are the ruins at Pen Dinas, one of the three hills overlooking the sea and its two beaches. The University of Wales (*Bryfisgol Cymru*) makes this a young and festive town

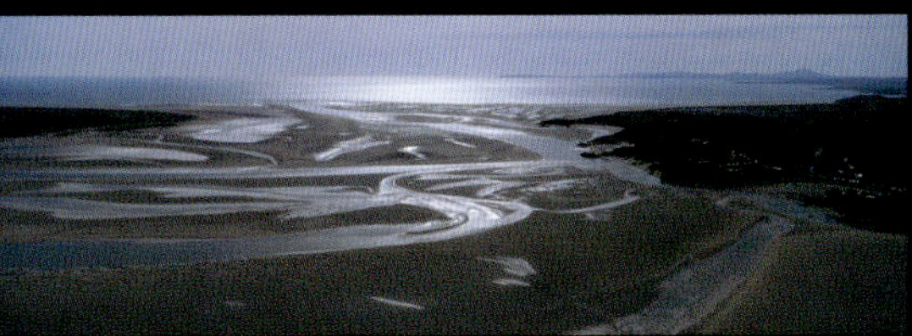

THE HEART OF GWYNEDD
The River Glaslyn flows into the mouth of Tremadog Bay where small islands scatter the horizon as far as Mochras or Shell Island. This is the heart of the county of Gwynedd, over which reigned the prince Owain, reputedly a contemporary of King Arthur. The beaches of Tremadog are highly regarded as the Gulf Stream warms the water.

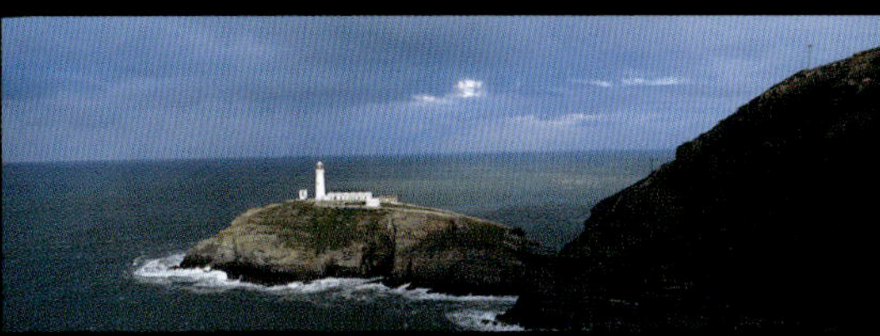

A BIRD PARADISE
The cliffs of Ynys Lawd (South Stack), the westernmost point of Holyhead, date from six hundred million years ago. They surround the lighthouse with its four hundred steps. In spring, the rocks provide nesting places for several thousand guillemots, razorbills and puffins.

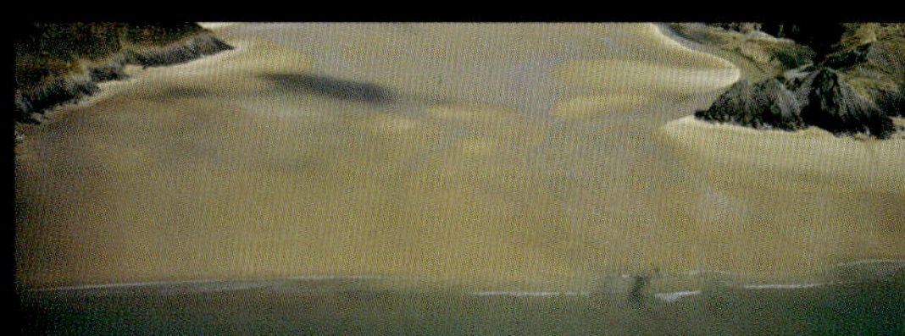

DUNES AND NATURE
Oxwich Bay, on the Gower peninsula in south Wales, is a favourite destination for ramblers. An hour's invigorating walk takes you through deep dunes, salt water marshes and small hills. It is also a popular spot for surfing and other watersports.

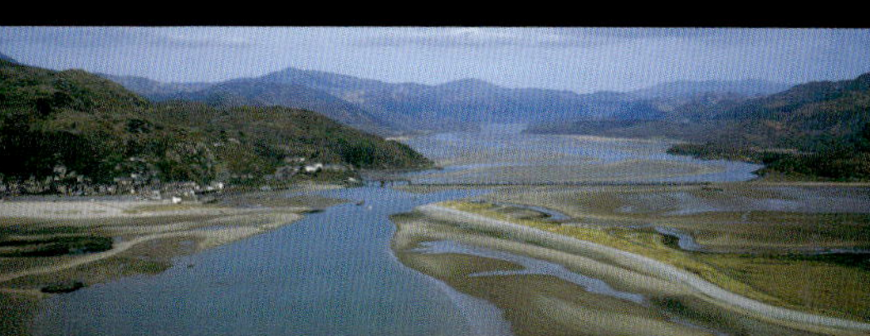

'CROESO!' WELCOME!
There is no better way to savour the view of Porthmadog than to fly over the Glaslyn estuary which winds along the Cambrian coast in Snowdonia. The ideal way is to take the *Rheilffordd Eryri* or Welsh Highland Railway, a restored steam railway line, which goes from Caernarfon to the village of Rhyd Ddu in the hills.

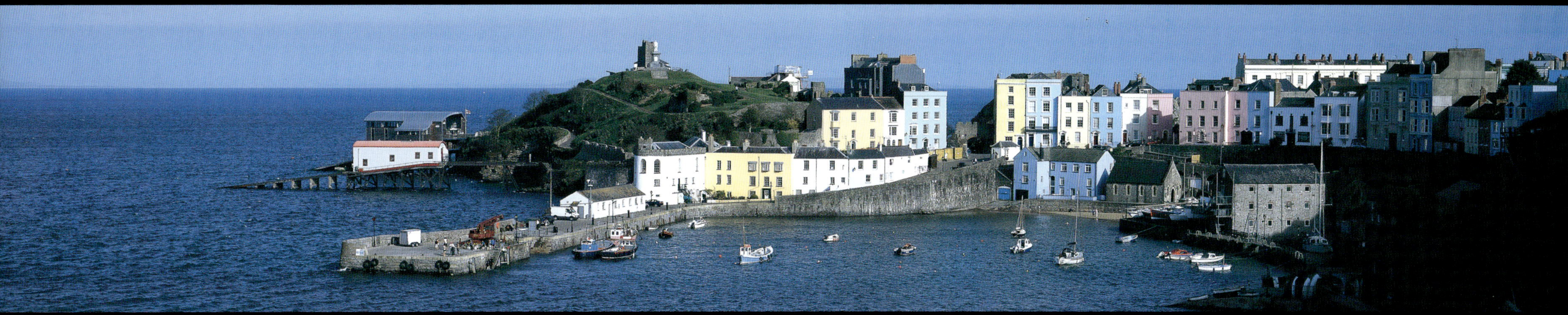

TENBY
Tenby is a pretty fishing port in Pembrokeshire in West Wales, overlooked by the remains of a 13th-century castle.

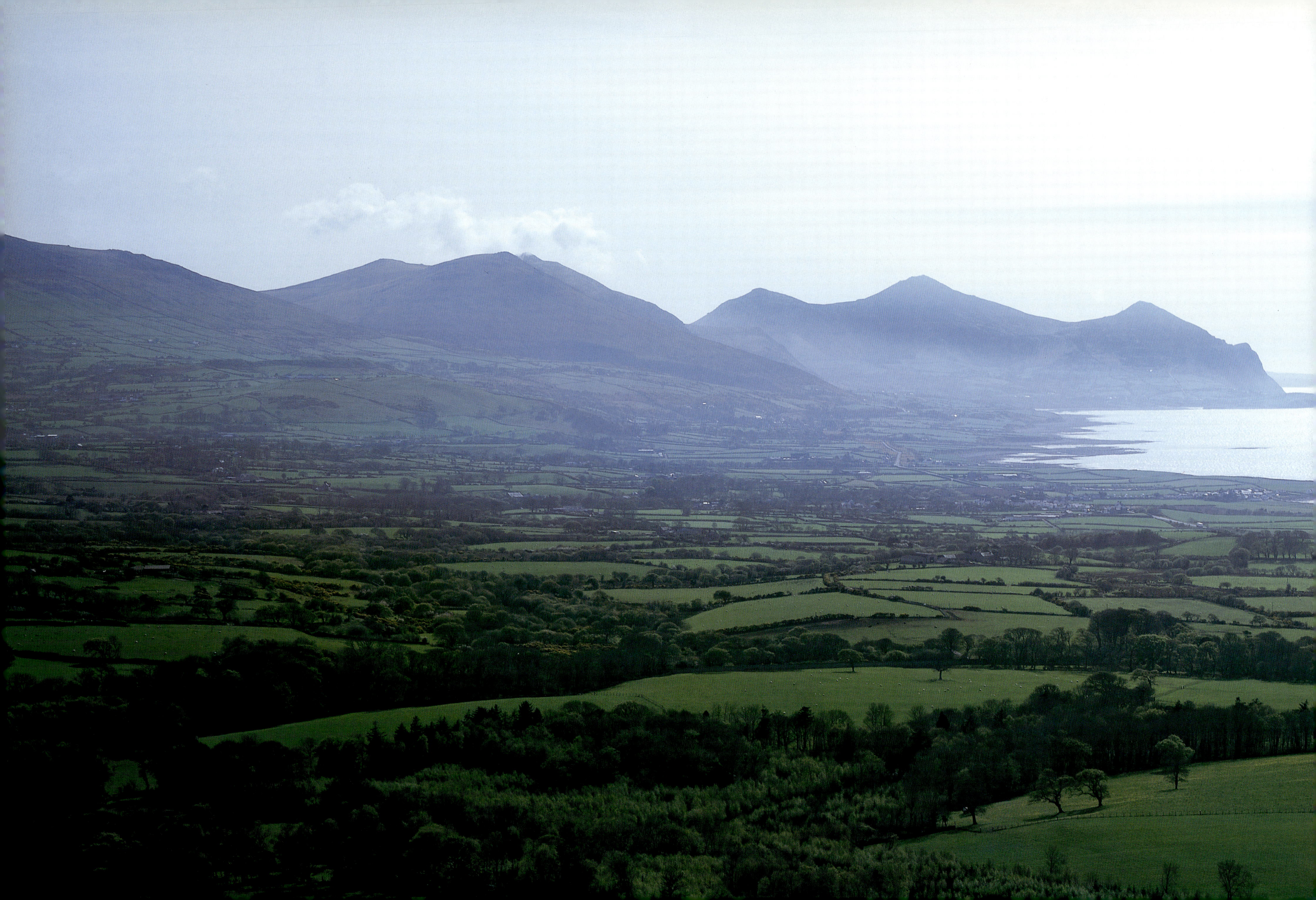

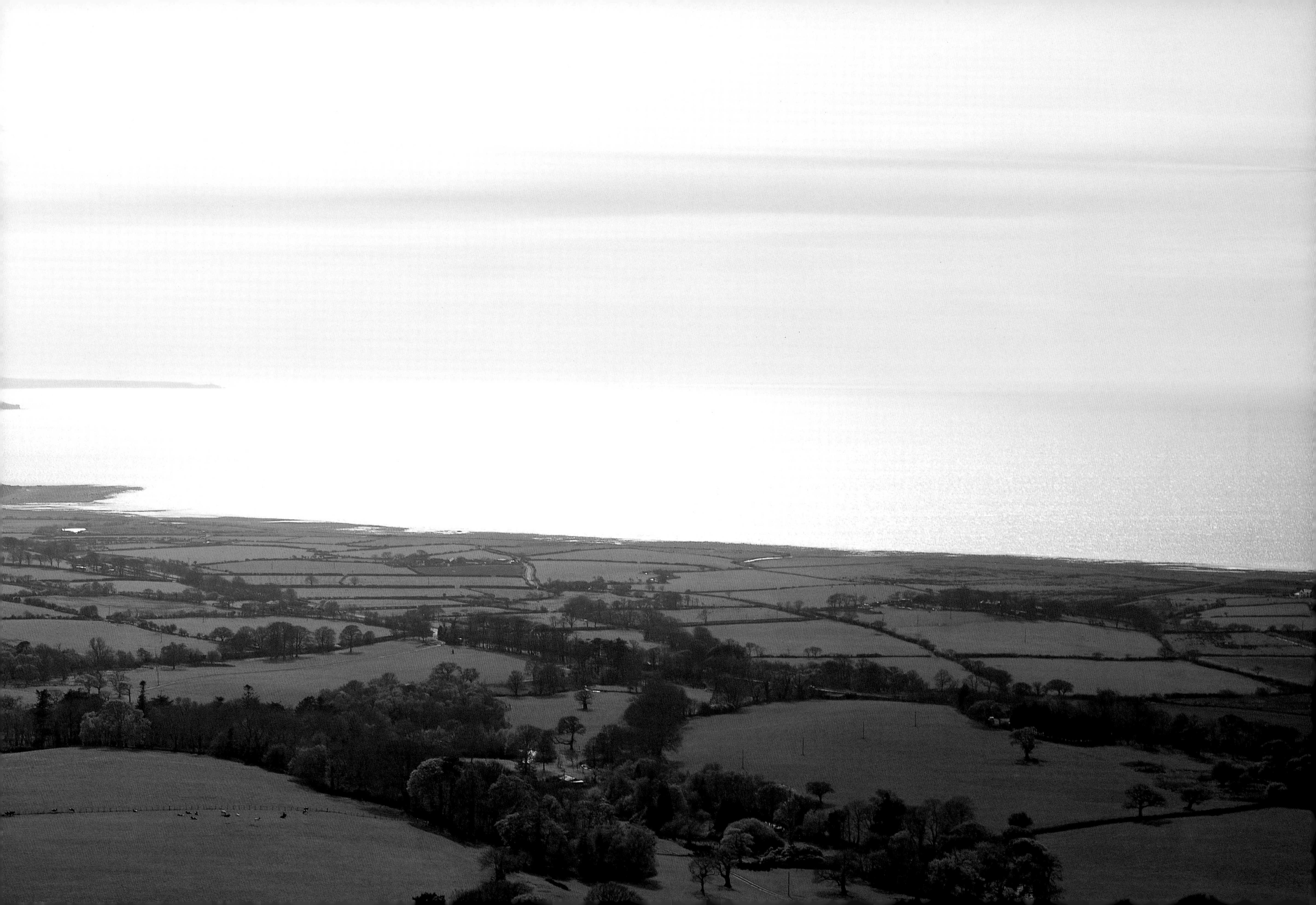

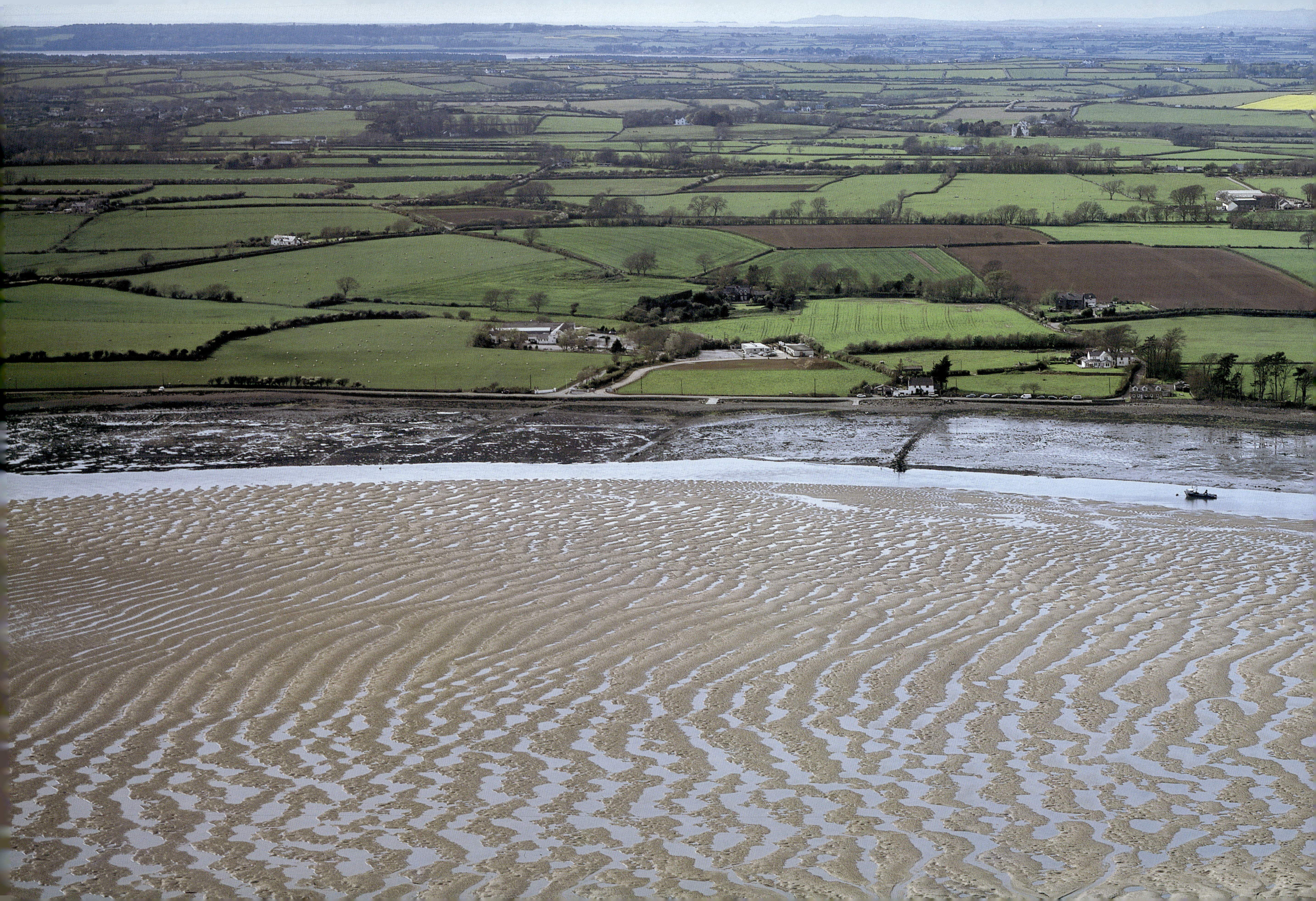

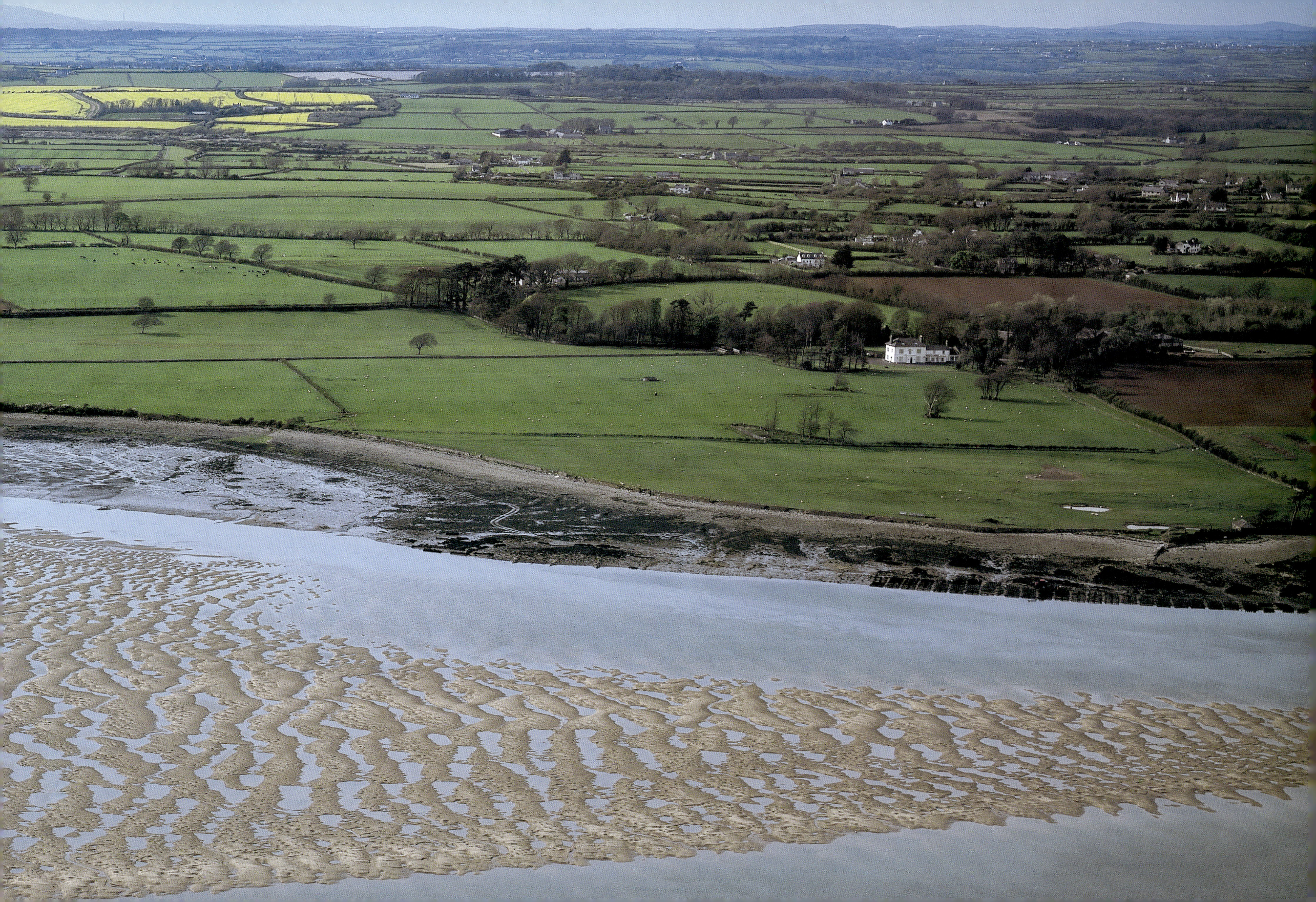

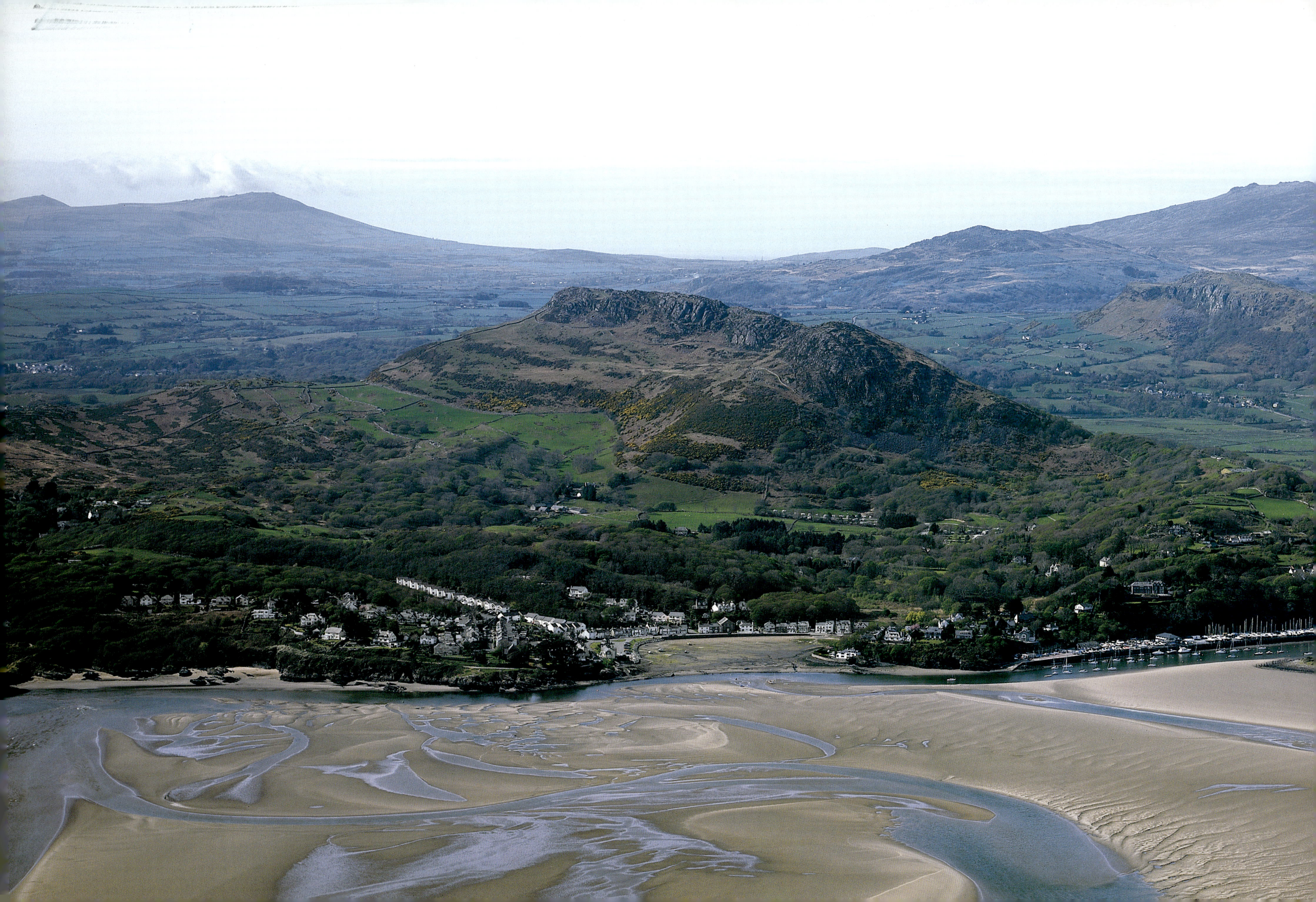

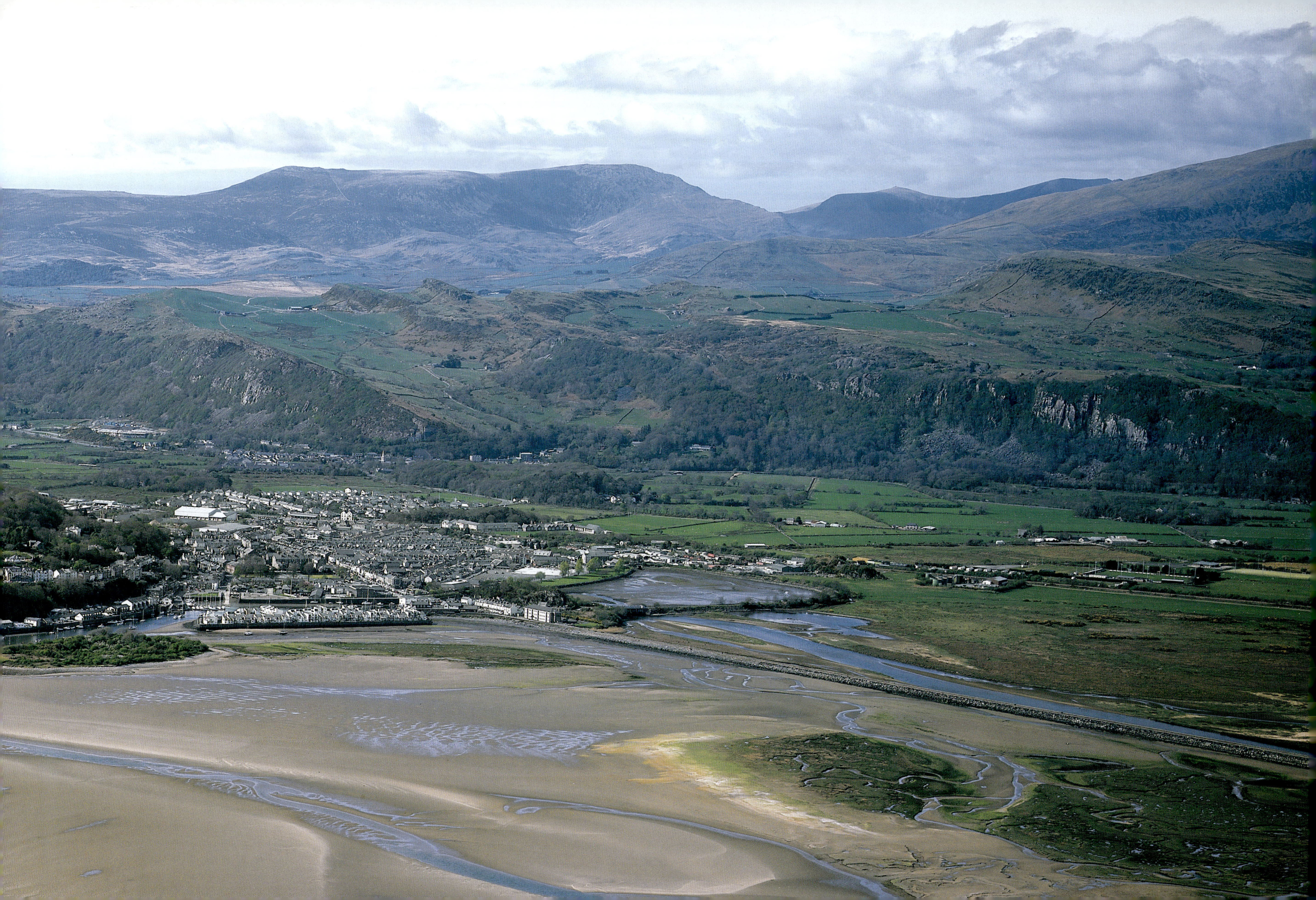

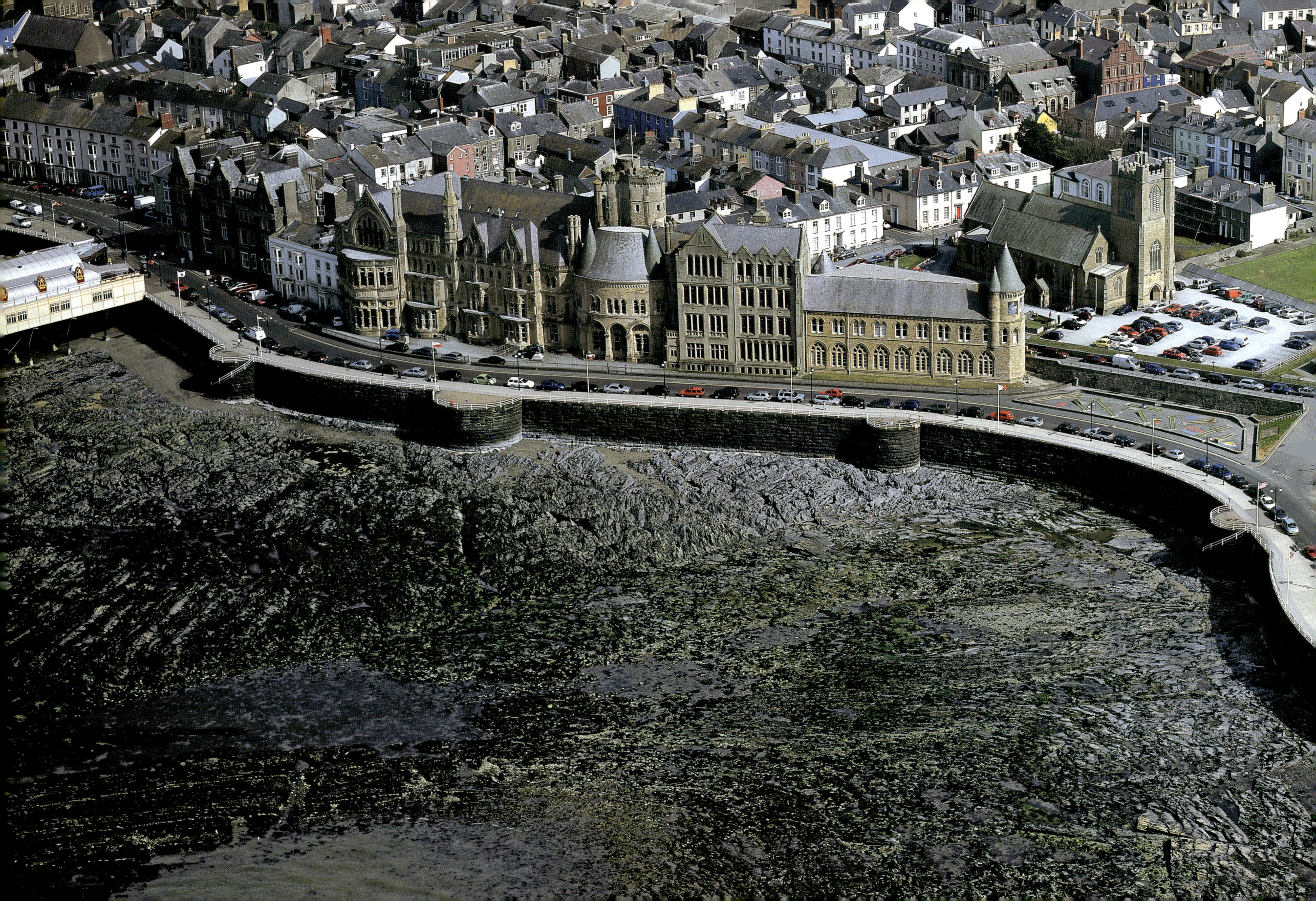

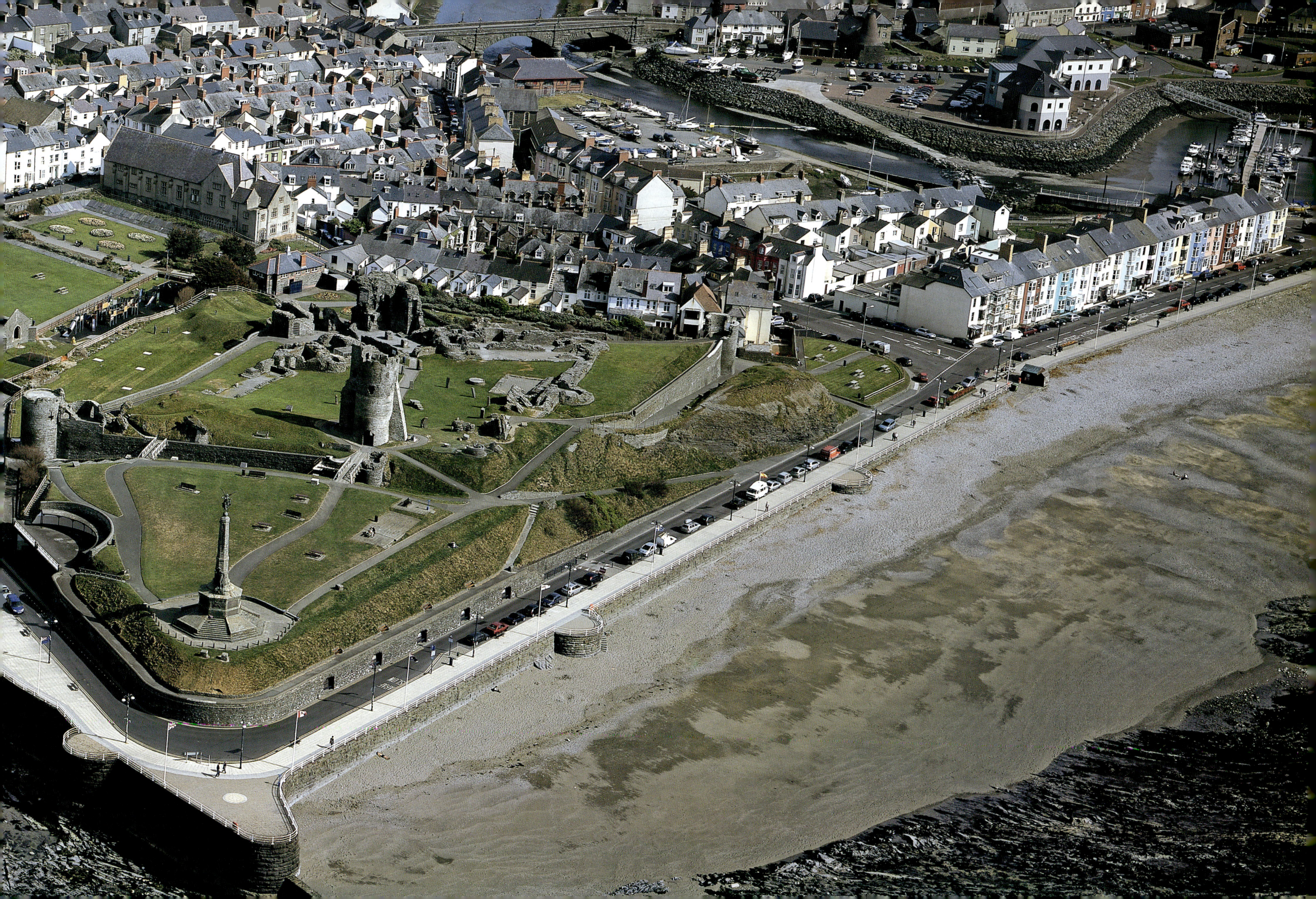

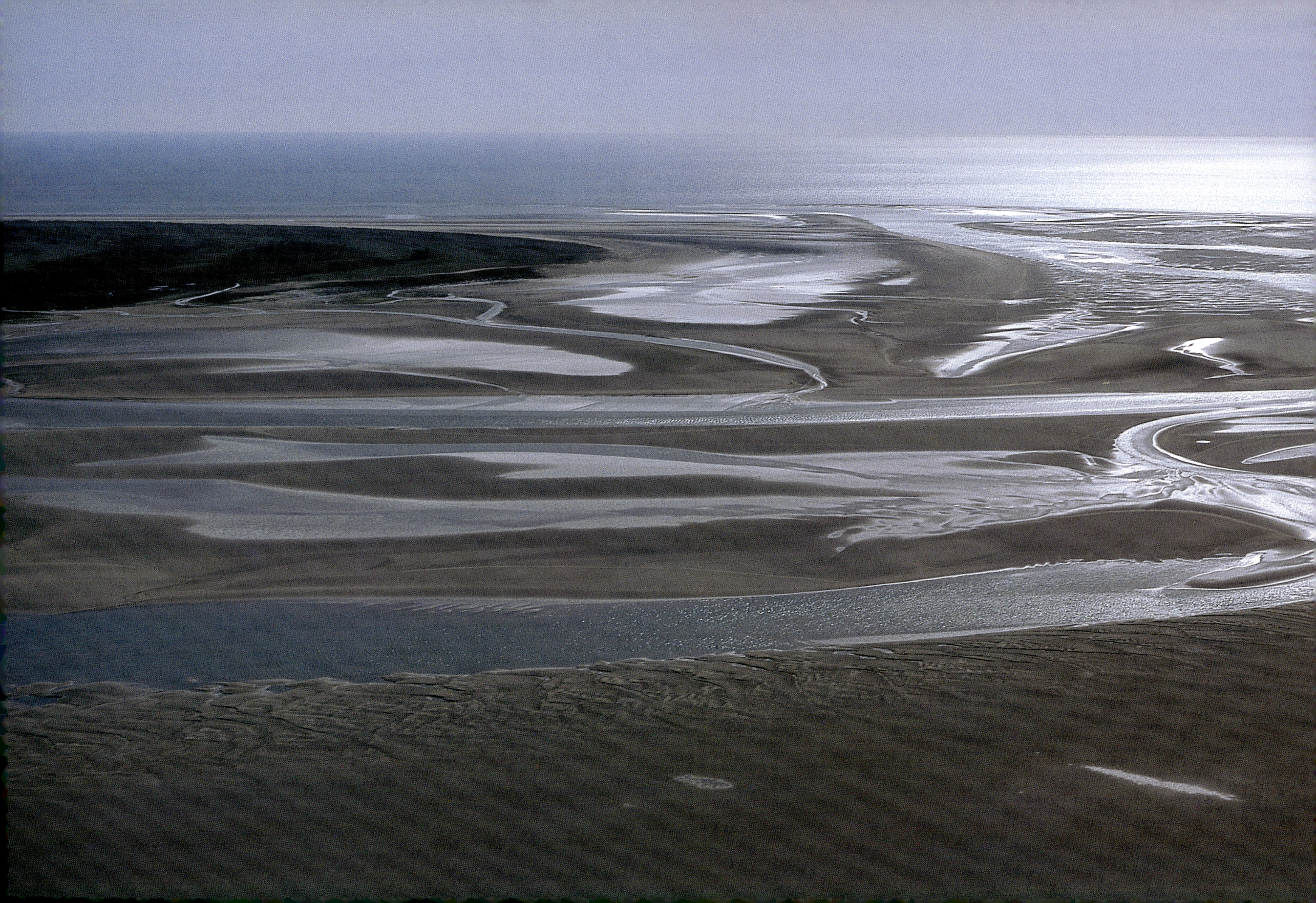

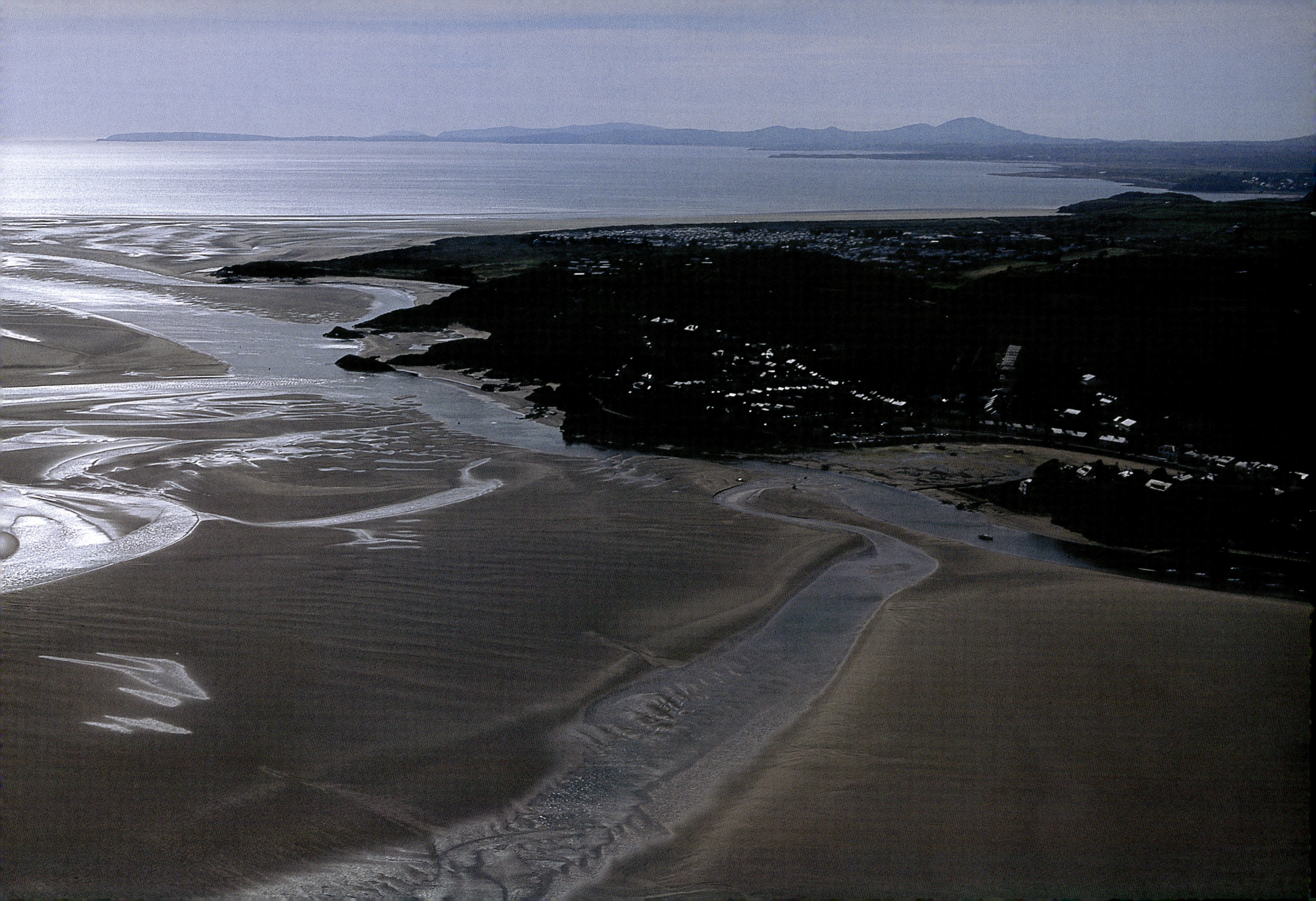

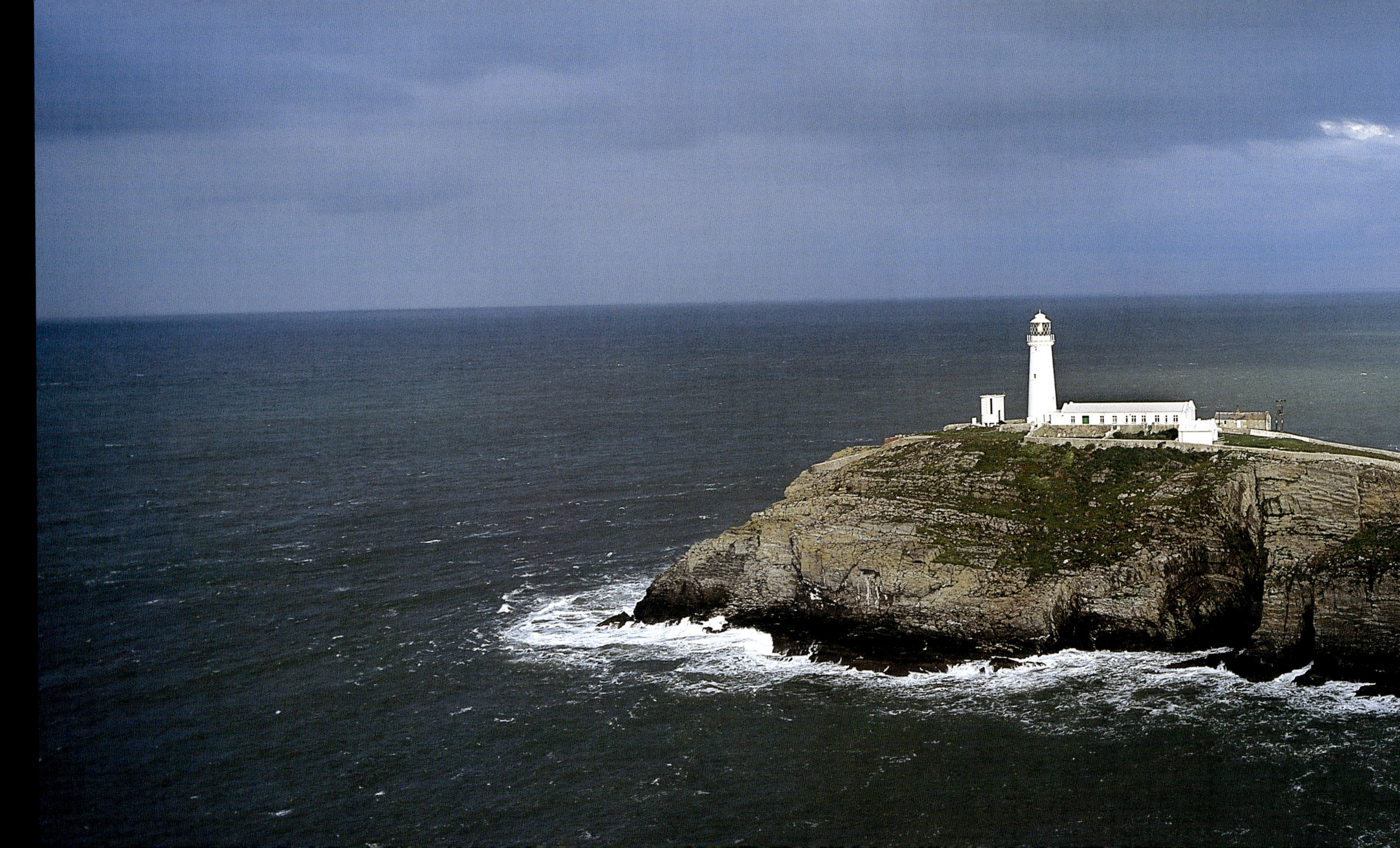

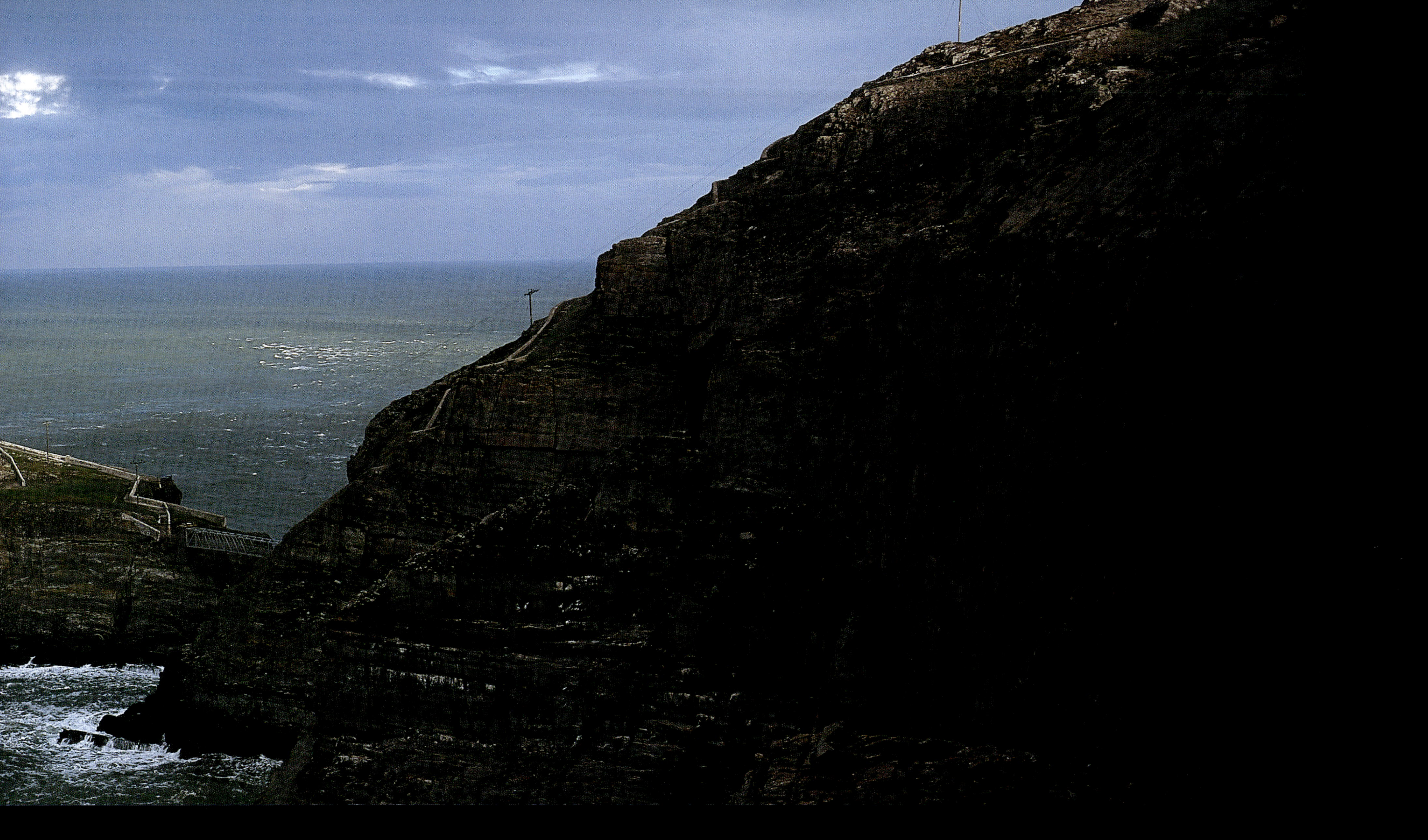

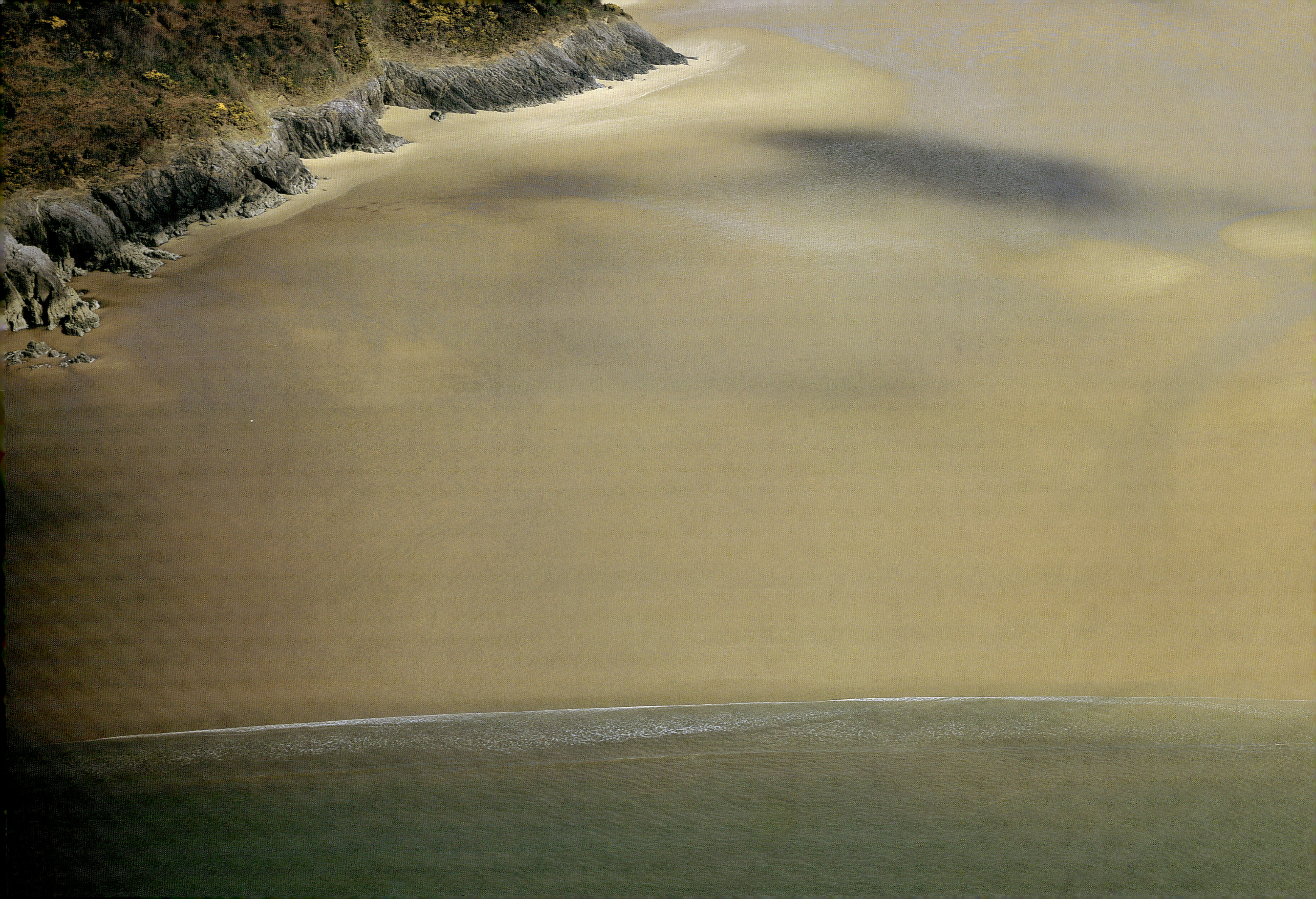

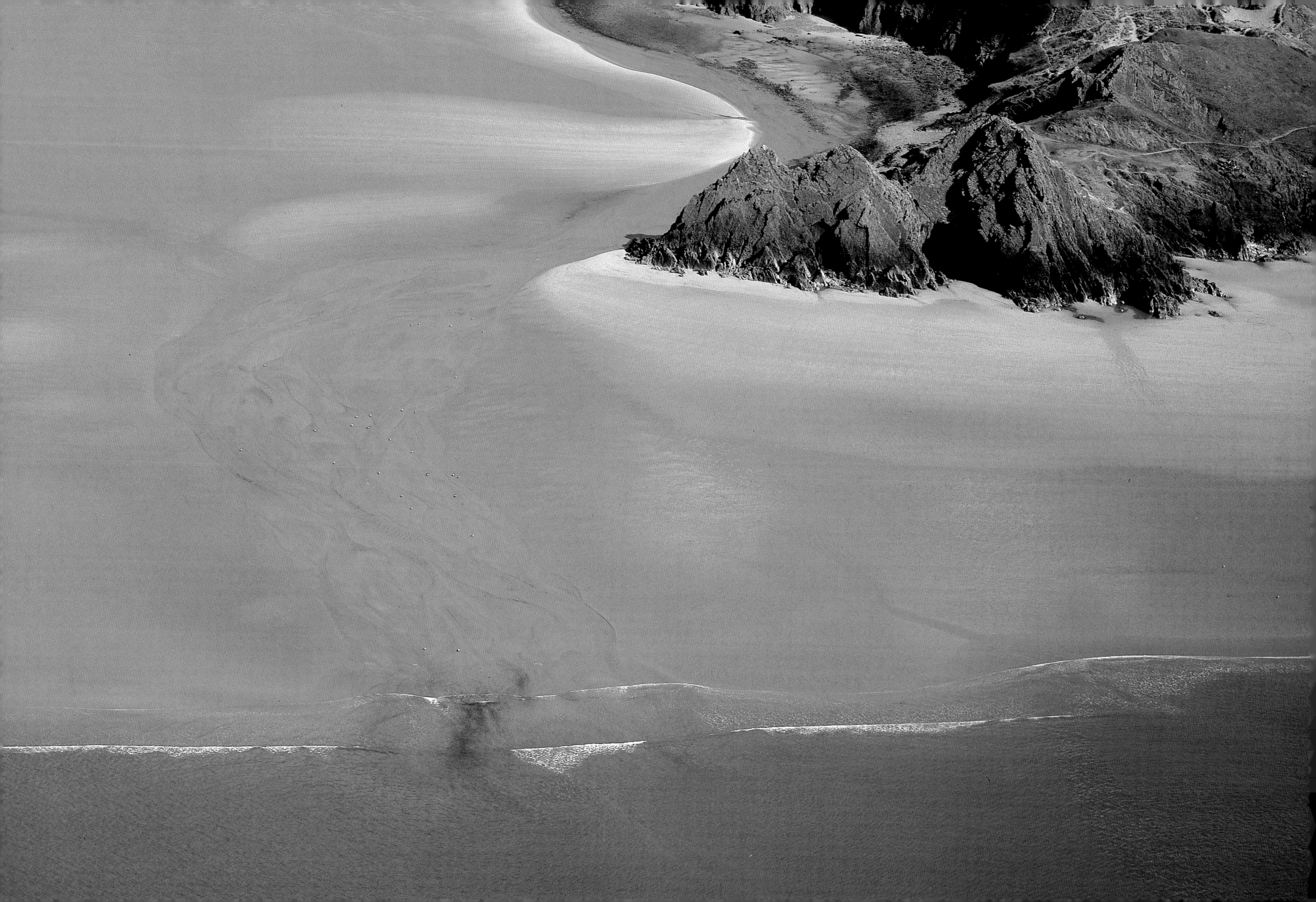

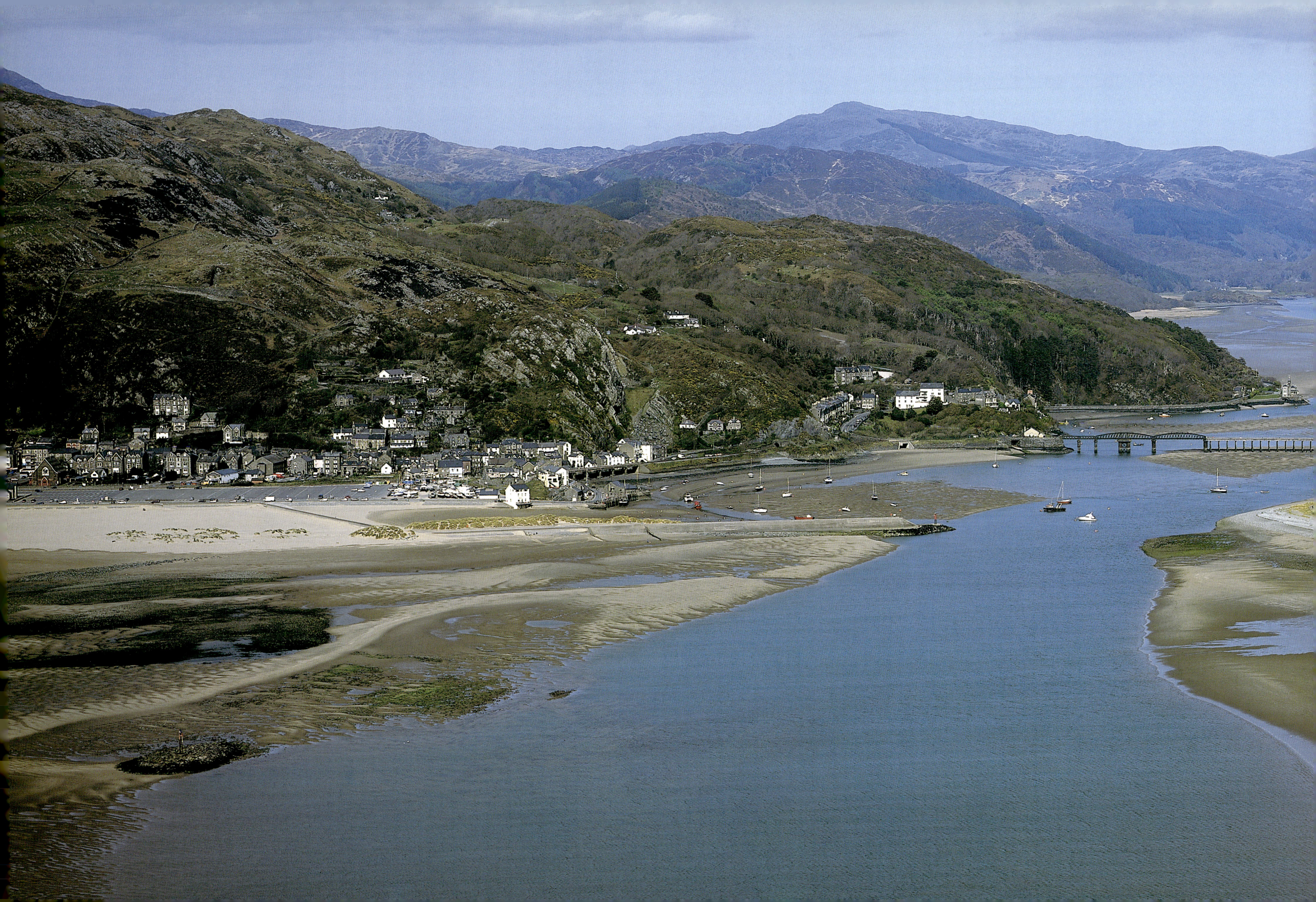

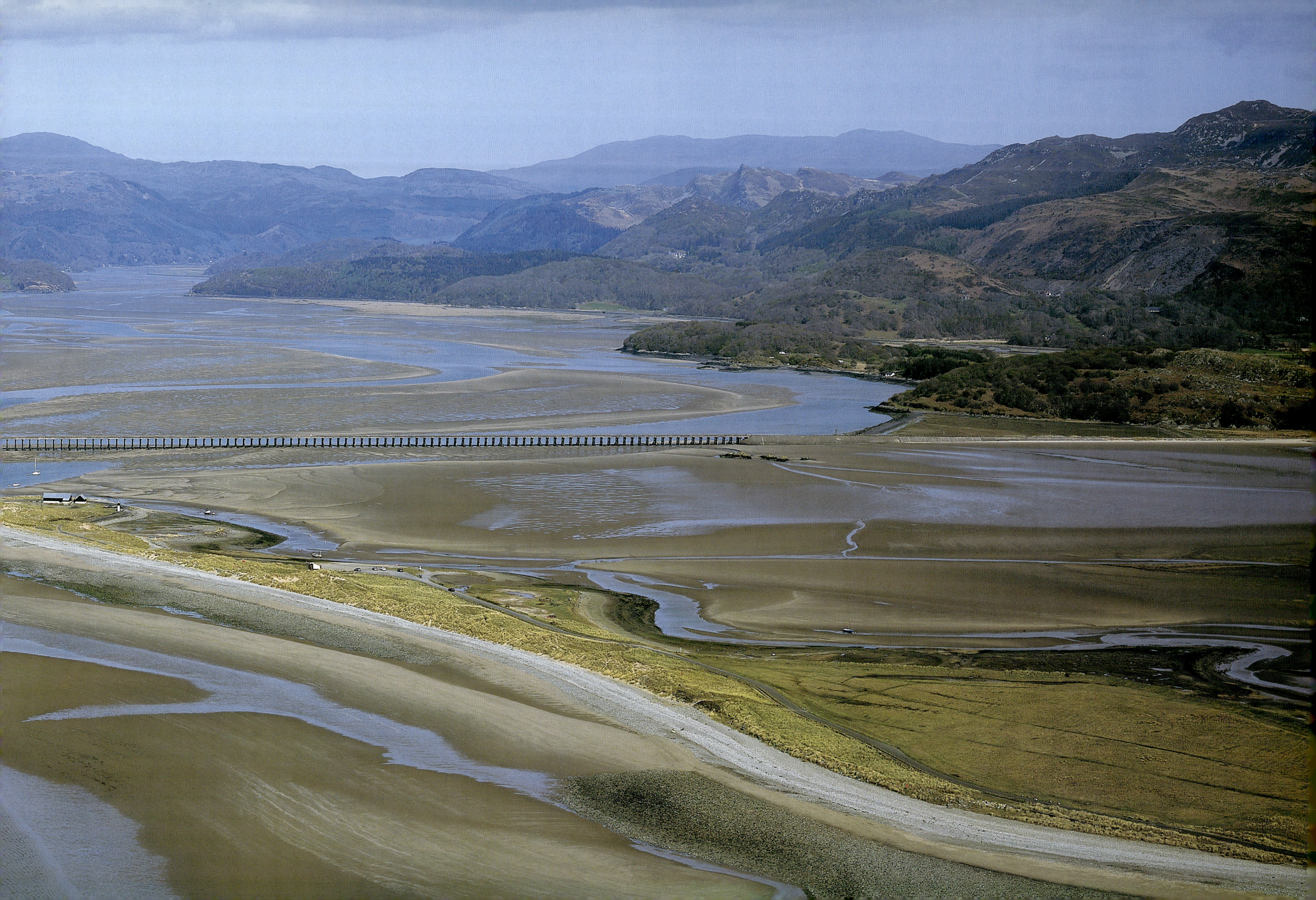

CORNWALL·KERNOW

ONEN HAG OL: **'ONE AND ALL'**, in Cornish. This is the motto of Cornwall, a garden peninsula, whose coast in the shape of a bow of a ship fends off the vastness of the Atlantic. Here the *Finis Terrae* is simply called Land's End.

Wedged at the foot of Wales, Cornwall is Brittany's closest relation within the Celtic world. The two share the same cliffs crowned with golden broom and purple heather, the same sharp-edged promontories, the same linguistic roots and the same saints. Sea trade brought the Breton 'Onion Johnnies', those sailor farmers who set off from the small harbours of Léon and Trégor to convert their crops of white, crunchy onions into cash in Cornwall. Finally, both countries fly black-and-white flags, Cornwall's white cross on a black ground matching Brittany's stripes and ermine spots.

To fly over Tintagel Castle, with its ruins winding over the top of the cliffs, is to open the great sacred book of the Arthurian cycle (12th–13th centuries). King Arthur was reputedly born here in the 5th century. Merlin, the druid magician, expounded his knowledge here. When Arthur rode south, armed with Excalibur, the sword taken from the sacred stone that made him king, he let himself be guided as far as the islet of St Michael's Mount, the last wild bastion jutting out into the vastness of the ocean. From this point he could contemplate the extent of his kingdom on the horizon. From the hills of Truro, towards the centre, his eyes swept across the Lizard Point and the Isles of Scilly.

Looking across the Breton Sea (*Mor Breizh*), he escaped into a fantastical royal dream to the mysterious forests of Brocéliande, the land of the fairies, where the Round Table welcomed his assembly of knights. There, pushed at sword point by the Angles and Saxons, thousands of Cornish and Welsh refugees were to settle behind their saints to build a new Britain in Armorica: Brittany.

The sovereign and great lord of Tintagel and Camelot, Arthur remains the fighting arm of the Celtic spirit, buried in the memory of generations. Legend says that the king 'fell asleep' after Sir Bedivere disposed of the sacred sword by throwing it into a lake. The royal ship carried Arthur to Avalon, the Celtic paradise, the mythical island glimpsed on the distant and dreamlike horizon. Arthur is everywhere in Cornwall: in the ruins on the cliffs of Tintagel, overflowing with purple flowers which grow in thick sprays and cascade down to the ocean, but also among the standing stones facing the sun, at sunset. Elves seem to sing for him around the stone circle of the Merry Maidens on the west coast. There, the country people with their wealth of timeless legends can take you through a round of tales and sagas transcending the Celtic imagination…

It is said that Arthur will one day return from Avalon, on the prow of his royal ship. He will cross back over the *Mor Breizh*. Then, he will take up his sword again and reunite, at last, all the Celtic lands. Forever.

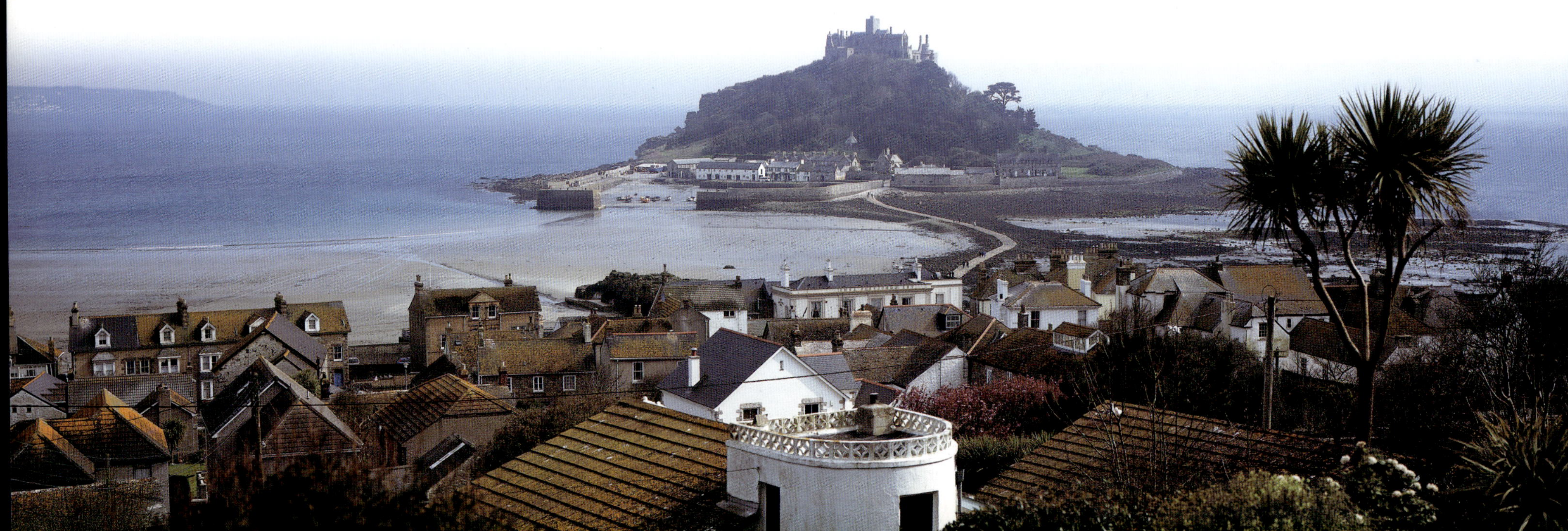

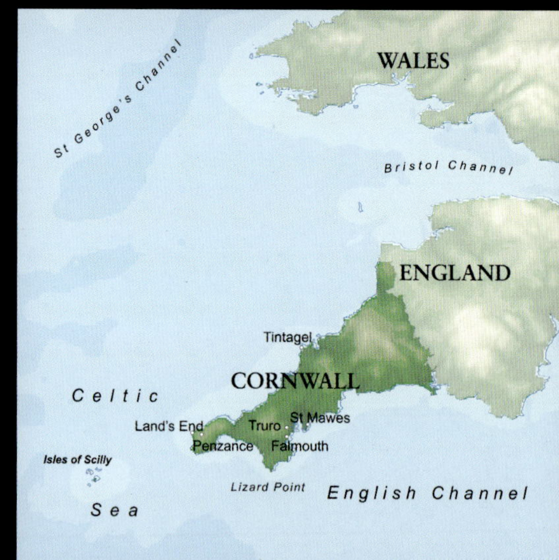

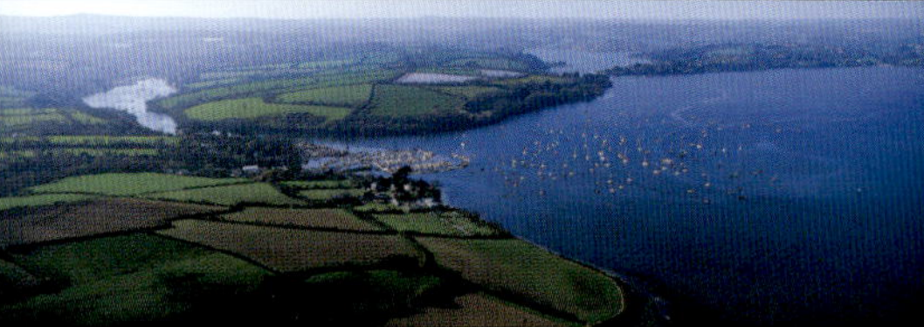

THE RIVER HELFORD
From the Lizard Point, you can head east towards Falmouth by boat along the elegant River Helford, after passing the former smuggler's caves at Nare Point. Sailing boats stop off in modern marinas. Falmouth is also home to the National Maritime Museum Cornwall.

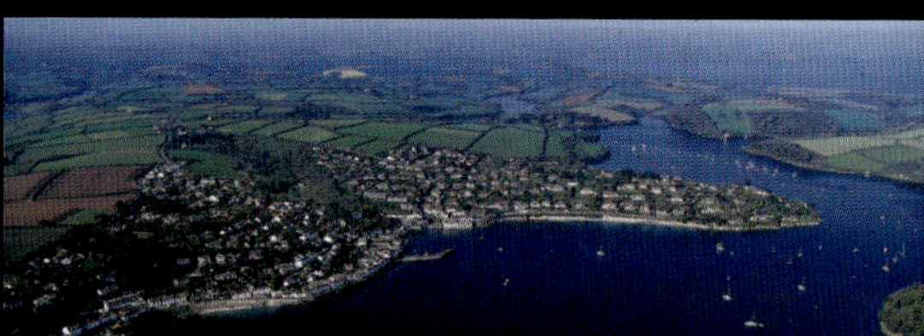

FLOWERS OF ROSELAND
The Roseland peninsula is a scenic part of Cornwall. Its heart is the little port of St Mawes, which marks the entrance to the waterway known as the Carrick Roads, leading up to Truro. The lighthouse of St Anthony has become an observation point for dolphins and (more rarely) whales in Falmouth Bay.

Opposite: A picture postcard view of Cornwall, from the houses of Marazion across to St Michael's Mount.

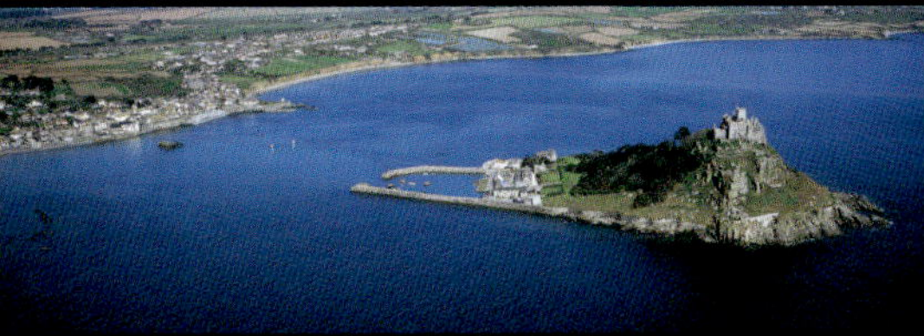

A PLACE OF PILGRIMAGE
A vision of the Archangel Michael emerged from the waters here in the 5th century. Cornwall's St Michael's Mount became a place of pilgrimage in the Middle Ages, as did Mont Saint-Michel in the Baie Bretonne, although it is now considered part of Normandy.

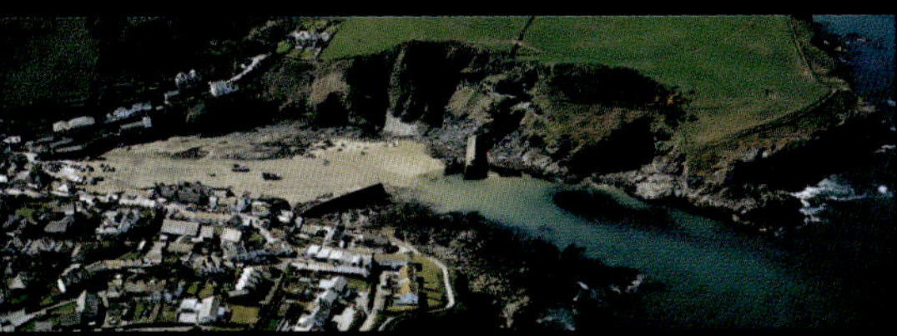

'LOBSTER HARBOUR'
The present-day Port Isaac (Porthusek, in Cornish) in North Cornwall began its life as Port Izzard or Portissyk. It is known for its fresh lobster and shellfish from the many fishing boats in the harbour, and for its 18th-century thatched cottages.

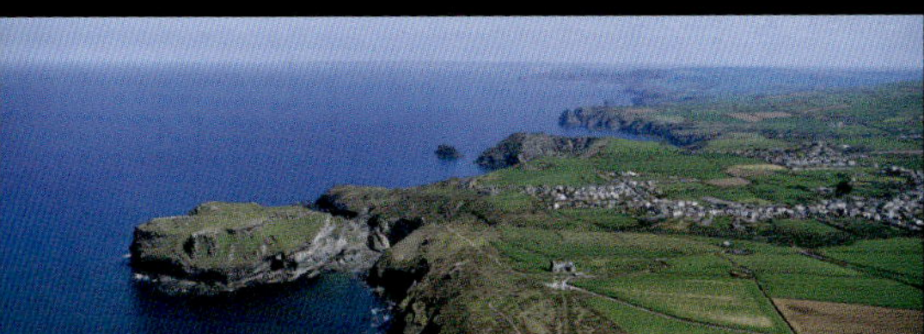

ARTHUR OF TINTAGEL
Faced with the legendary King Arthur, the Saxon invader seemed destined for a rout. Arthur, king of Britain and of Brittany, reigned over his court at Camelot, a few miles from his castle at Tintagel overlooking the sea, built on four hundred metre high cliffs.

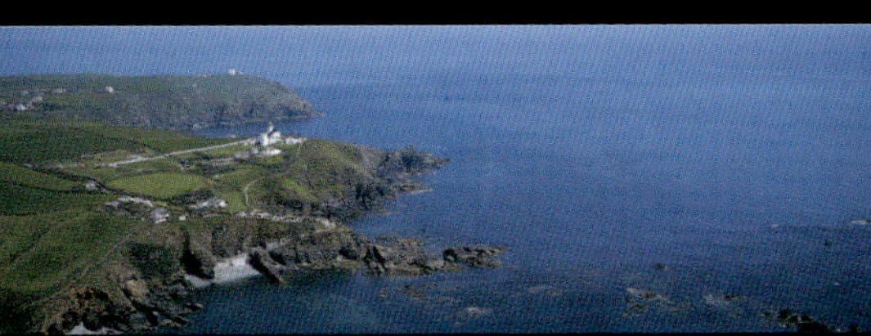

THE RECORD POINT
Like twin sisters facing the open sea, the Lizard Point lighthouse has two towers. It is here, at the foot of the signalling tower, that transatlantic sailing records are judged. Charlie Barr took 12 days, 4 hours and one minute to sail from New York in 1905. Éric Tabarly lowered the record to 10 days, 75 years later.

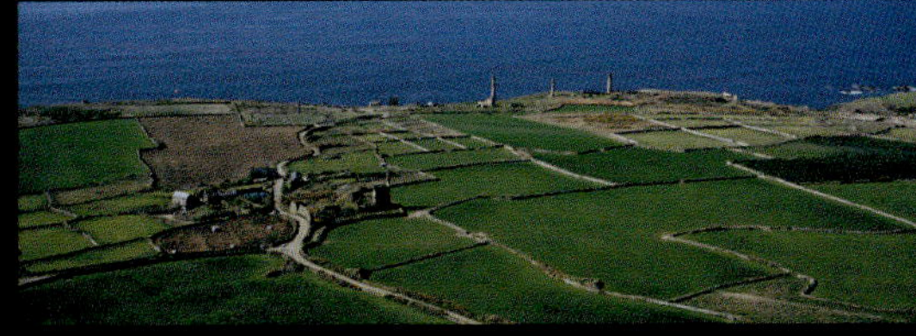

CHIMNEYS BY THE SEA
At the foot of the Pendeen Watch lighthouse, in the west, is a coast studded with chimneys. These are relics of the Levant tin mine, between Land's End and St Ives. To shore up the workings, the Cornish fetched wood from La Trinité sur Mer in Brittany!

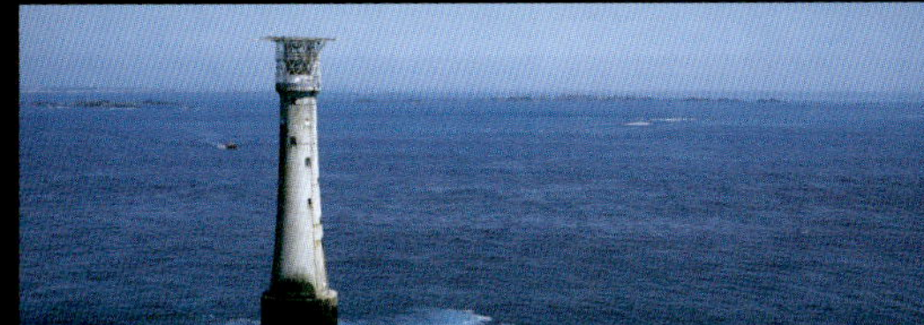

AT THE COURT OF BISHOP ROCK
Bishop Rock lighthouse is the last sentinel facing the vastness of the ocean. Next stop, America! It towers above the waters off the Scilly Isles, holding court to the other lighthouses within its orbit: there are eight within a fifty-mile radius.

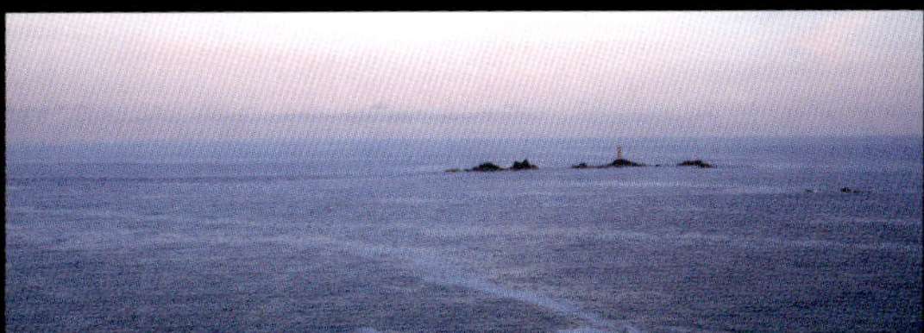

LAND'S END
Every five seconds, a red flash and a white flash shine from the Longship lighthouse some twenty-five nautical miles from the Isles of Scilly. It was in the waters around Land's End that Éric Tabarly was thrown overboard in January 1996 from his yacht *Pen Duick*, which was heading for Scotland.

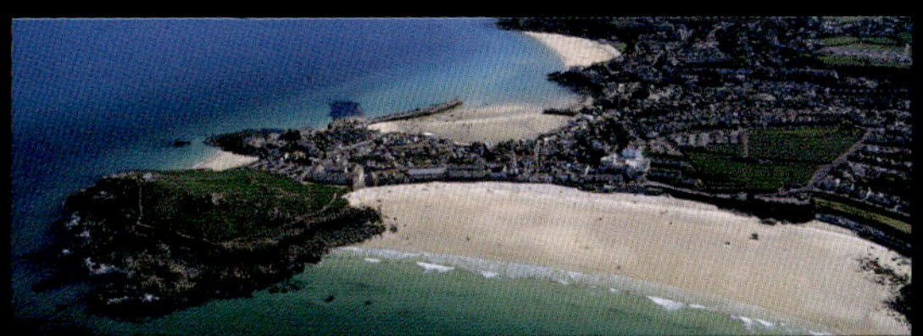

ST IVES
Cornwall's patron may be St Piran, but the town of St Ives – Porth Ia in Cornish – takes its name from an Irish princess and martyr, St Ia (or Hia). Its two beaches, Porthgwidden and Porthmeor, are popular with fishermen and surfers.

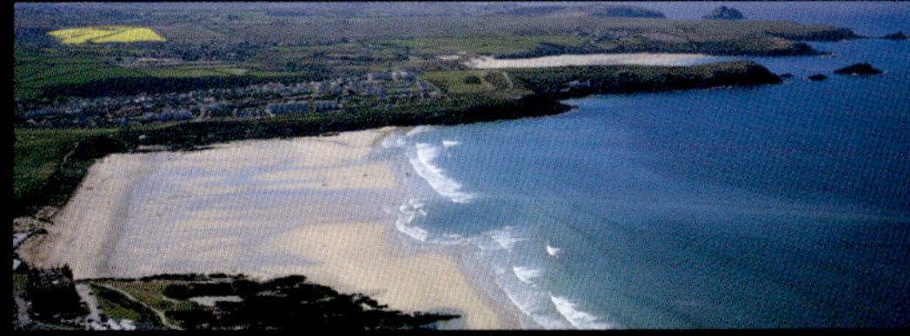

GOLDEN BEACHES
Fistral Bay is one of the most popular beaches on Cornwall's west coast. To starboard, some Iron Age remains. To port, a golf course on the water's edge. In the centre lies Newquay, its lively port a famous gathering place for surfers.

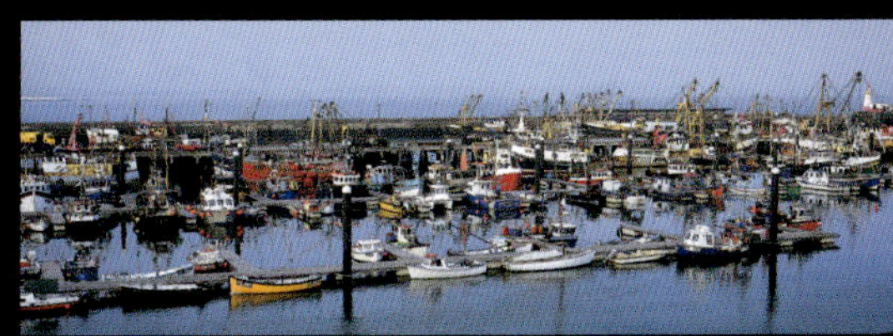

REQUIEM
Just outside Penzance in Mount's Bay is Newlyn, Cornwall's largest fishing port. A number of the trawlers photographed here are headed for the maritime cemetery for the benefit of less industrial fishing. Sailors here still mourn the wreck of the Breton ship *Bugaled Breizh* in 2004.

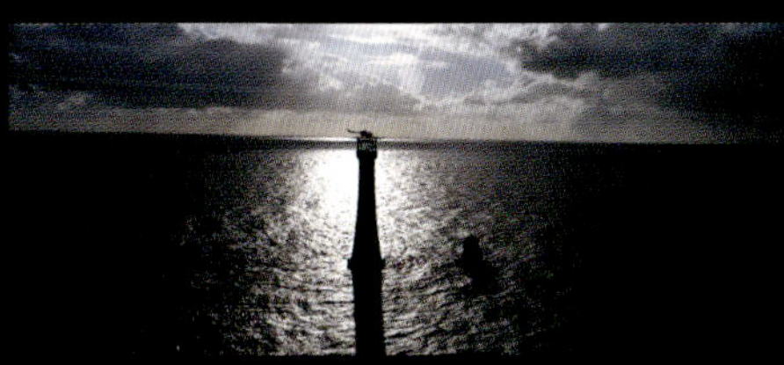

HELICOPTER...
The Eddystone Lighthouse stands in the sea off Plymouth, and marks the meeting point of England and Cornwall. The first lighthouse on this site was built in 1696, but the current one was opened by the Duke of Edinburgh in 1882. One hundred years later it became fully automated. Note the helicopter on its platform.

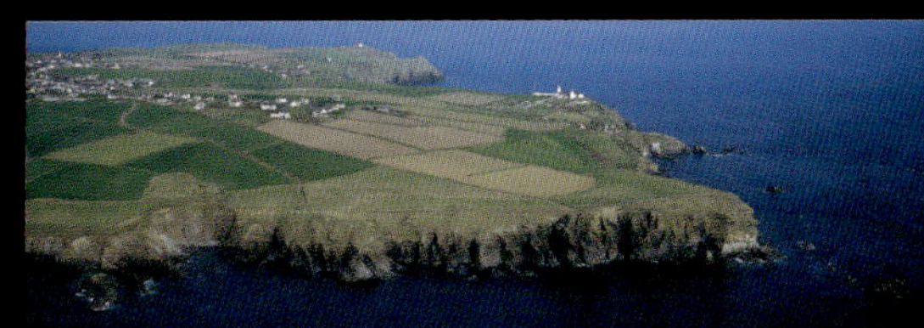

LIZARD POINT, THE ATLANTIC TERMINUS
On 29 July 1588, an armed fleet of one hundred and twenty boats was sighted off Lizard Point, the southernmost point of Cornwall. This was the Spanish Armada with its 29,000 men. It was defeated by the English navy. Today Lizard Point is often used as a starting point or end point for transatlantic speed challenges.

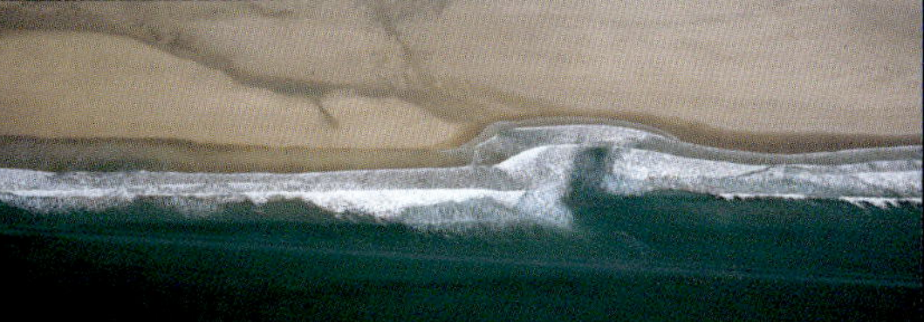

A BEACH FIT FOR A SAINT
Cornwall's endless beaches are lapped by the froth of the waves. St Ives is a cheerful town full of gardens with tropical plants and an impressive collection of sculptures and other modern art.

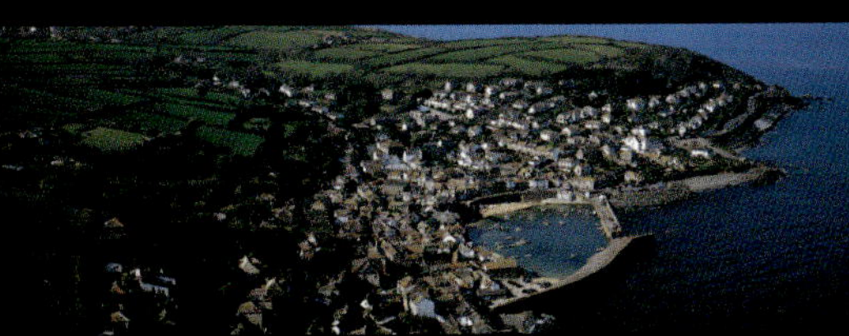

CORNISH WAY
The village of Mousehole was sacked by the Spanish in 1595. Just one house survived, and still stands today. The port is now filled with local fishing boats, and pleasure boats in the summer. All around lies 'The Cornish Way', a flower-strewn balcony overlooking the sea.

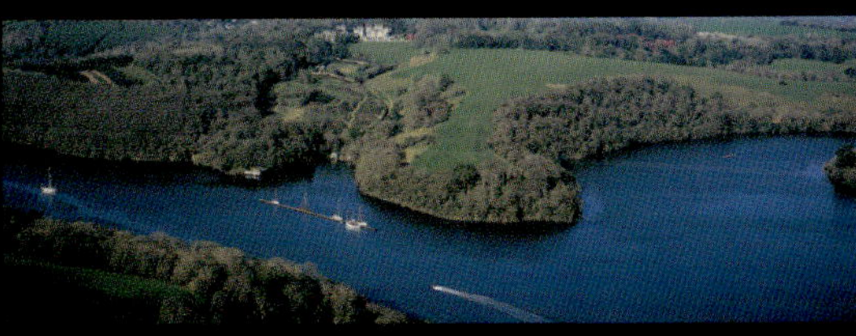

NOBLE TRURO
Truro, a magical name. Cornish settlers who left for the New World gave the name to their encampments in Nova Scotia and Massachusetts. Truro by the edge of the Carrick Roads and the River Allen hides Loe Pool, invisible from the road.

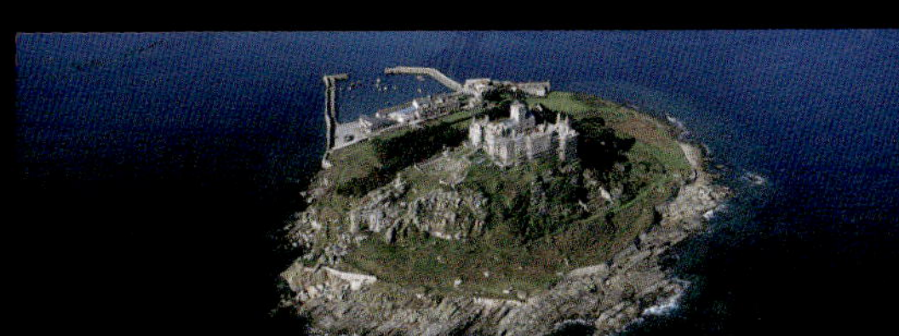

A PLACE OF SANCTUARY
Another view of St Michael's Mount. As well as being a pre-druidic and druidic sanctuary, according to legend it was built by the giant Cormoran who was eventually defeated by Jack the Giant Killer. It later served as a monastery and military garrison.

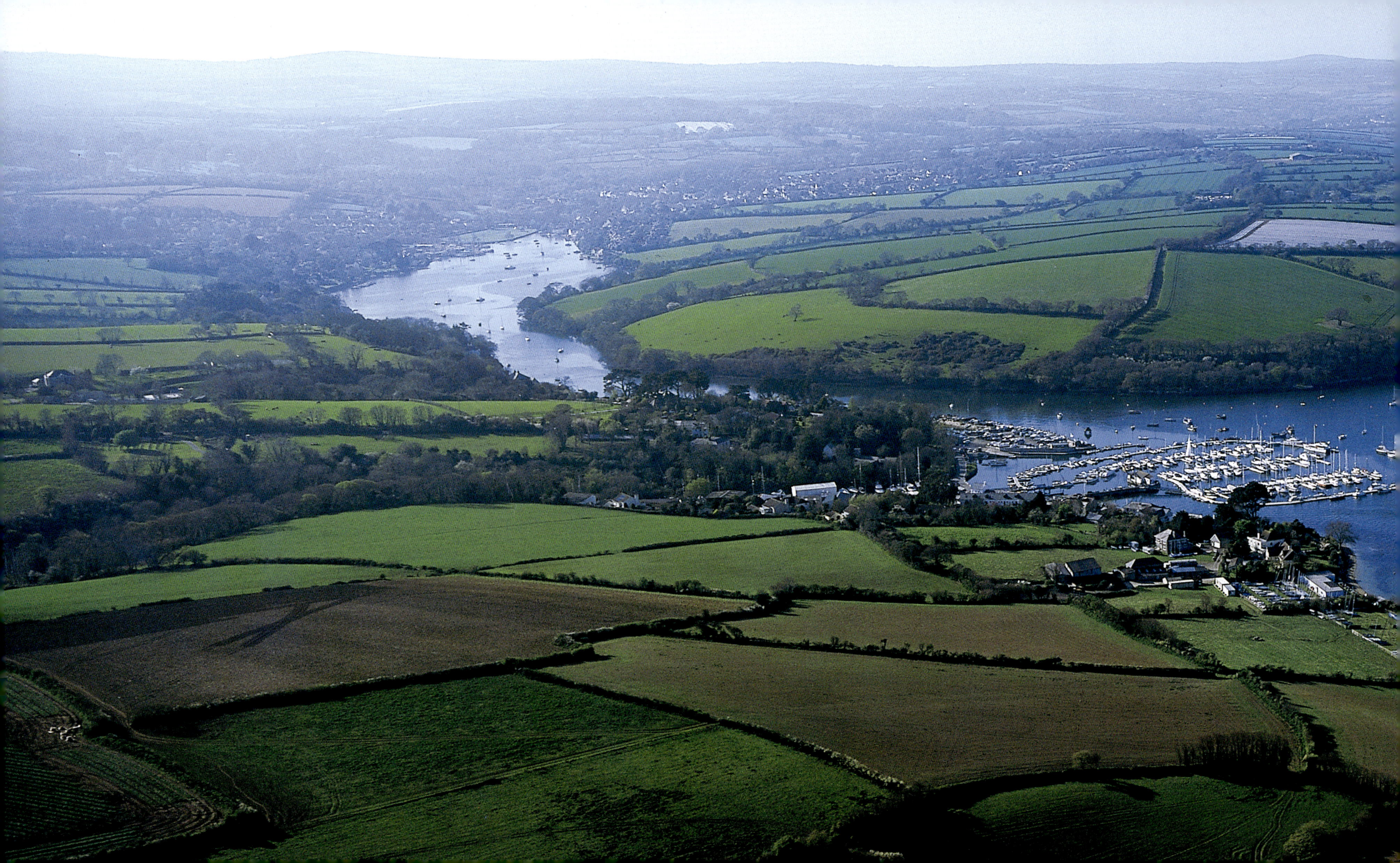

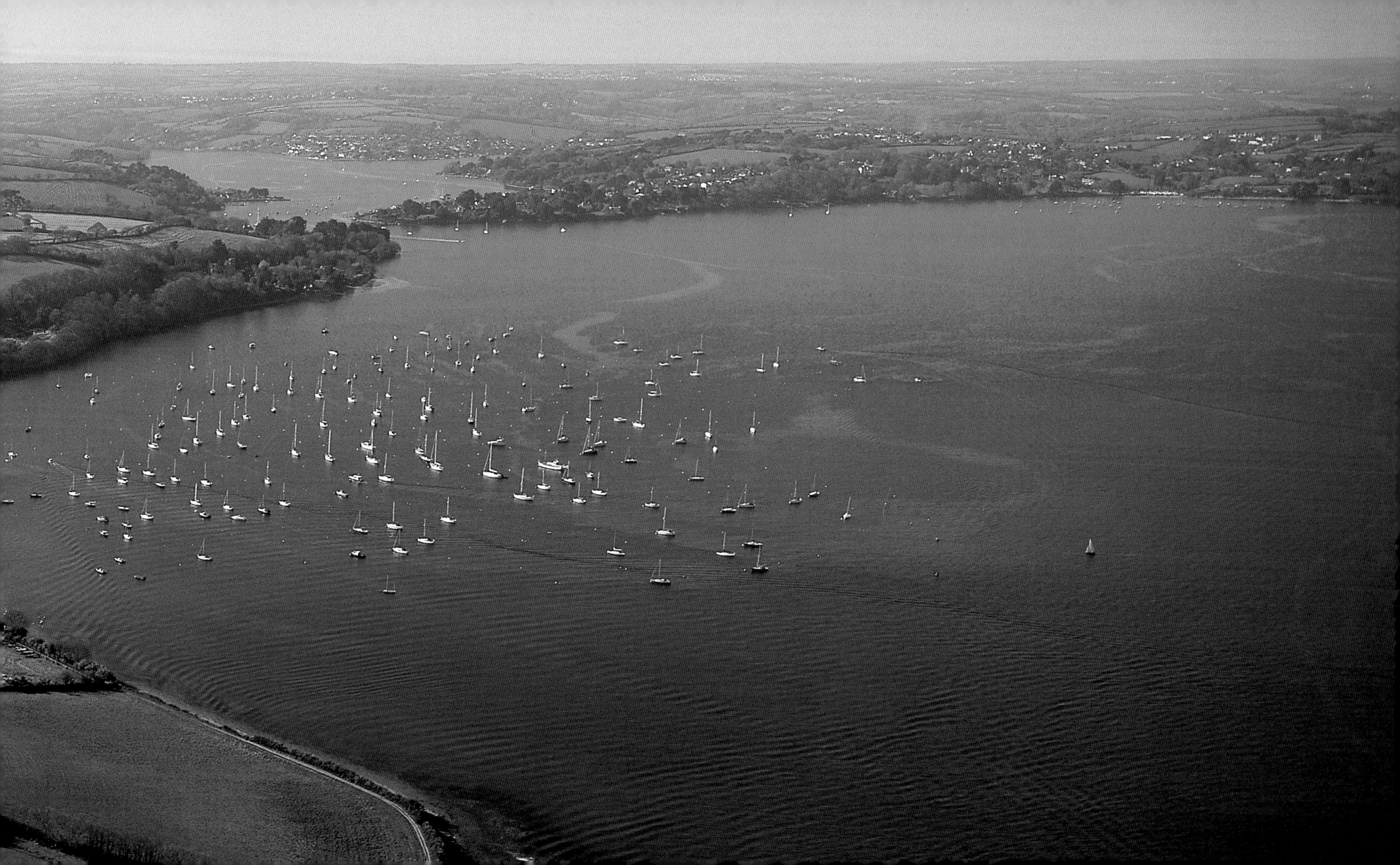

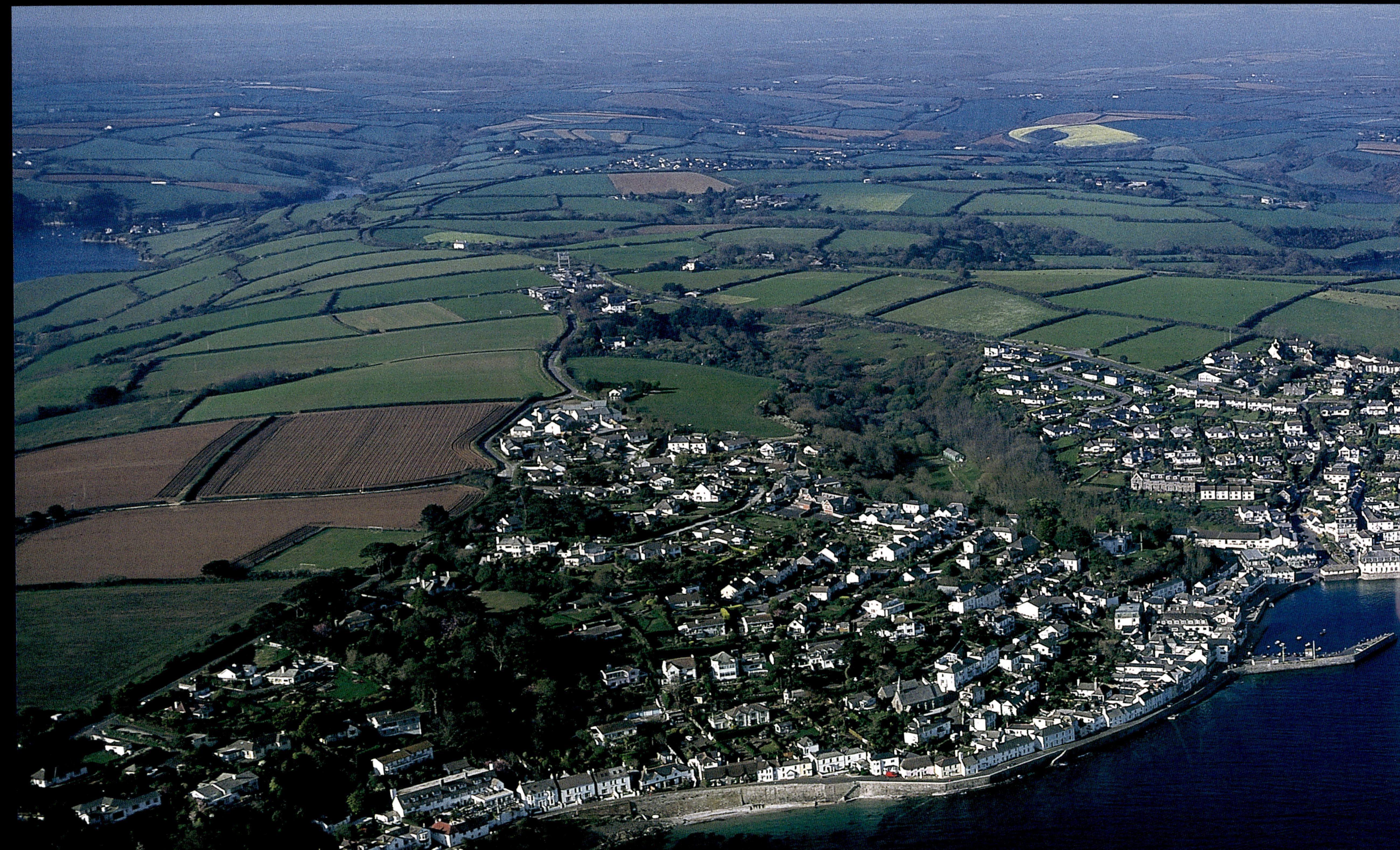

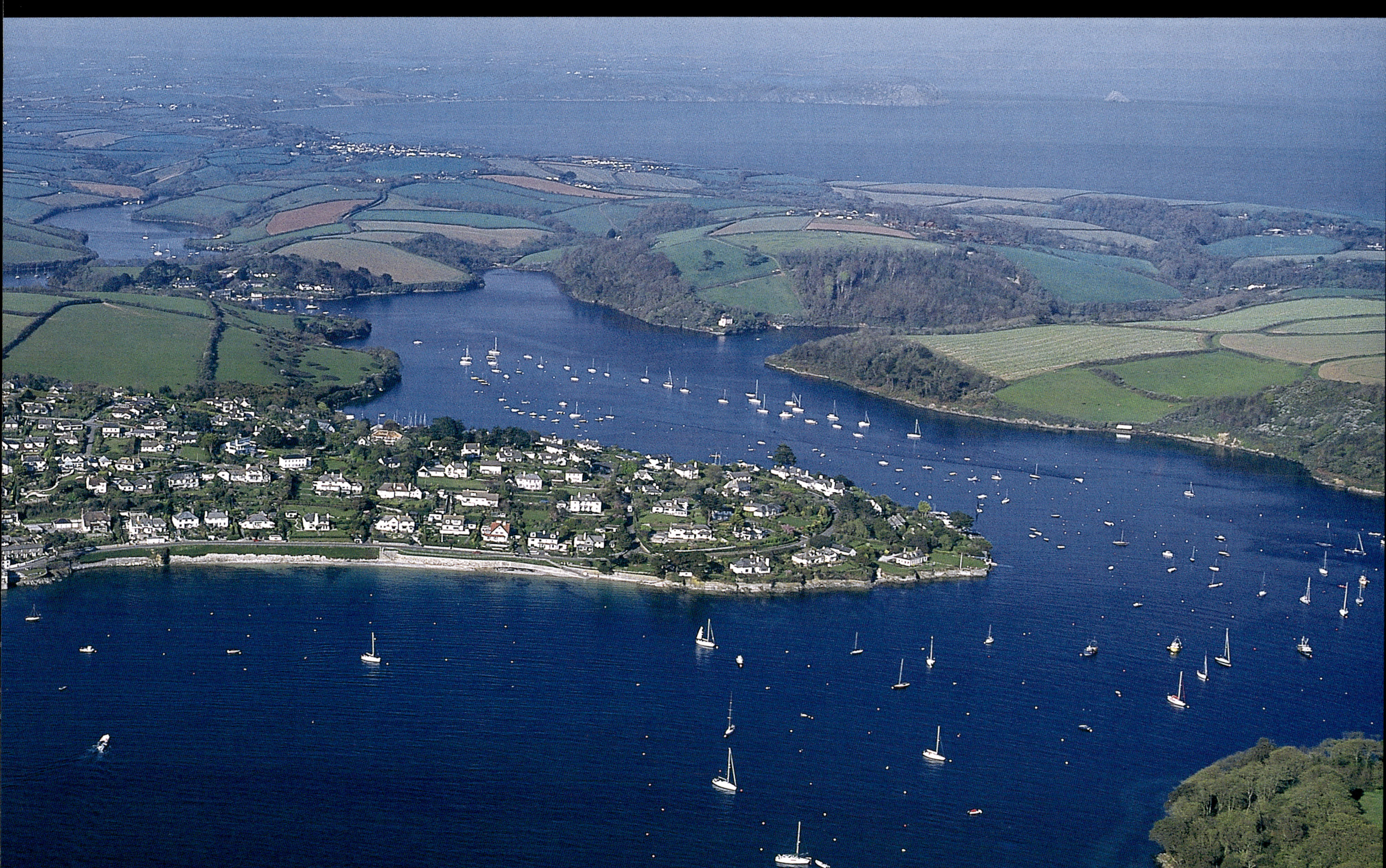

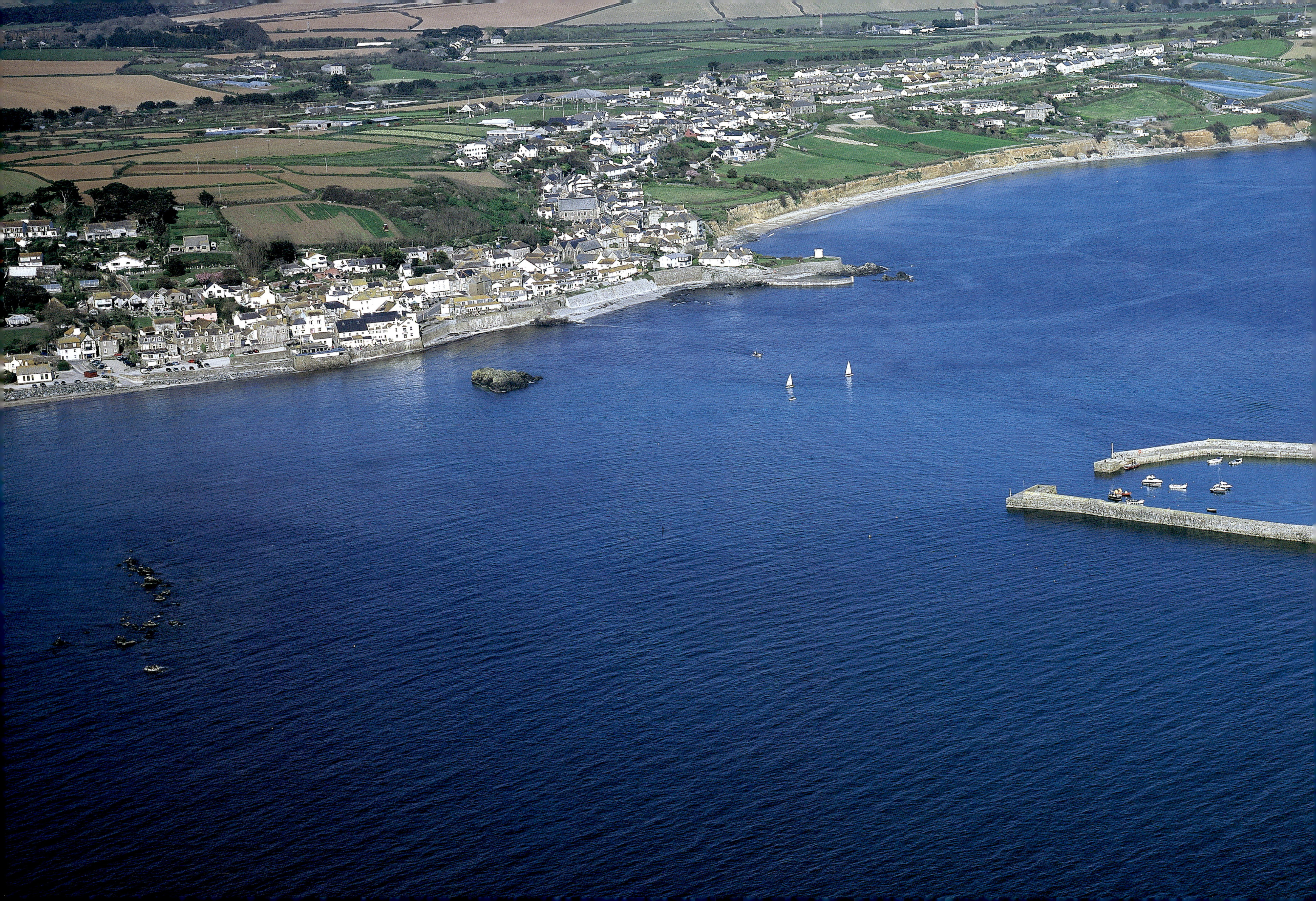

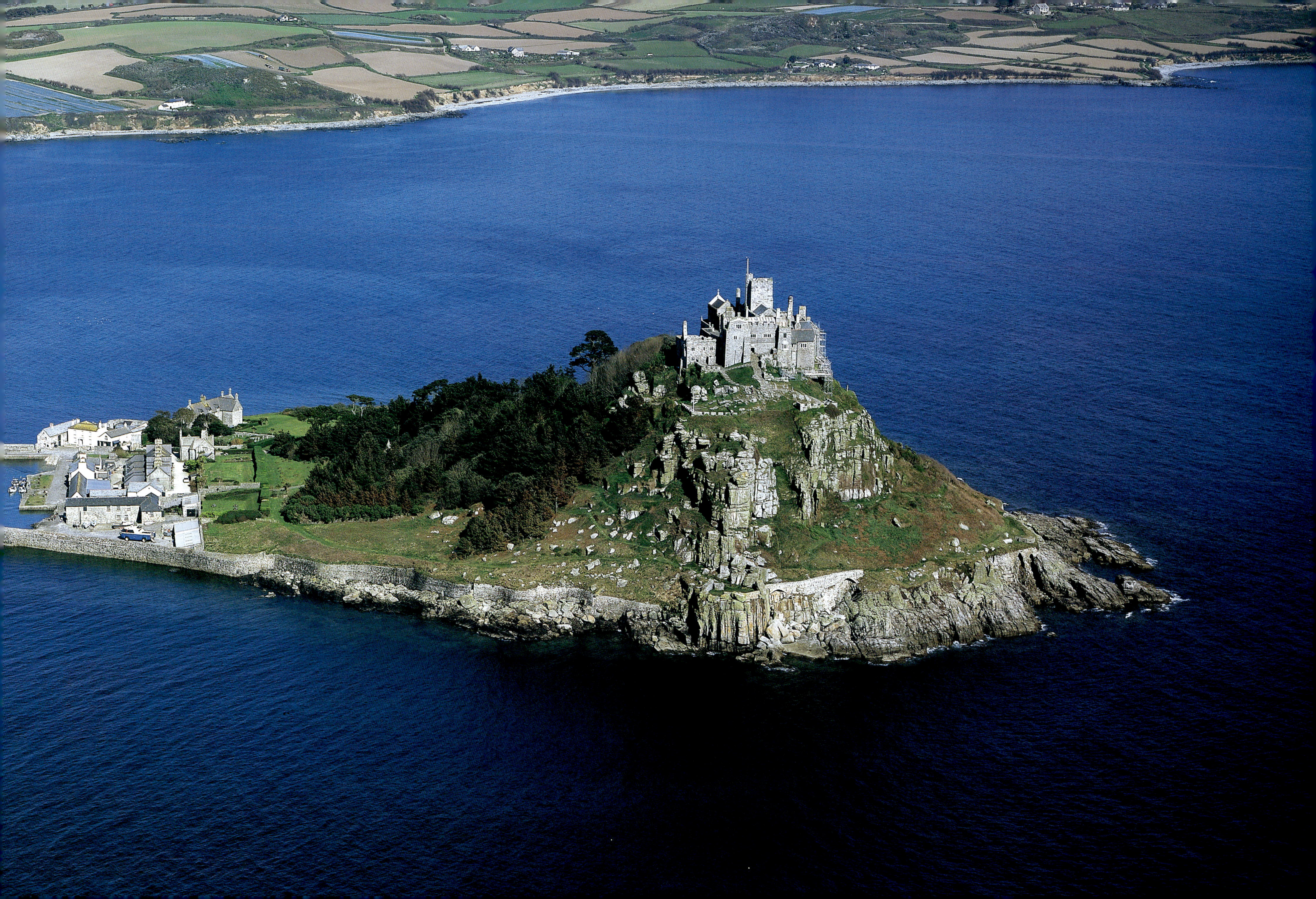

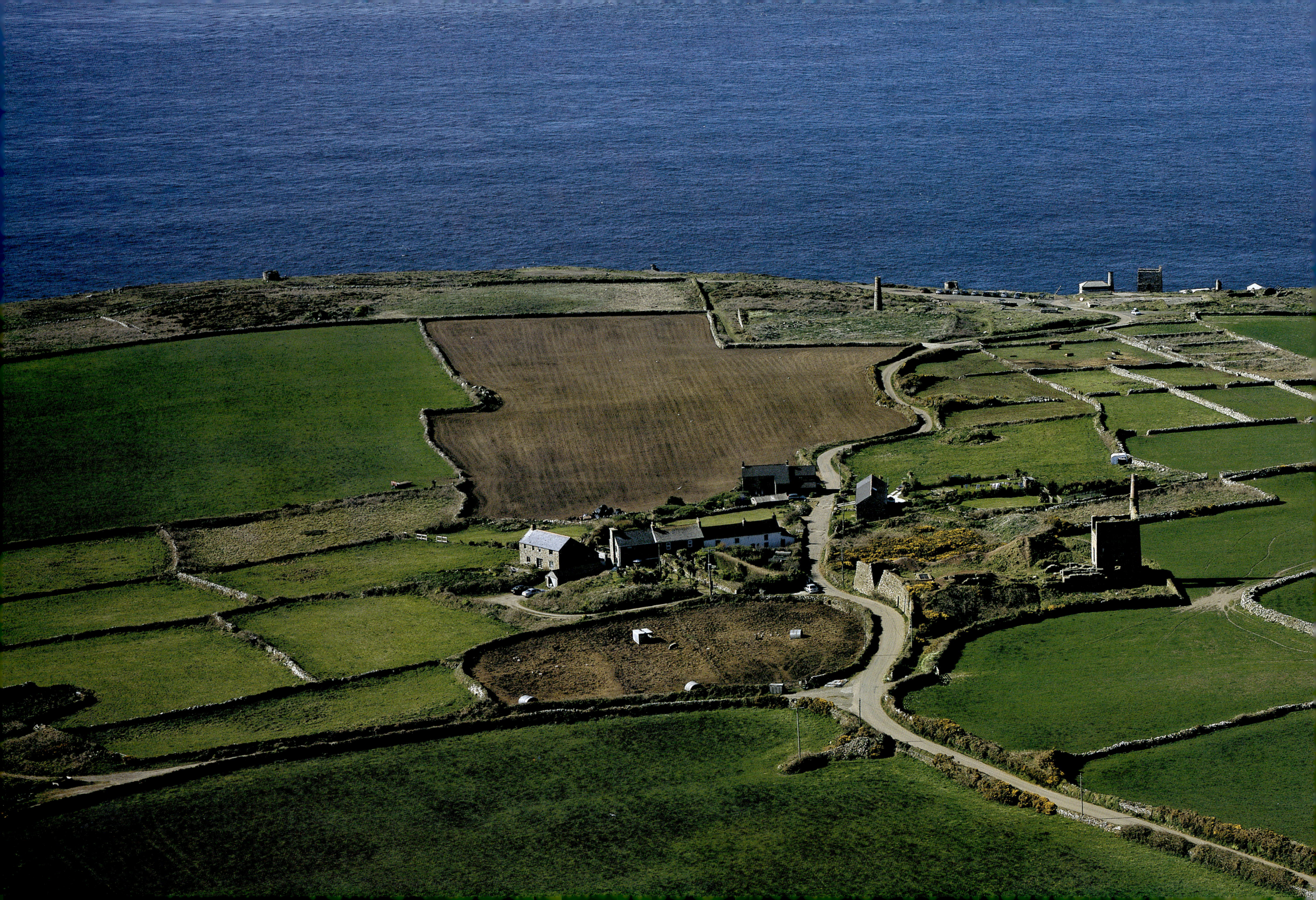

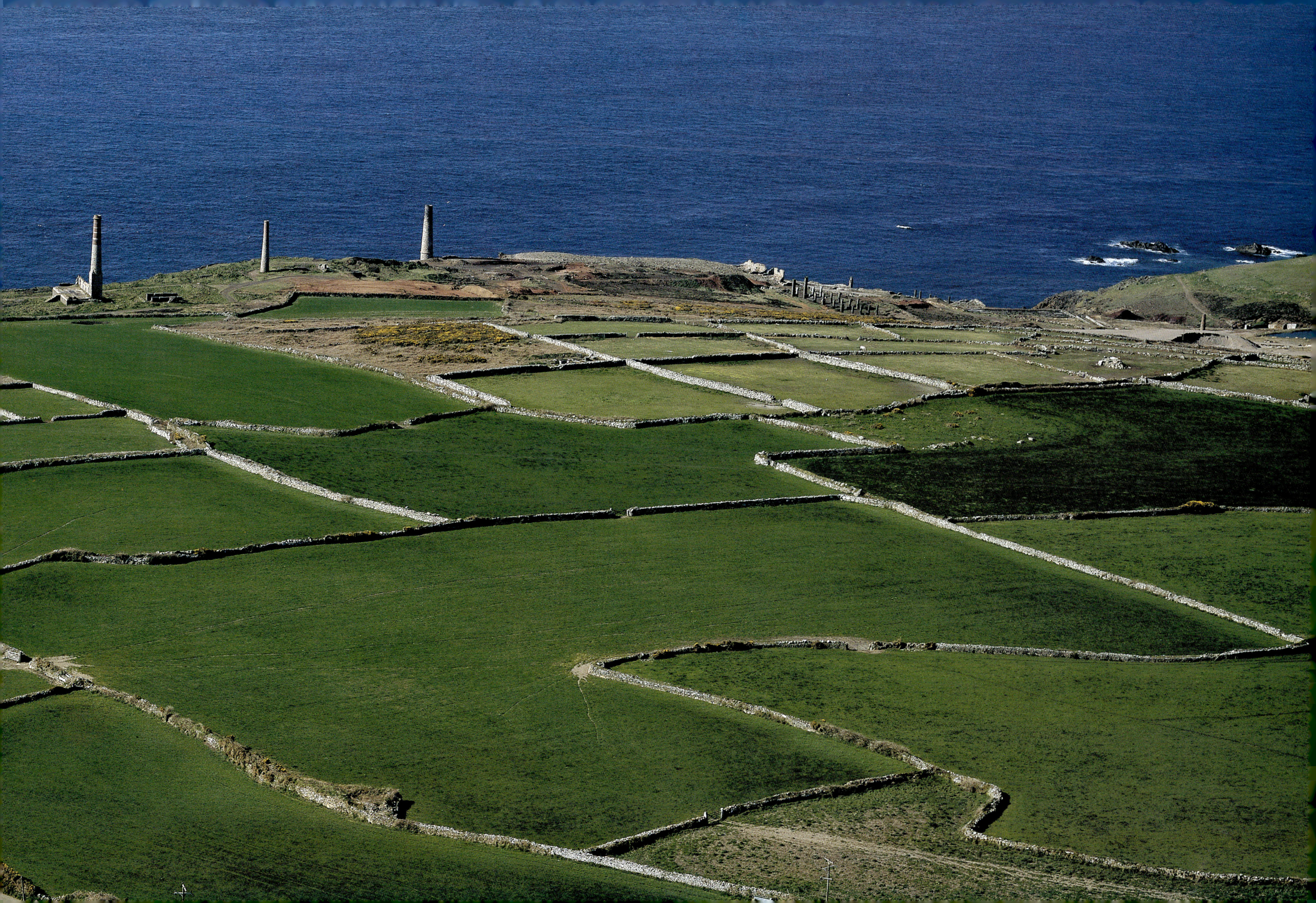

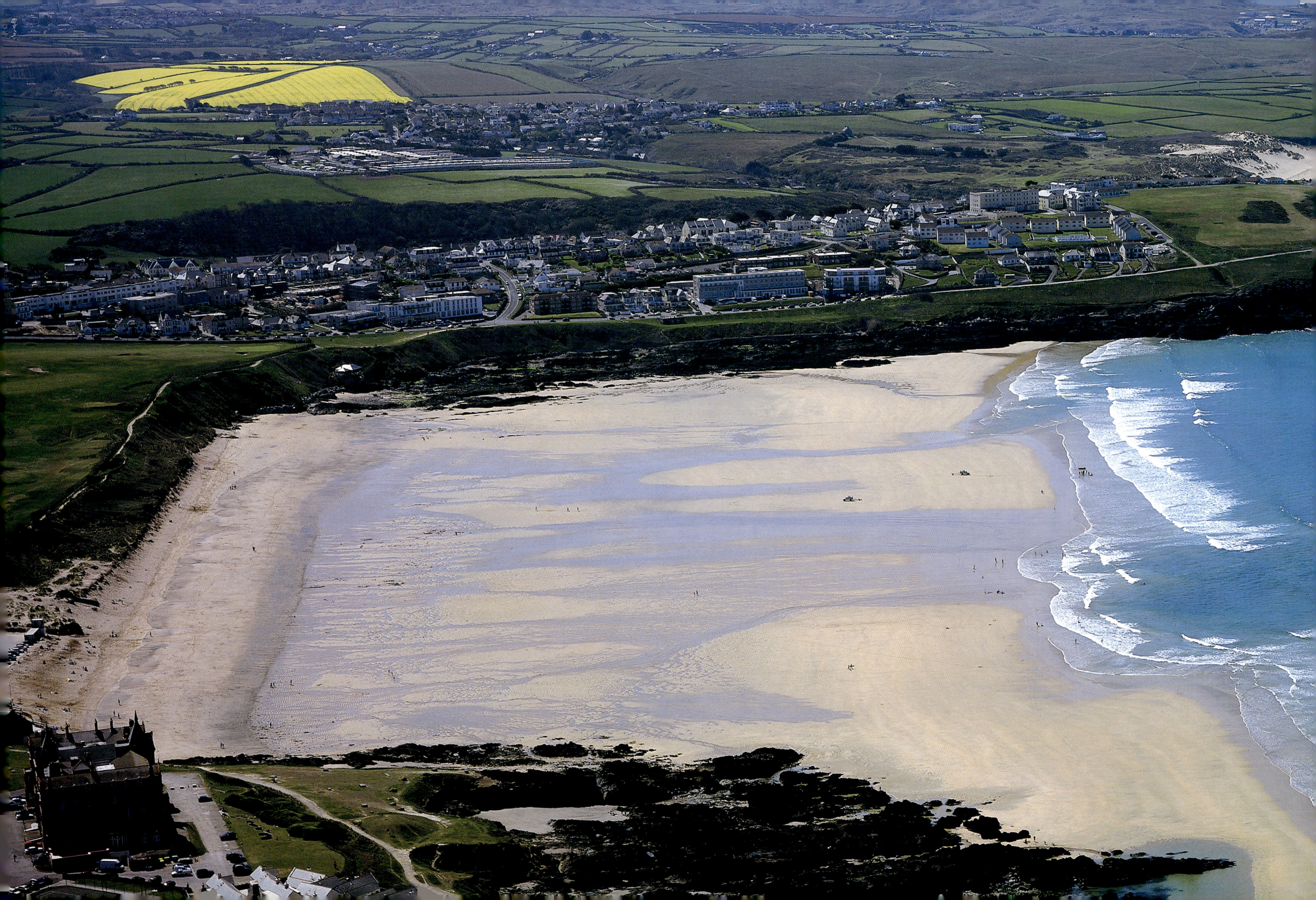

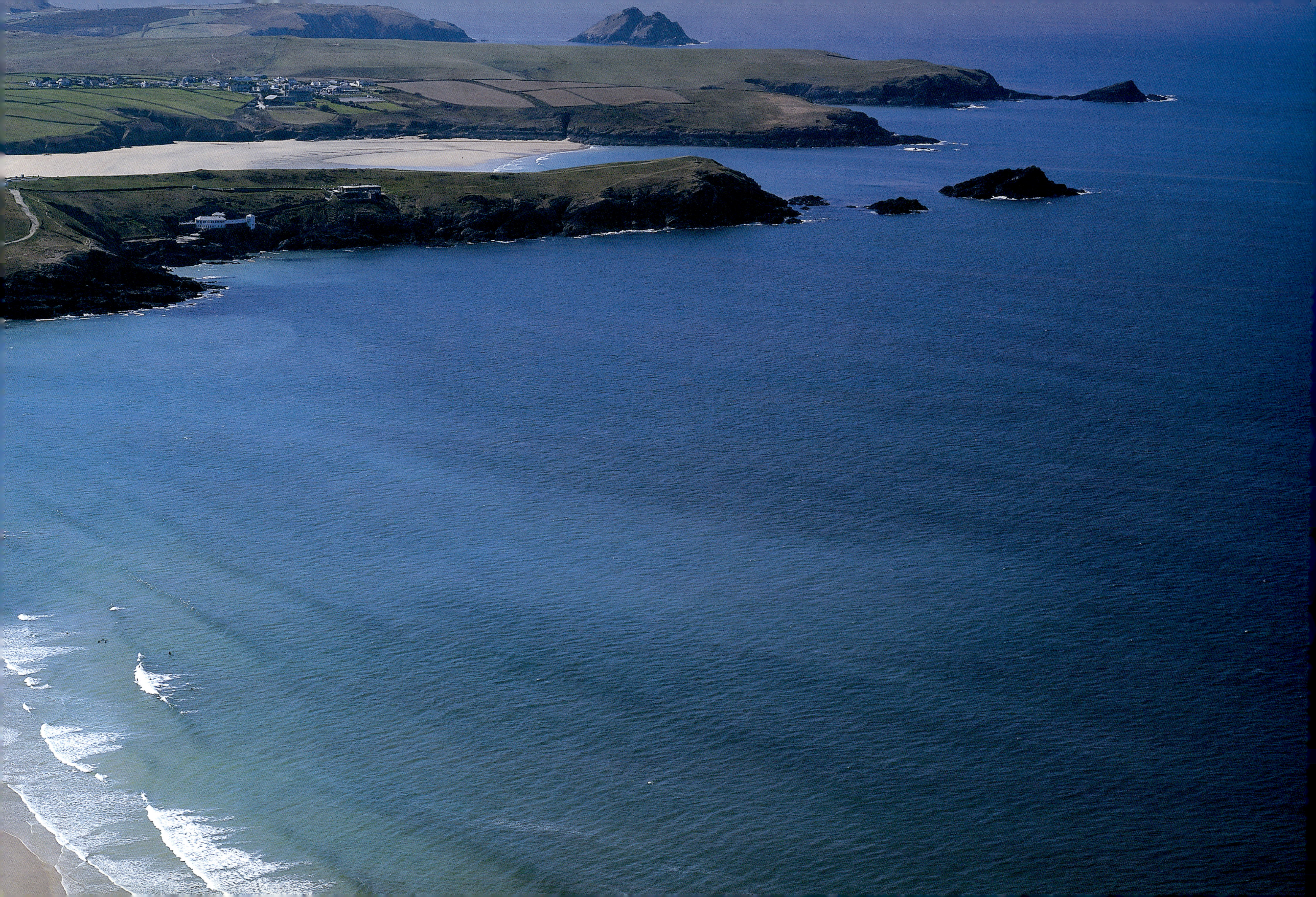

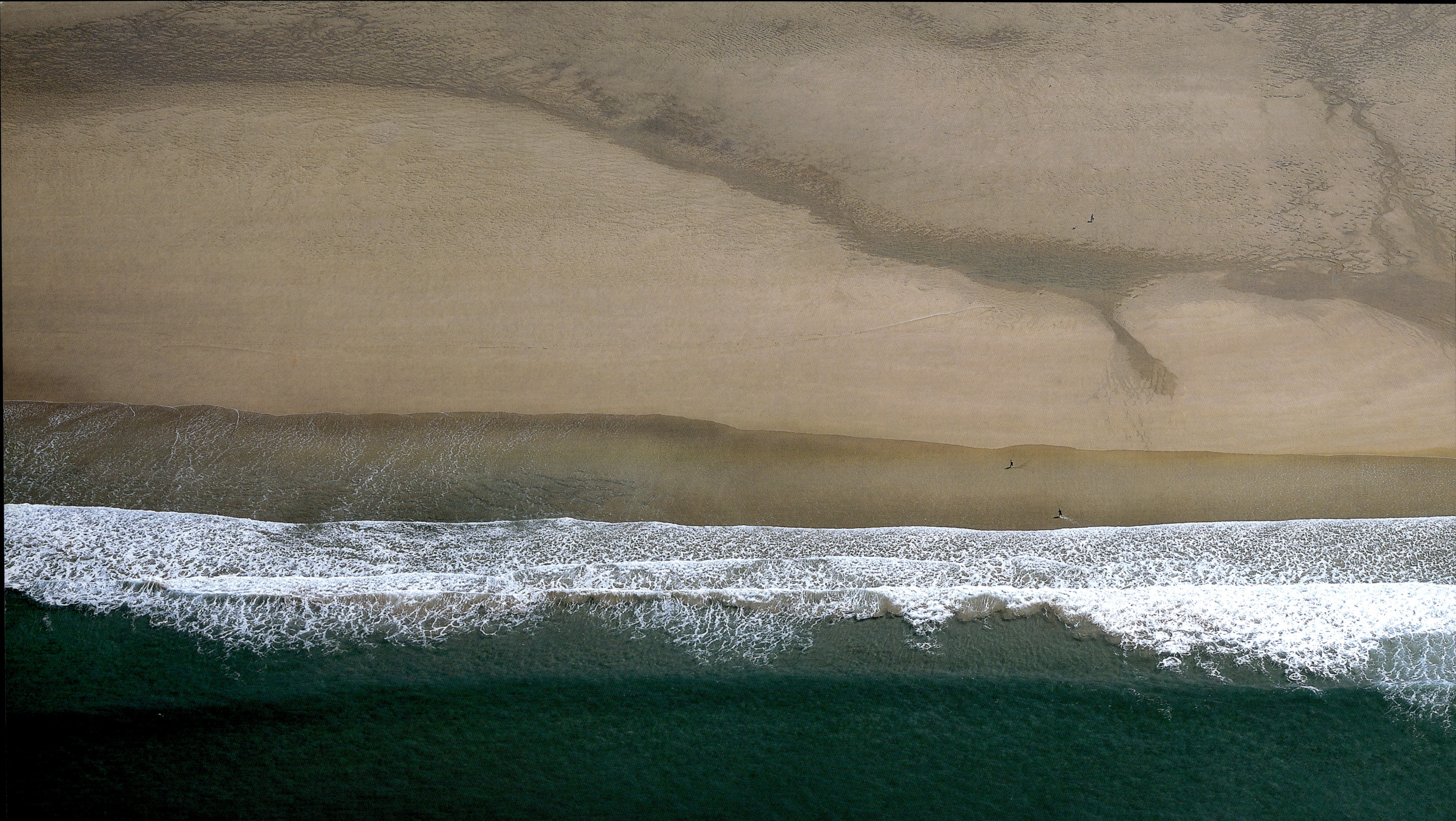

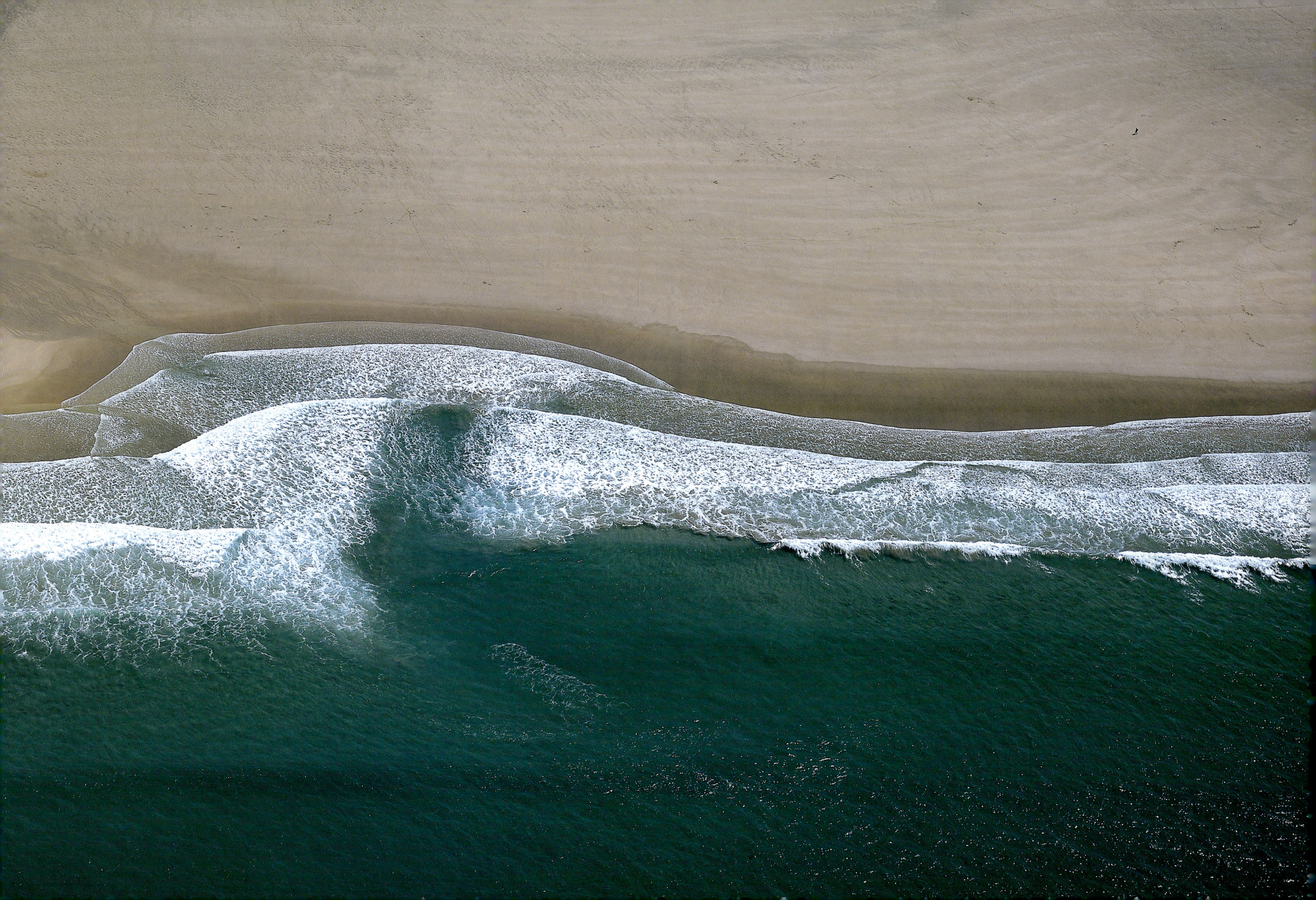

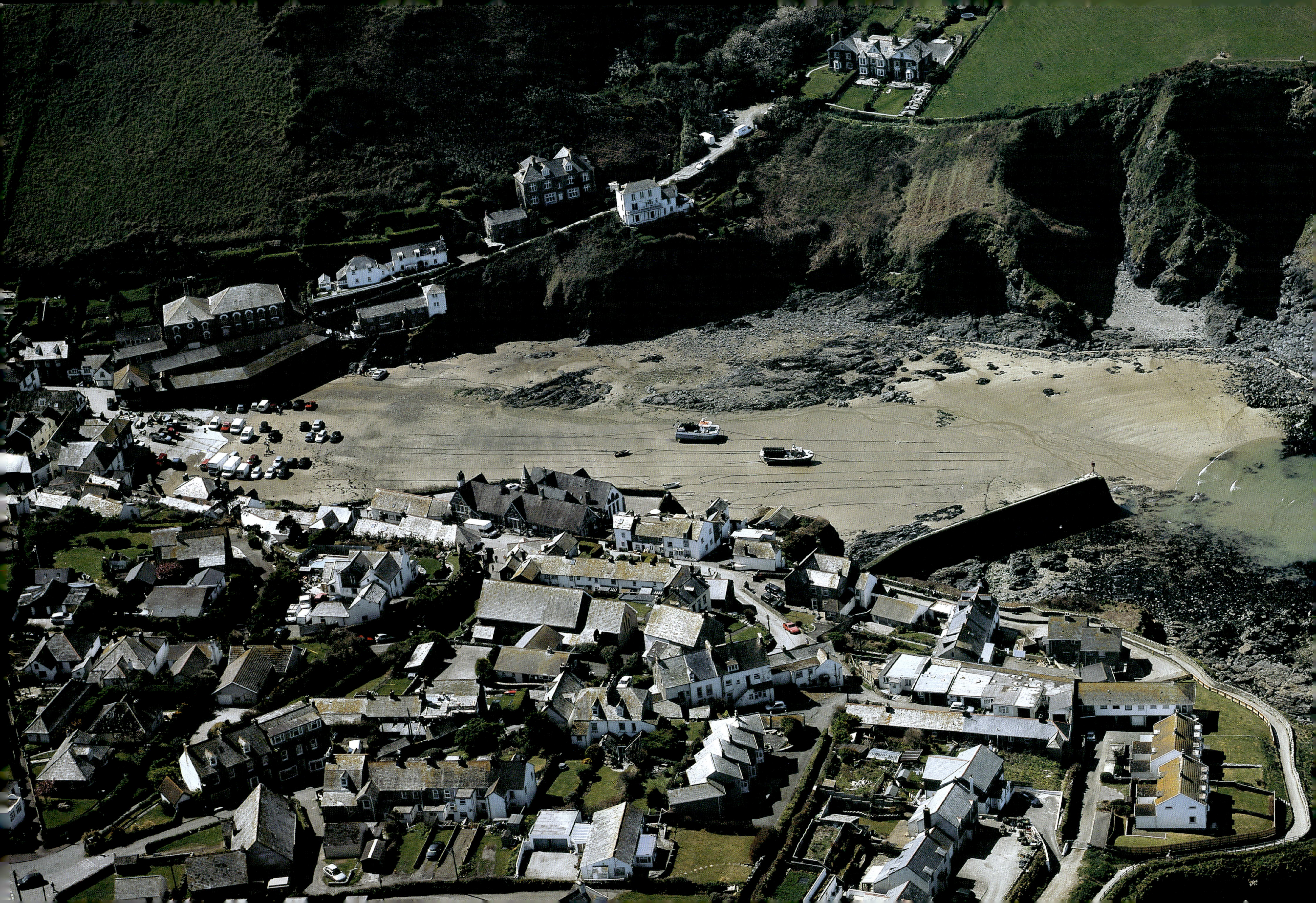

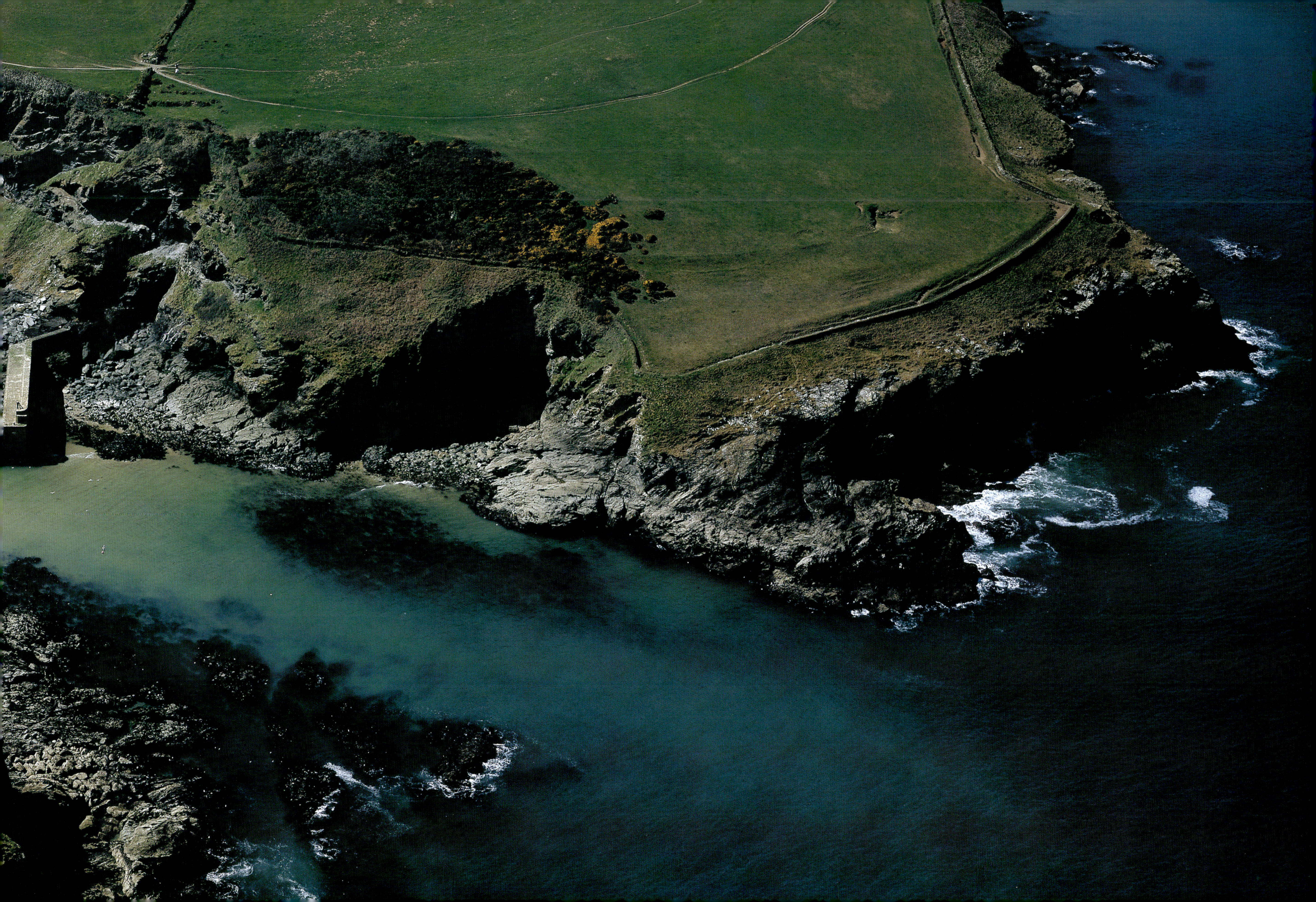

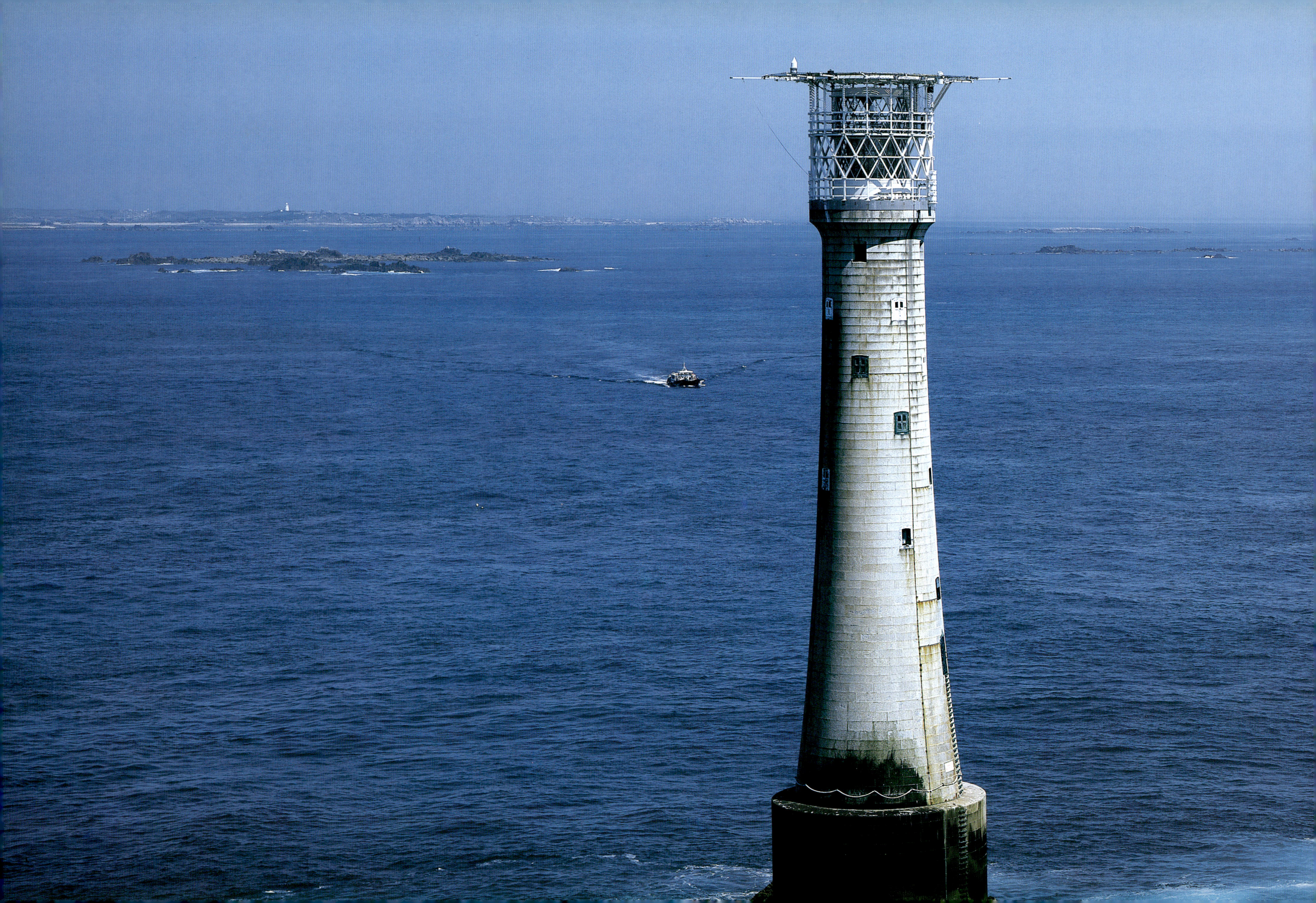

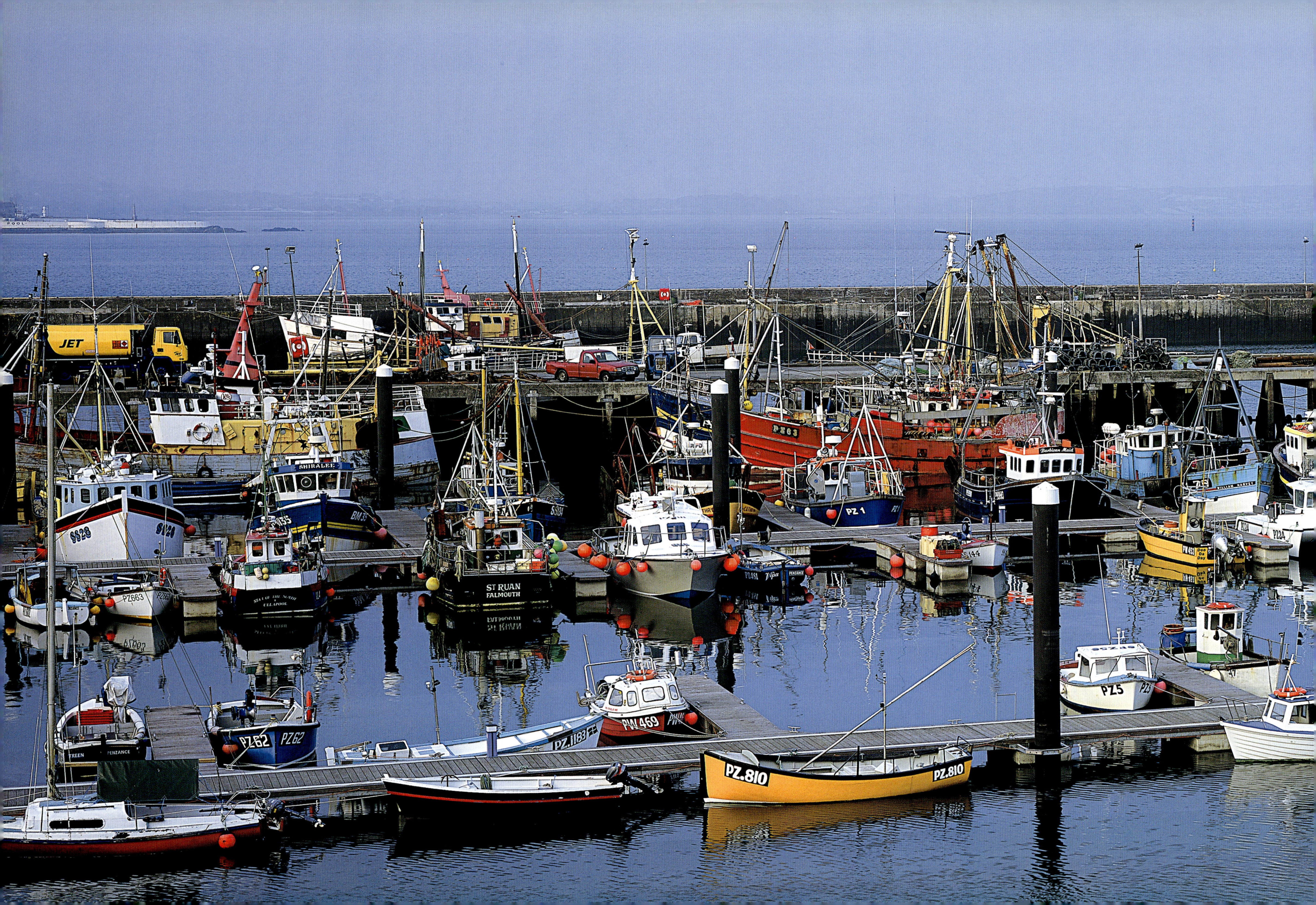
JET
SS29
ST RUAN
FALMOUTH
PZ62
PW469
PZ5
PZ.810

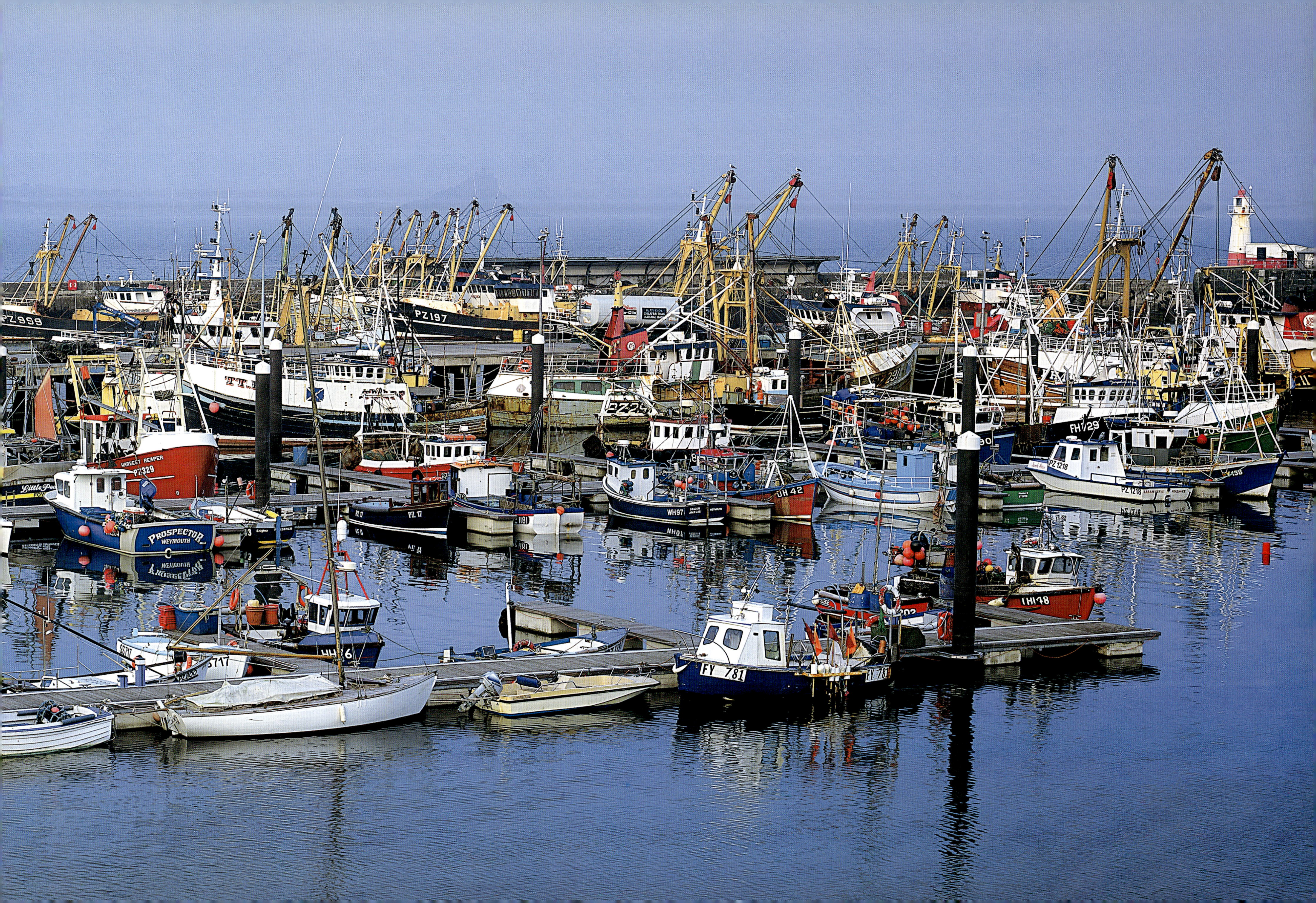

PZ999
PZ197
HARVEST REAPER
PZ329
PROSPECTOR
WEYMOUTH
FY 781

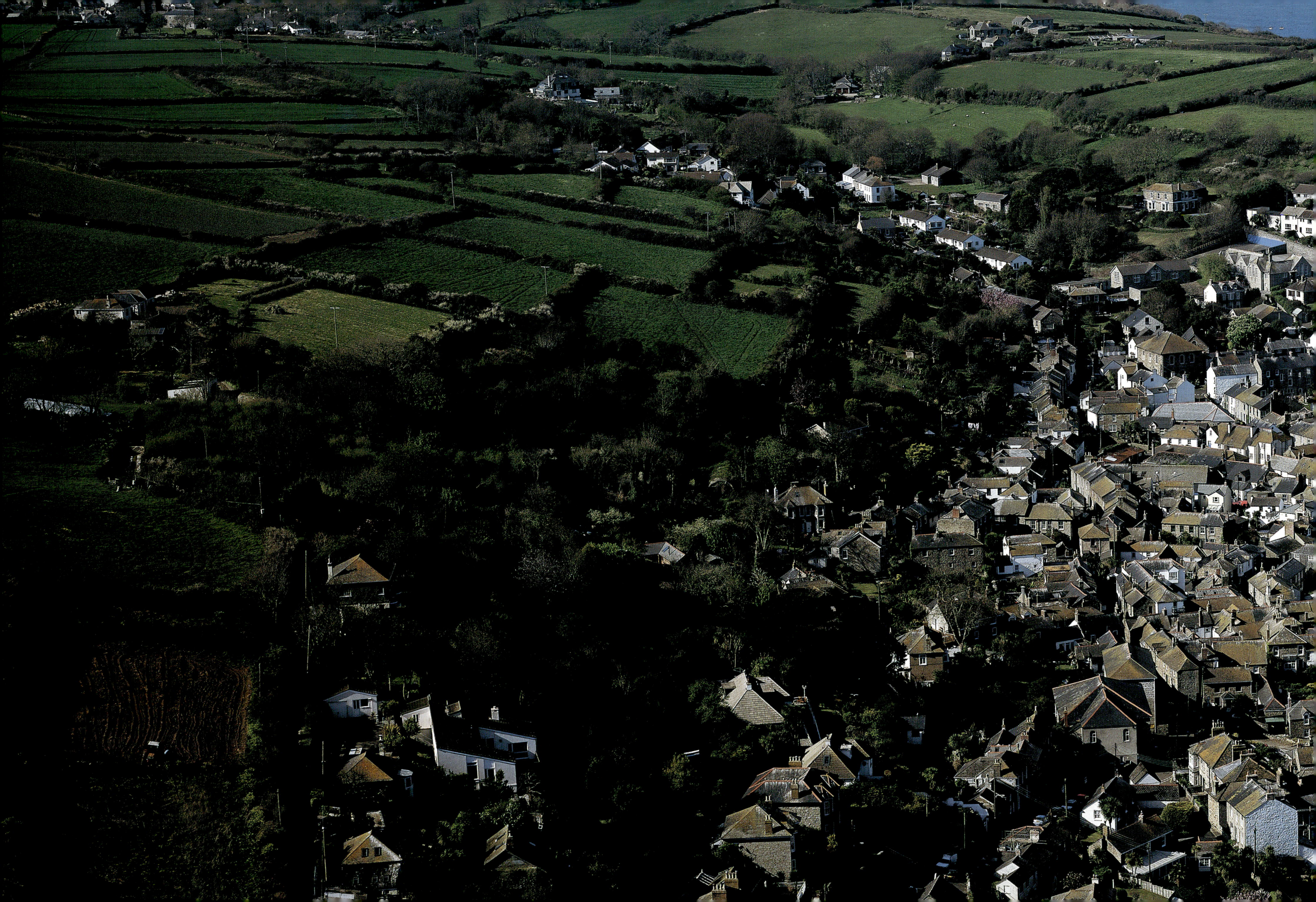

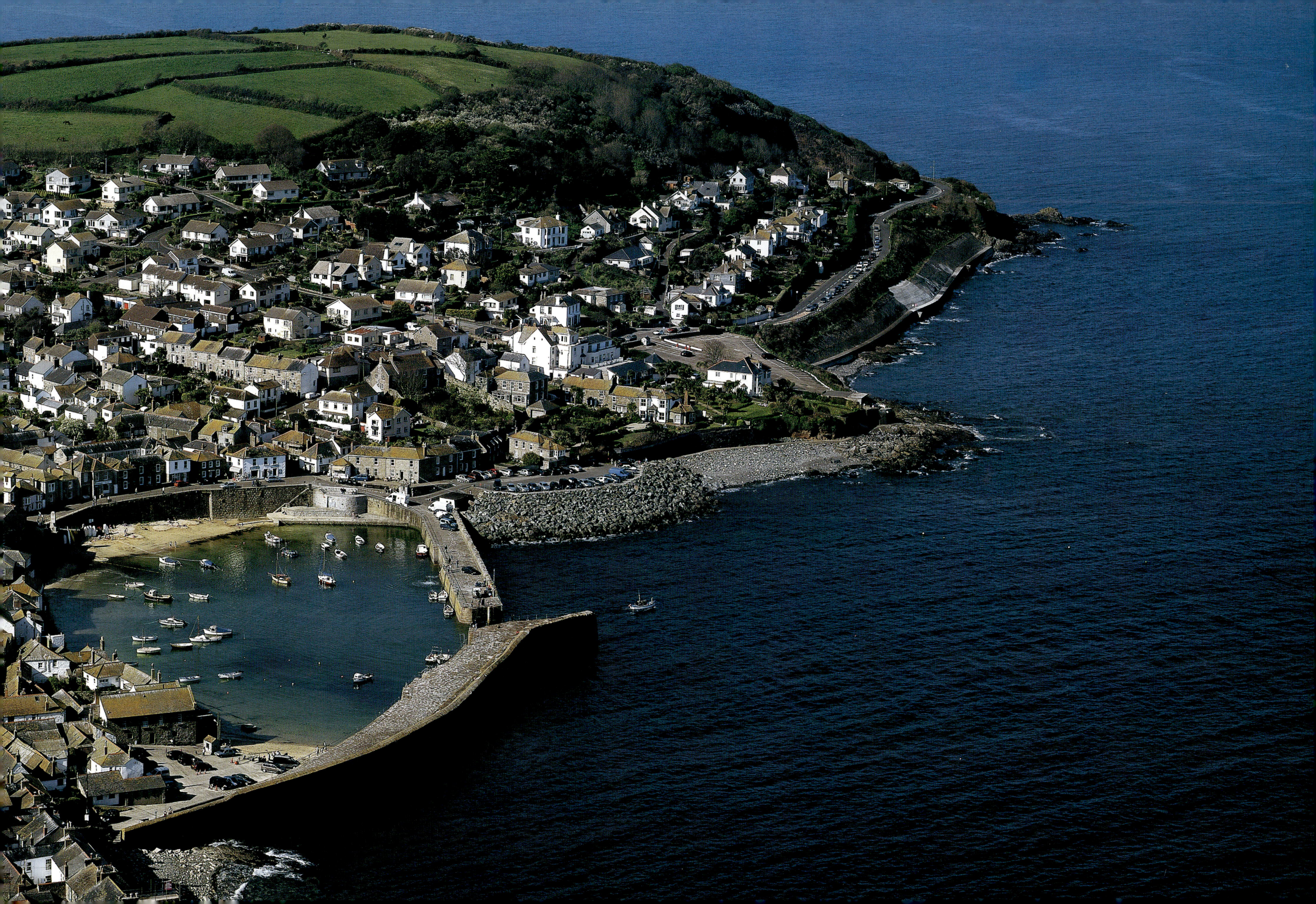

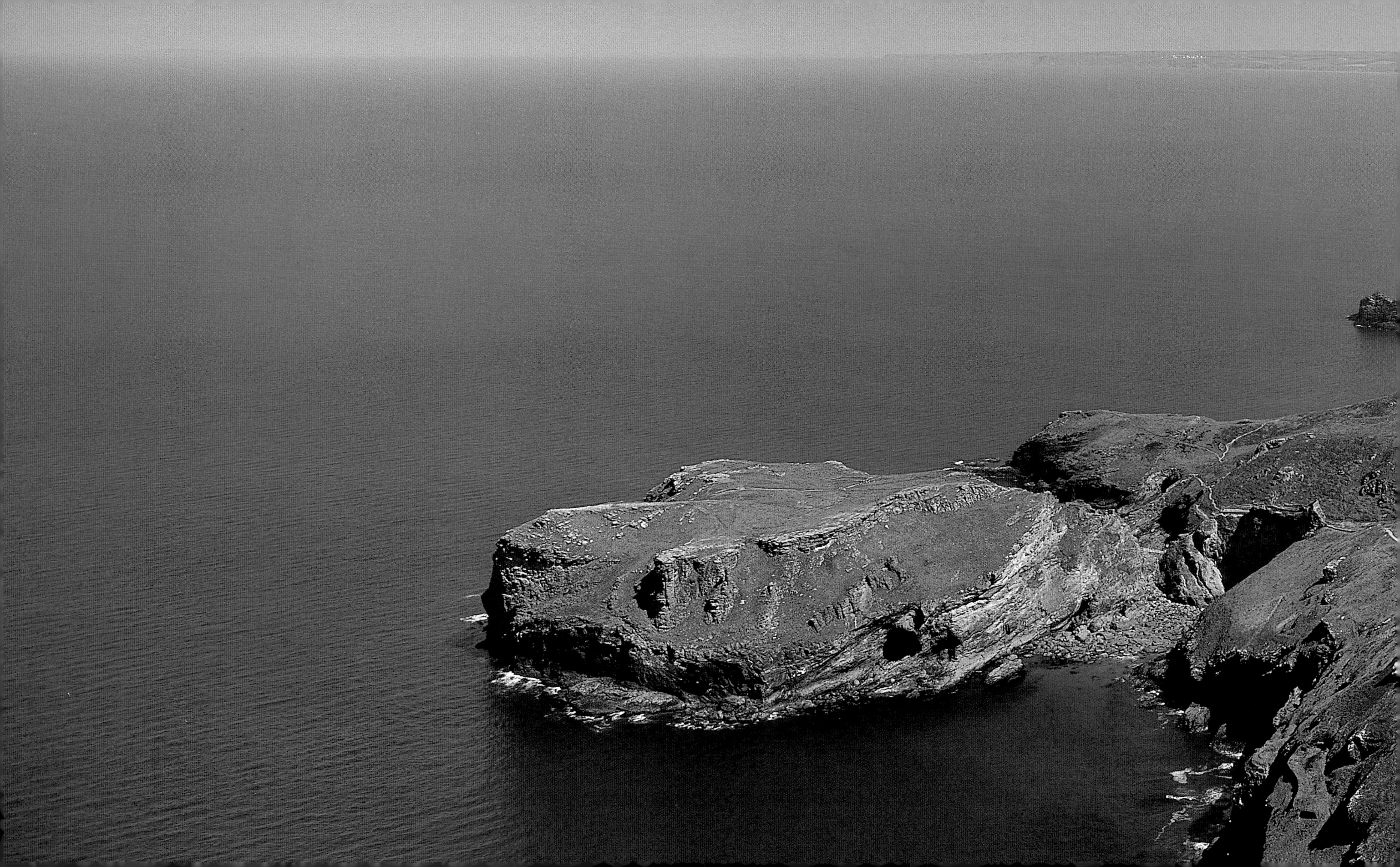

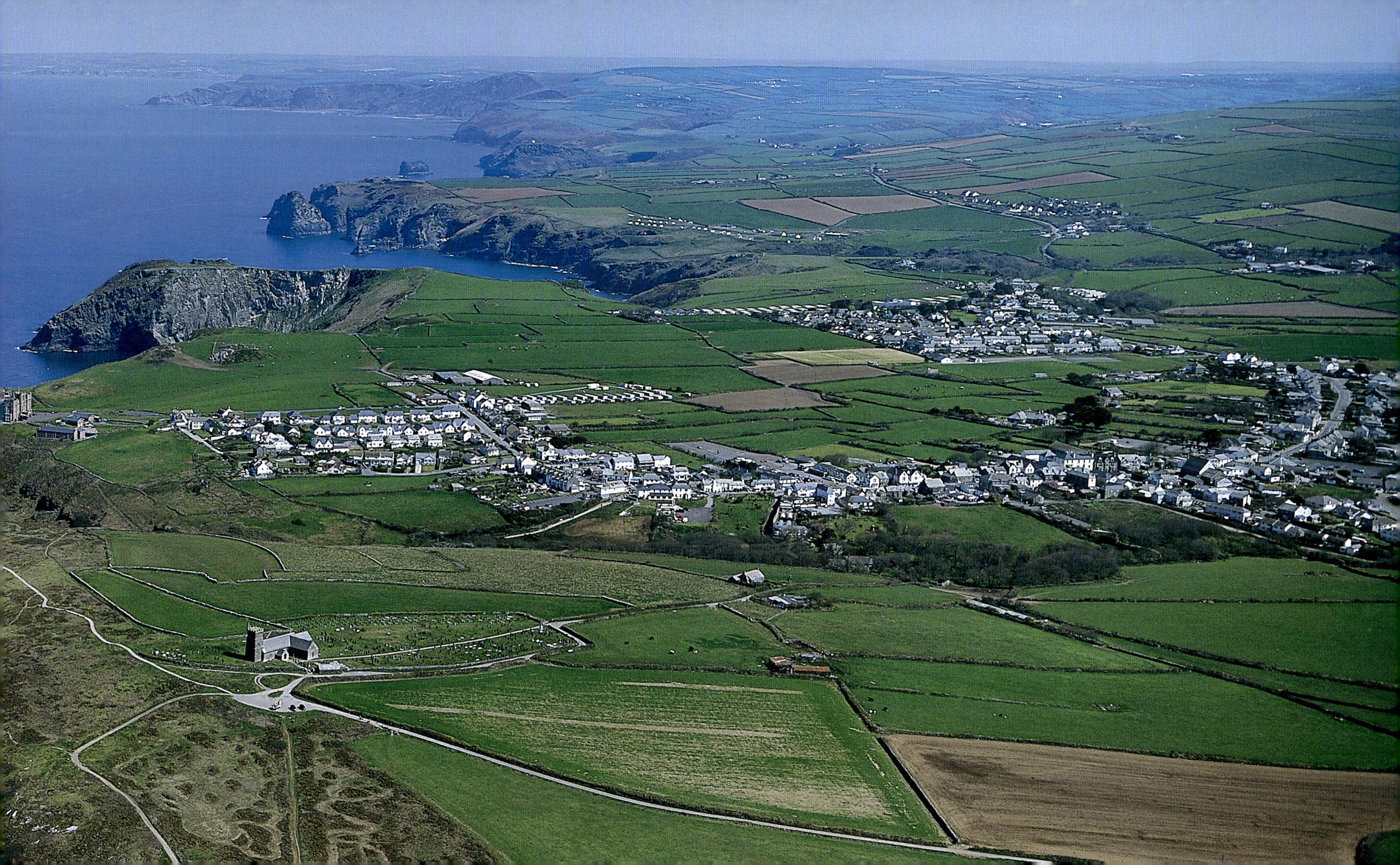

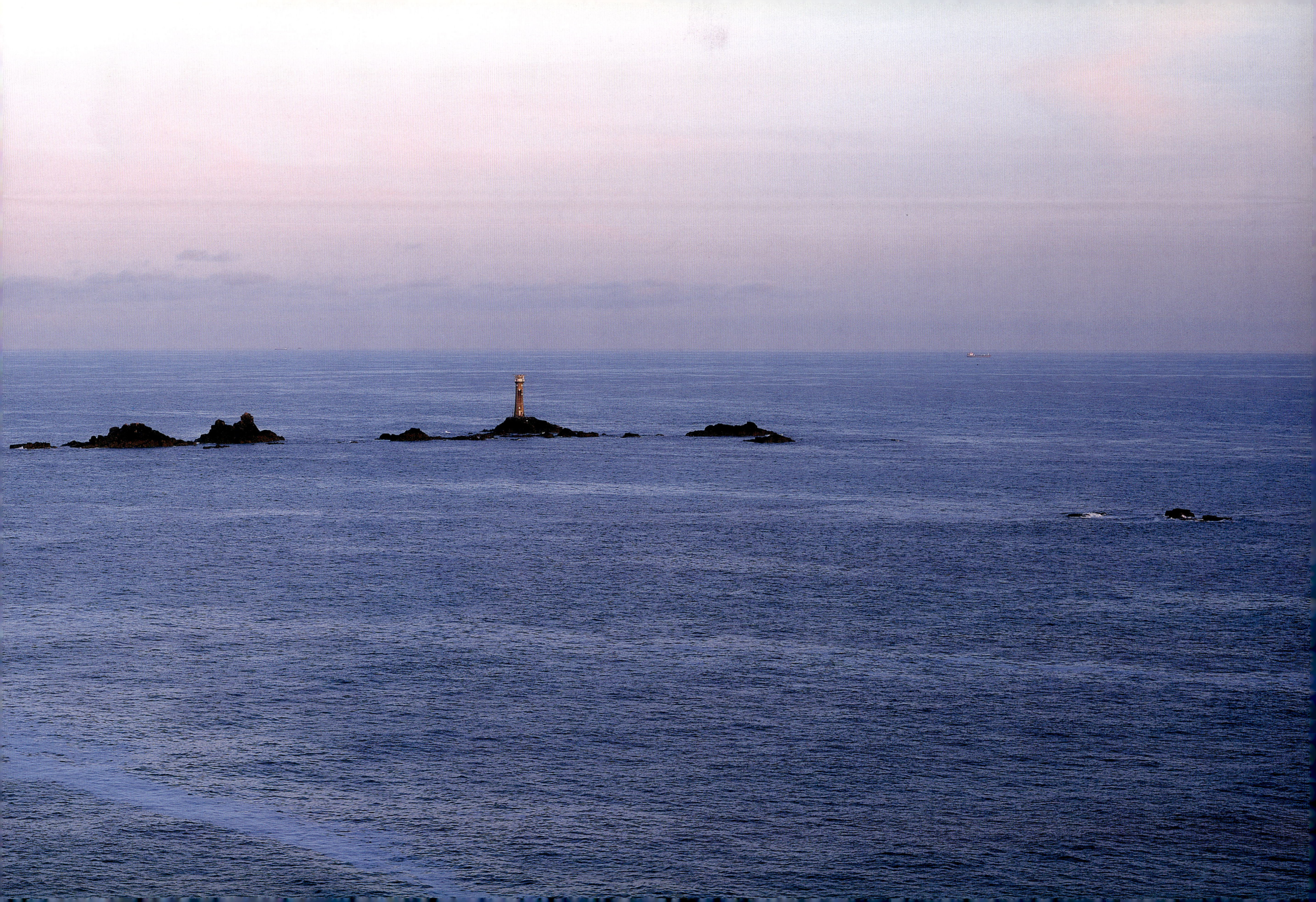

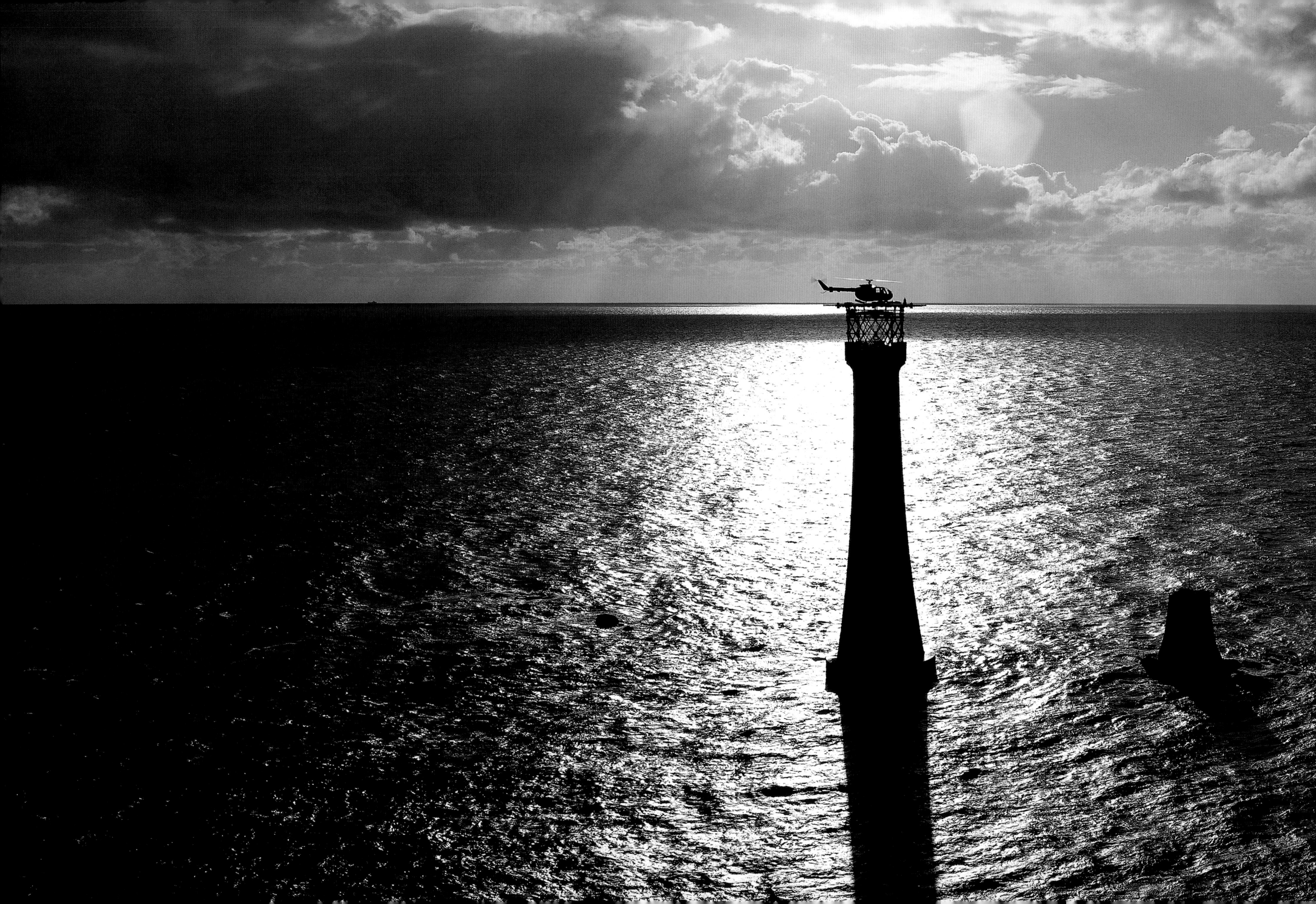

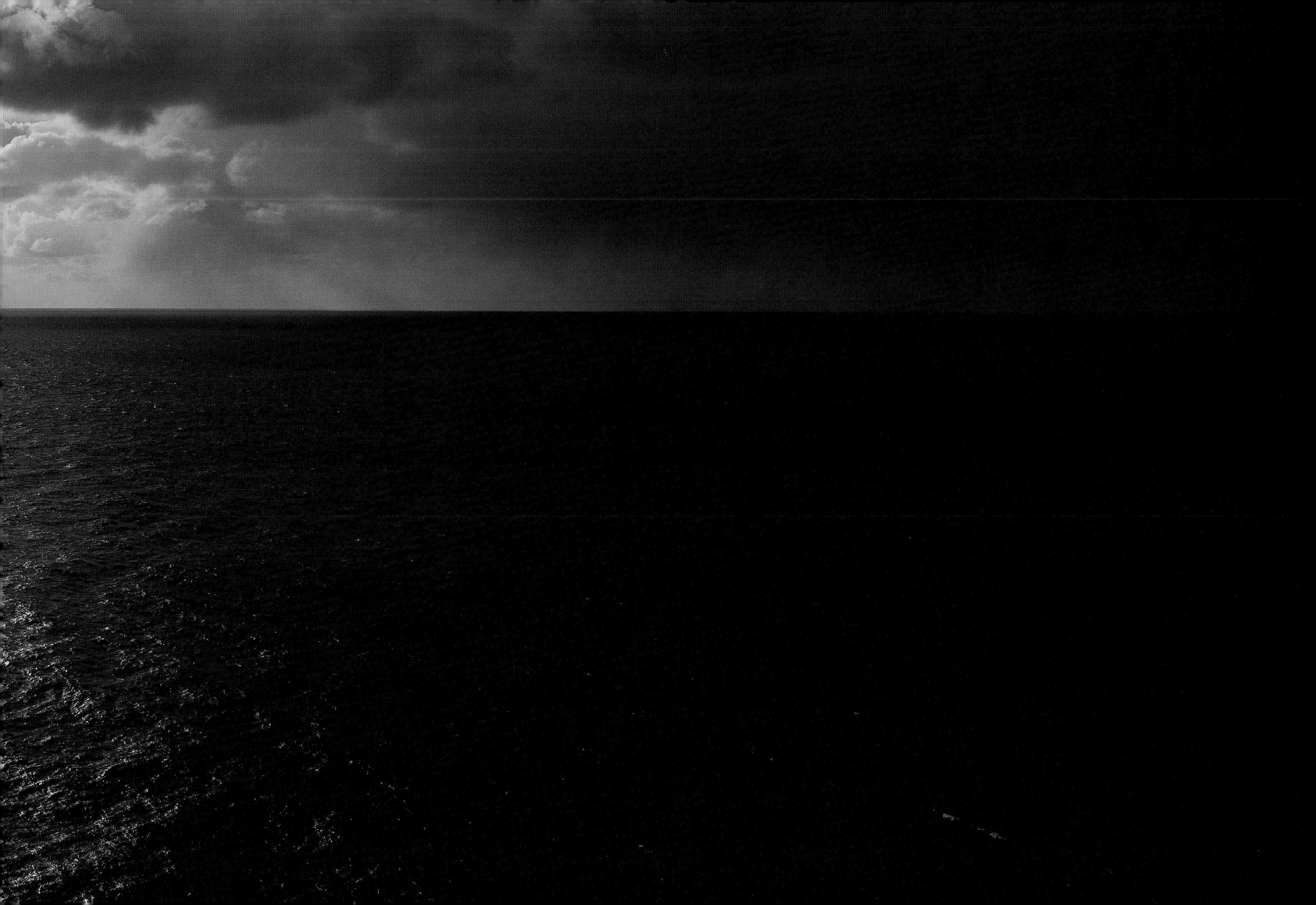

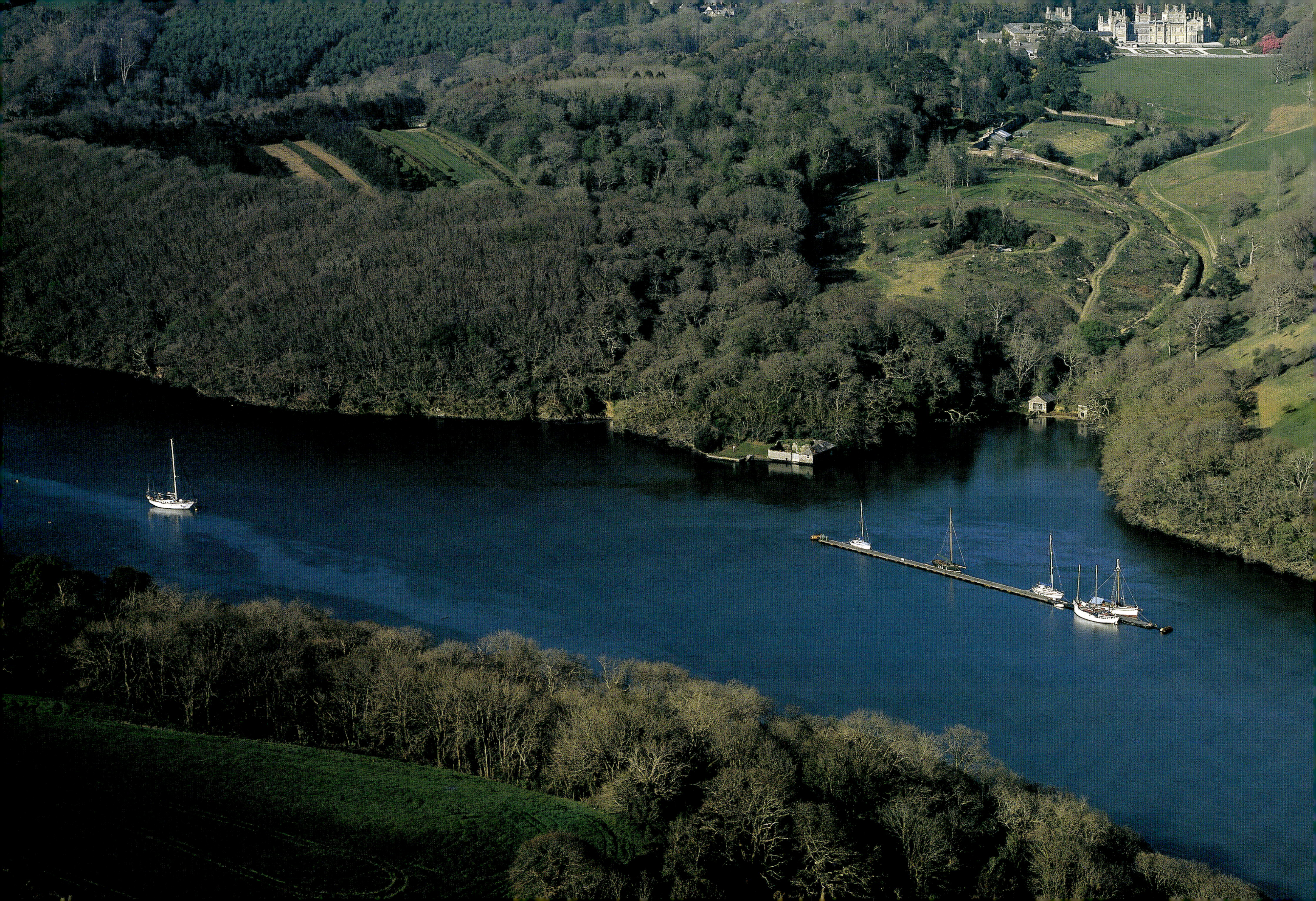

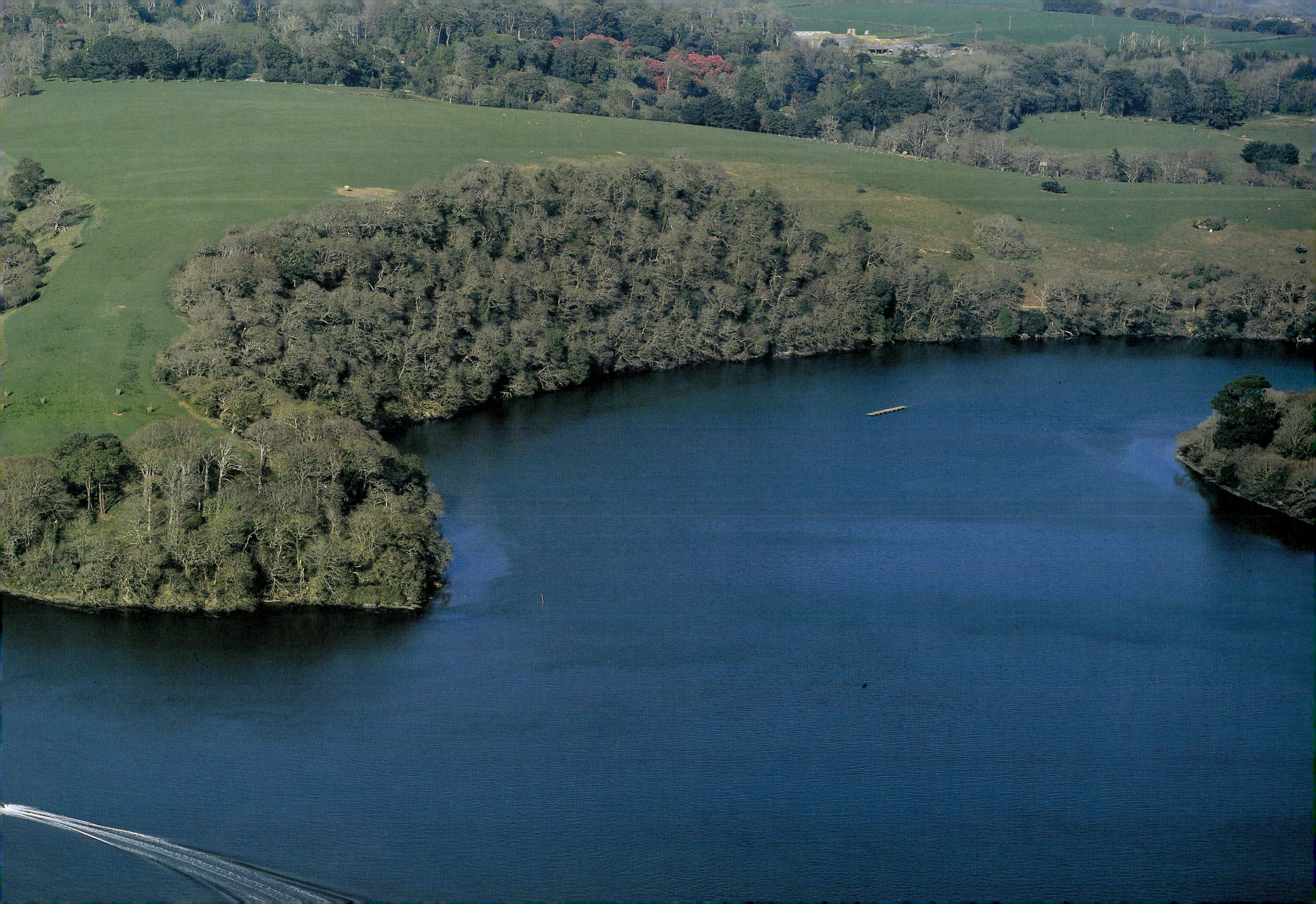

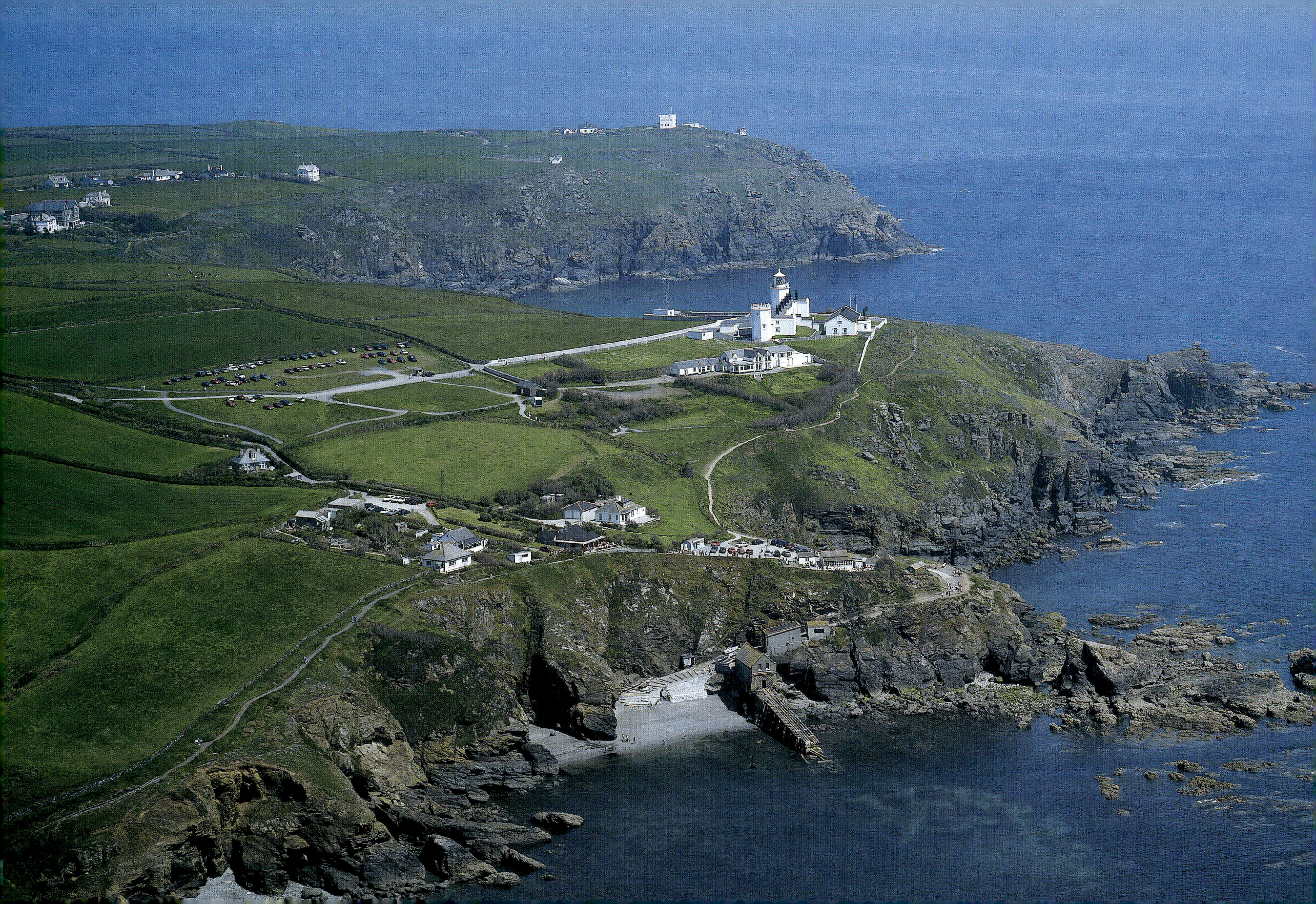

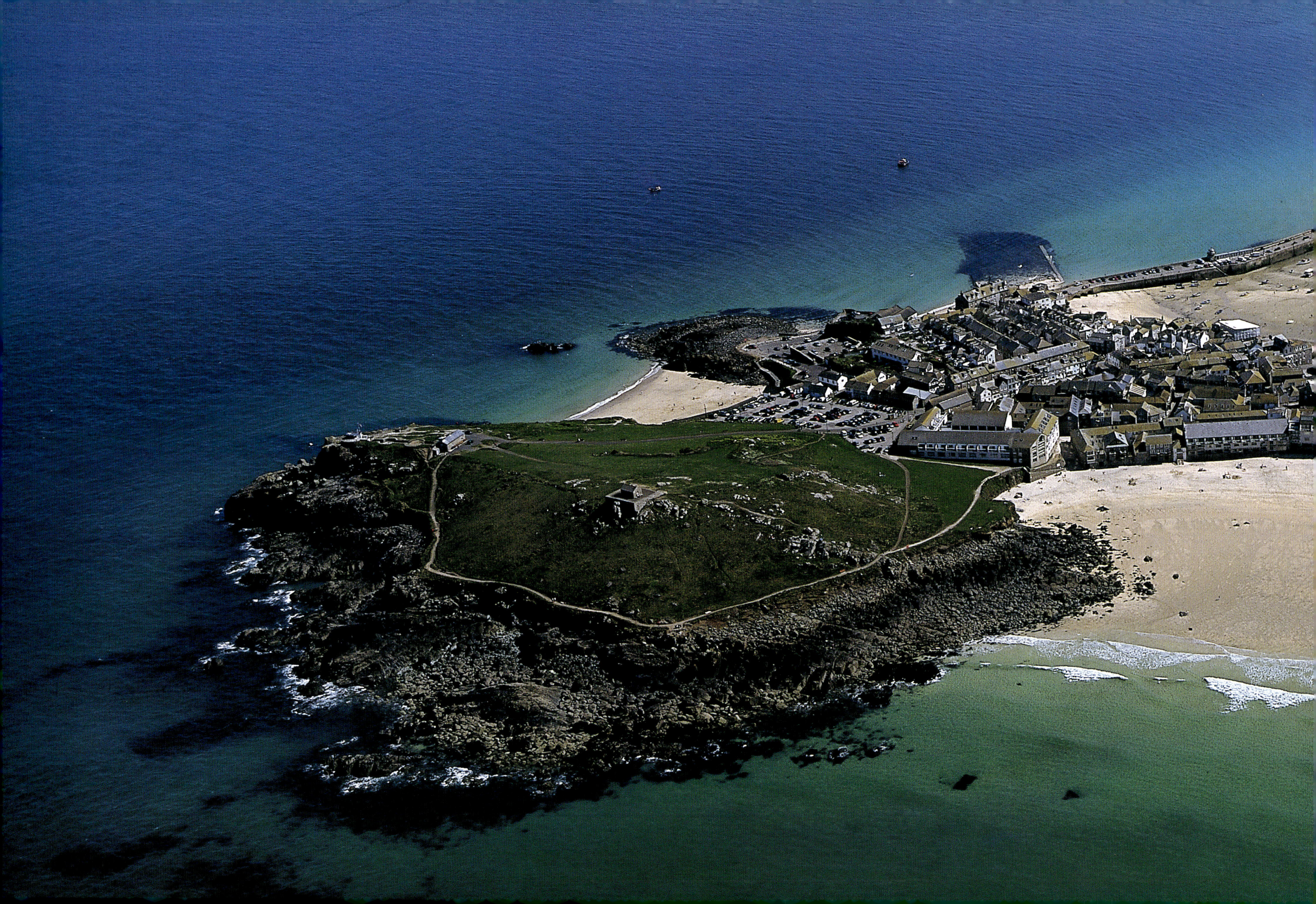

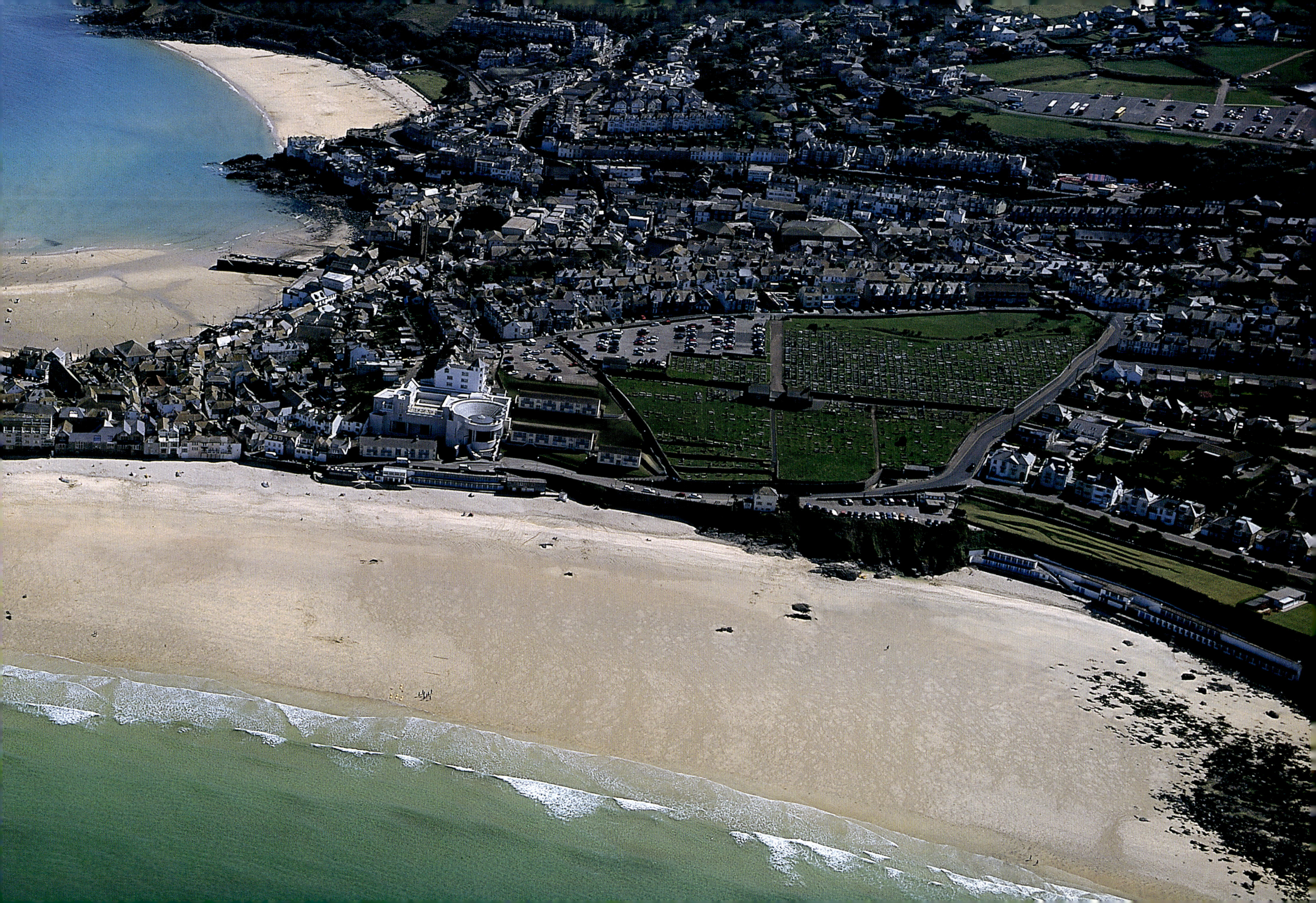

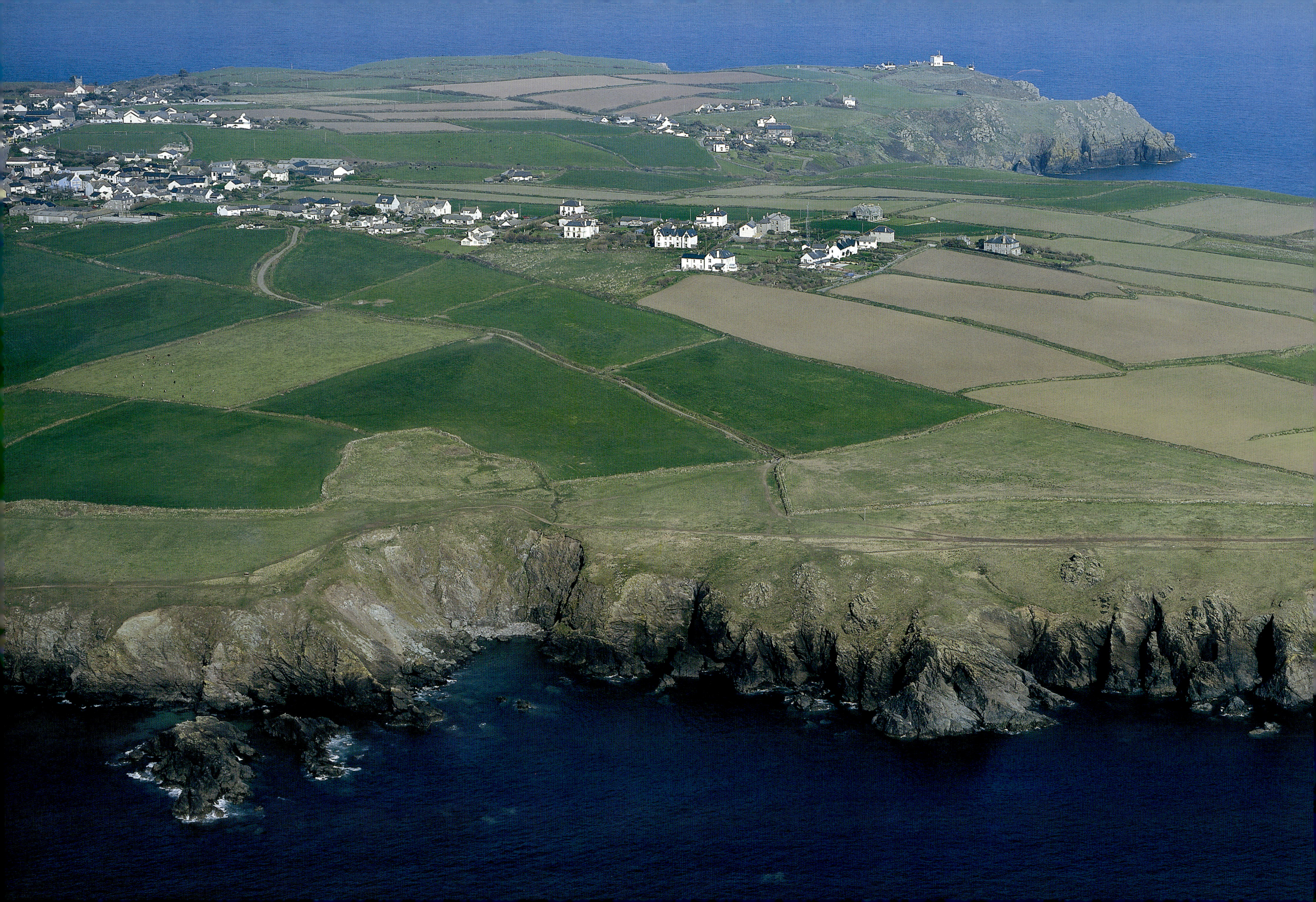

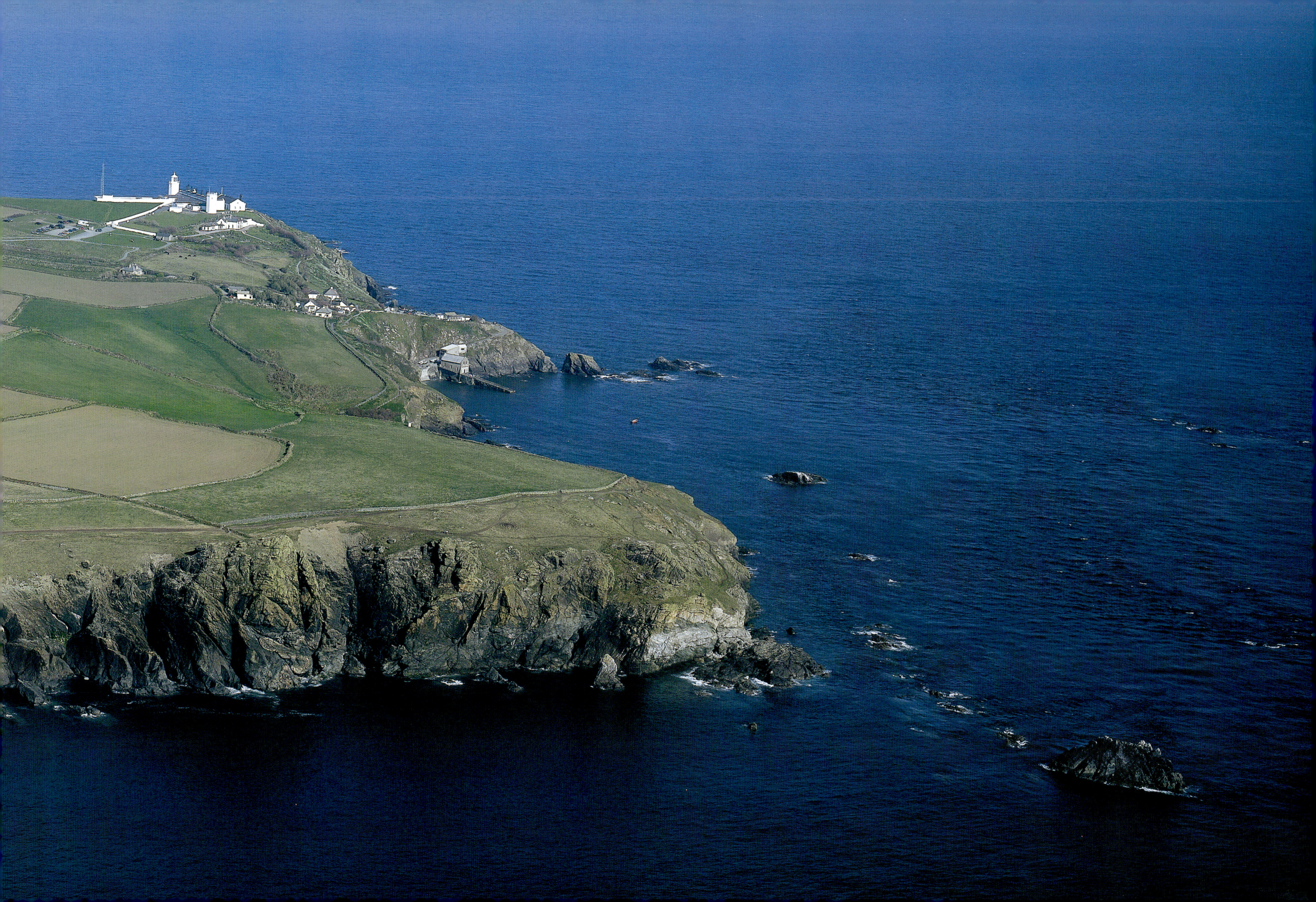

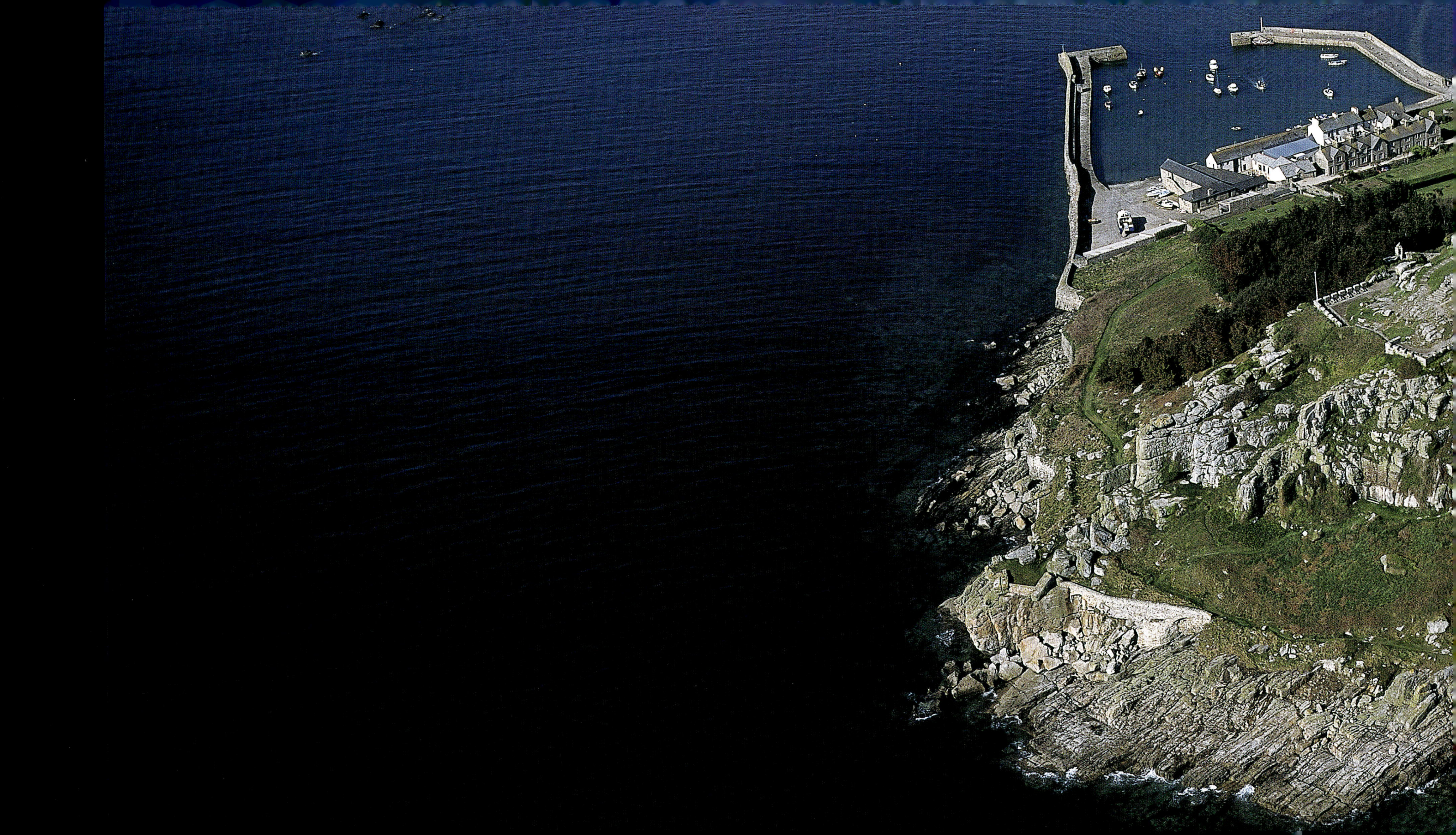

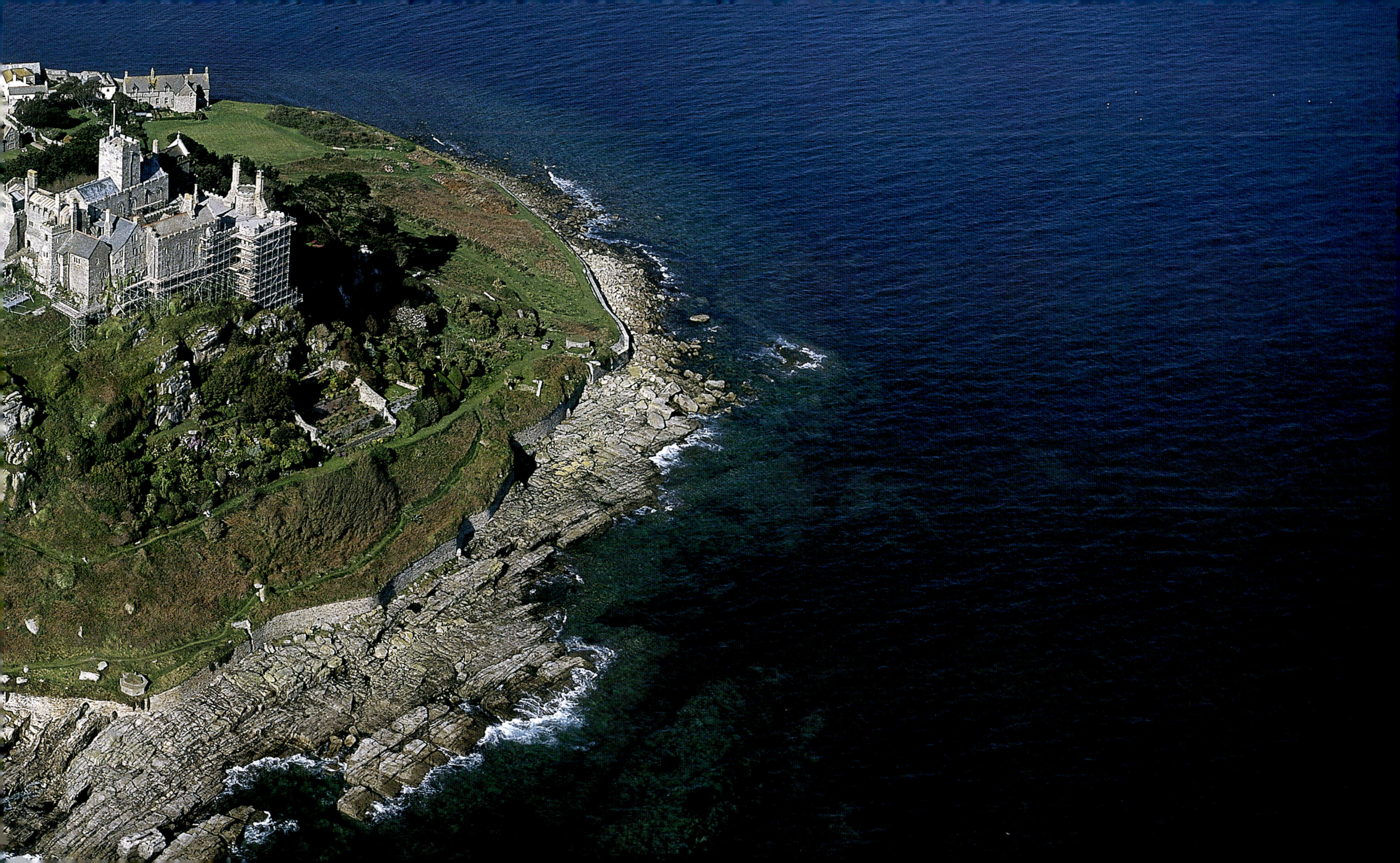

BRITTANY · BREIZH

When the 'blue flag' is raised over the coasts and shores, Brittany takes out its winner's yellow jersey: not the yellow oilskins worn by holidaymakers keen to dress up as fishermen for a souvenir photo in front of the café by the port, but the yellow jersey of a perpetual leader in the race to have the most prized sea coasts. It is true to say that the coastline girdling the rocky peninsula has a ribbon of golden sand some 750 miles long.

As the tides come in and out, the beaches are left exposed. There is nothing more exhilarating than exploring the expanse uncovered after high tides, where the ebb and flow of the waves with their dull roar are governed by the eternally seductive dance of the moon, sun and ocean. Wild coasts, peaceful creeks, sailors' harbours, bays and inlets run along a coastline as long as the distance between Paris and Nice. It is easy to forget that this ancient land of Armorica ('land by the sea') is larger than Belgium.

Brittany is half the size of Scotland or Ireland but larger than Wales and Cornwall put together. For a thousand years, it withstood the covetous actions of its powerful neighbours: the royal armies of England or the kingdom of France against the ducal troops. The knell sounded for the latter in the grey valleys of Saint-Aubin-du-Cormier, on the threshold of the 16th century. Anne of Brittany lost her freedom to marry any royal suitor other than Charles VIII of France, the victor over her father, Francis II, who died of grief one month after the surrender. Requiem for the duchy.

It was at Pornic, a fishing port now popular with yachtsmen, that Duke Alain Barbetorte fixed the southern sea border of Brittany before choosing Nantes as its capital. From there, though now broken up into five departments, each with its own distinct character but united by its heritage, Armor's coast ran all the way to Mont-Saint-Michel in modern-day Normandy, a mirror image of St Michael's Mount, across the Channel in Cornwall.

A sea-faring people, Bretons have now become ocean travellers seeking new horizons: merchant sailors from Nantes and Saint-Nazaire, long-haul captains and fishermen from the gulf of Morbihan, weatherbeaten crews from the Bigouden area, lifeboatmen from the islands of Cornouaille and the estuaries of the Léon area, conquerors of the world's sea routes – to the Indies or to Canada and Louisiana – as well as today's legendary racing yachtsmen – Tabarly, Kersauson, Peyron – and yachtswomen – Arthaud, Autissier, Chabot, Fontenoy. Together they make up an incomparable mosaic of adventure and legend. It is as if the sea, the water of life, was the water of survival.

In this land lined with lighthouses mounting guard against the breakers while sweeping the waves with a protective beacon, you only need to watch out for a rising squall to notice the helicopter of Philip Plisson flying ahead of the storms. The gulf with its sparkling clear waters or the Glénan archipelago with its Polynesian colours are forgotten – those cheerful islets lying just off Concarneau and Pont-Aven where Gauguin sharpened his paint brushes before sailing off to Tahiti... This is our Breton sea: *Mor Breizh* – a majestic work of strength and ocean light under a sky which, at times, seems on friendly terms with both hell and heaven.

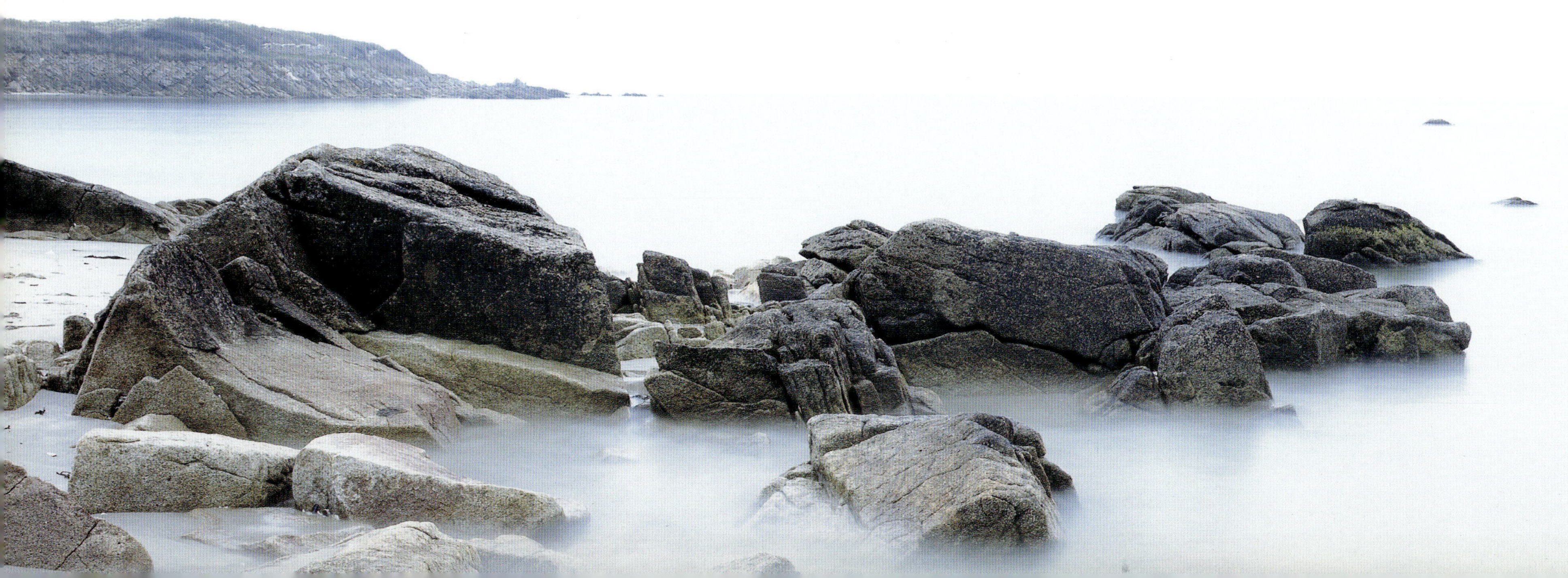

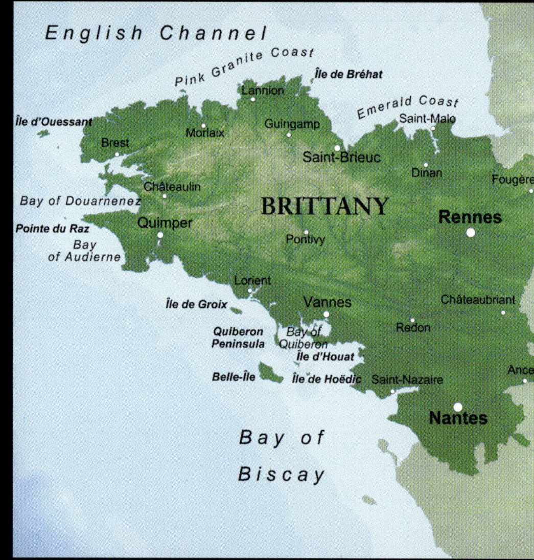

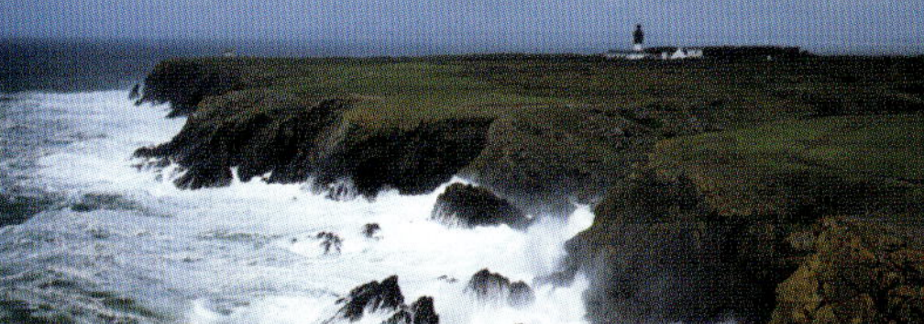

ÎLE DE GROIX
'He who sees Groix, sees joy,' claims a local saying. Below Pen Men lighthouse, where migrating birds nest on the rocks, the beacon sweeps the waves in memory of the tuna boats that once battled the winds in the Bay of Biscay. Île de Groix, *Enez Groe*, the 'true island', is where the first Bretons found refuge in the 5th century.

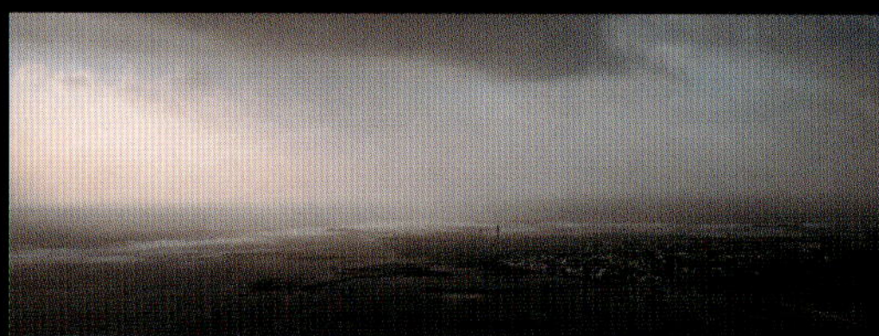

WAVES CRASHING AT PENMARC'H
It is known as 'the sentinel of Bigouden'. The Pointe de Penmarc'h is surrounded by reefs. In stormy weather and high winds, the waves crash onto it sending up spectacular foam. Two small ports frame Penmarc'h: St-Guénolé has made langoustine fishing its speciality, while Kérity is famous for yachting.

Opposite: Between La Trinité-sur-Mer (An Drinded) and the family beaches at Carnac, sheltered in the bend of Quiberon Bay, and opposite Belle-Île, lies Kervillen cove, a jewel below the dunes and a classified nature reserve on the Morbihan coast.

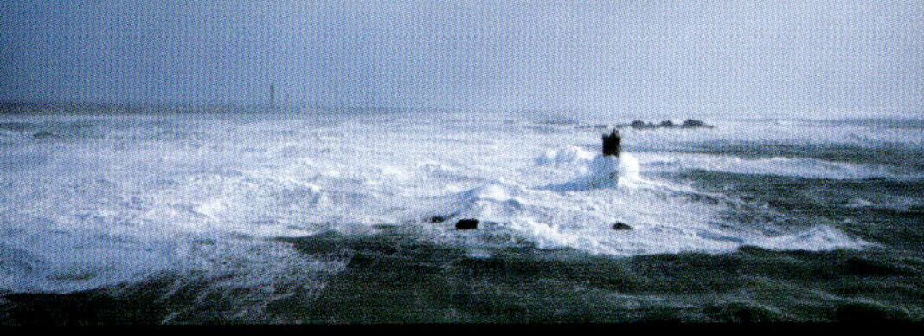

LOOK-OUT POST

Another lighthouse rises from the waves. Here we are off Penmarc'h, the last look-out post of the Bigouden areas. Round about are other fishing ports, including St-Guénolé and Kérity. The lively atmosphere of the quays and the thrill of the tales of the sea can be found everywhere.

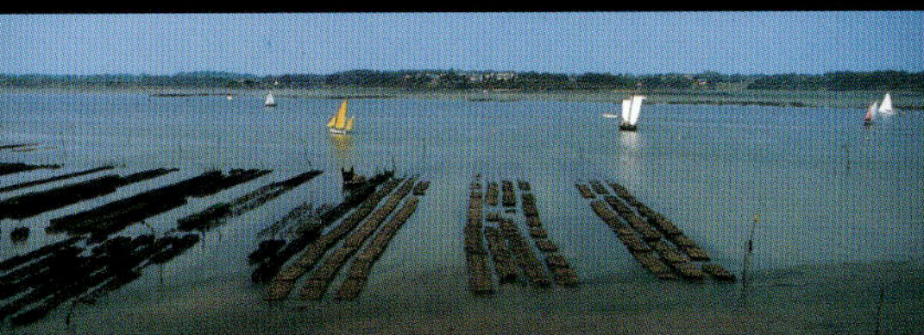

A SMALL SEA

The gulf of Morbihan (*mor bihan* means 'small sea') extends from Locmariaquer and Port Navalo, its mouth, to the port of Vannes. According to legend, it contains 365 islands and islets. Oyster beds line some of the coasts, such as in the River Auray or, further on, in the Étel estuary, its little sister.

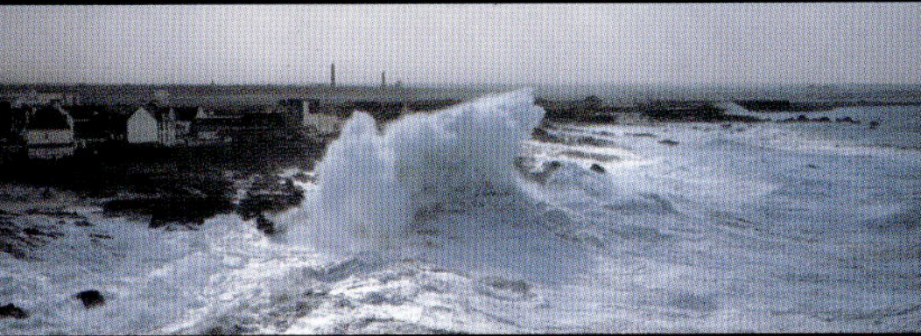

HEADING TO PENMARC'H

A few miles south of the Raz de Sein is the Pointe de Penmarc'h, riddled with shelves and reefs – a legendary Breton headland. Eckmühl lighthouse, named after one of Napoleon's marshals, stands 200 feet tall. With the old lighthouse at its side and the imposing beacons, it forms a stone rampart amid the sea swell.

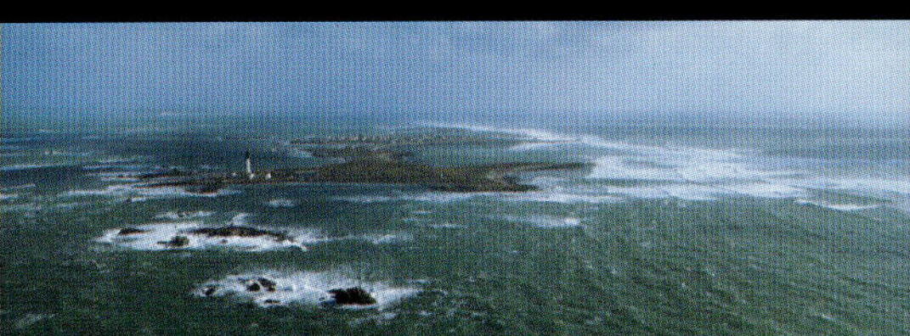

AT THE LEVEL OF THE WAVES

One mile long and half a mile wide, Île de Sein (*Enez Sun*), 8 miles from the Raz de Sein, is shaped like a crab's pincers. It barely skims the top of the waves – the highest mound is only 20 feet above sea level. No trees, no bushes, just a few sea walls for protection. And five hundred inhabitants, the women wearing their traditional black headdresses.

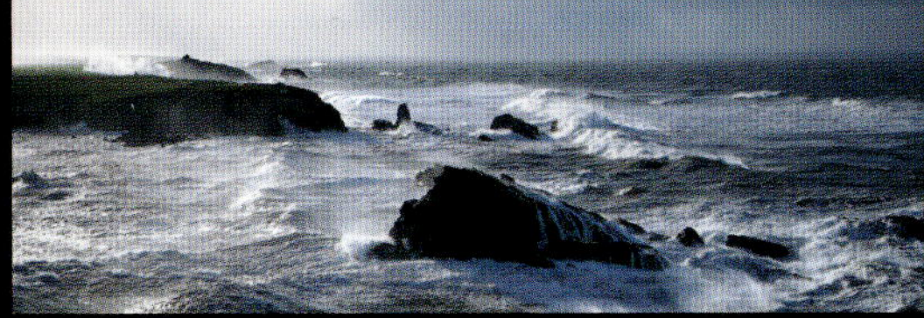

QUIBERON: THE WILD COAST

Quiberon (*Kiberen*), as slender as an island, on the Penthièvre isthmus, is proud of its rocky coast. It has been a conservation area since 1936. Not far from there, in 1795, a fleet of royalist Emigrés landed in support of the peasant soldiers led by Georges Cadoudal during the French Revolution.

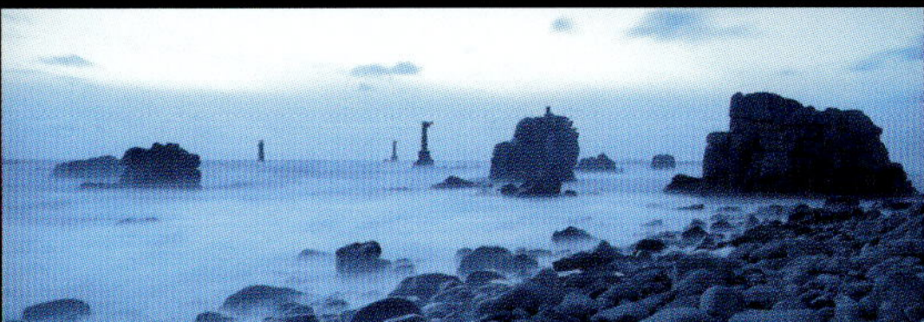

ENEZ EUSA: OUESSANT

'He who sees Molène sees suffering, he who sees Ouessant sees his blood.' Thus *Enez Eusa*, Brittany's highest island (200 feet), wards off the curse of the elements. Wind and mist beat down on this island inhabited by a thousand sturdy islanders, half farmers, half fishermen.

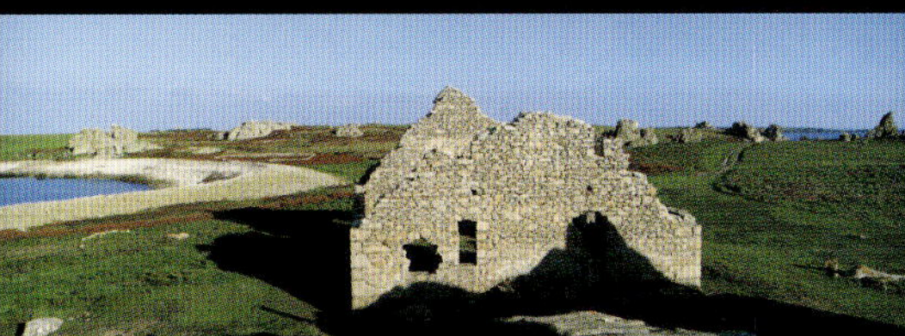

THE MOORS OF OUESSANT

The island of Ouessant has tongues of sand, white rocks and stone huts from another age. Nesting sea and migratory birds add to the local wildlife. On the windy moor, a breed of small black sheep grazes, and among the hollows of the rocks, a colony of seals makes its home.

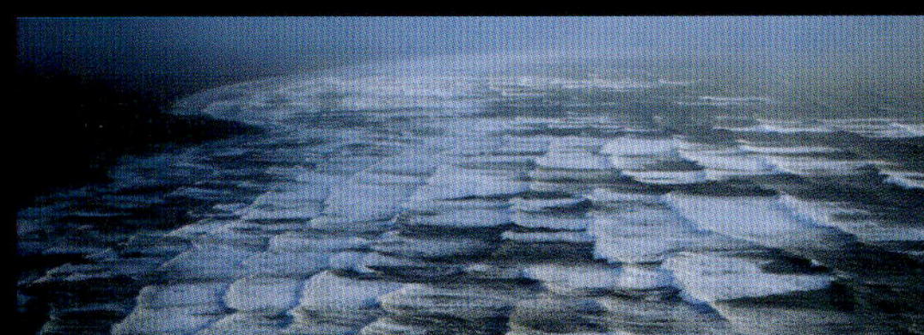

AUDIERNE BAY

Foam-edged waves form a chequerboard pattern as they break in the bay of Audierne (*Gwaien*), south of Cap Sizun and the Pointe du Raz. There is a lively fishing port here with a fleet of multi-coloured boats, as well as a cemetery for langoustine fishermen in Locquéran cove.

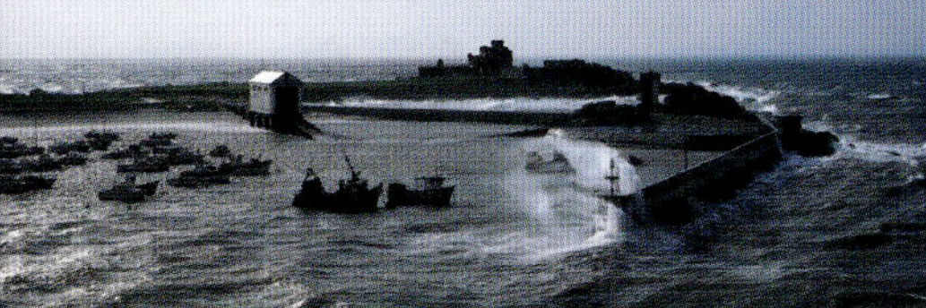

POINTE DE TRÉVIGNON

The rocky coast near Tregunc, a few miles from Concarneau, in the Cornouaille area of Finistère, runs for 15 miles, punctuated by creeks, river estuaries and many white, sandy beaches. The Pointe de Trévignon, jutting into the sea beyond the dunes and salt marshes, shelters a lively fishing port and a maritime museum.

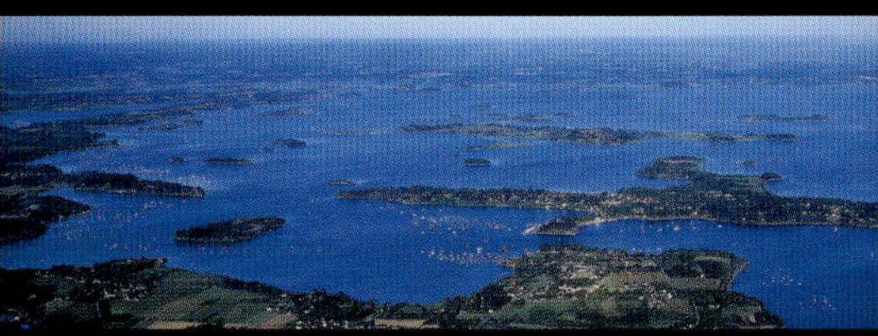

THE GULF OF MORBIHAN

'Fest Mor Bihan': festival on the small sea. This could be the title for Gulf of Morbihan Week. In early May, nearly a thousand old sailing ships hoist their sails in this sea garden with its 365 islands and as many legends: from Vannes to Locmariaquer, the Île d'Arz to the Île aux Moines and from Arradon to Port Navalo.

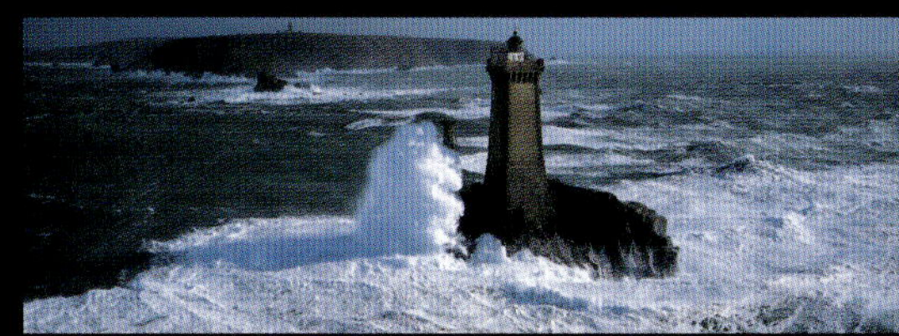

POINTE DU RAZ

The Pointe du Raz lighthouse and its neighbour, Pointe du Van, mark the Baie des Trépassés (Bay of the Dead), where wandering shipwrecked souls are said to roam. The site has become a nature reserve, and a symbol of the region of Finistère – *Finis Terrae*, 'land's end'.

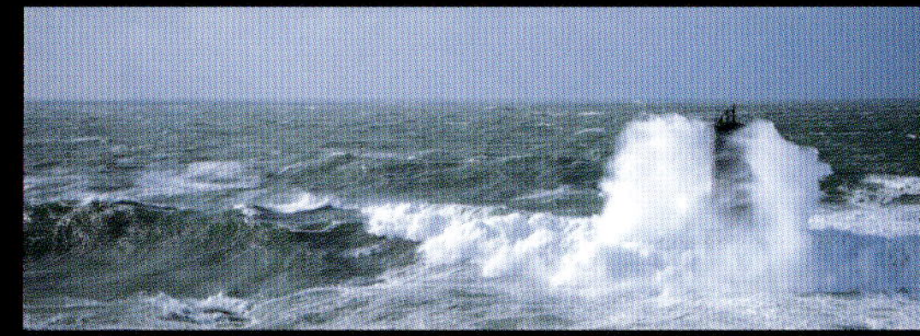

STORMING NIVIDIC

Facing the island of Ouessant stands Nividic lighthouse, 90 feet above the waves.... except when the waves storm and engulf this stone tower which took fourteen years to build.

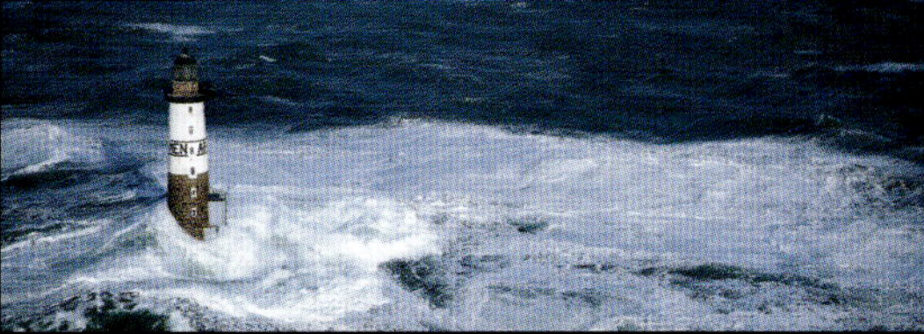

AR MEN LIGHTHOUSE

One of the most famous Breton lighthouses, Ar Men (meaning 'head' or 'point') dominates the submerged rock, constantly lashed by the swell. It took six years to build it at the end of the 19th century. From 120 feet above the waves, its light sweeps the sea near the Île de Sein.

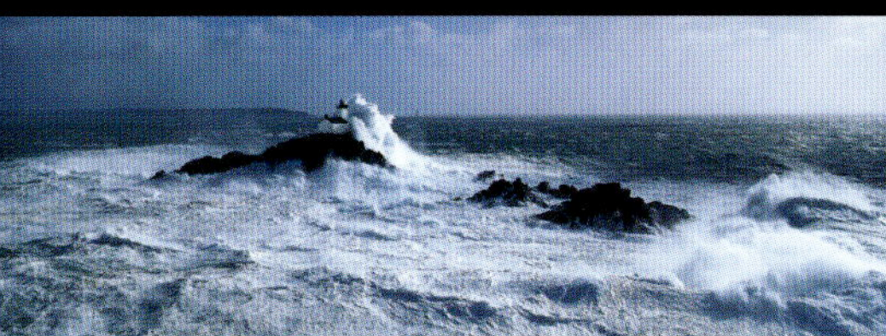

THE LEGEND OF TÉVENNEC

Tévennec, north of the Raz de Sein – a lighthouse always whipped by the spray, standing nearly 100 feet above sea level. Yet another challenge for man and for wandering souls. The legends and superstitions of Cap Sizun speak of the *bag ar noz*, the night boat that carries *an anaon*, the souls of the shipwrecked.

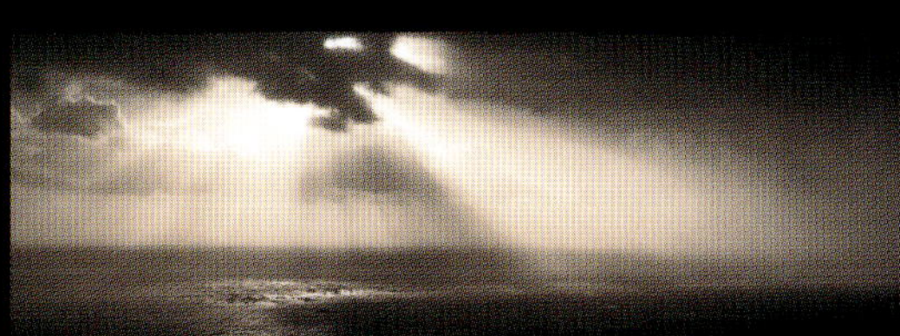

THE SEIN CAUSEWAY

Sunset over the Sein Causeway. The mythical passage extends from Île de Sein – 'He who sees Sein sees his own end' – to Ar Men lighthouse, whose construction took fourteen years of hard labour. Here the waves flow between two seas: the *Mor Breizh* (the English Channel) and *Mor Braz*, the Atlantic Ocean.

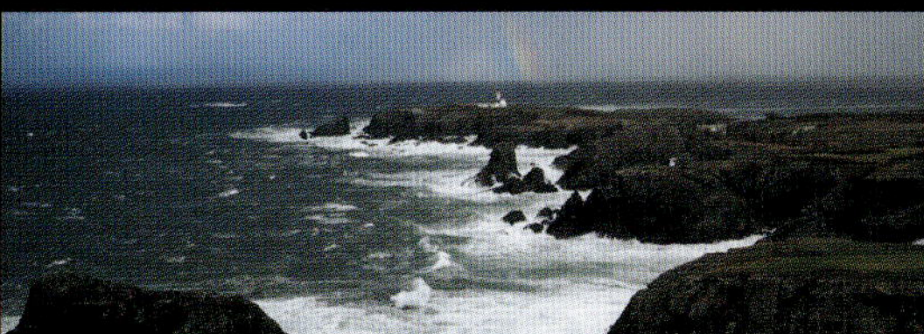

POINTE DES POULAINS

North-west of Belle-Île stands the Pointe des Poulains, 60 feet above sea level. In bad weather, the waves crash onto the rocks and the spray drowns the wild moor.

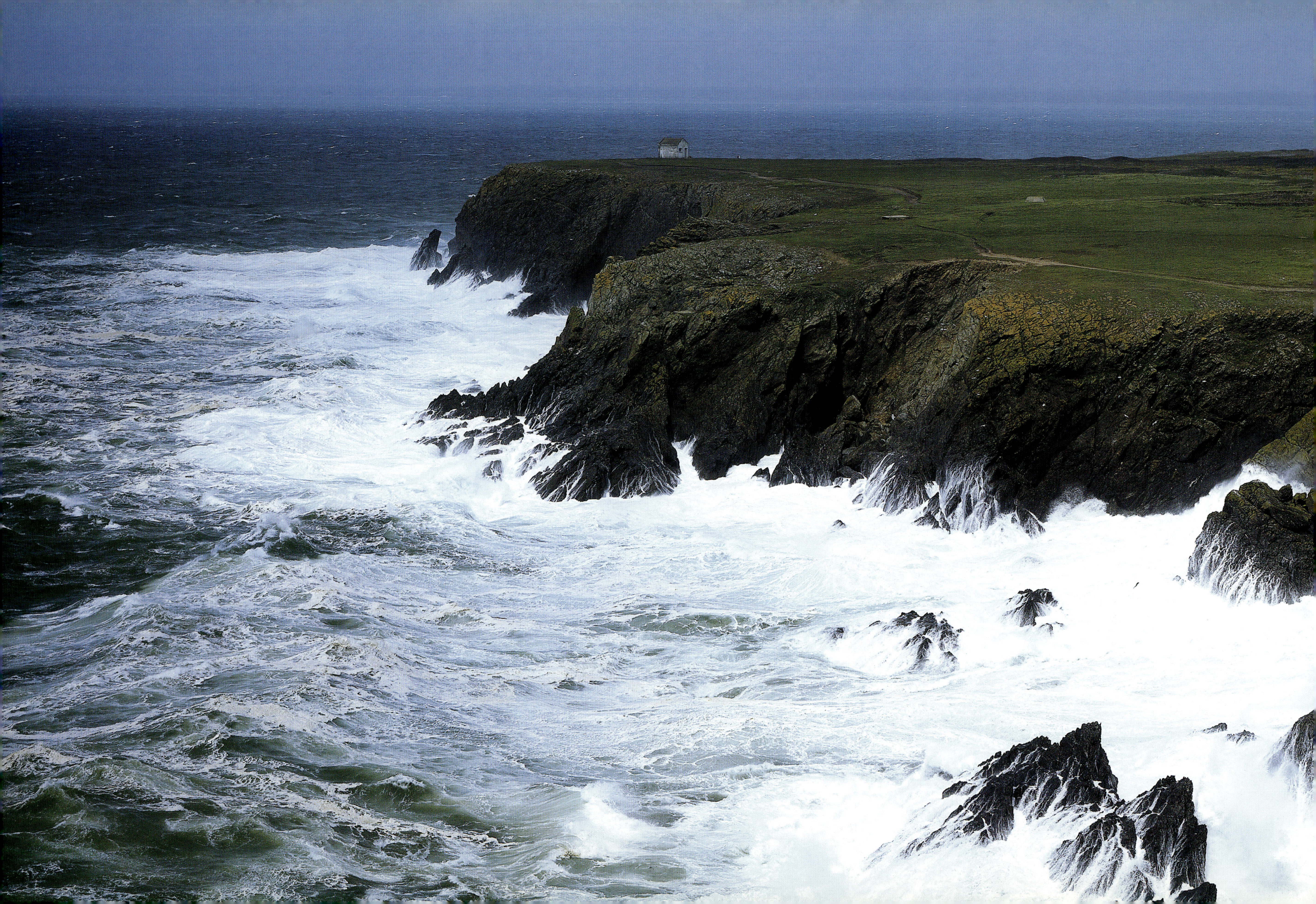

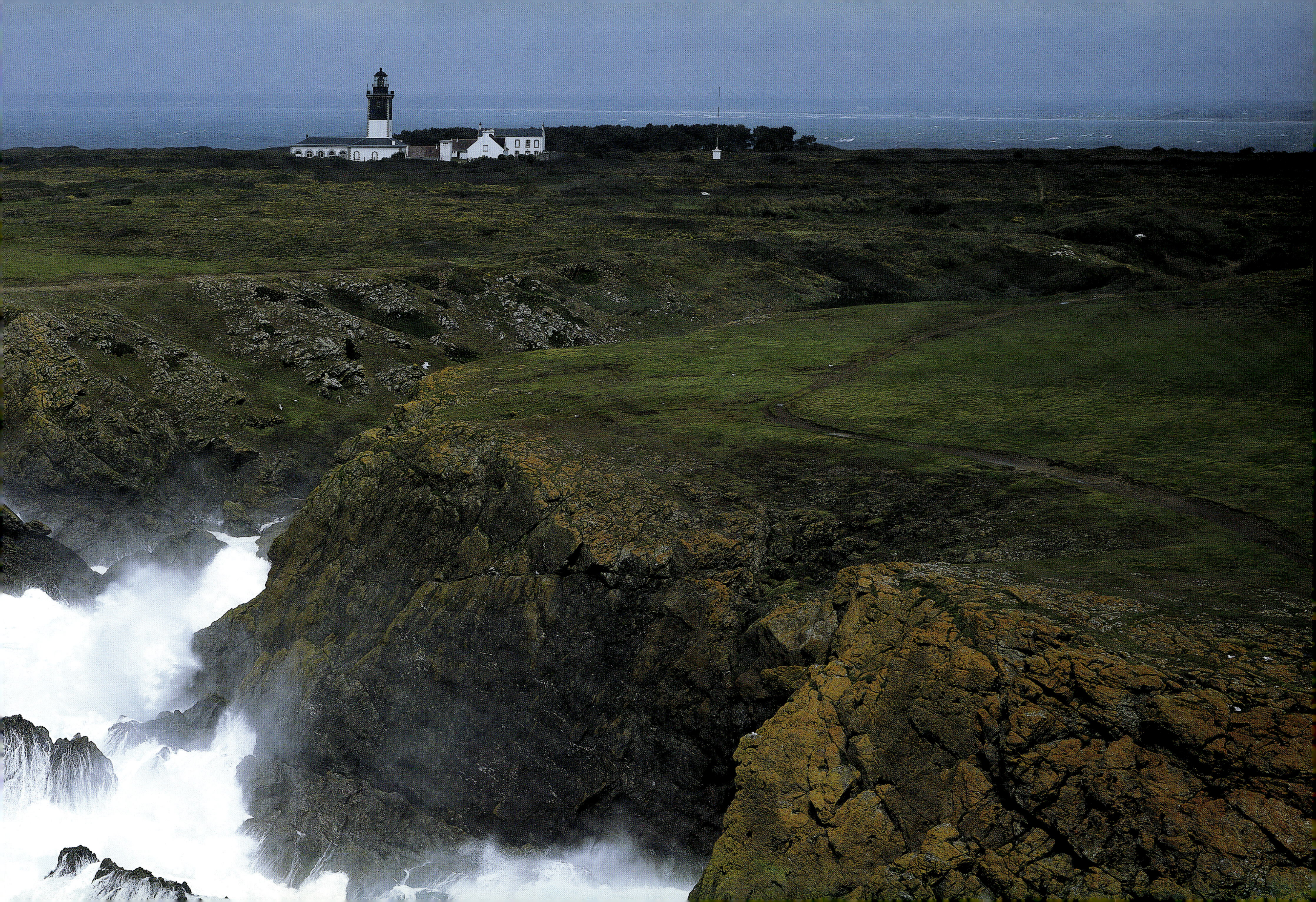

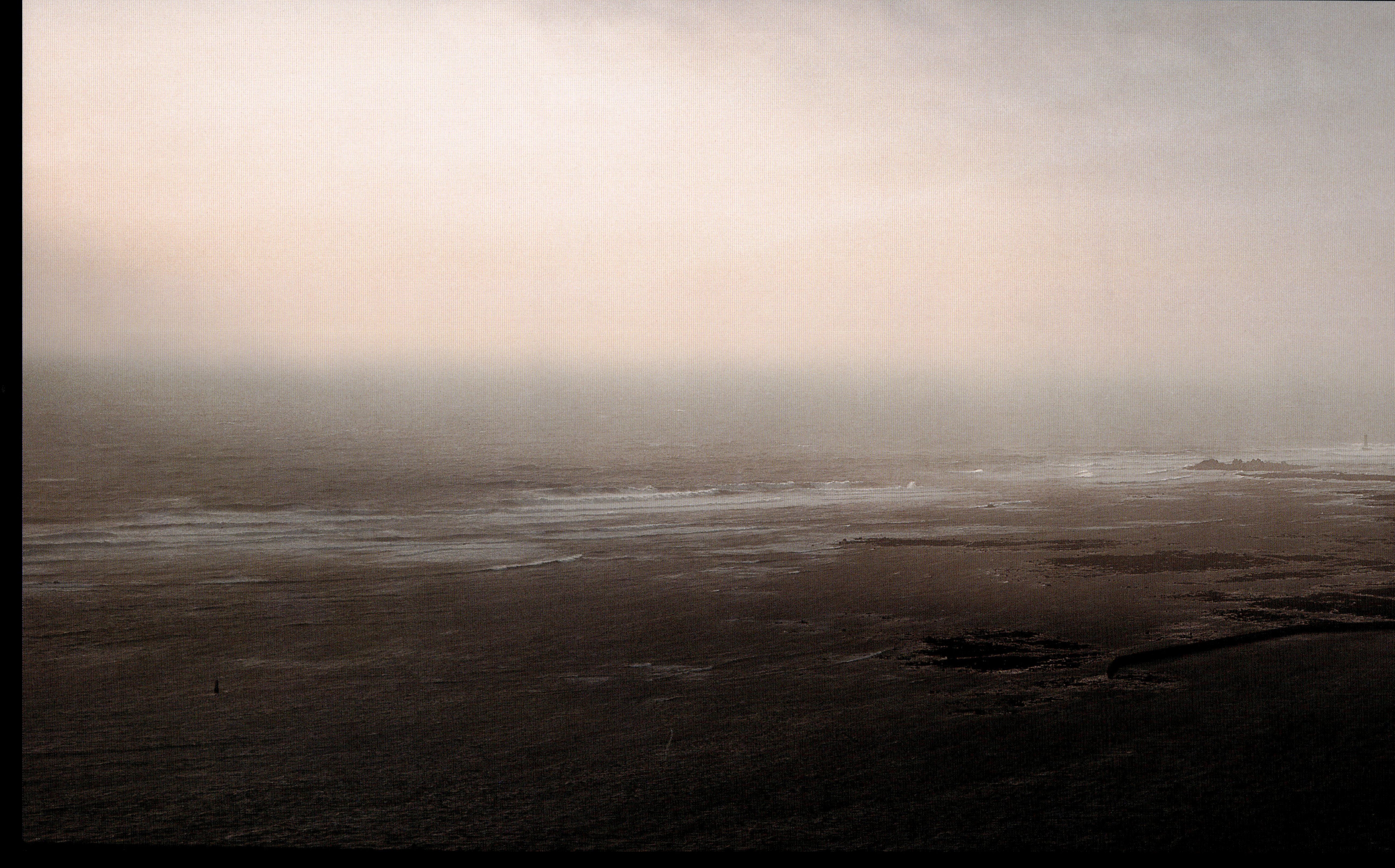

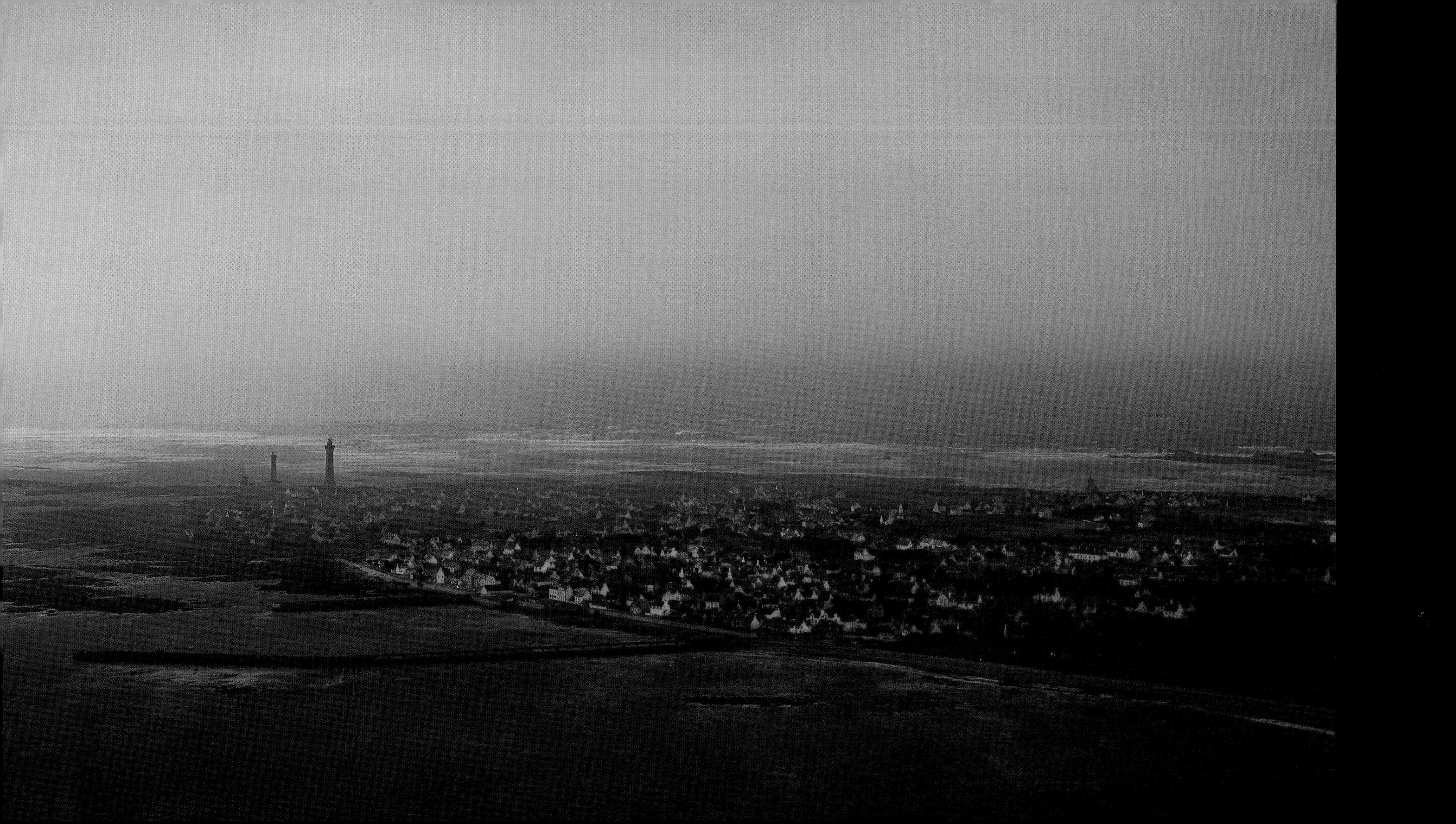

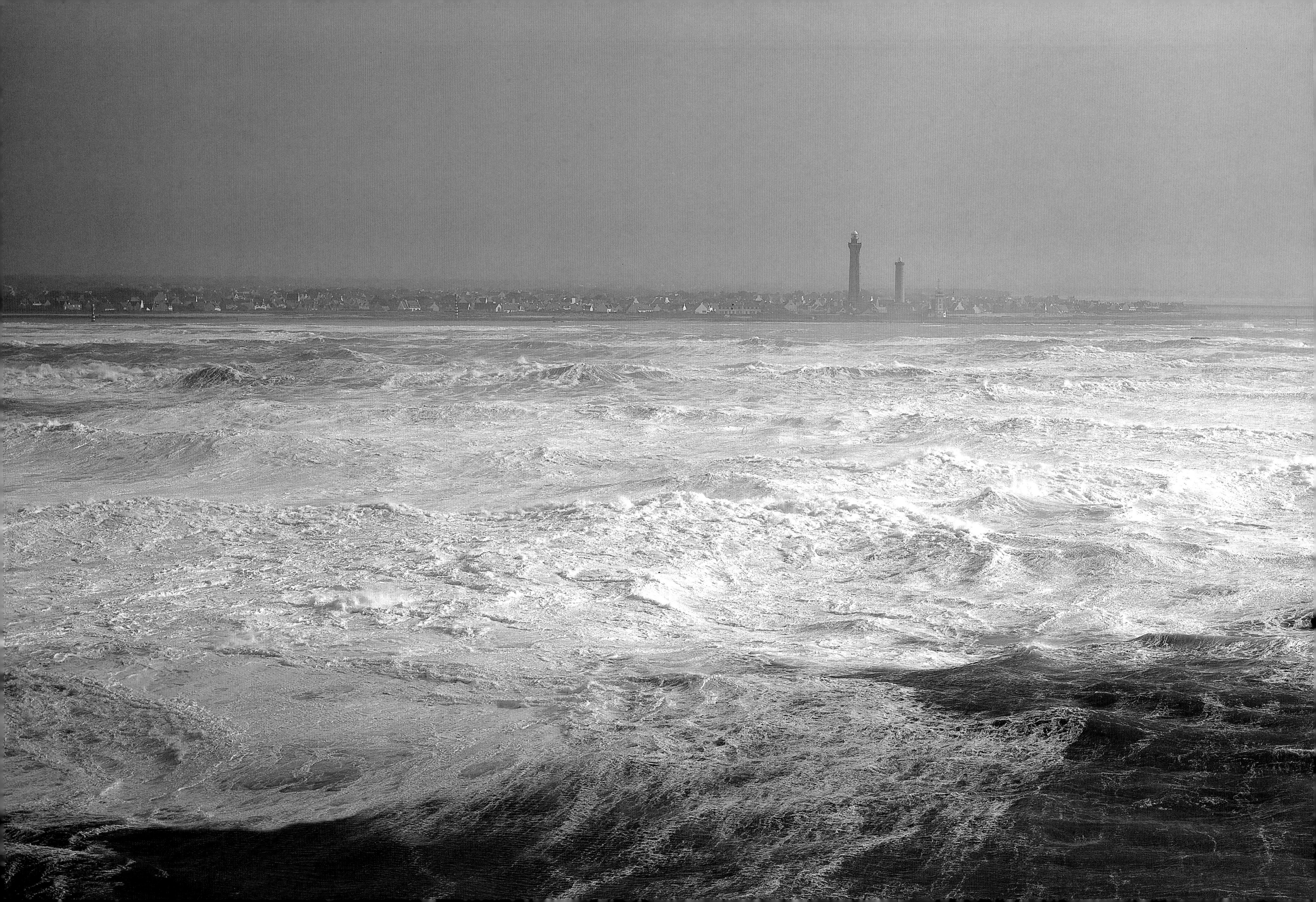

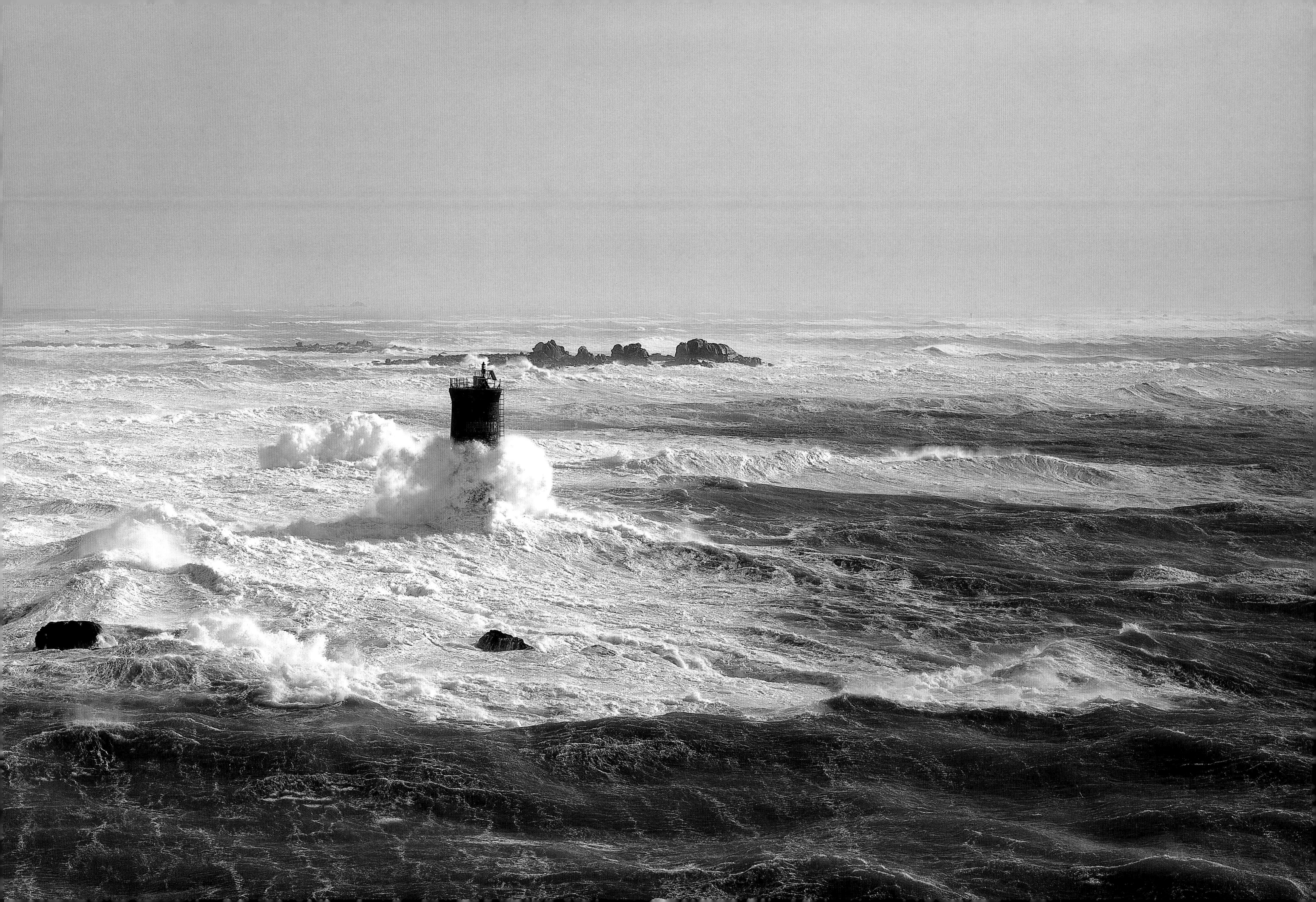

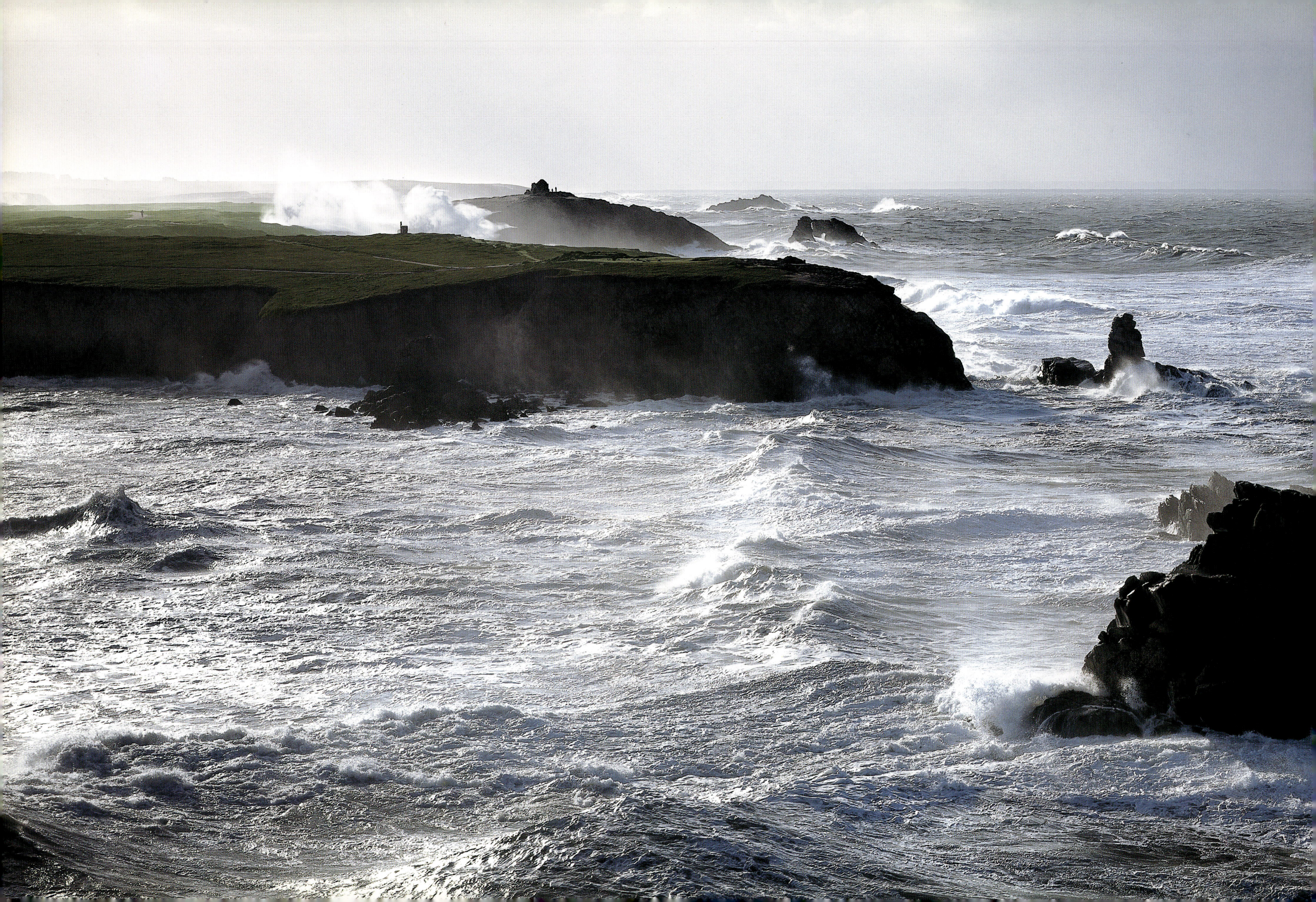

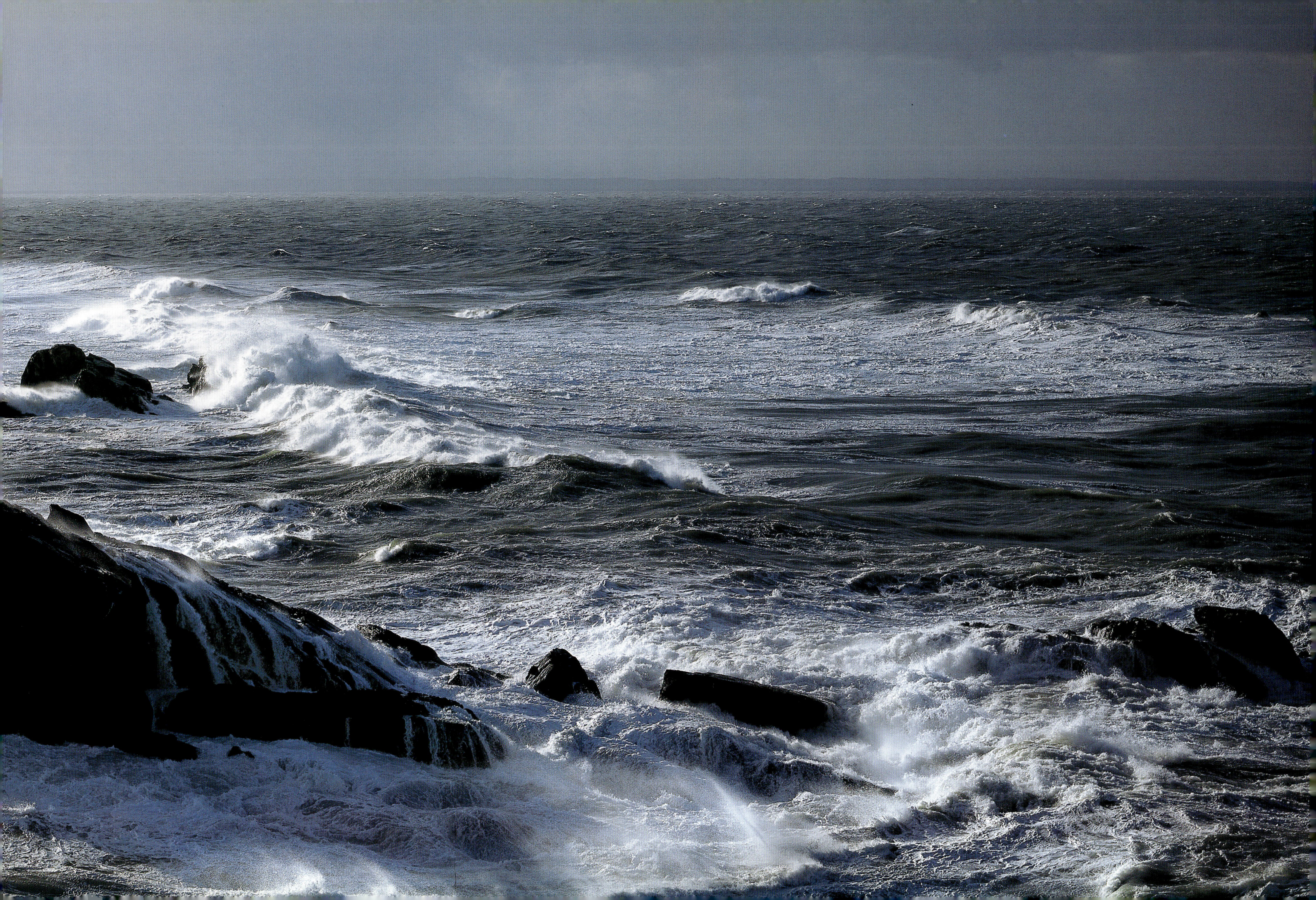

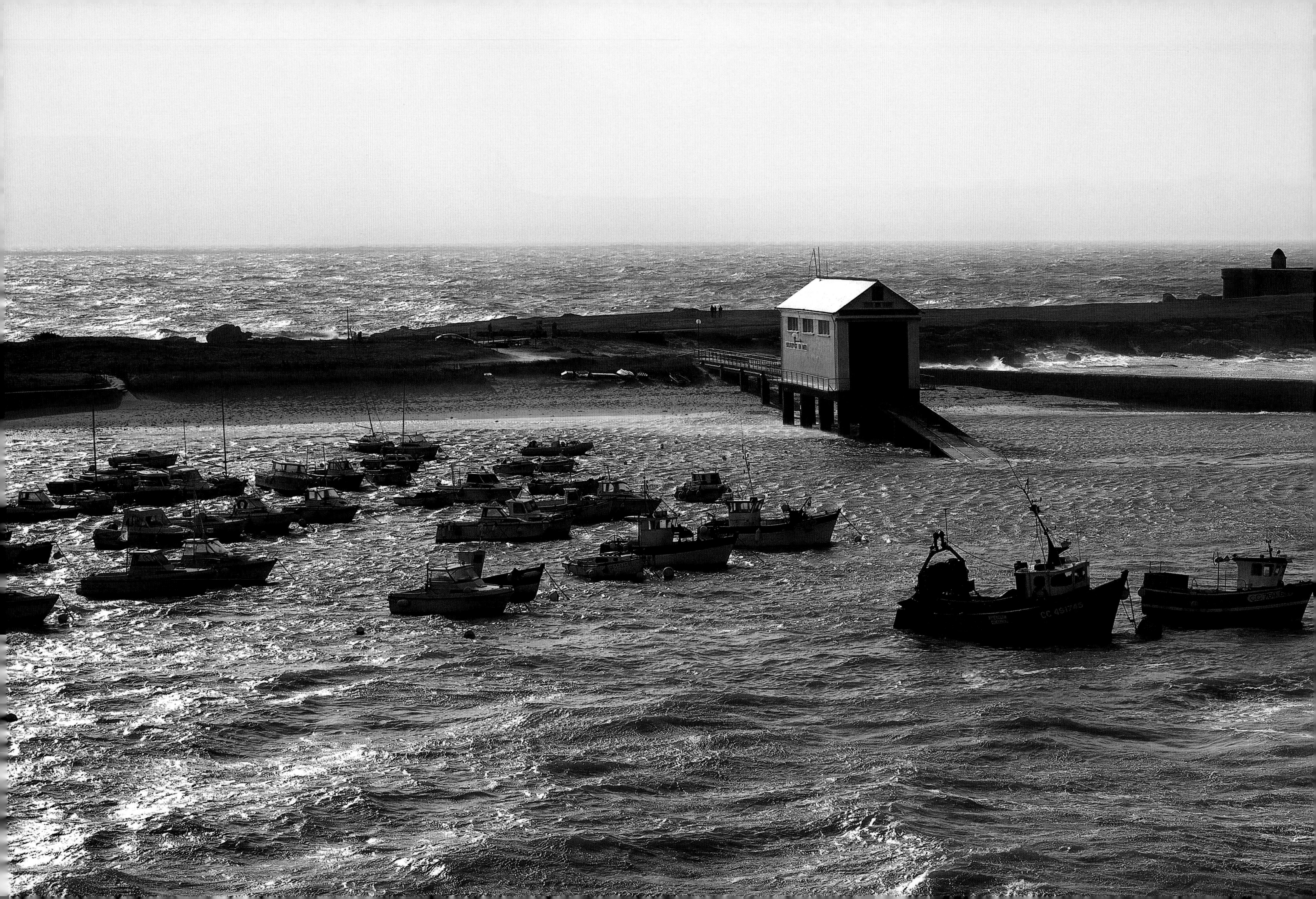
CC 491745

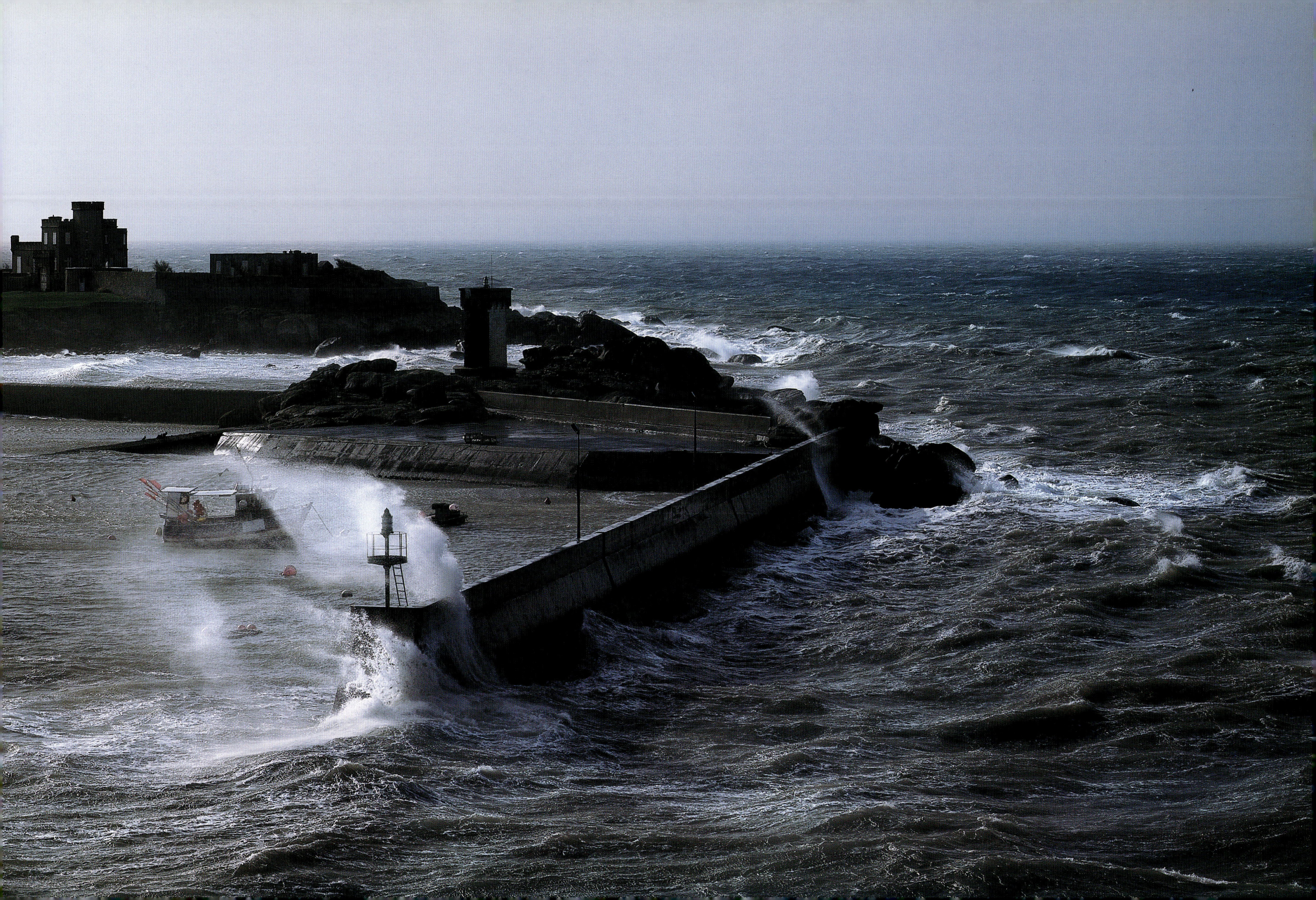

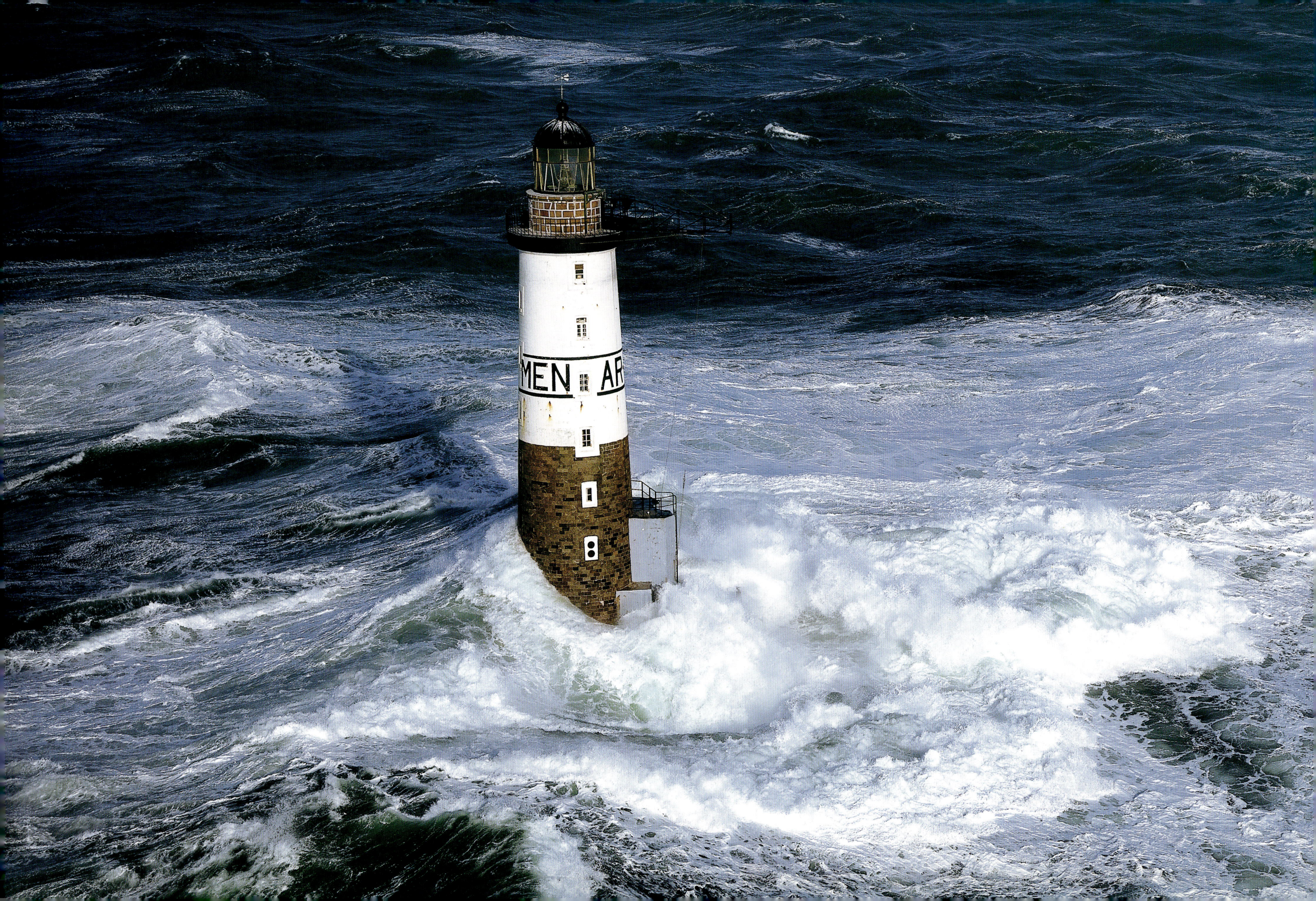
MEN AR

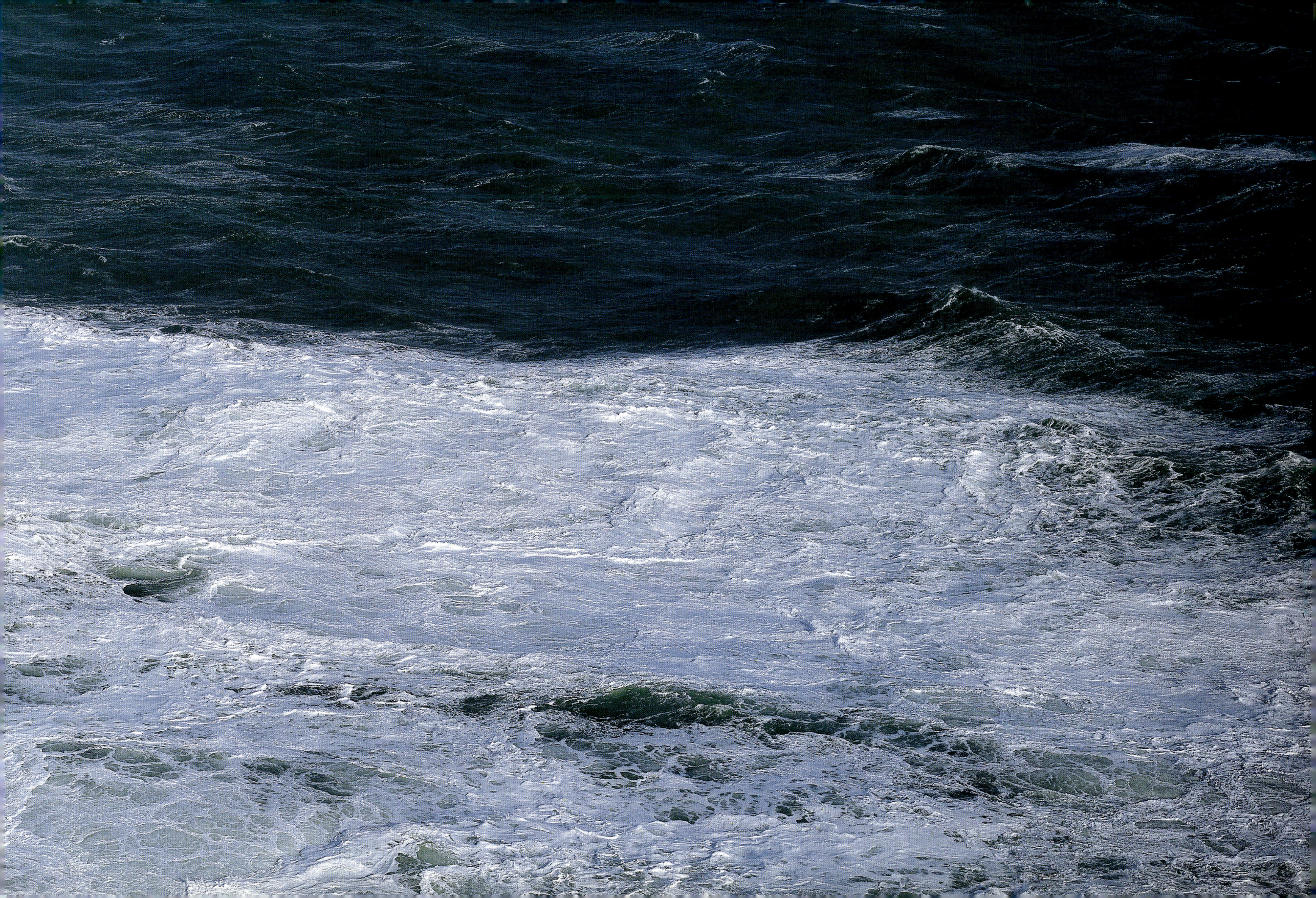

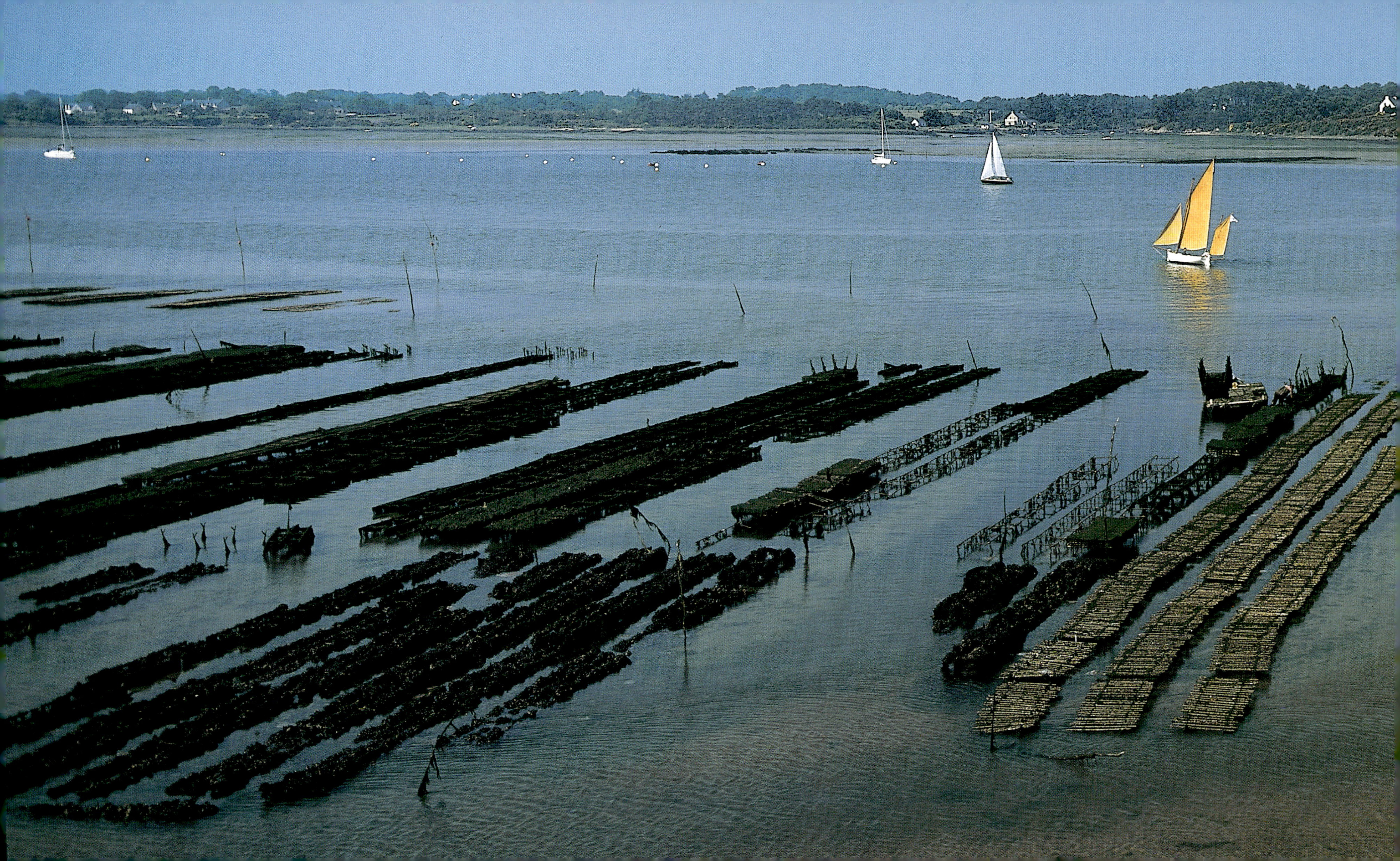

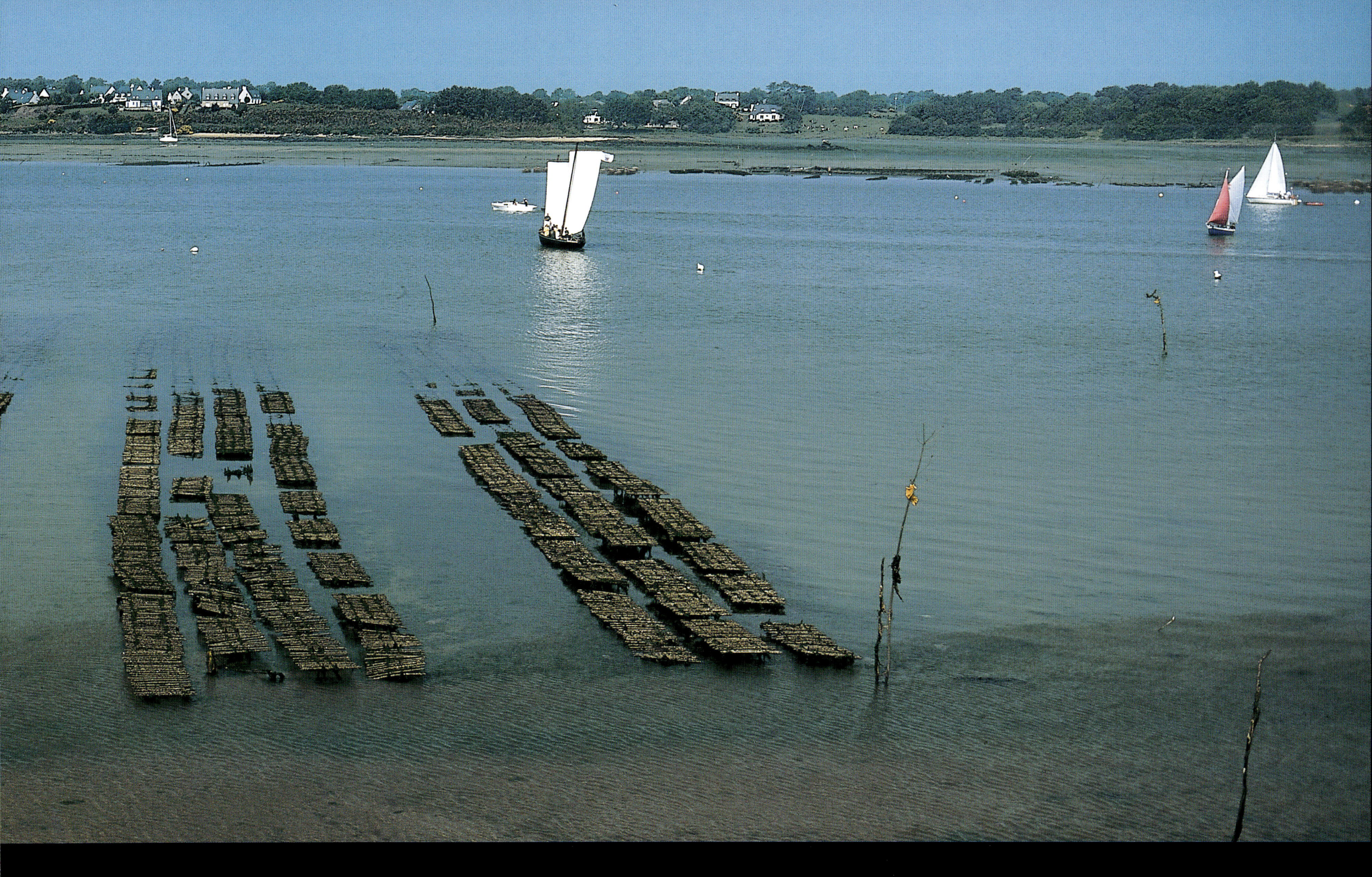

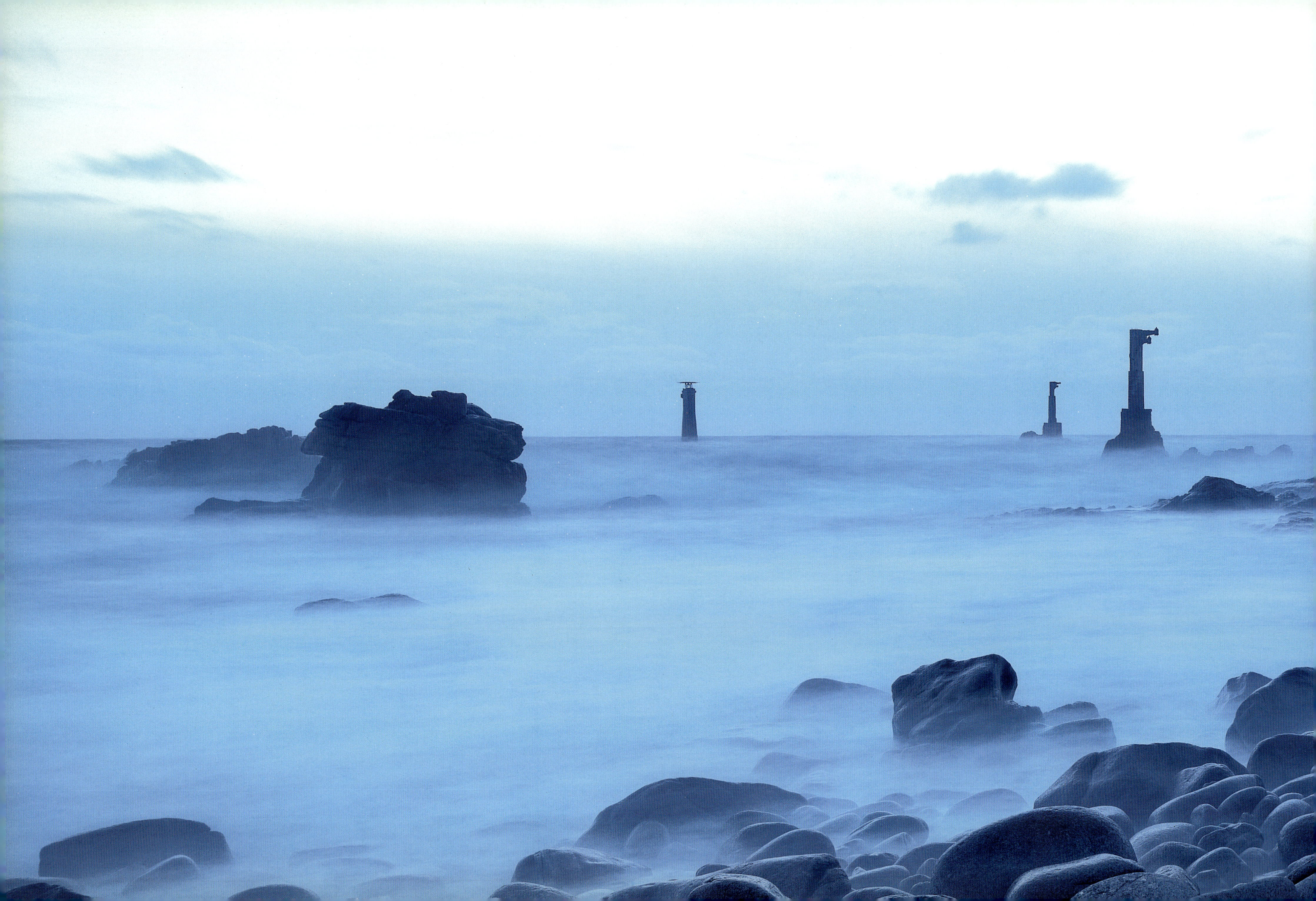

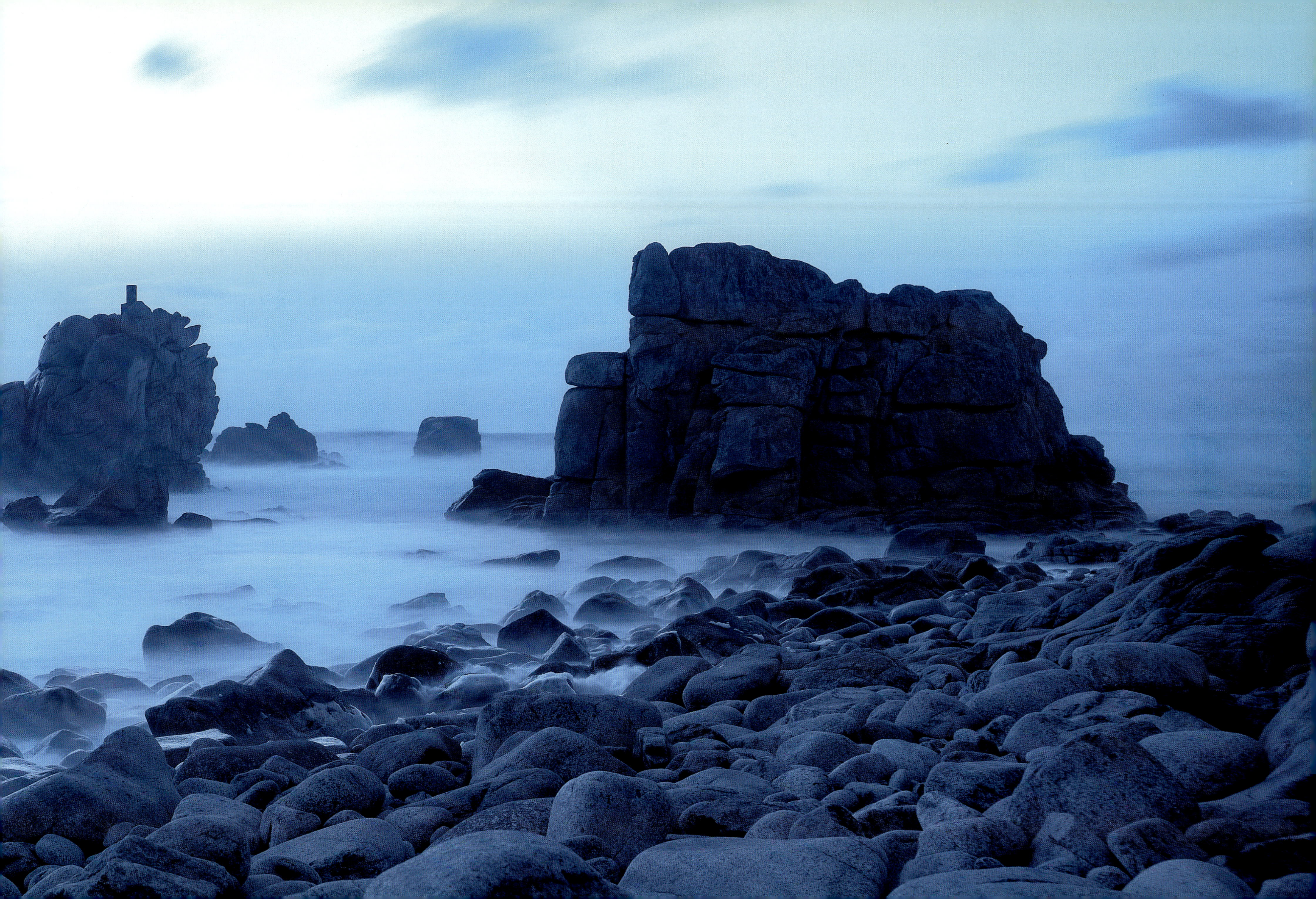

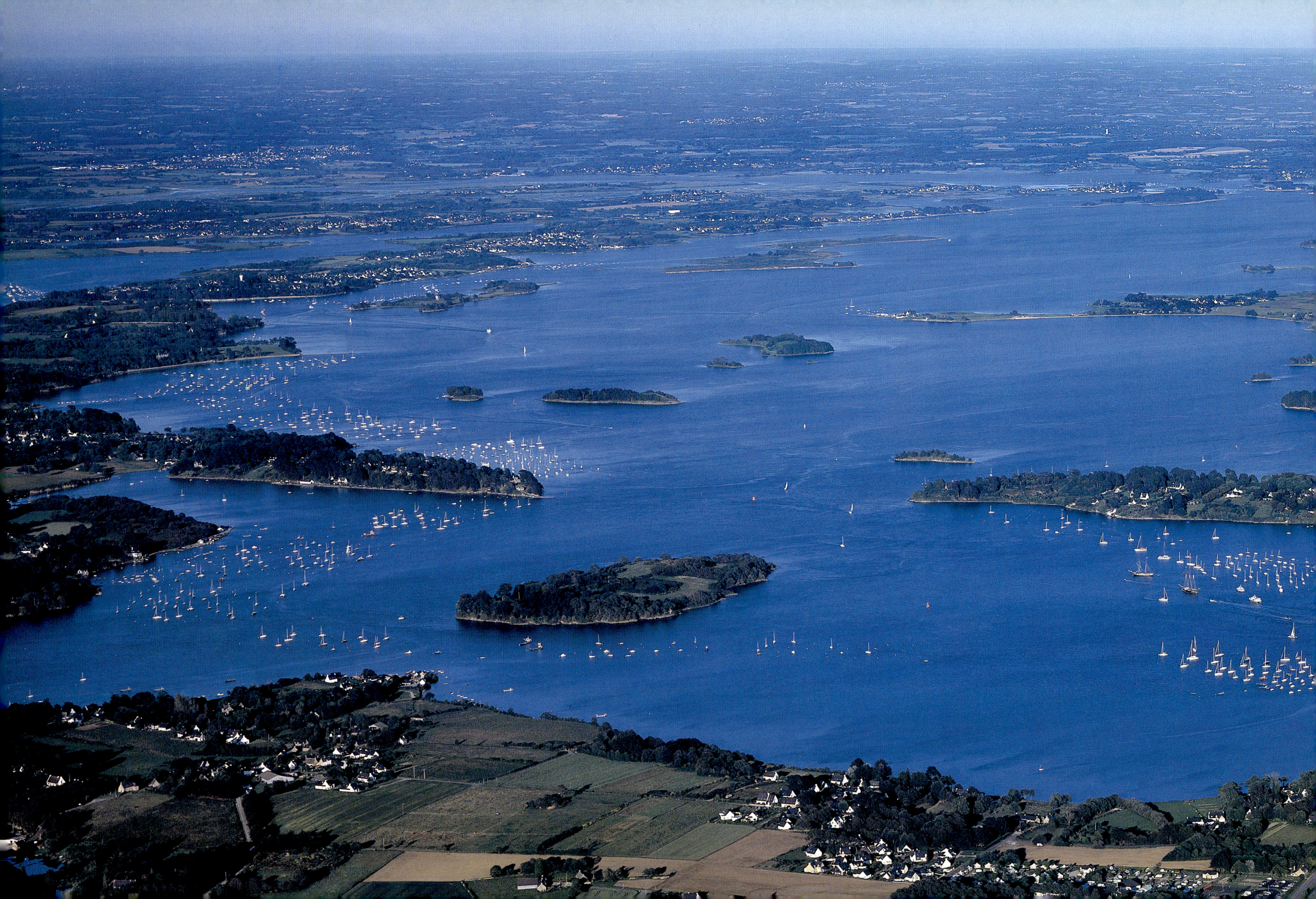

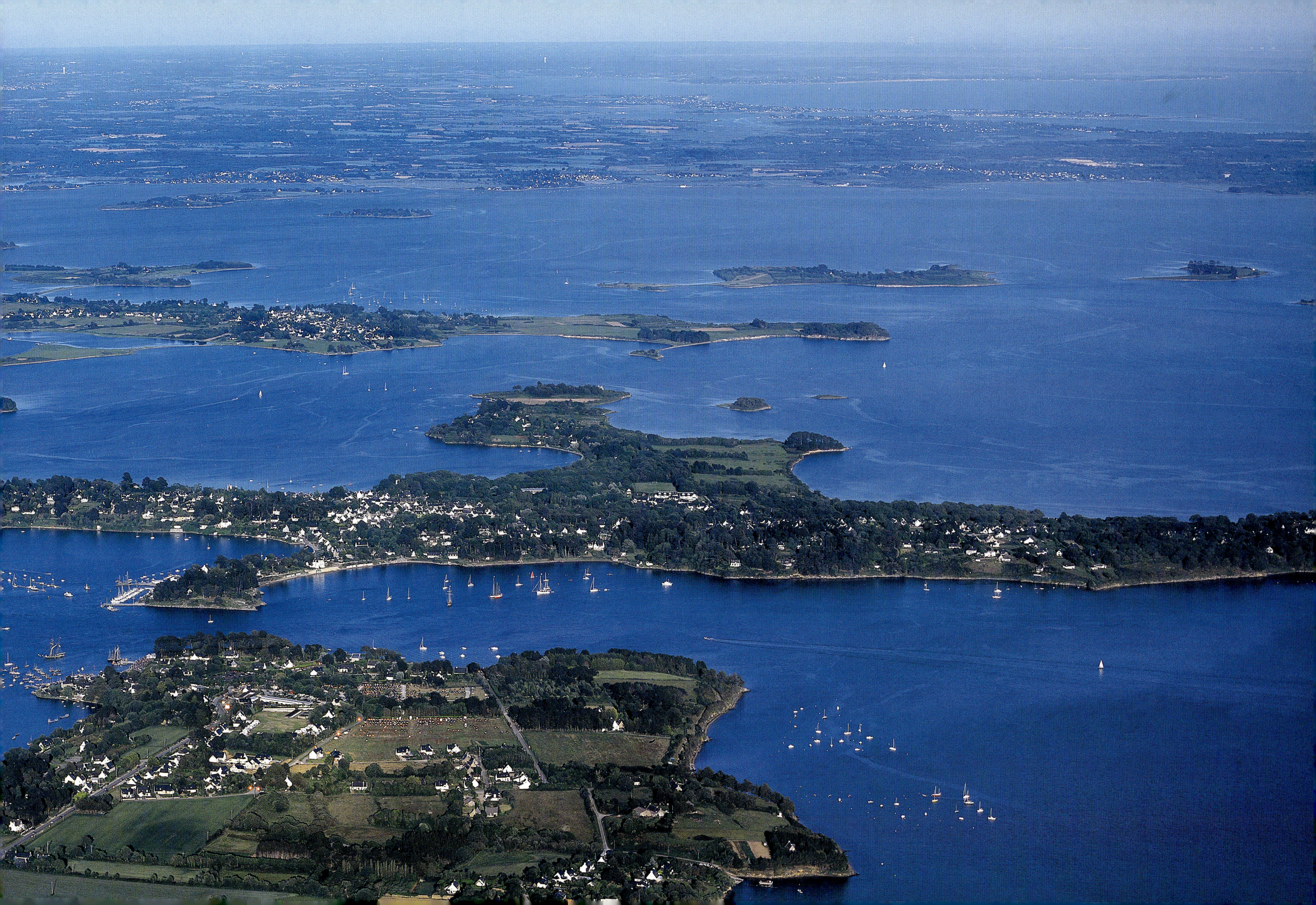

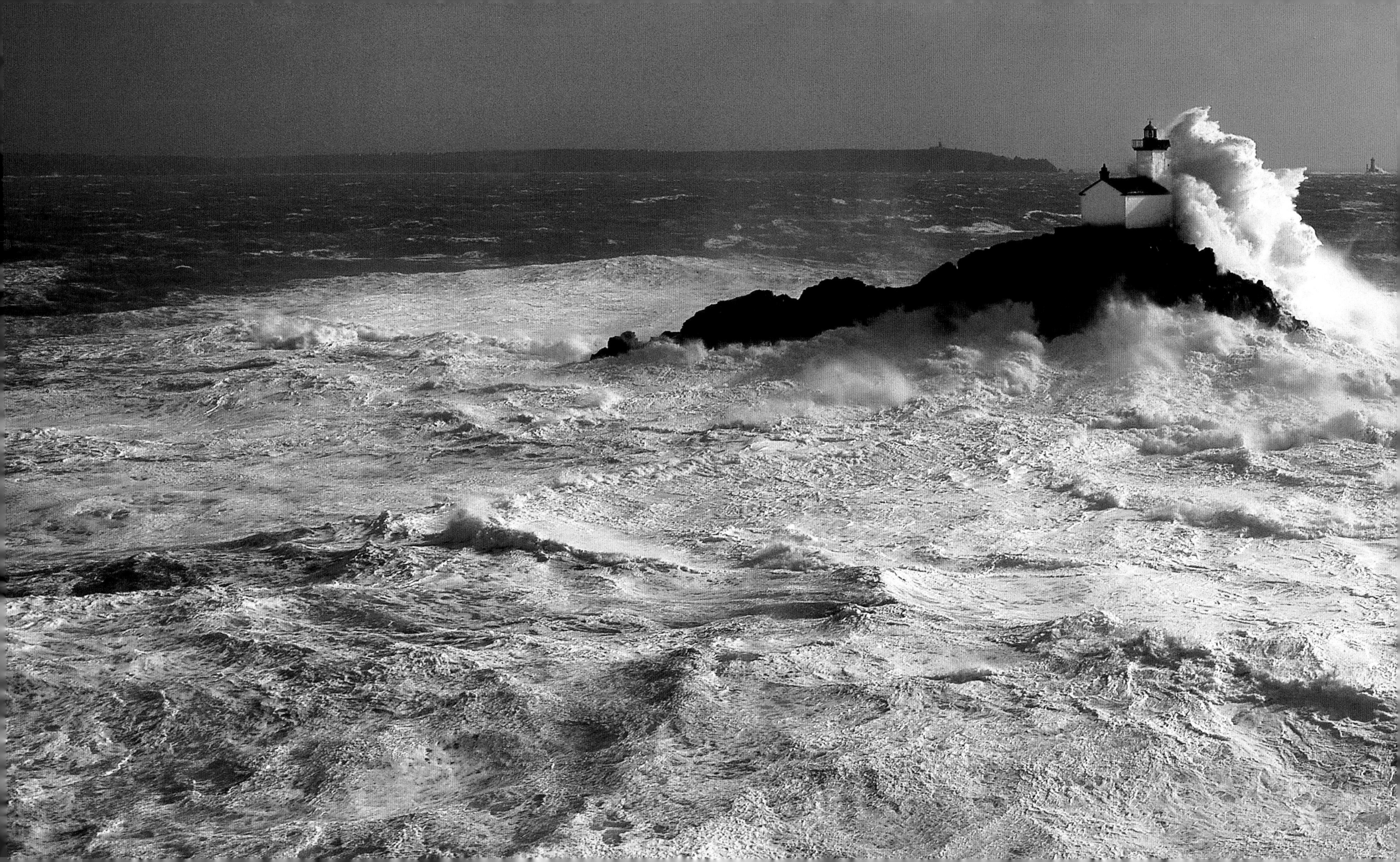

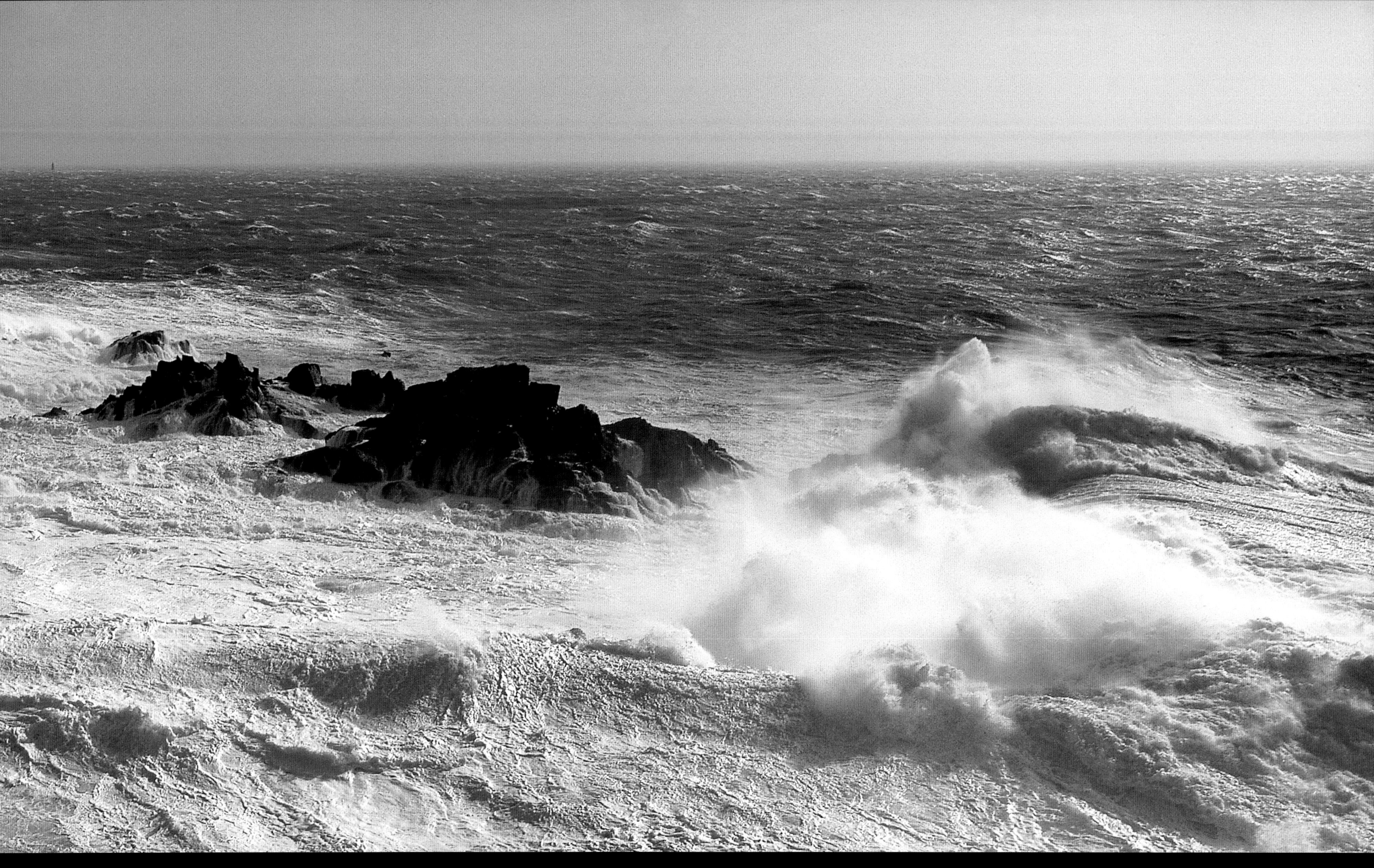

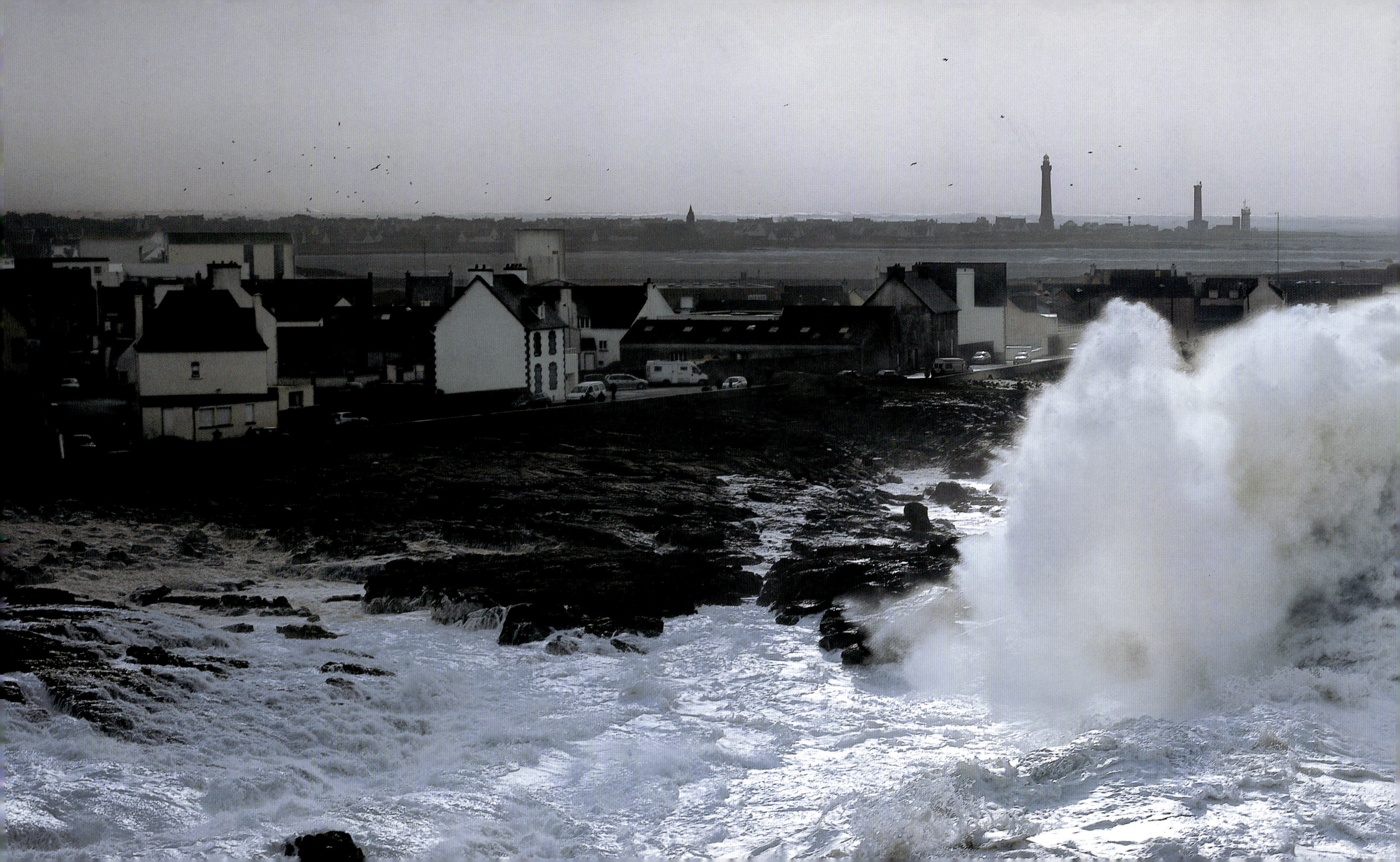

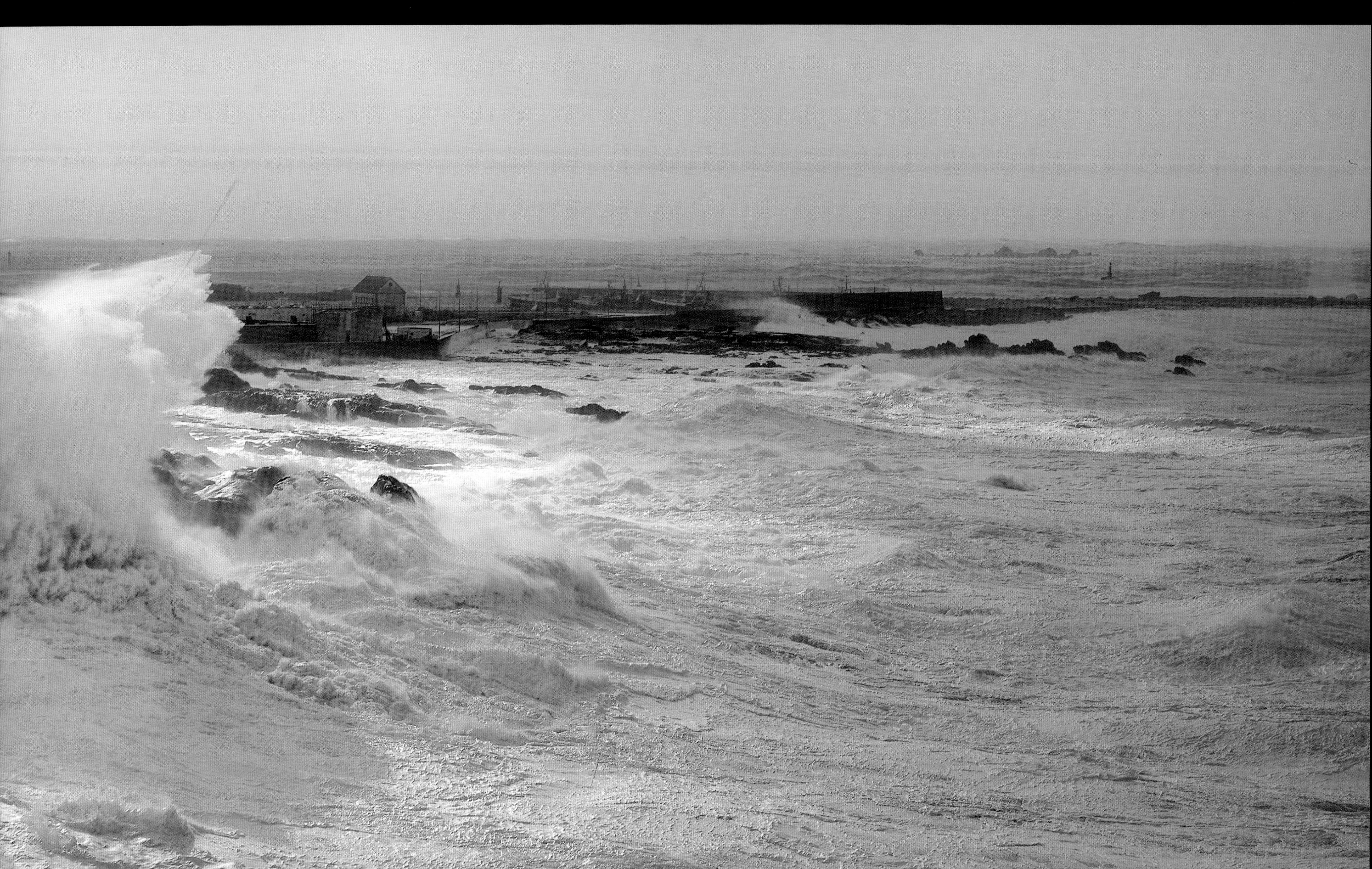

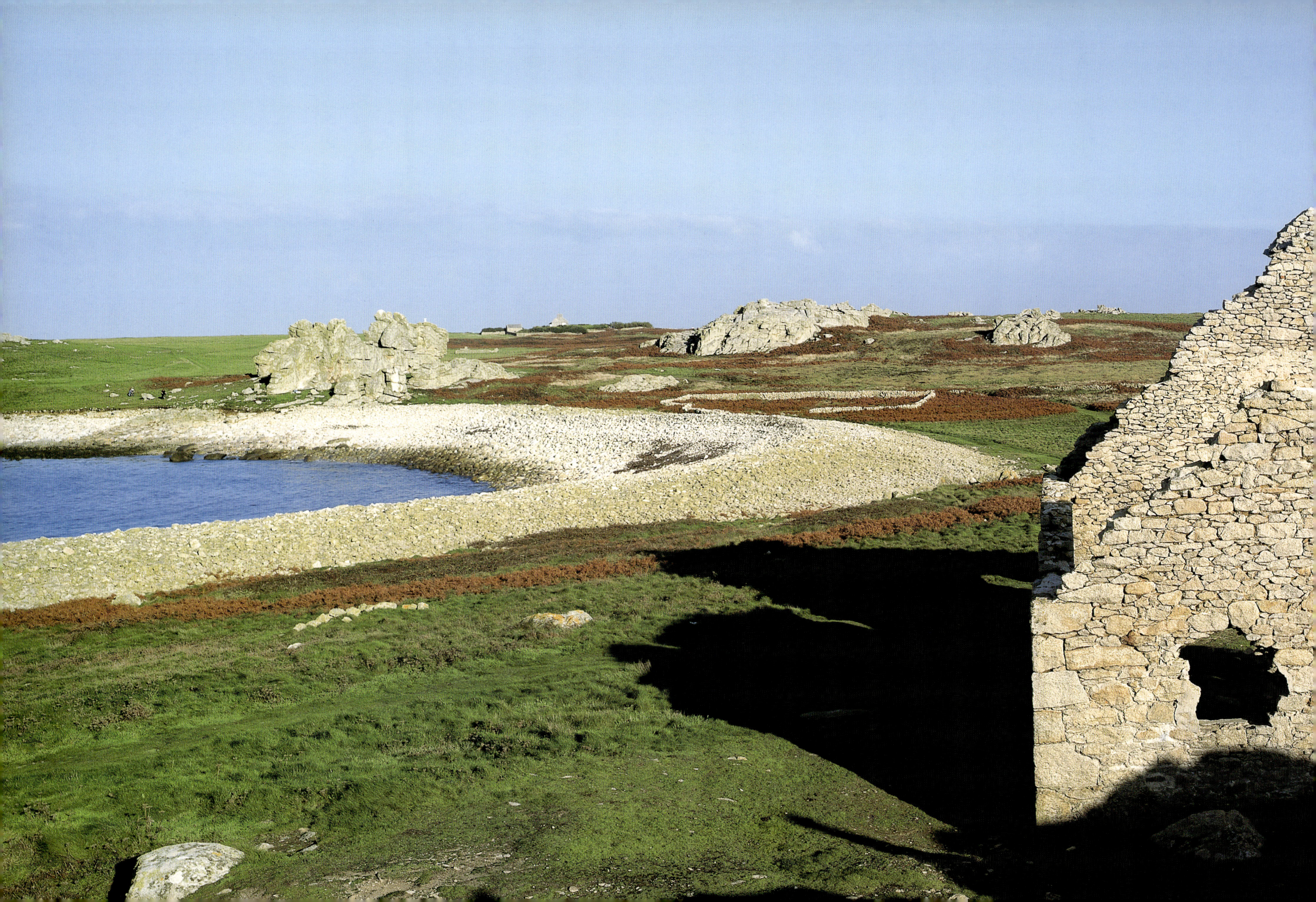

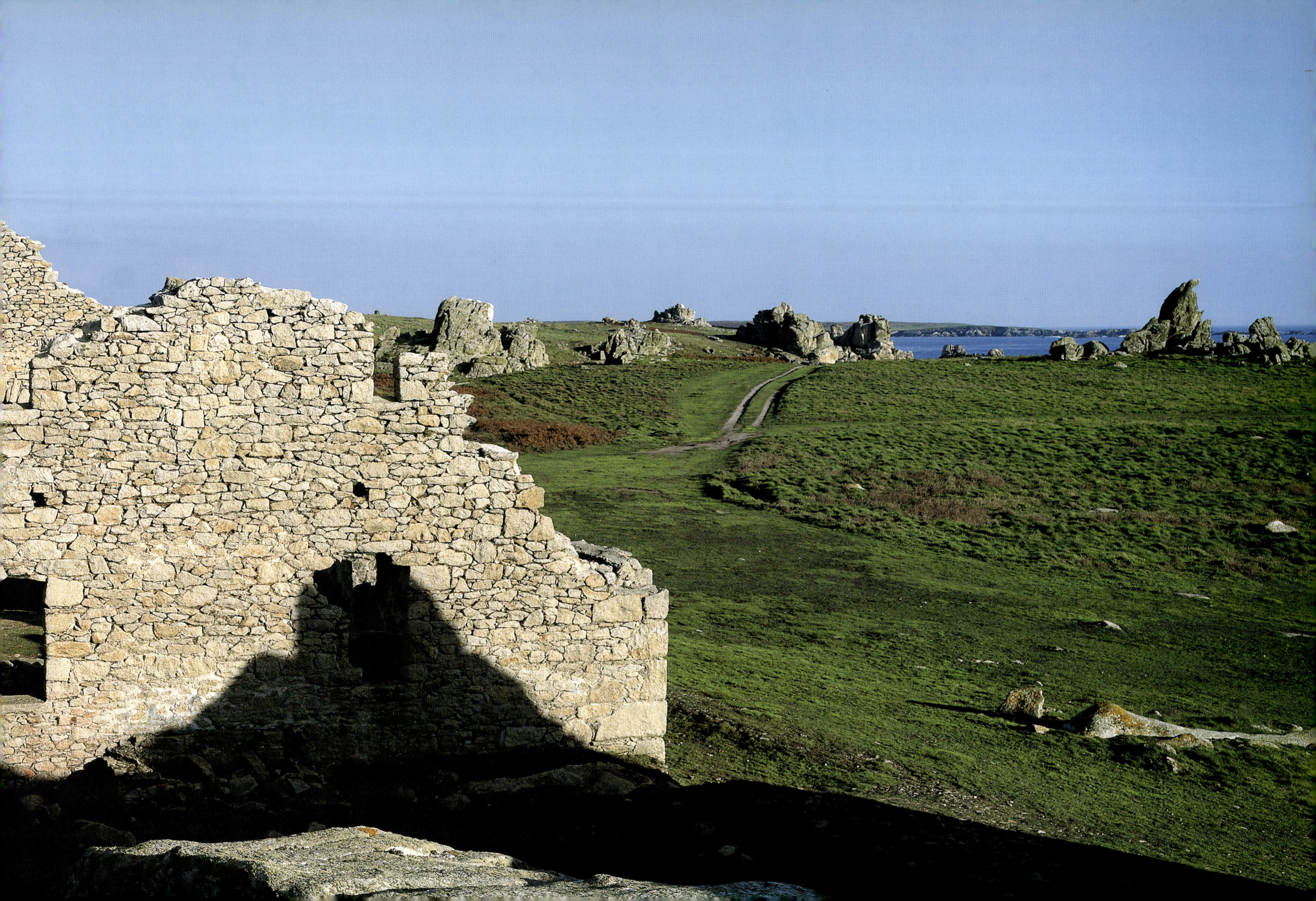

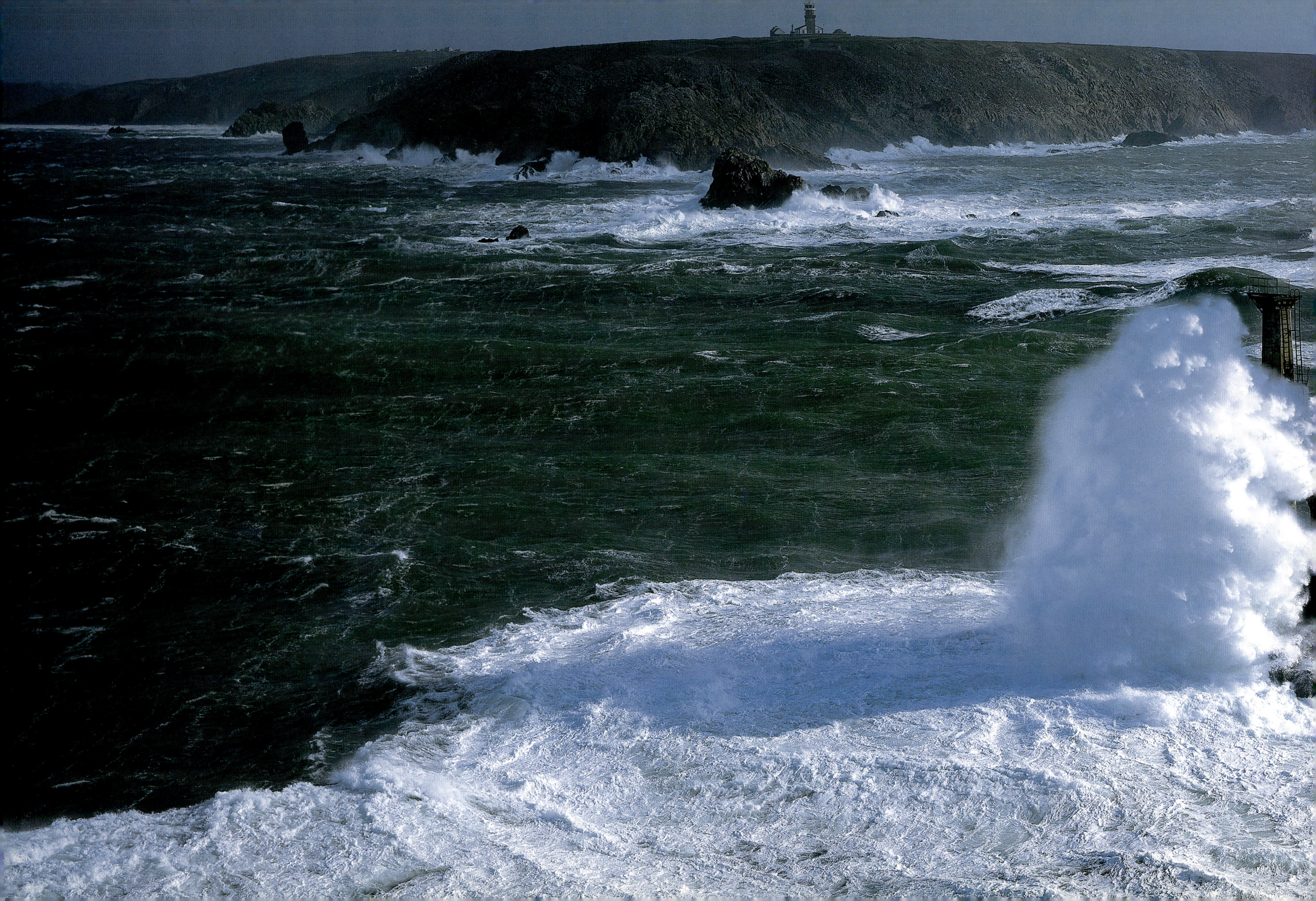

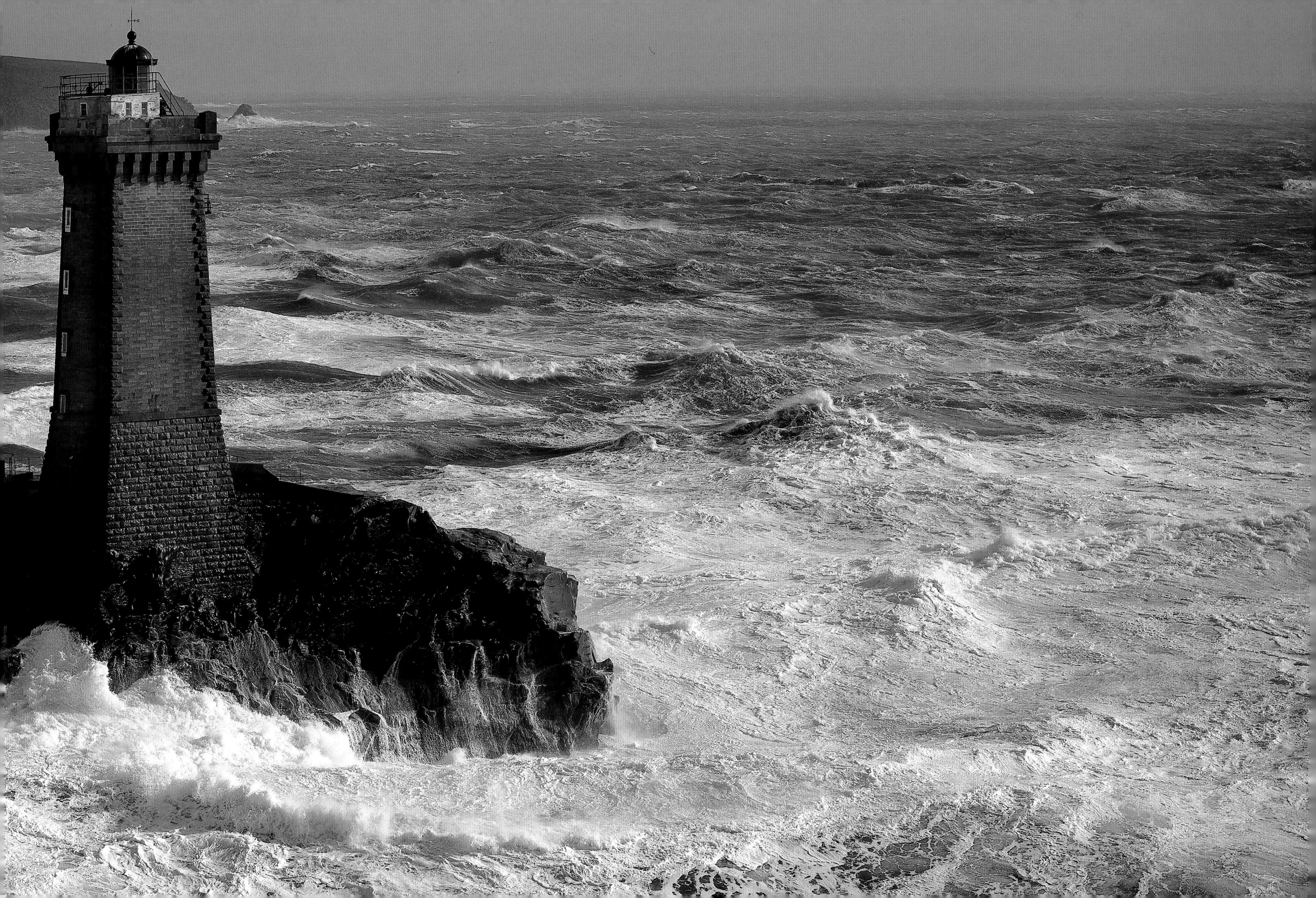

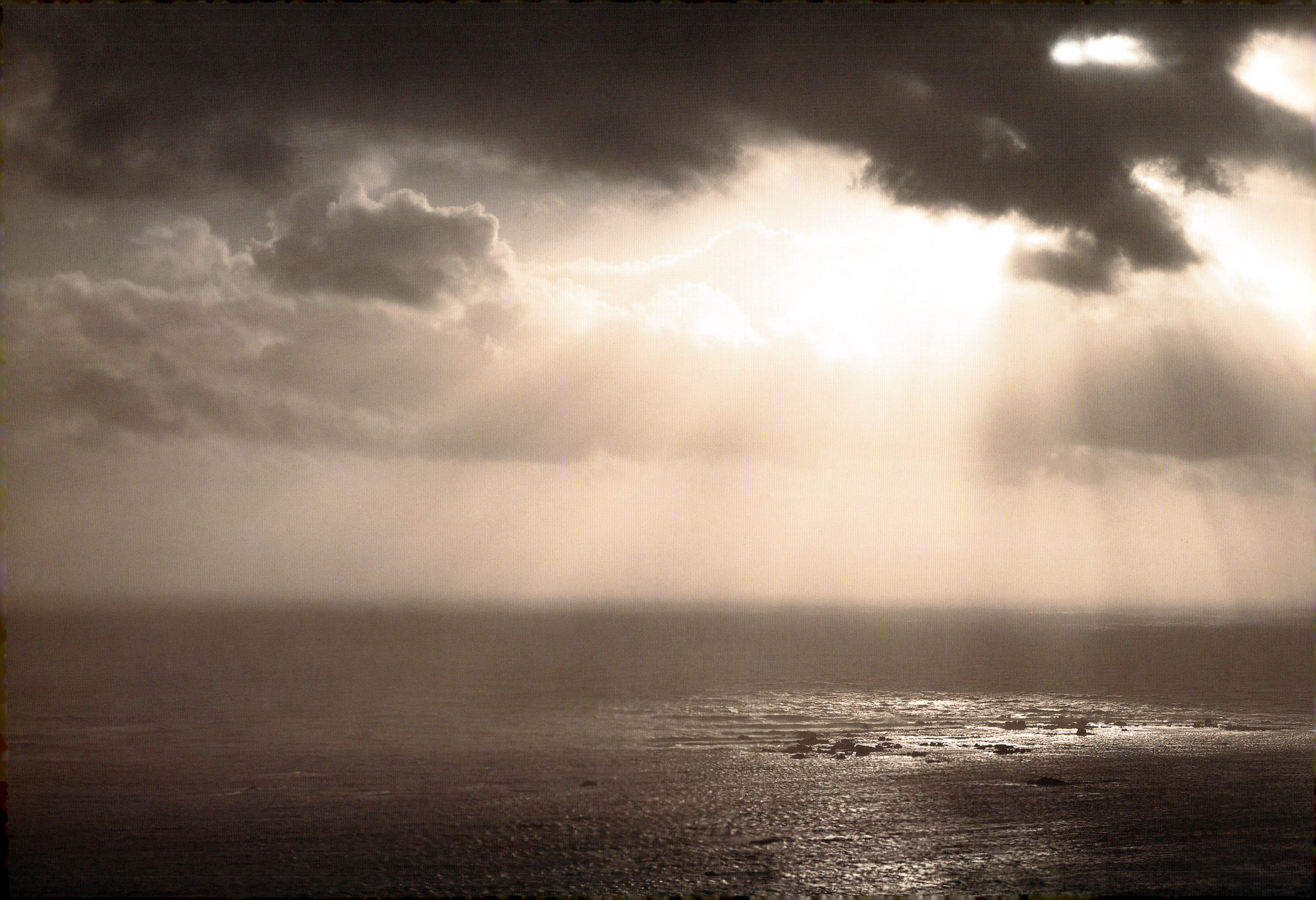

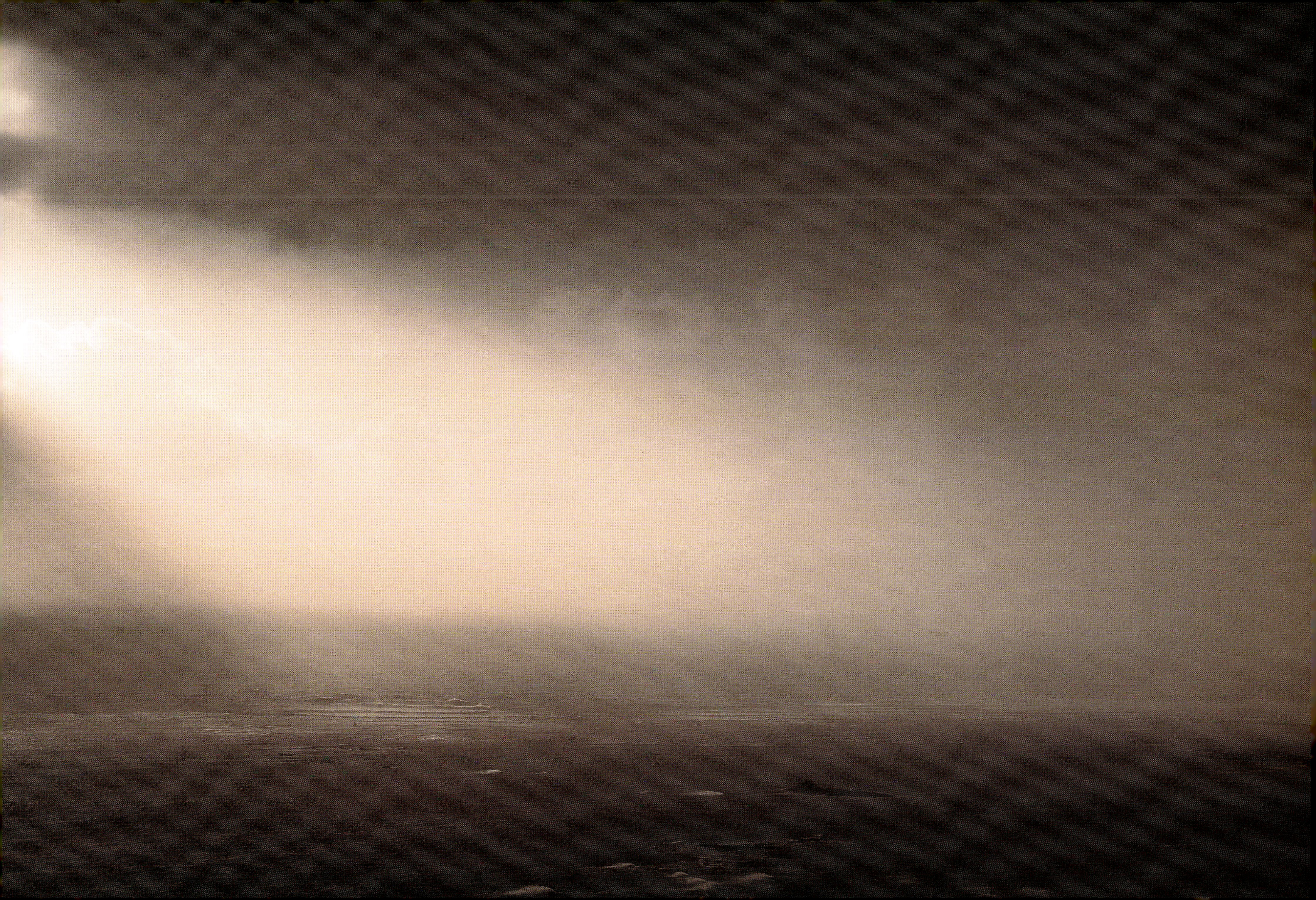

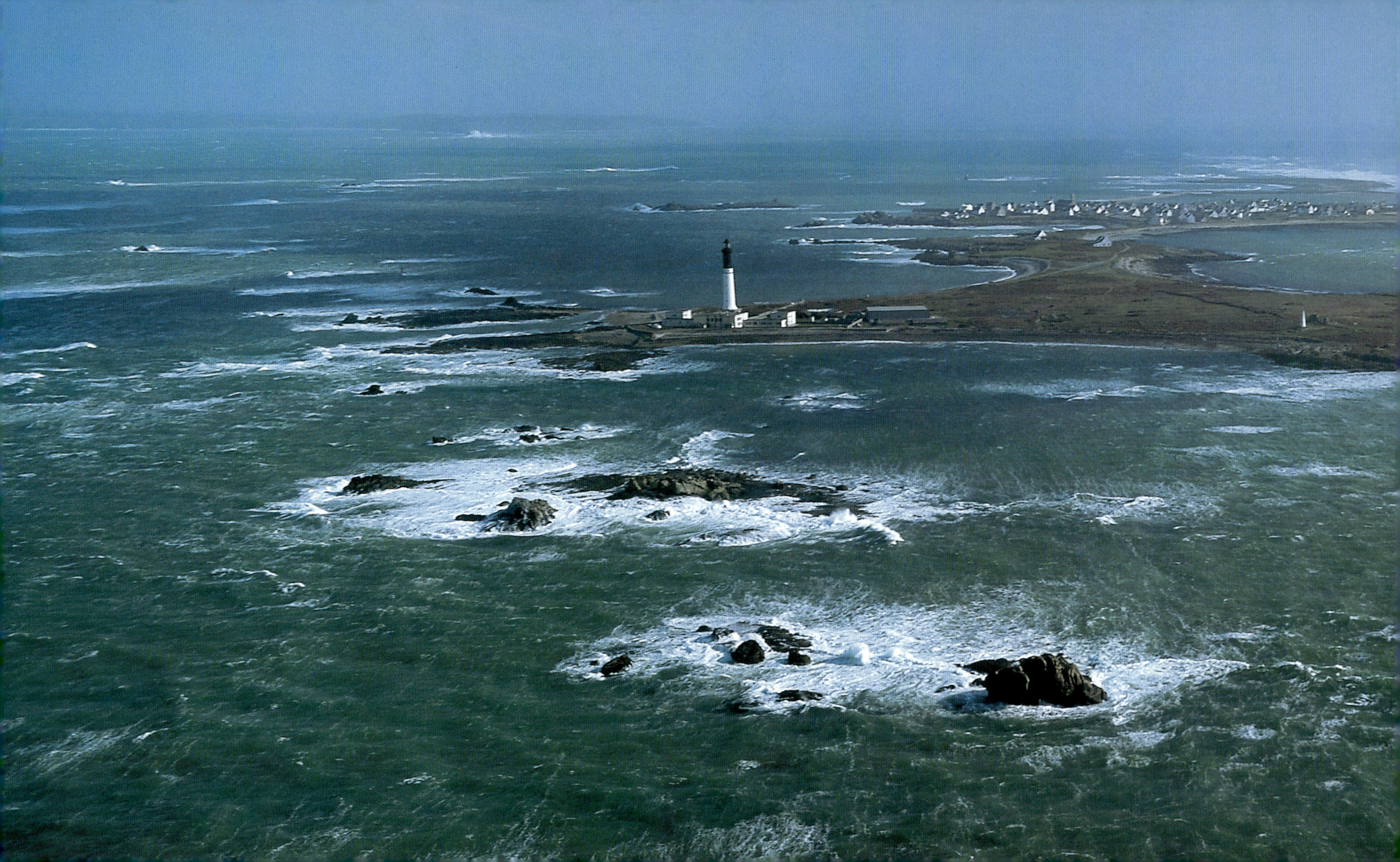

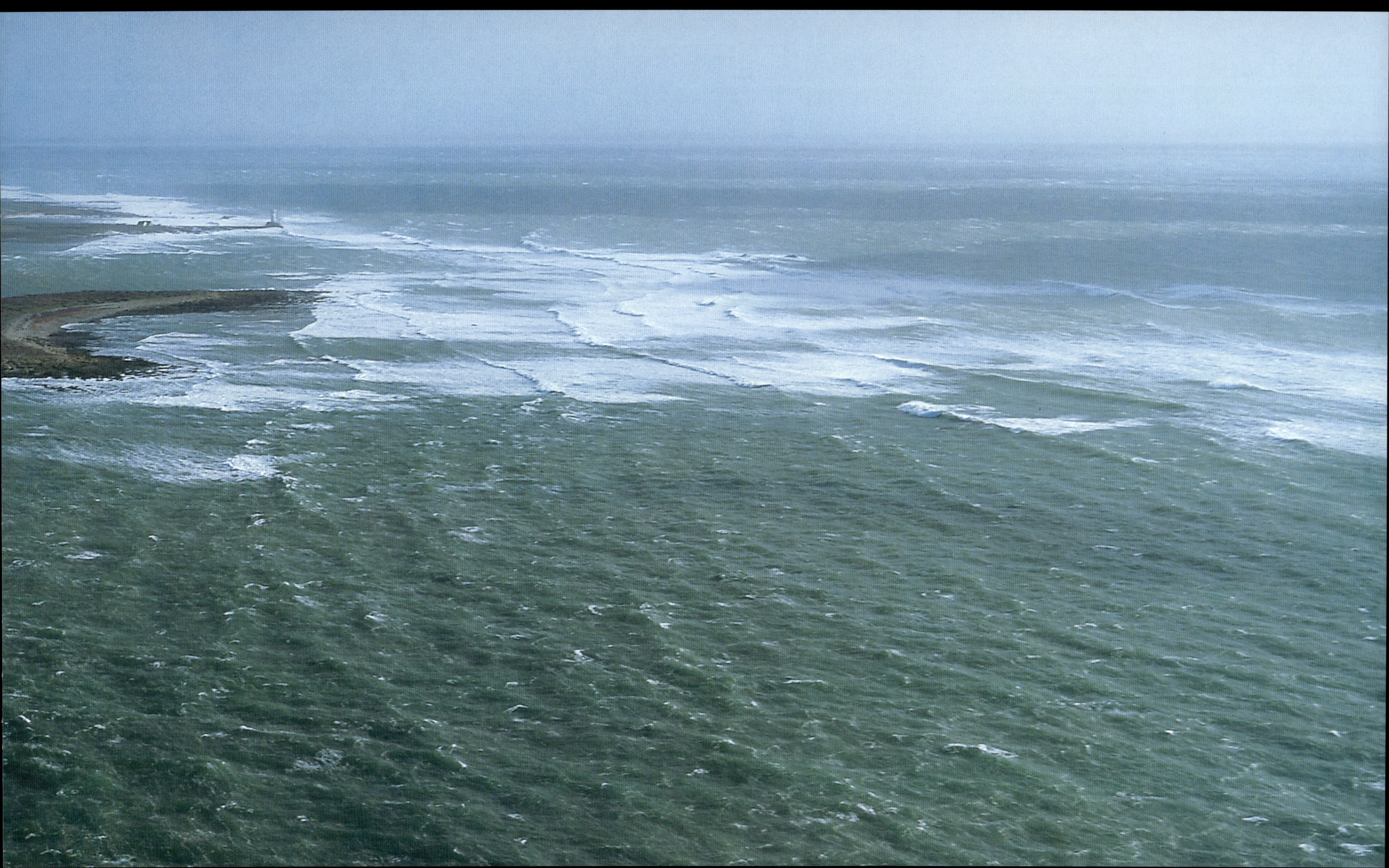

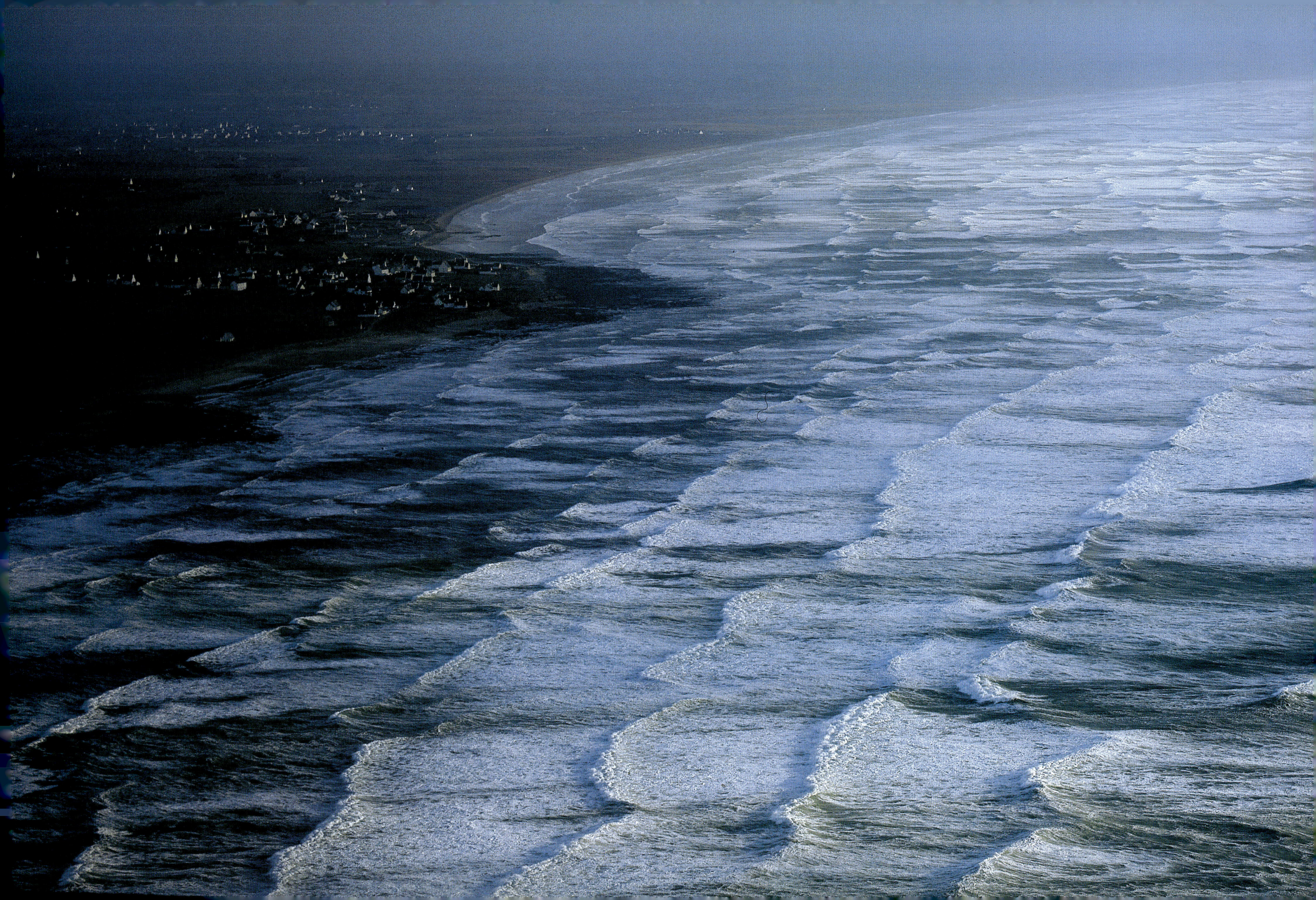

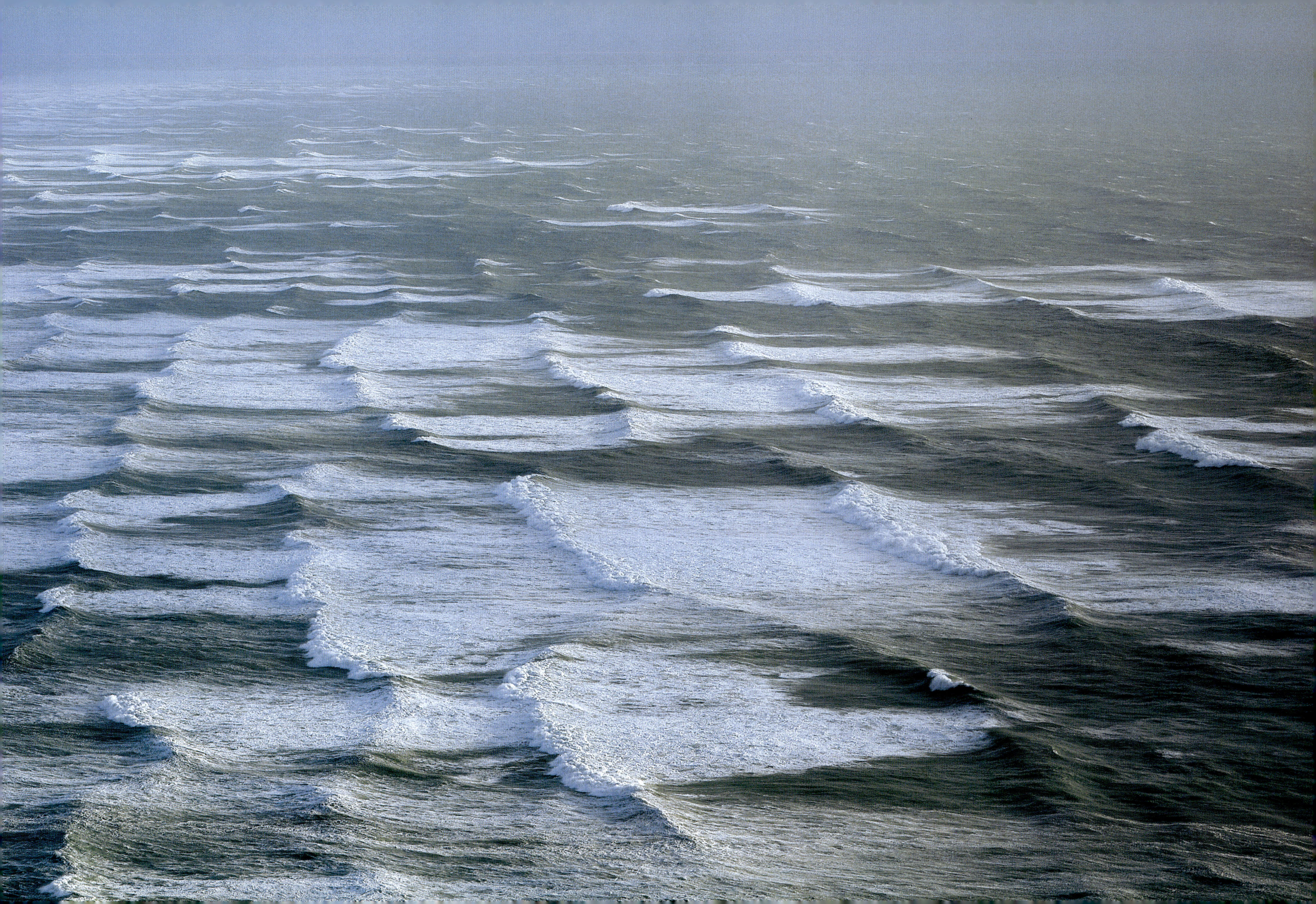

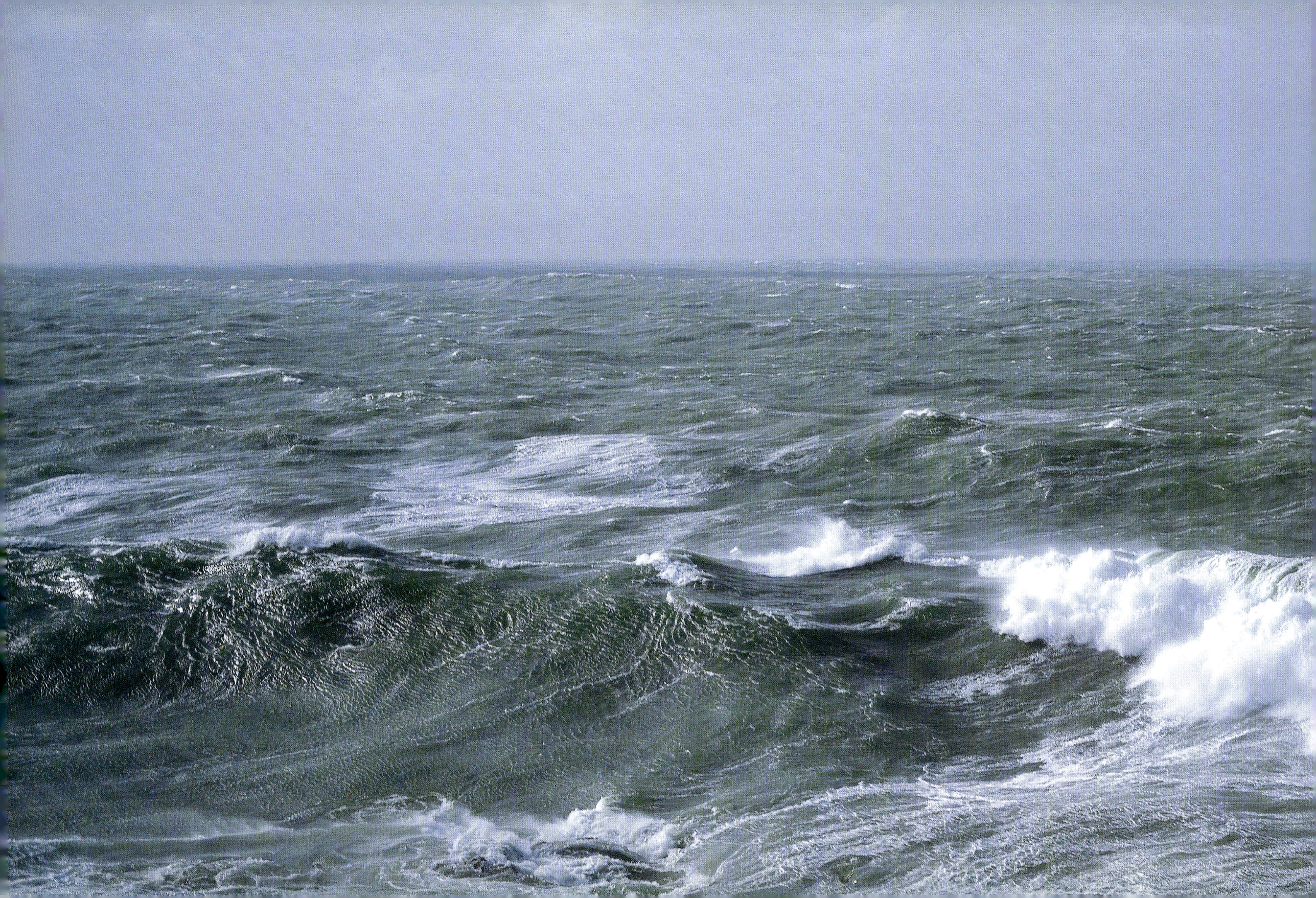

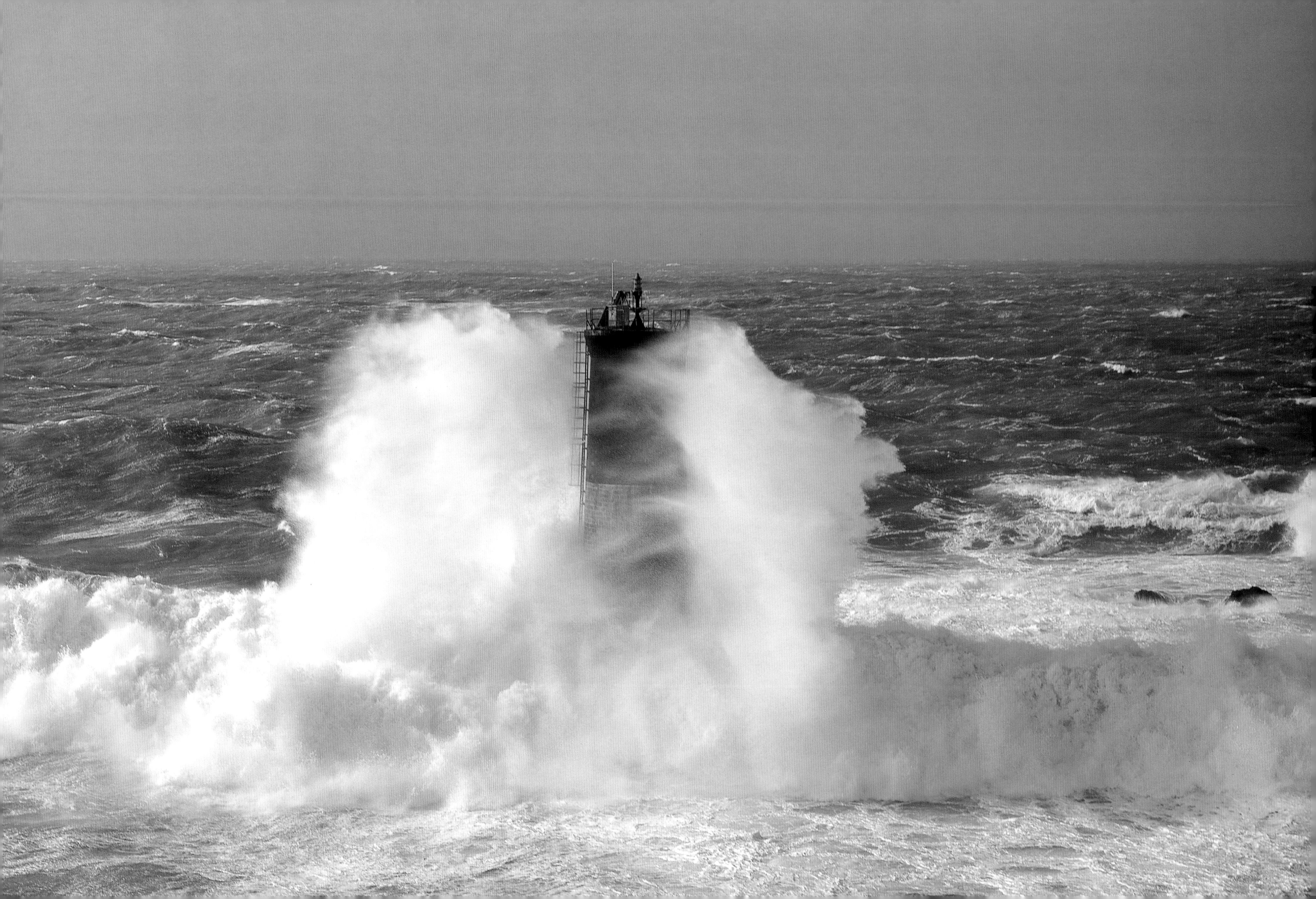

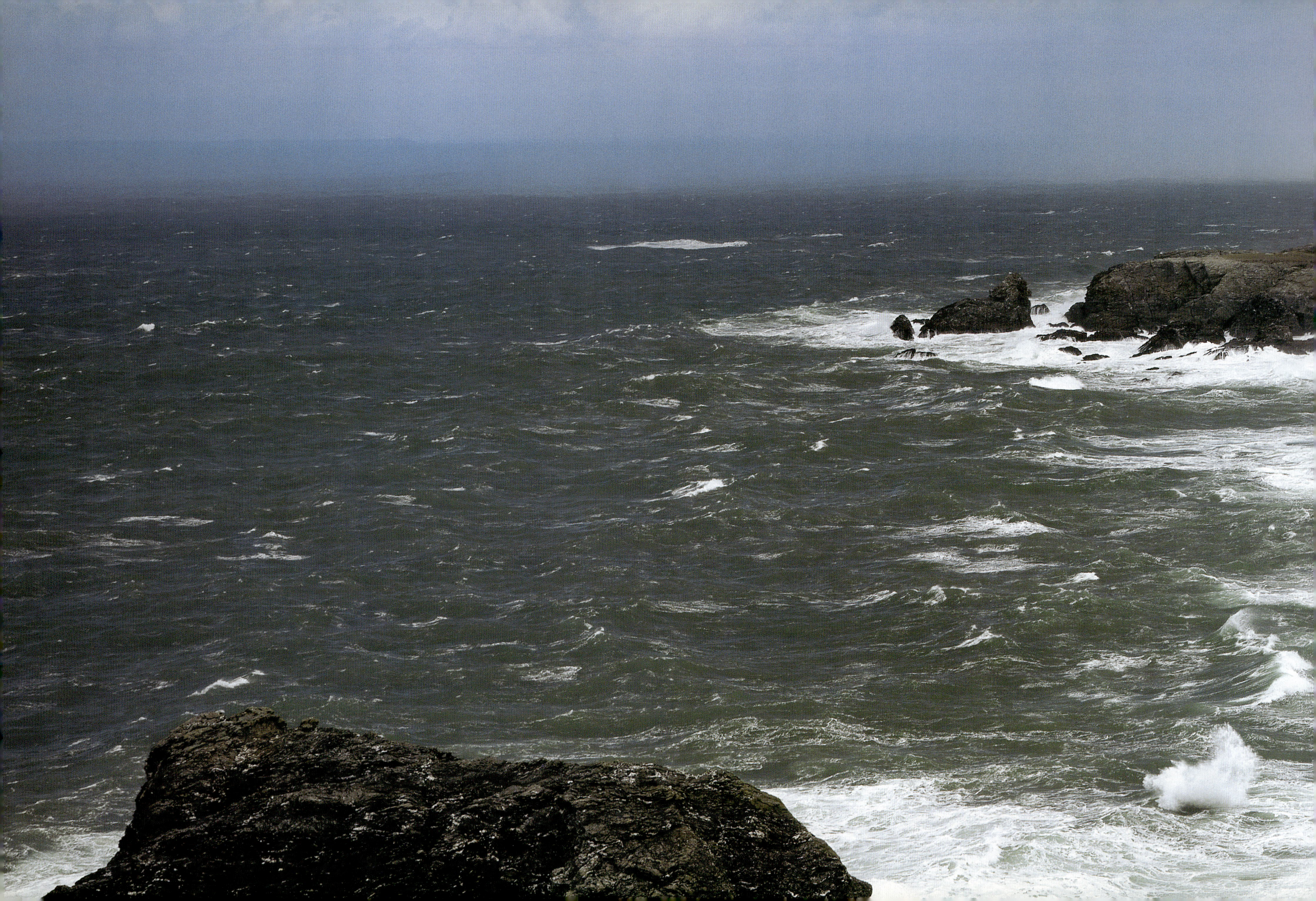

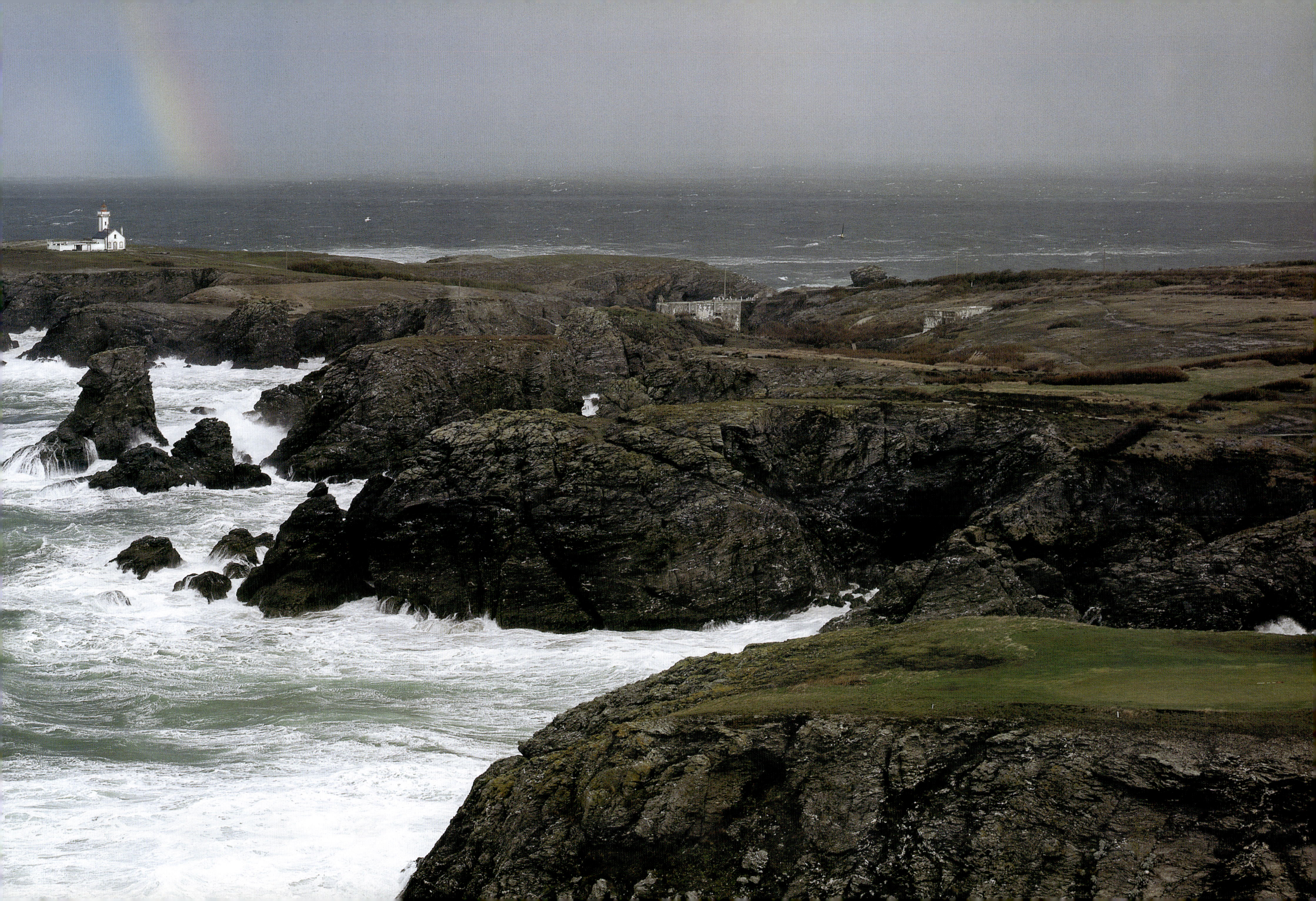

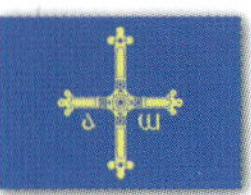

ASTURIAS·ASTURIAS

Noite Celta – 'Celtic night'. This is how the modest town of Porcia invited tourists, idling in the Cantabrian region, to come and join in the evening dances which, like the Scottish *ceilidh* or Breton *Fest Noz*, perpetuate the ancestral traditions of Asturias. The response of Oviedo, the local capital, was to found a summer festival, symbolically called *Celta Oviedo*. A wave of folk-inspired music groups began to stream to these get-togethers which became a huge success, with age-old traditions tailored for modern tastes.

It was in 1987 that Asturias, a Celtic cousin in Iberia, was first invited to take part in the Inter-Celtic Festival held each year in Lorient, Brittany. This long journey is not always understood by Celtic purists, even though it was the Pan-Celtic Festival in Killarney in Ireland which first issued an invitation to them. Those who resist their integration into the Celtic world see the port of Gijón as nothing more than the harbour town in a region with a million inhabitants wedged between green mountains and the sea, set amid some 180 miles of coastline. Backed up against highlands which rise to peaks over 6,500 feet high, the land seems to be 'forged from the almost mystical fury of the Cantabrian Sea and the magical serenity of its mountains.'

It is true that the Asturian language does not have Celtic roots. It is of Romance origin, like the Gallo language traditionally spoken in eastern Brittany. It is understood by two out of three Asturians, and spoken by one in three. The revival of interest in Asturian culture has led to the forming of *bandas* (musical groups) to perform at parades and parties. Based on a traditional repertoire of songs and drum percussion, the most daring musicians look towards the musical heritage of their Galician neighbours. The *gaita*, a bagpipe a little smaller and with a higher sound than its more famous Scottish counterpart, is now played at many of the festivals which proliferate during the summer when the Asturians, even those from the mountains, descend to dip their feet in the sea. *The Night of the Celts*, a half-classical, half-traditional piece composed by Ramón Prada, now reverberates under the stars until even the starfish dance!

The connections that give the Asturian shores their Celtic roots are ancient ones indeed. In the 5th and 6th centuries, Celts from Wales and Cornwall, fleeing the Angles and Saxons, crossed the sea and travelled beyond Brittany, heading south towards other distant lands. Many landed in the estuaries of Galicia, but some weighed anchor in the creeks of San Salvador, north of Oviedo and the mountains that bar the way to the hinterland like a natural fortress.

Archaeological excavations are now turning up pre-Roman remains. There are no standing stones, but there are sun cross symbols which are evidence of Celtic rituals and ceremonies. These feed the nostalgia of the bards of the banks and fields. Their songs and stories reflect the melancholy of the Portuguese *saudades* and *fado* traditions, the melancholy music which came down from the Tagus and rolls like the waves of the sea.

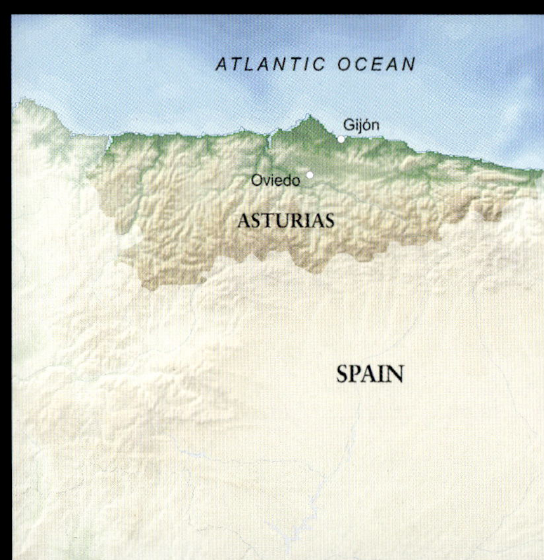

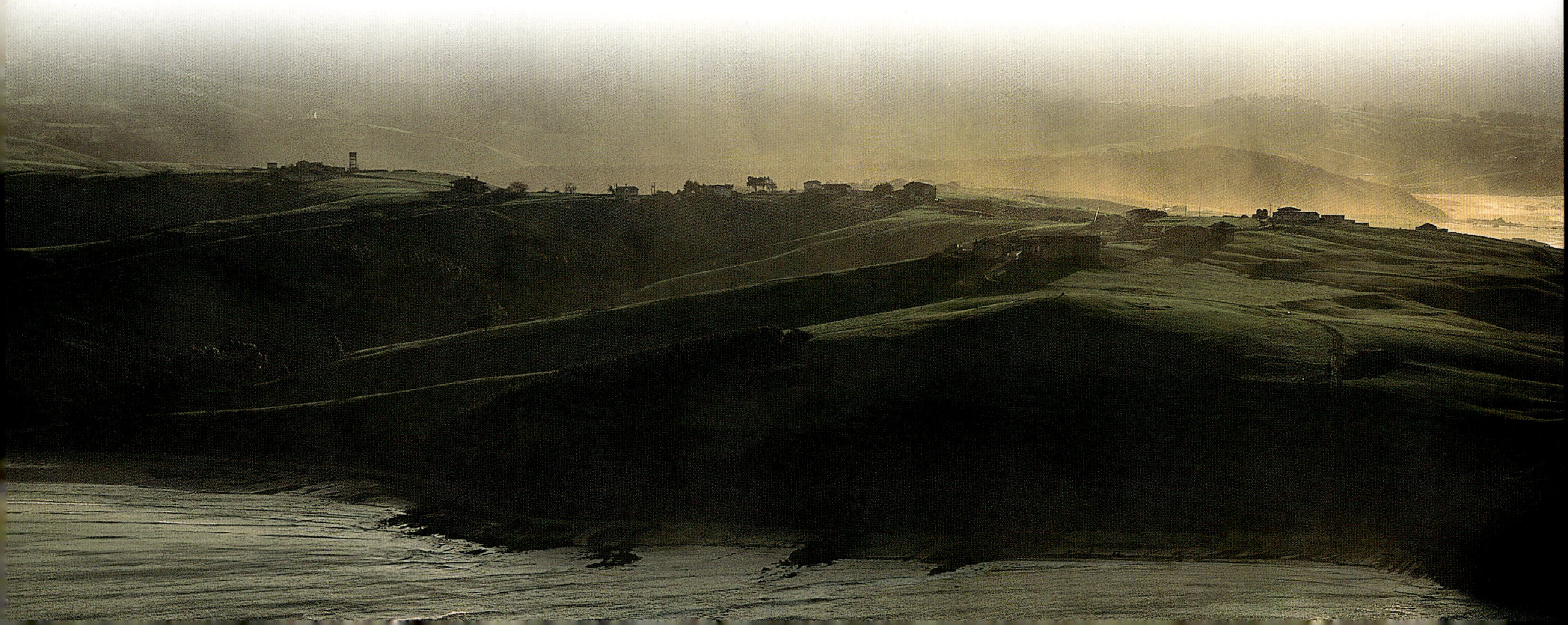

Opposite: *España Verde* – Green Spain. A fitting name for the land of Cantabria, Asturias and Galicia, united by mountains and sea.

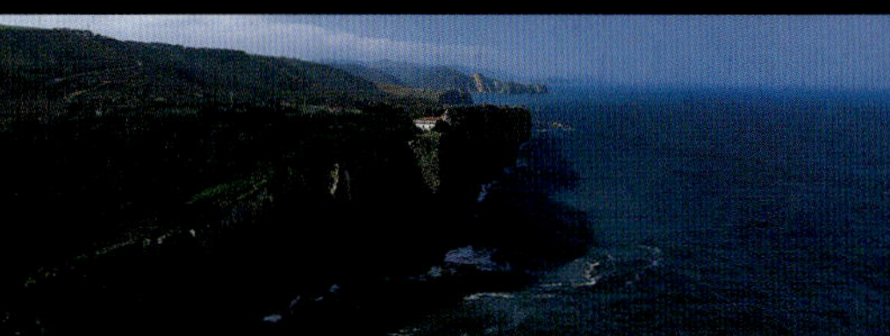

A BALCONY OVER THE SEA
Like the sheer rocks overhanging the Costa Verde, the whole coastline of Asturias resembles these cliffs near San Emeterio. It forms a 150-mile balcony stretching to the Galician border.

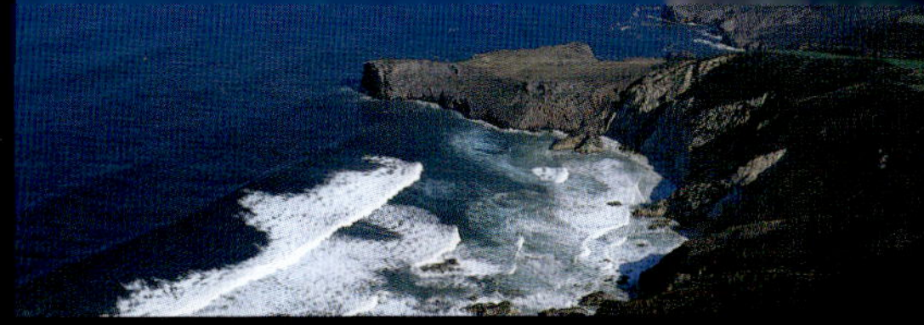

WILD COAST
You never get tired of Oyambre. Its headland, a green mass planted like a spearhead, bars the horizon. Just a few miles away, beyond the Punta de la Barrera and the Tina Mayor estuary, is the start of the Asturian sierra and its wild, majestic coast.

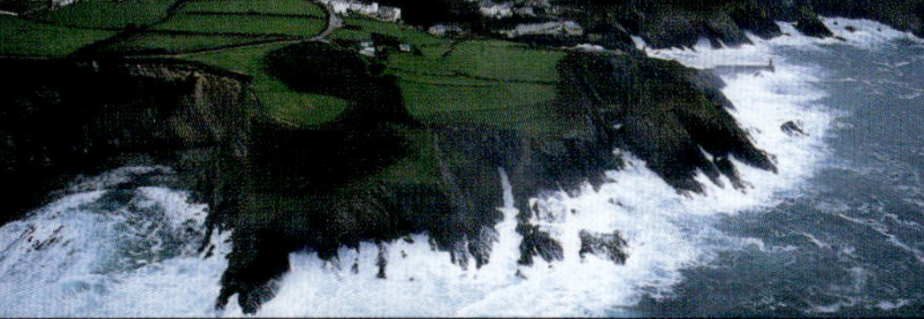

THE LAST RESERVE
The Oyambre nature reserve, near San Vicente de la Barquera, offers a foretaste of the splendours of Asturias that lie beyond the Tina Mayor estuary. It is the start of a panoramic coastal route.

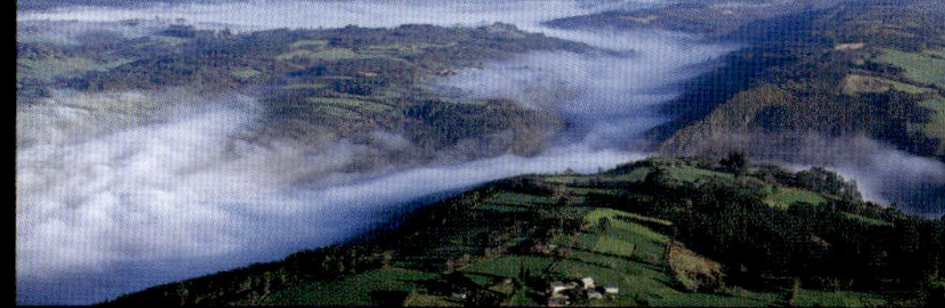

A MAGICAL SPOT
A house on a rock – far from the sea, the spray, the waves and storms, but not from the winds from the Cantabrian Sea which swirl in gusts before rushing into the sierra. Everything ahead is blue. Behind, everything is green.

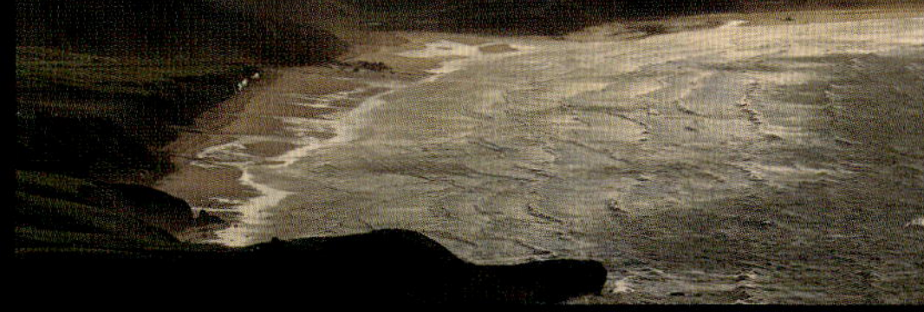

GOLDEN SAND
There is more than a mile of fine golden sand, between Punta Lumbreras and its wild headland: this is the famous beach of Oyambre. It is the perfect approach to Asturias and is popular with all those who love the tranquillity of the Cantabrian coast.

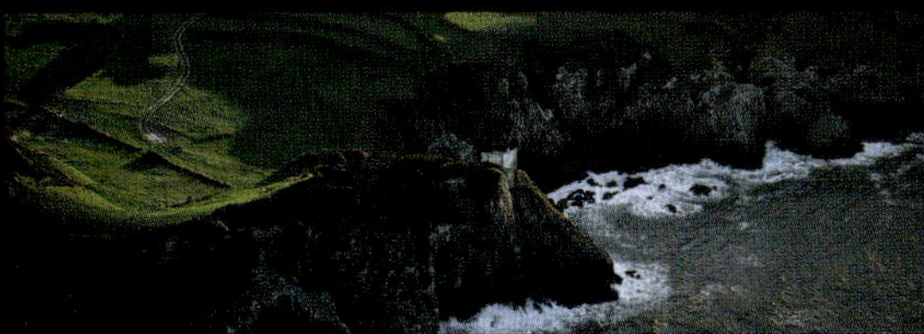

ROMAN REMAINS
The cape of Atalaya: one of the three headlands between La Caridad and Porcia, where salmon travel upstream in June and July. Nearby Viavélez is a popular site with archaeologists. It contains *castros*, fortified buildings from the Roman period.

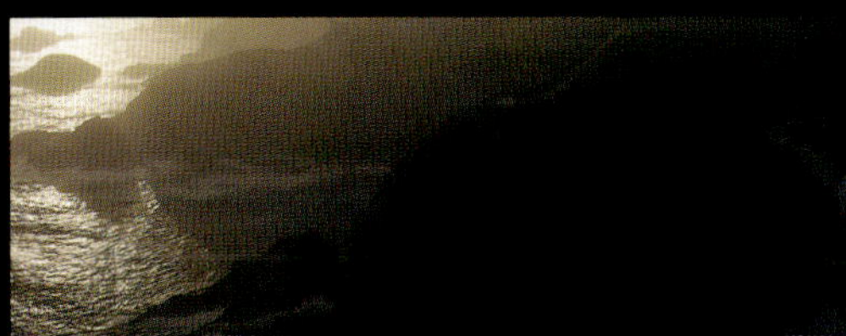

IBERIAN CELTS
Cabo Vidio: a mountain in the sea. Its lighthouse shines for up to 25 nautical miles. Driven out by the Angles and Saxons from the 5th century onwards, a few Celts from Wales and Cornwall landed here, having bypassed Brittany: they became the first Iberian Celts in Asturias.

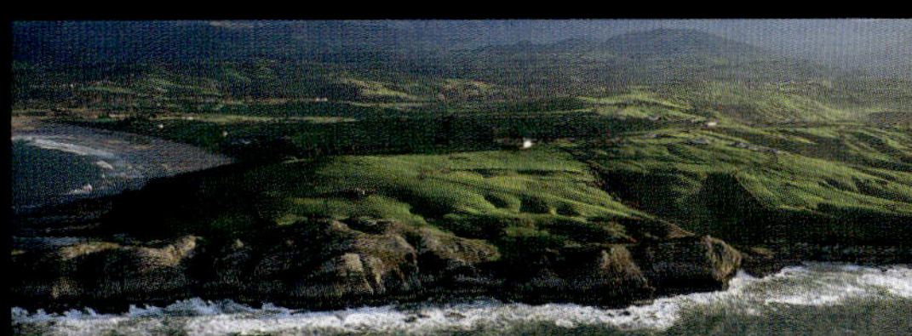

A CARPET OF GREEN
The Cabo d'Oyambre once again. When the sun shines at its brightest, the grass looks like a green carpet. The sea shimmers with an infinite variety of blues, but turns to soft jade where it merges with the sand of the *calas*, *penas* and other creeks.

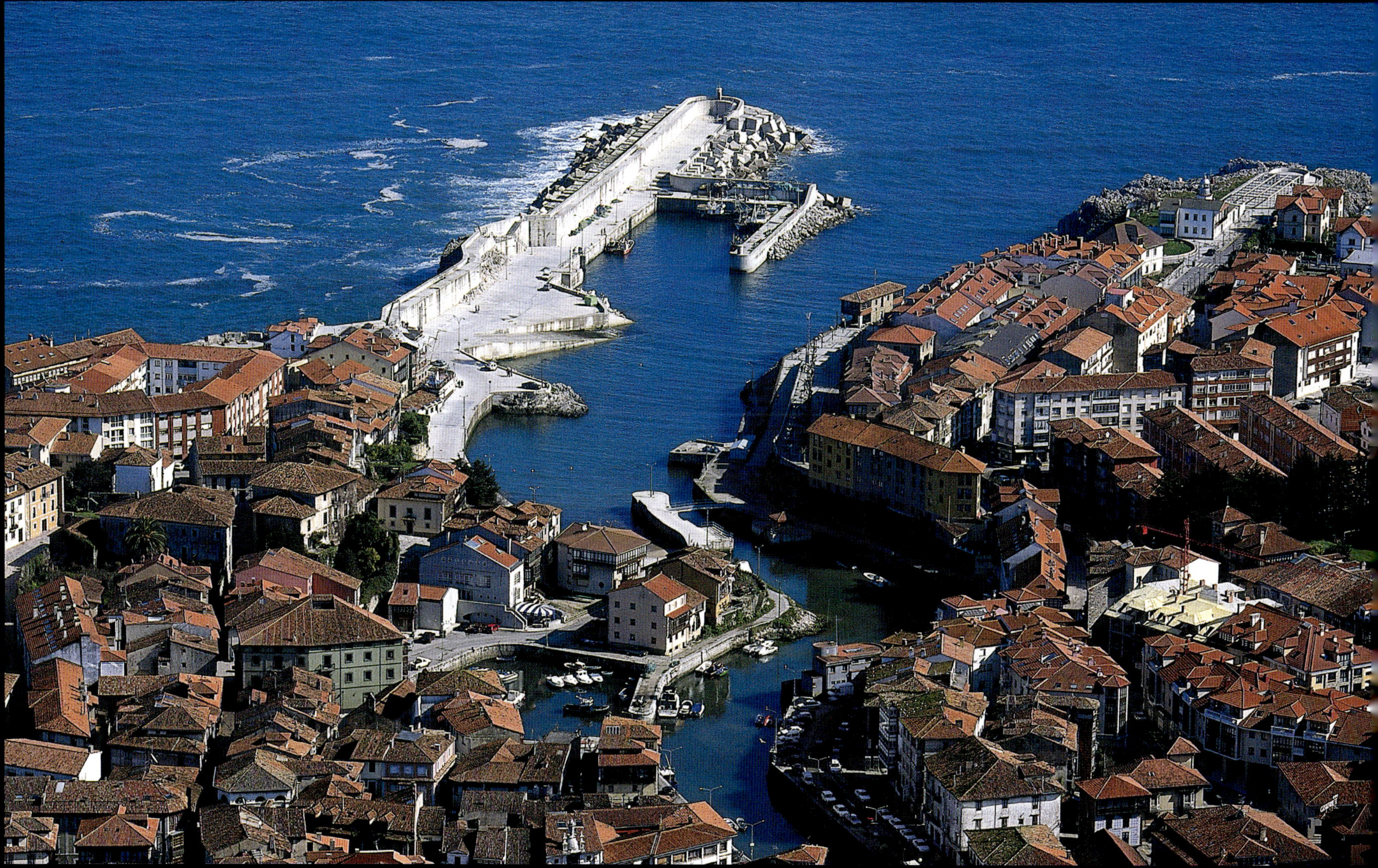

A WELCOMING HARBOUR
Llanes was the largest town in Asturias in the Middle Ages. It is a lovely boat trip from Puertu Chicu, the 'little port', down to the beach of Sablon The town is bordered downstream by the foothills of the Sierra del Cuera

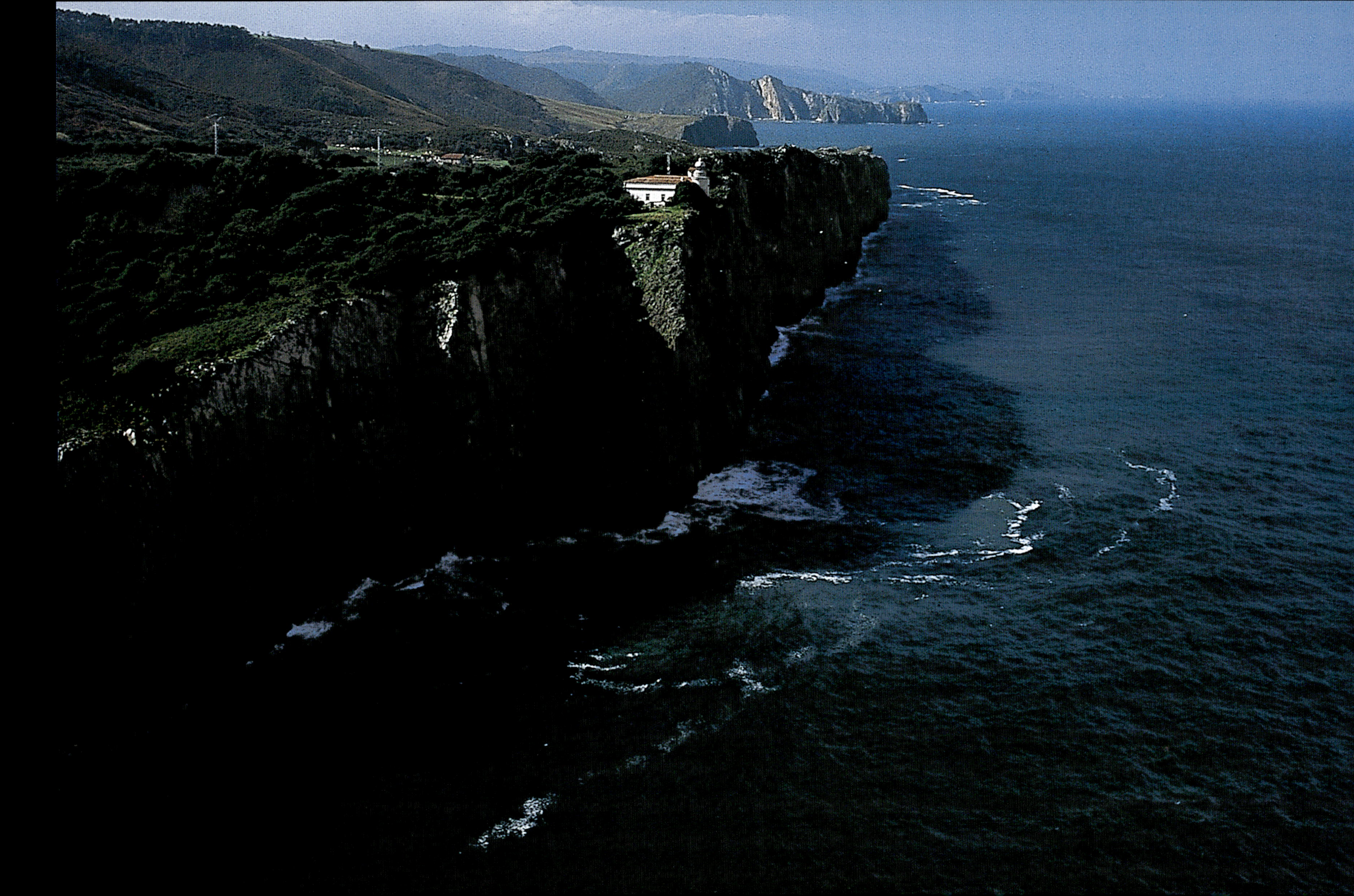

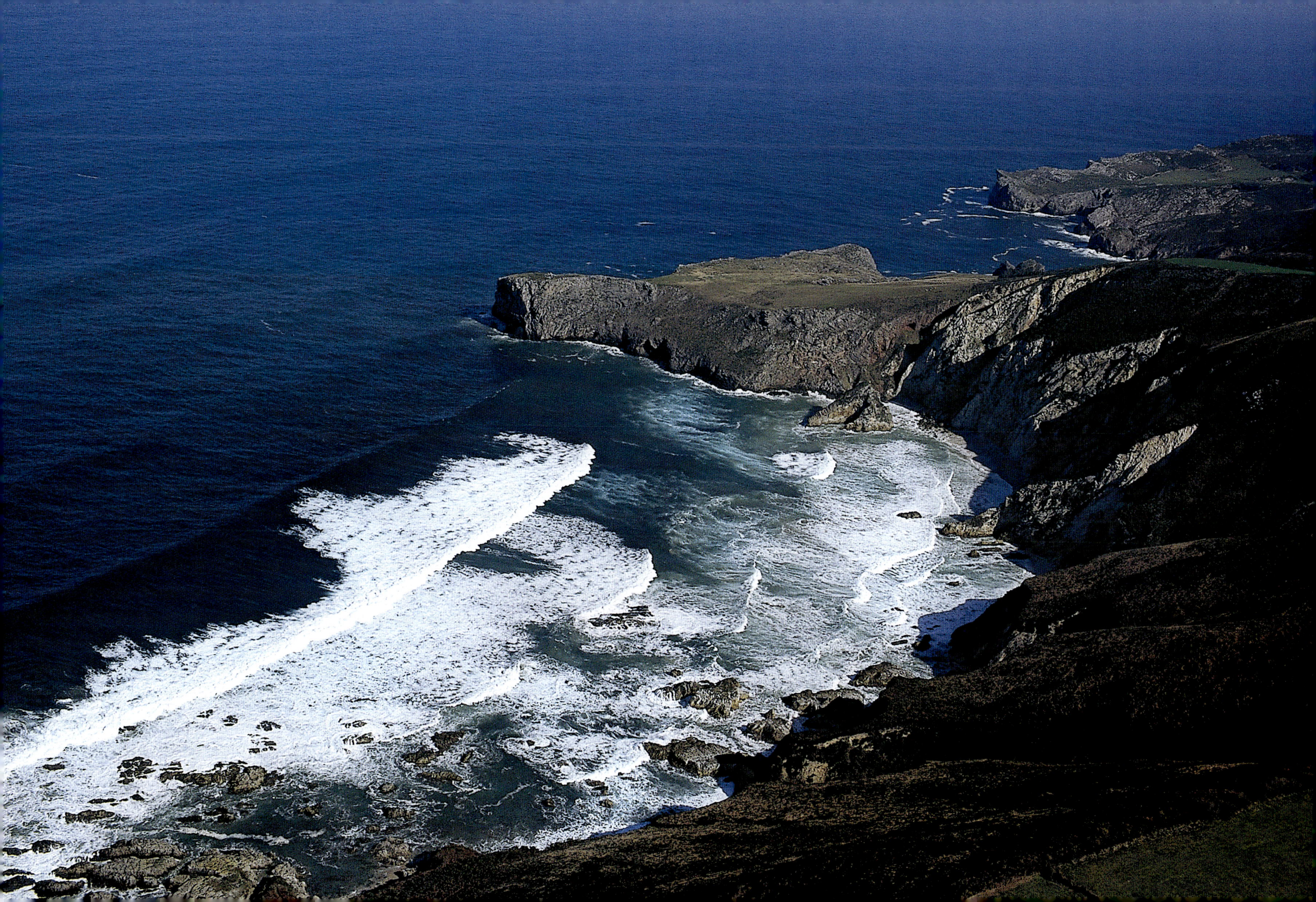

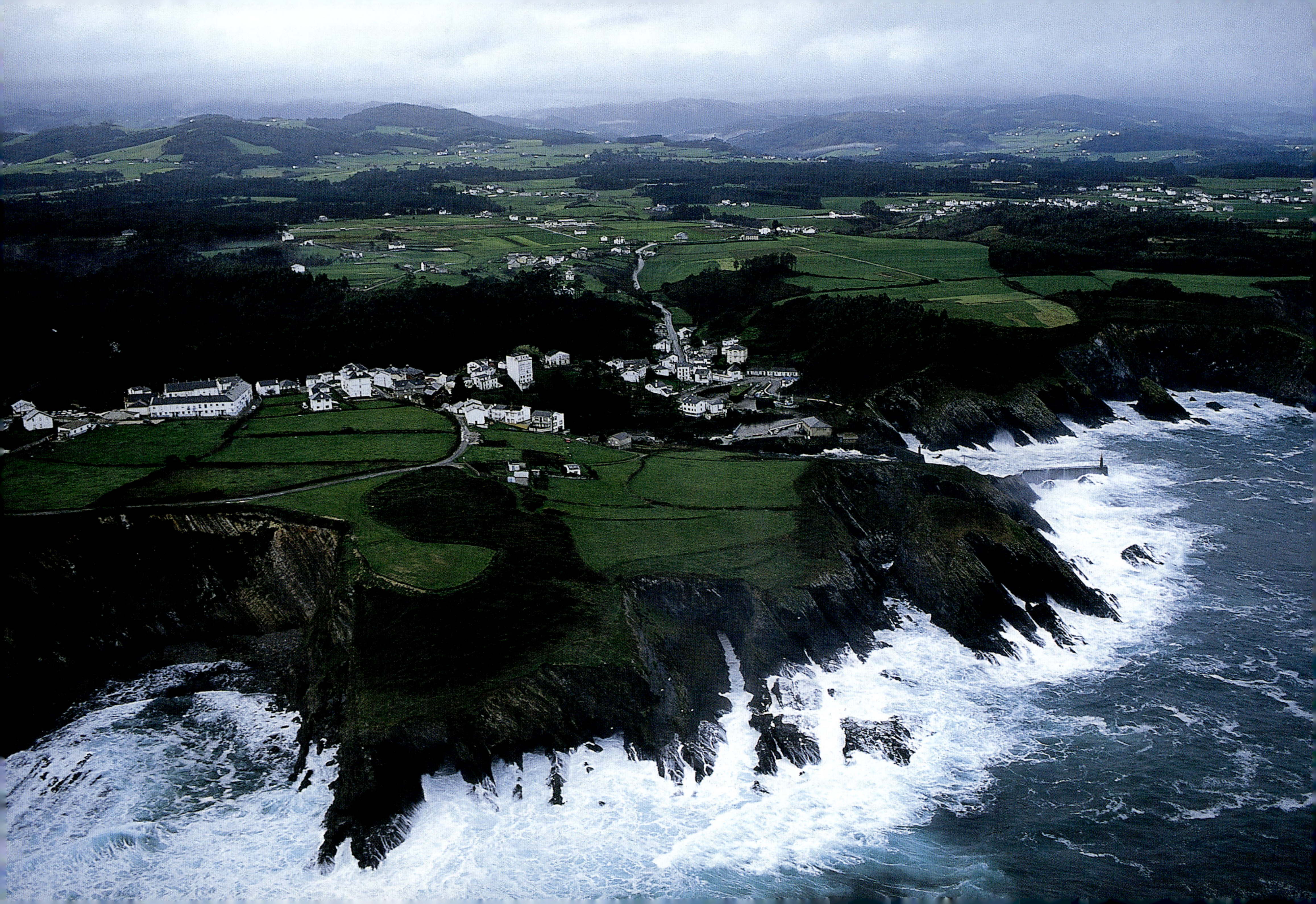

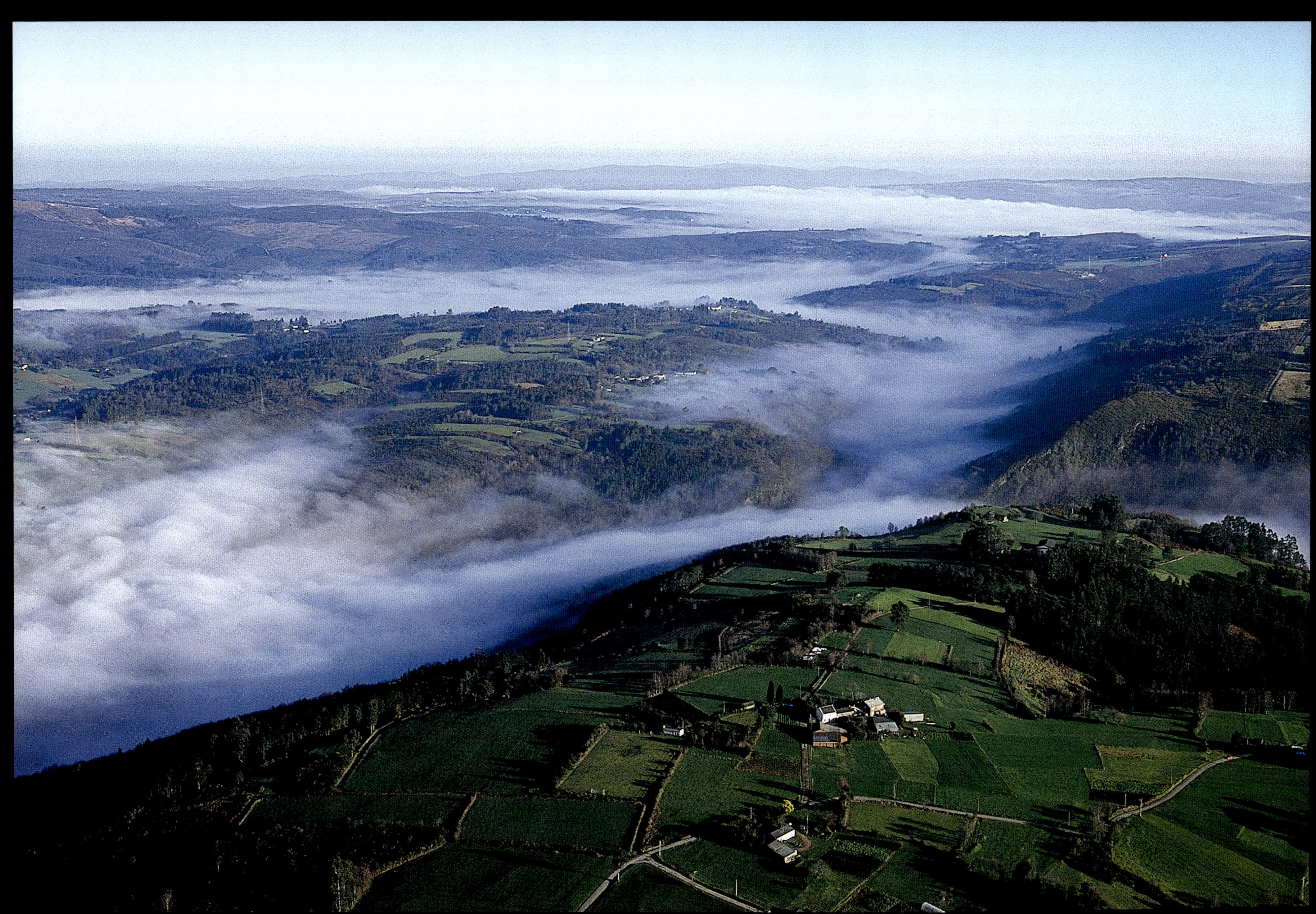

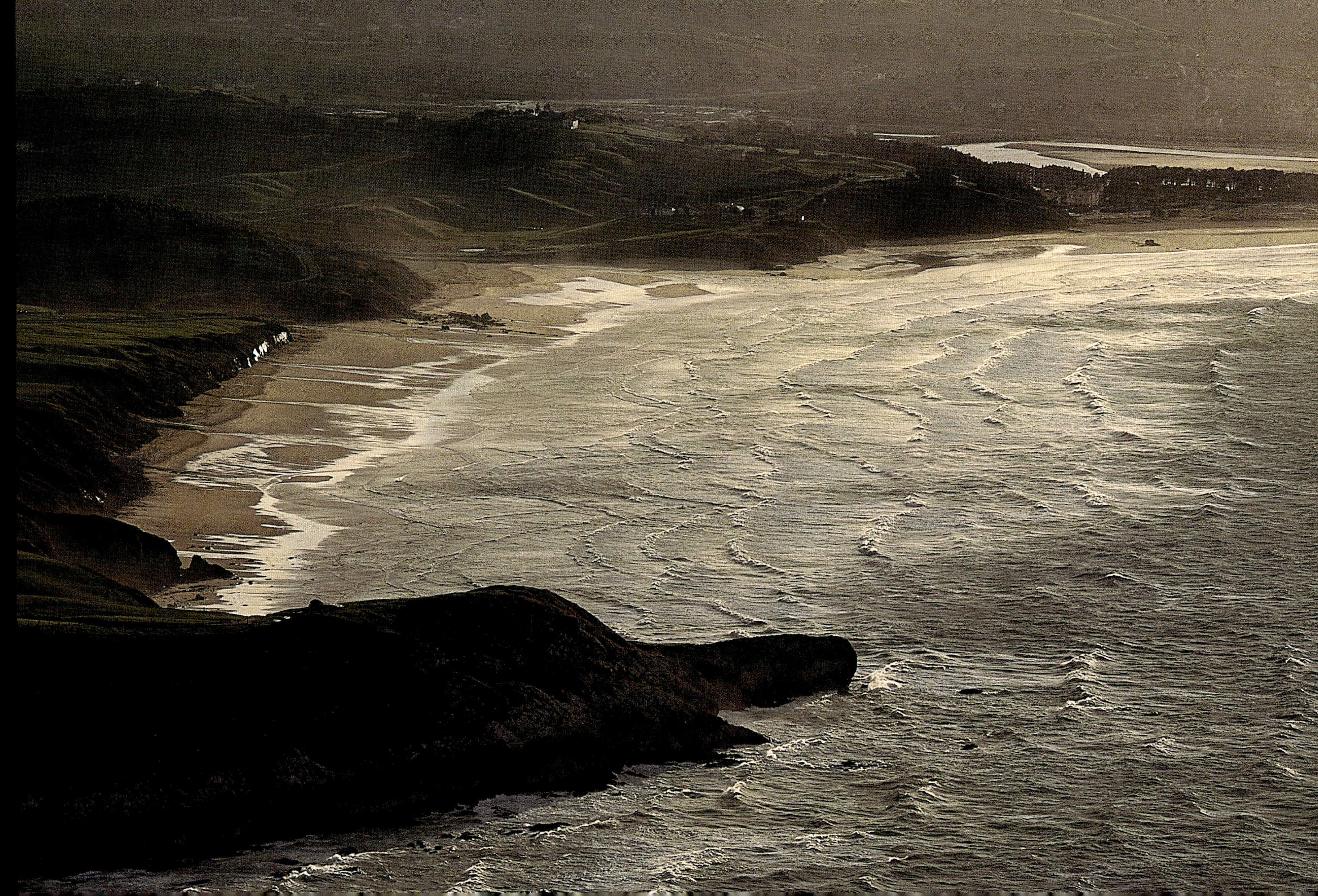

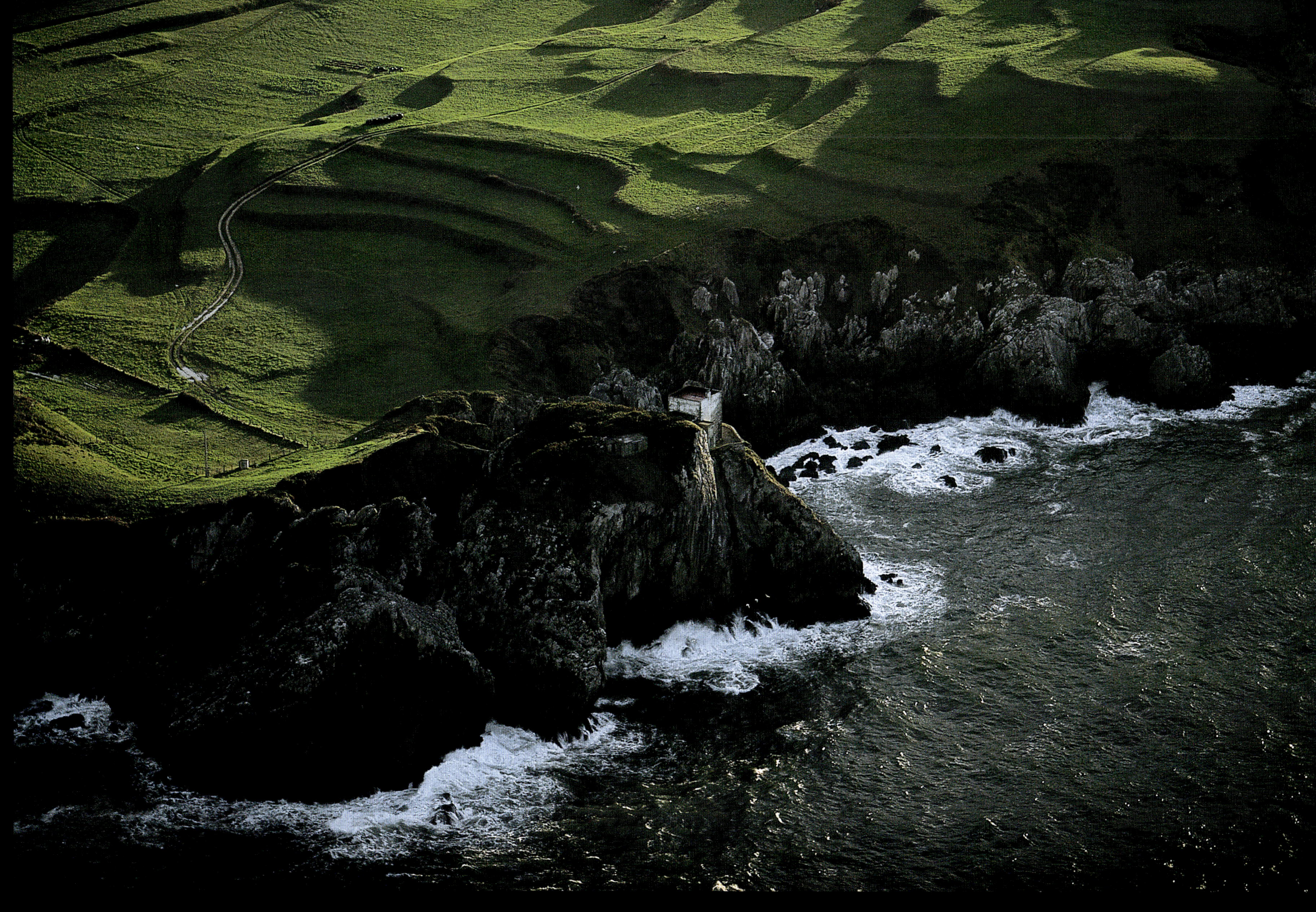

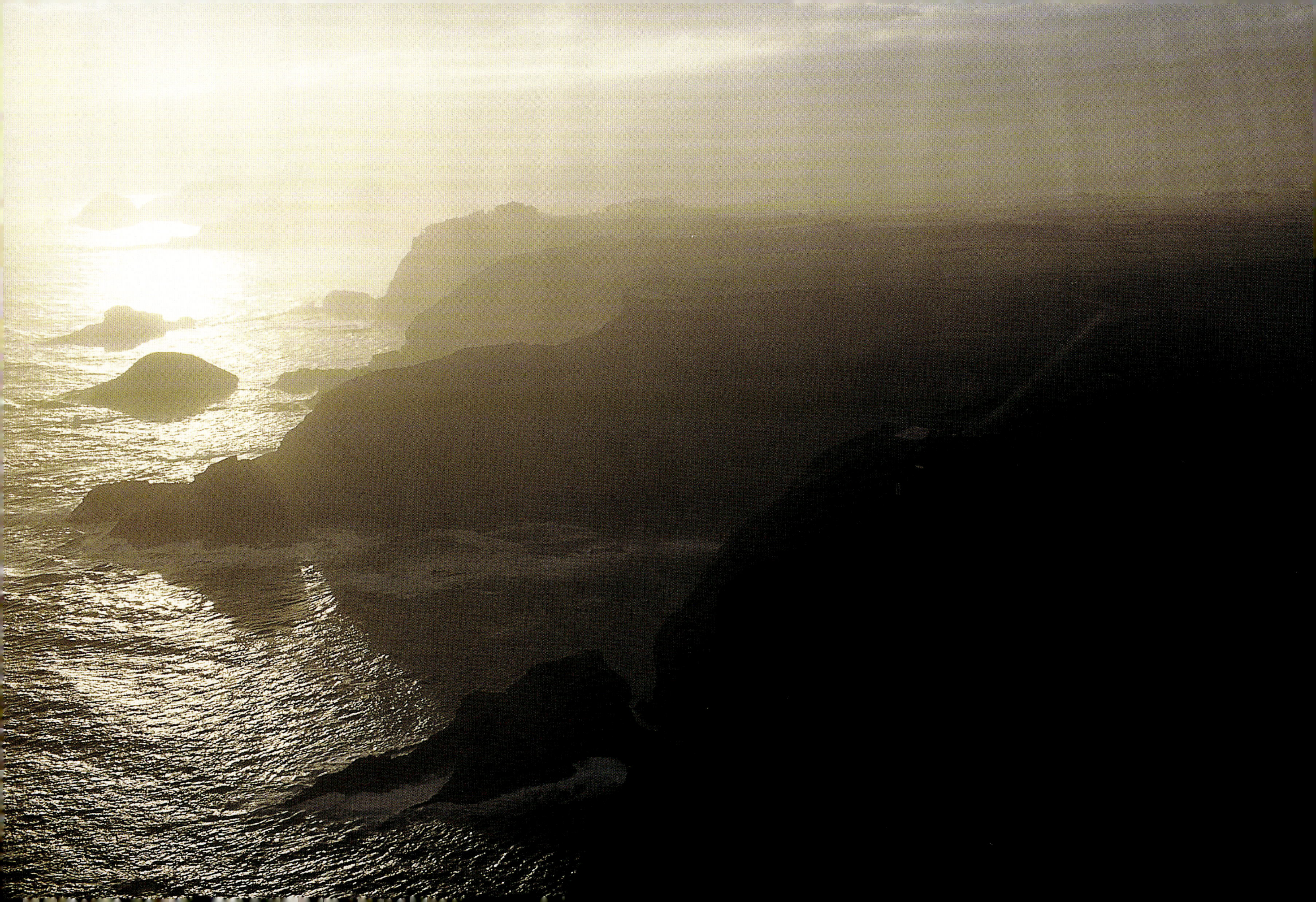

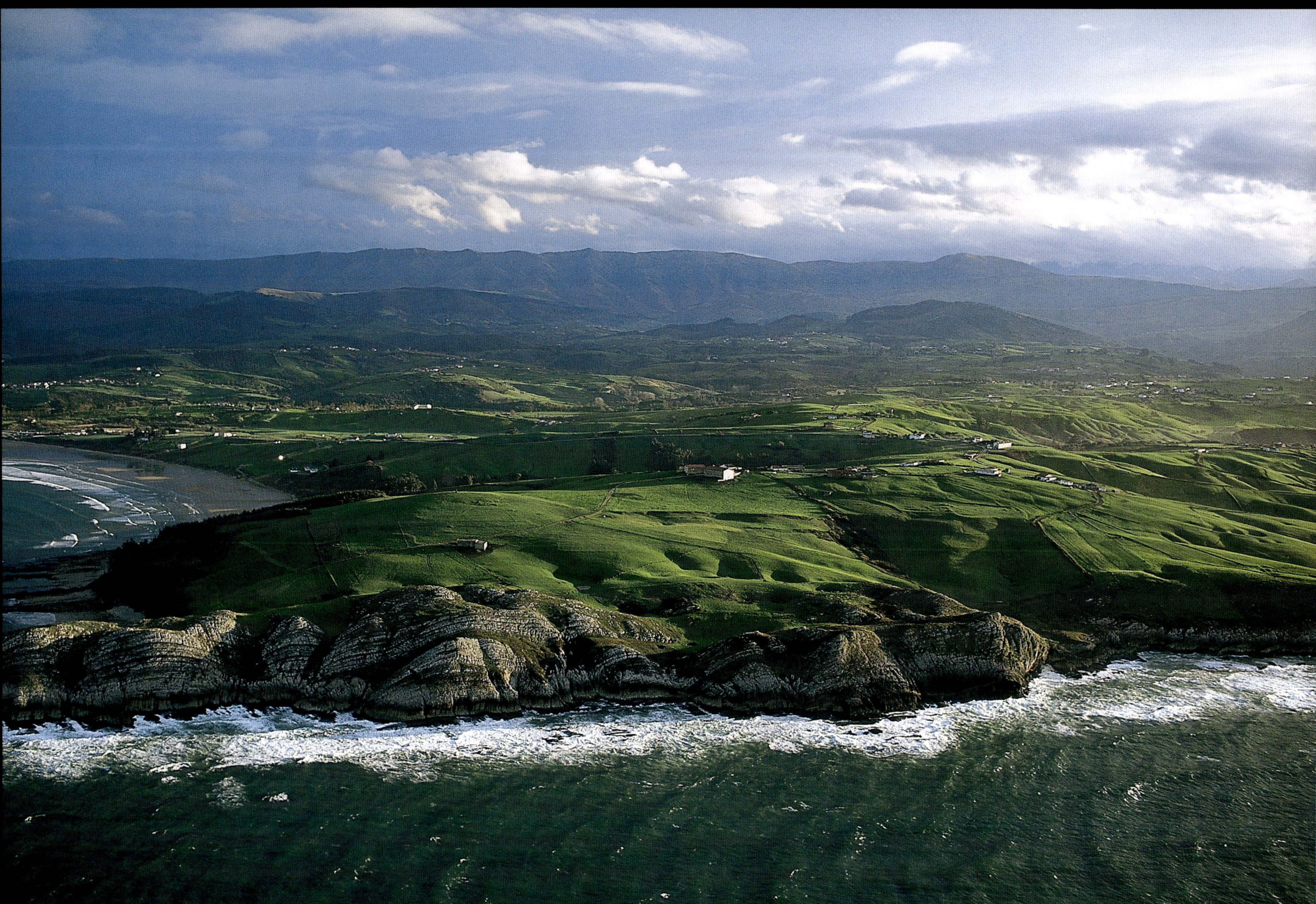

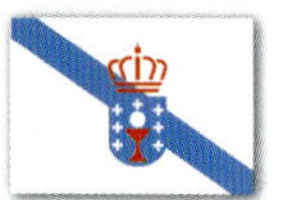

GALICIA · GALICIA

BRITONIA. Around the remains of a fifteen-centuries-old bishopric, this is the most northerly point of Galicia, its own Land's End, set to music by both the Breton Dan Ar Braz and the local bard, Carlos Nuñez. More than the *Finis Terrae* of the ancients, it recalls Brittany's wild and tormented *Penn Ar Bed* (literally 'the head of the world').

It was against these rocks, sheltered from some estuary, that monks fleeing the invading Angles and Saxons for the same reasons which led the Britons of Wales and Cornwall to Brittany, led a makeshift squadron of refugees in an unprecedented exodus by sea. This tormented shale coast has a prophetic name: Costa da Morte, the 'Coast of Death'. Many have been broken on it. As if the requiem of the centuries was not enough, more recently its coastline was devastated by a viscous oil slick from a damaged tanker, the ill-fated *Prestige*.

Today, Galicia is forgetting the nightmares of the past. It thrills to the exploits of its football club, called Celta de Vigo. Yes, there is a Celta in Vigo, in the same way as there is a Celtic in Glasgow. And in Boston, the American city of the Celts, there is a basketball version, the Celtics.

Galicia closely resembles Brittany. Its steep cliffs facing the sea are dotted with megaliths as old as the standing stones of Carnac or the circle of Stonehenge. Its inlets, a short distance from the plains of Lugo, recall the coast of Brittany. And its bard, also from Vigo, is popular across the world like a timeless messenger in the guise of a rock star. With his hair hanging loose, Carlos Nuñez, the pilgrim of Galicia, blows a Celtic storm across the continents. Nothing and nobody resists him with the wind at his heels: neither his Galician cousins who ran aground after being exiled on the Rio de la Plata, in Argentina, nor even the Gaelic community of Japan, withdrawn into its pubs selling their dark, frothy Guinness marked with a shamrock, who welcome him in a state of grace on St Patrick's night.

In Spain, the beautiful women of Andalusia swoon in front of the matador. In Galicia, they fall in front of the *gaitero* or pipe-player. The Celtic people recognize in the son of Vigo the only player capable of bringing together in a melodious trilogy – *The Three Pipers* – the majestic bagpipes of Scotland, the Uilleann pipes of Ireland and the gaita of Galicia. Fire, water and earth.

Like Kenneth White, the Scottish poet and minstrel of the isles, living on his hill by the sea in the Léon area of Brittany, Carlos Nuñez has set up camp on a headland reaching out into the immensity of the *Mare Nuestru* (the Atlantic). Sometimes he dreams of seeing the waves part and the mythical town of Ys re-emerge... With his music and triskelion symbols on stage, and inspired by the ancient bardic tradition, Nuñez has given Galicia and its three million inhabitants (plus one million exiles) a place of honour at the table of the Celtic nations. In his wake, Susana Seivane, a red-haired siren, adds a touch of glamour which lightens people's spirits.

Those who, rucksack on back, take the road to Santiago de Compostela to kneel before St James, must also take the time to cross this ancient land where at nightfall the souls of the *Kallaikoi* (those who live among the stones) rise up.

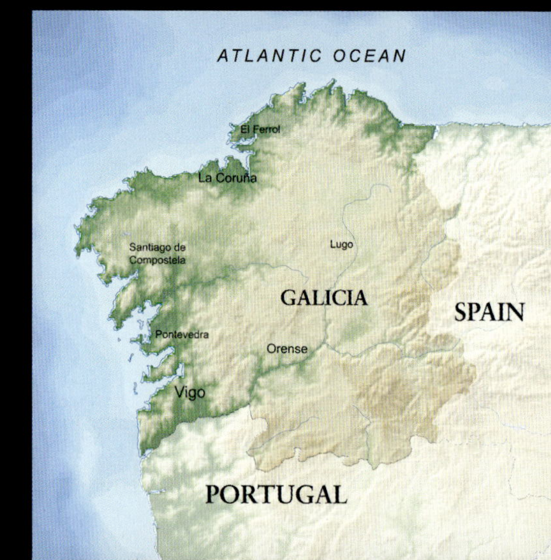

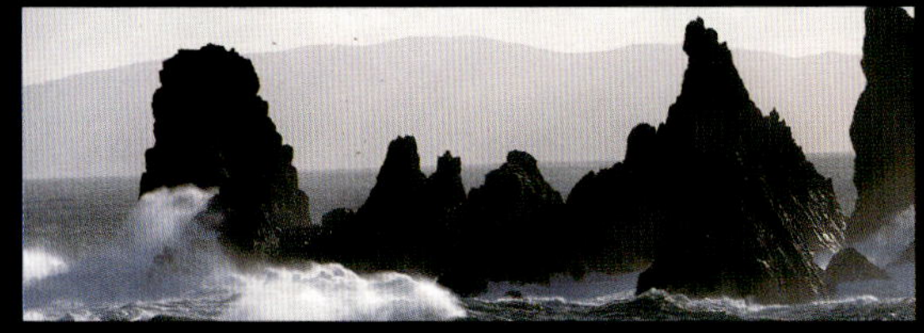

THE CAPE OF HELL

To navigate these waters, you need to know each rock as well as the lines on your hand. This is how fishermen talk of Cabo Ortegal, in the far north, and of its needles of rock emerging from the waters – a geographical feature shared by all the Celtic lands.

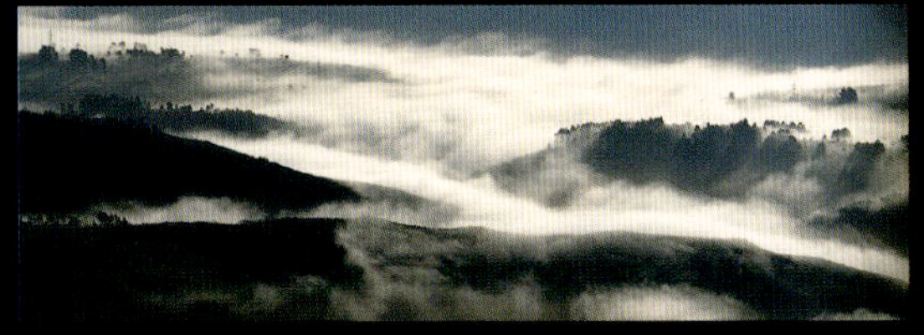

A VIEW OF ETERNITY

Blue sky, the sun peeping over the clouds, mountain tops and the sea below. As in its neighbouring cousin, Asturias, golden streaks, green summits and steep valleys, dark rocks and deep blue water compose a picture of eternity.

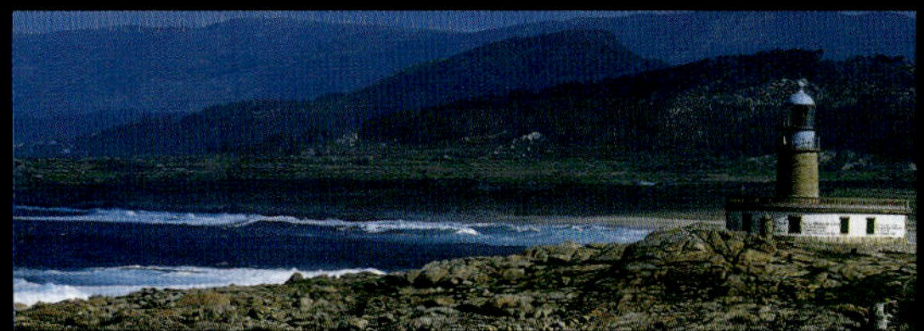

THE POETS OF NARIGA

This is the birthplace of Eduardo Pondal, the greatest Galician poet. Above the plunging Punta de Nariga stands the hermitage of Nosa Senora do Faro, bringing its divine blessing to the place.

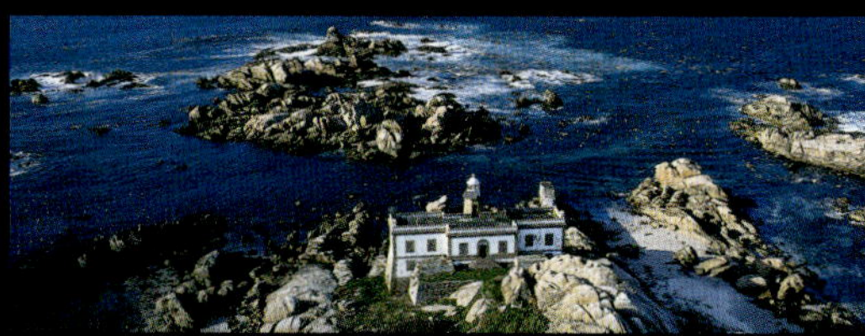

THE ENDS OF THE EARTH

There are many ways to describe the land's end: Cap Finistère in French, Penn-ar-Bed in Breton, Land's End in English – and Cabo Fisterra in Galician, a linguistic relative of Portuguese. The island of Lobeira Grande and its majestic lighthouse stand at the westernmost point of Galicia, gazing out across the Atlantic.

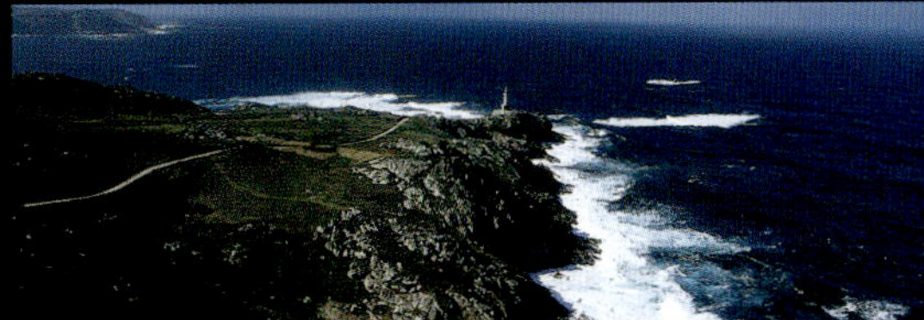

THE LIGHTHOUSE OF THE BARDS
At the end of the pilgrim's path to Santiago de Compostela lies the vastness of Cabo de Corrubedo, below the Mirador de la Curota. It is surrounded by two deep rias (estuaries): to starboard, Muros and Noia; to port, Arousa. In the middle stands a lighthouse, celebrated in local song.

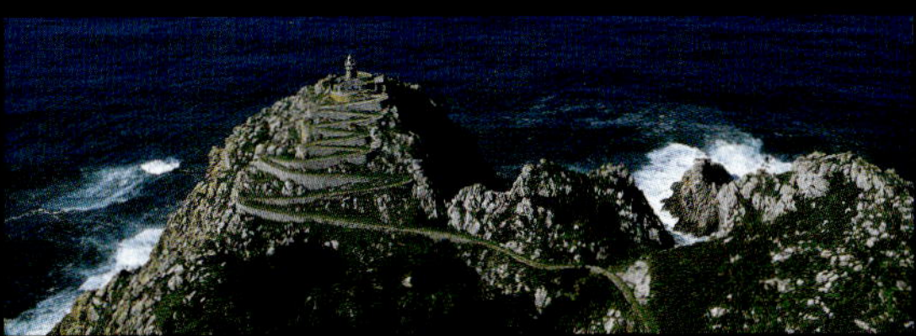

ISLANDS OF THE GODS
A veritable inland sea, the Ria de Vigo is protected by the natural wall of the Islas Cíes. This archipelago bears the envied nickname of the 'Islands of the Gods'. The many archaeological remains testify to the region's ancient Celtic heritage.

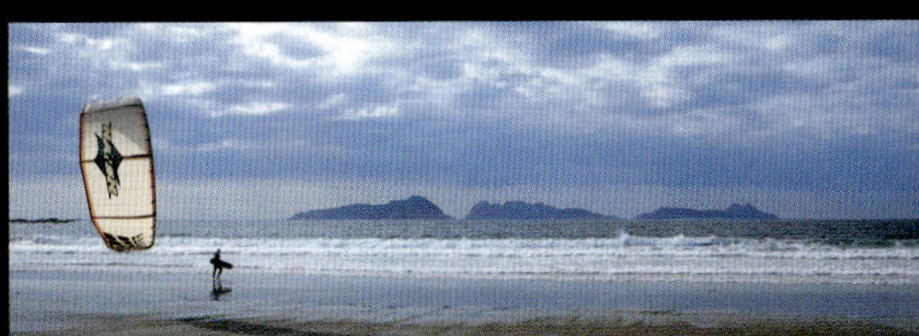

FLYING IN THE WIND
The beaches of Galicia are a paradise for watersports enthusiasts. From beach to beach, locations for surfing and paragliding vie for the wildness of their settings.

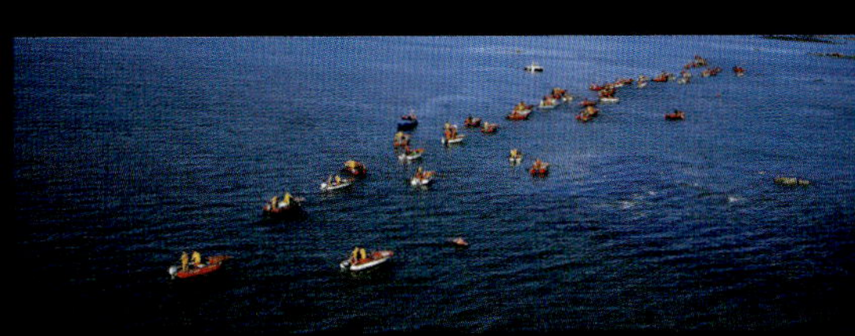

BOATS ON PARADE
In the morning, they leave in a colourful fleet. In the evening, they return at the same time, loaded with the day's abundant catch. These boats are a sign of the ongoing success of the traditional Galician fishing industry.

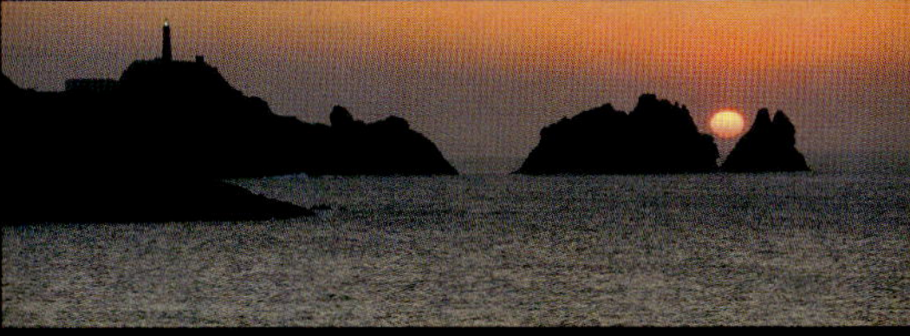

THE COAST OF DEATH
Cabo Villan lighthouse, south of La Coruña, dominates the sea on its rocky peak. Here the most violent winds of Galicia blow. Here the legend of 'the coast of death' was born. There are stones and rocks, but no refuge before the port of Camarinas.

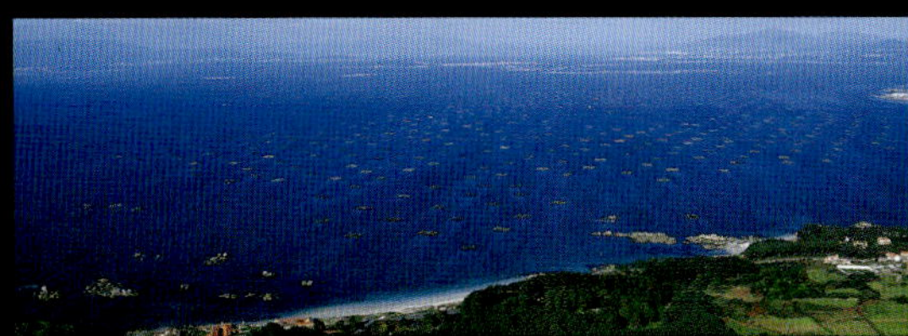

A NATURAL BARRIER
Like the Islas Cíes near Vigo, the even wilder Isla de Ons bears the brunt of the crashing waves in bad weather and protects the entrance to the Ria de Pontevedra. In fine weather, its countryside also seems blessed by the gods.

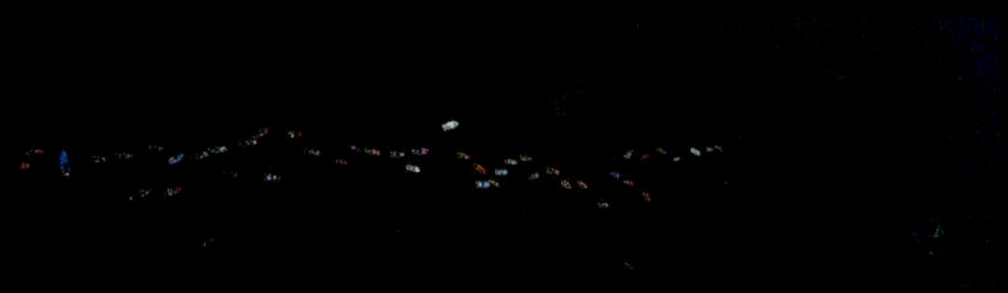

A LAND OF FISHERMEN
The social and cultural tradition of fishing is celebrated throughout Galicia with boat-blessing ceremonies. These are performed in even the smallest ports: this one is Arousa.

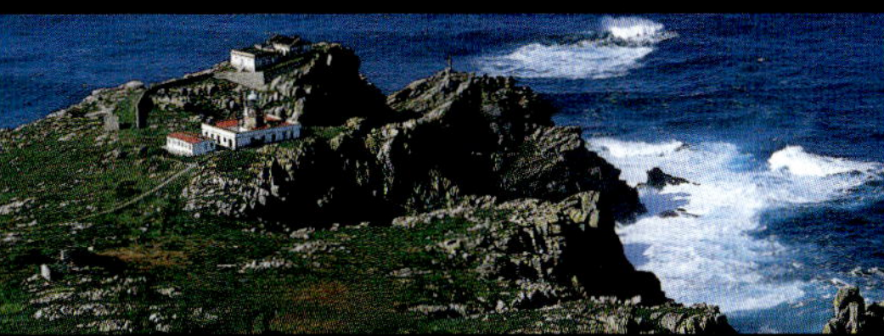

WILD EDEN
Legend says that Isla Sisargas, planted on the edge of the Rias Altas, west of La Coruña, is a piece of Cabo San Adrian that went off to live its own life a short distance away. It is a paradise for birds and several rare plant species. The rocks are covered with

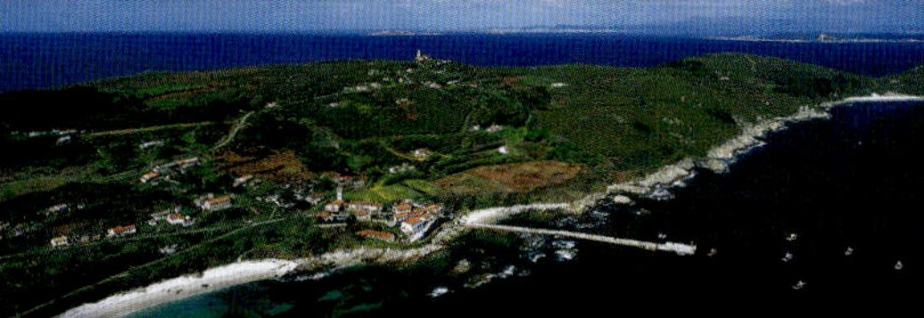

A BEAUTIFUL BAY
The bay of Pontevedra is surely one of the finest in the world. From the heights of Sanxenxo, you can admire the horizon broken by the Isla de Ons (above) and its little sister, Onceta.

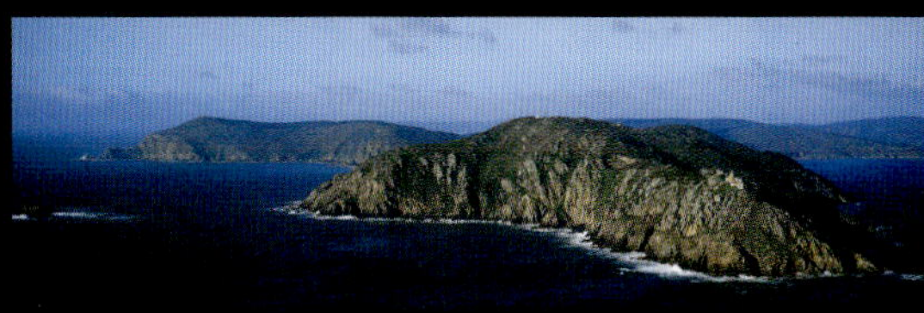

CABO FISTERRA
When sailors, going along the Galician coast, leave the Rias Gallegas to go down towards the Rias Baixas in the south, they pass the intimidating Cabo Fisterra peninsula. On the summit of Punta Saurade, the lighthouse stands 75 feet tall.

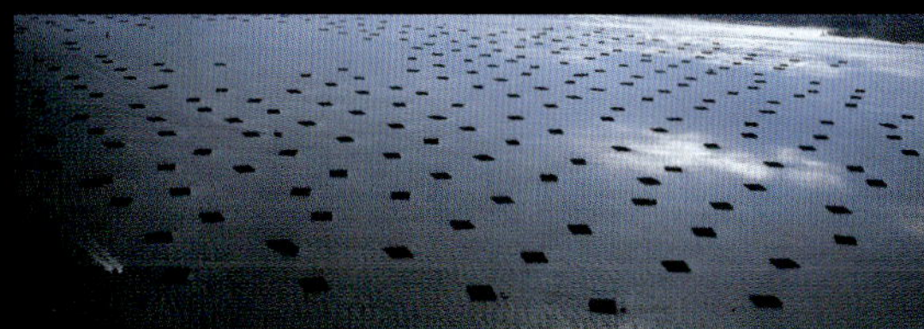

MOORINGS AND SHELLS
Shells collected by fishermen from the creels of the Ria de Arousa adorn the stalls of village markets. Luis Seone has made tapestries from them and Carlos Maside has turned them into highly respected pictures.

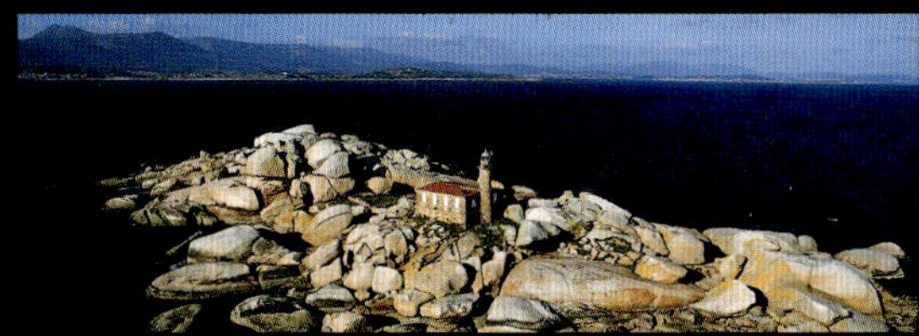

PINK GRANITE
Isla Rùa, at the entrance to the Ria de Arousa between Ribeira and La Toxa. These ancient stones recall the pink granite coast of northern Brittany.

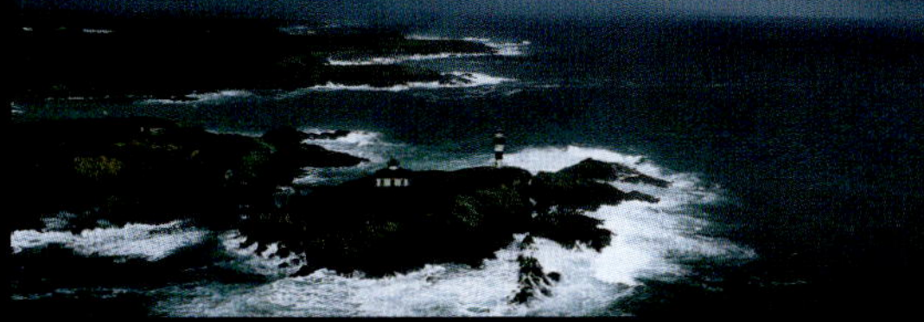

ISLANDS BY THE SCORE
Islands in the very north, creeks in the far west, rias right in the middle of the windy coast, off Santiago and Pontevedra as far as Vigo. And yet more islands in the open sea, including Arousa, Ons and the three Islas Cíes. This is the Isla Pancha lighthouse on the rocky coast.

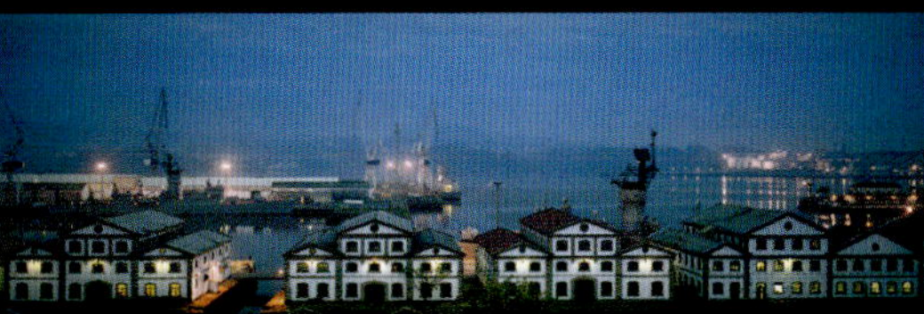

THE QUAYS AT FERROL
Ferrol is an attractive port opening onto the Rias Altas. One hundred thousand inhabitants have made it the maritime capital of northwestern Galicia. Classical and neoclassical buildings are a feature of the Magdalena district, not forgetting the architecture of the port with its straight lines.

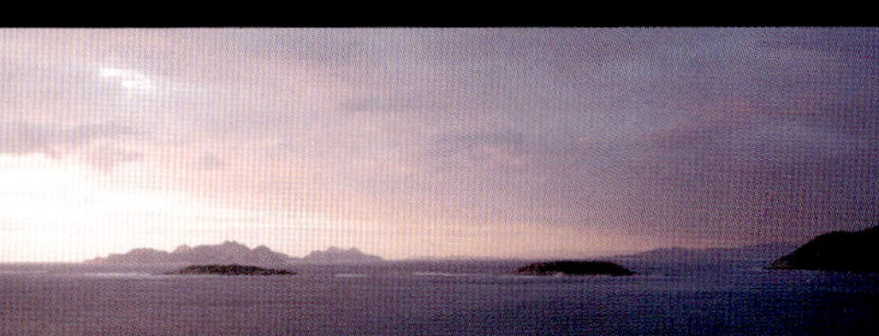

ISLAS CÍES
The Islas Cíes lie a mile and a half from the coast and 9 miles from the busy city of Vigo, whose football club – Celta de Vigo – honours the Celtic tradition. These islands are studded with standing stones and Roman remains.

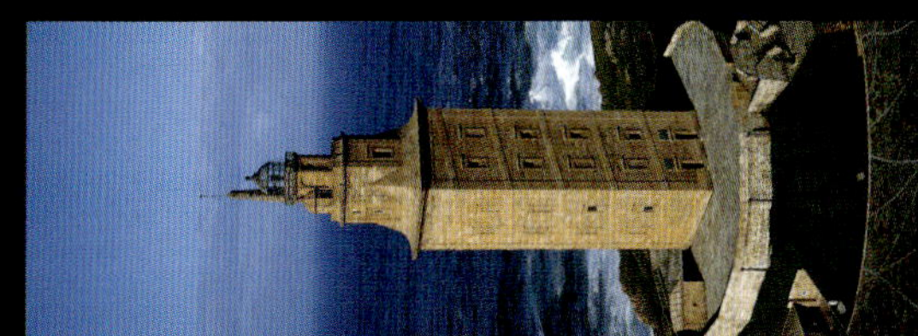

THE TOWER OF HERCULES
It stands 185 feet tall, and is the oldest lighthouse in Europe. The Tower of Hercules marks the entrance to the seaside town of La Coruña. It was built by the Roman emperor Trajan some nineteen centuries ago.

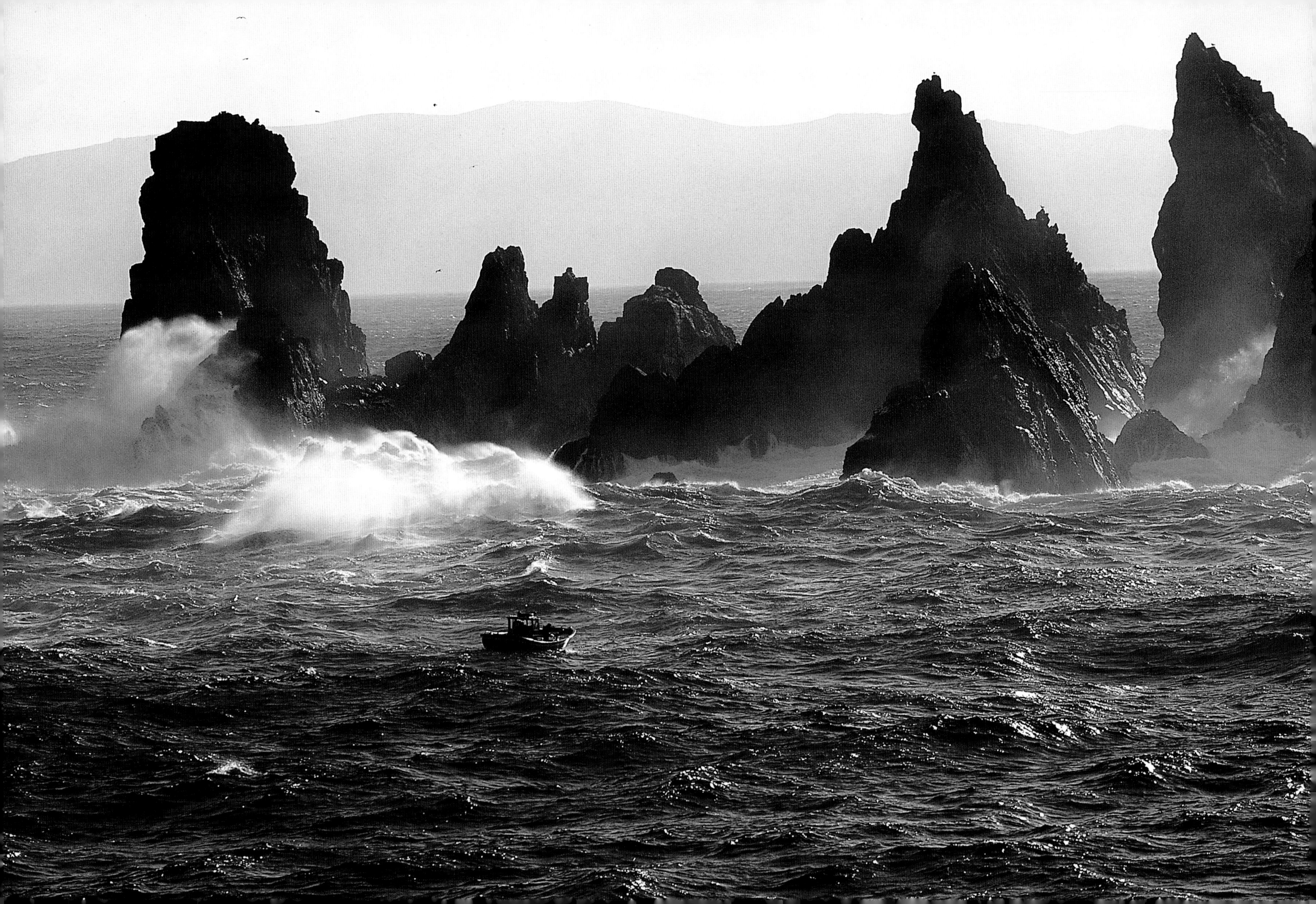

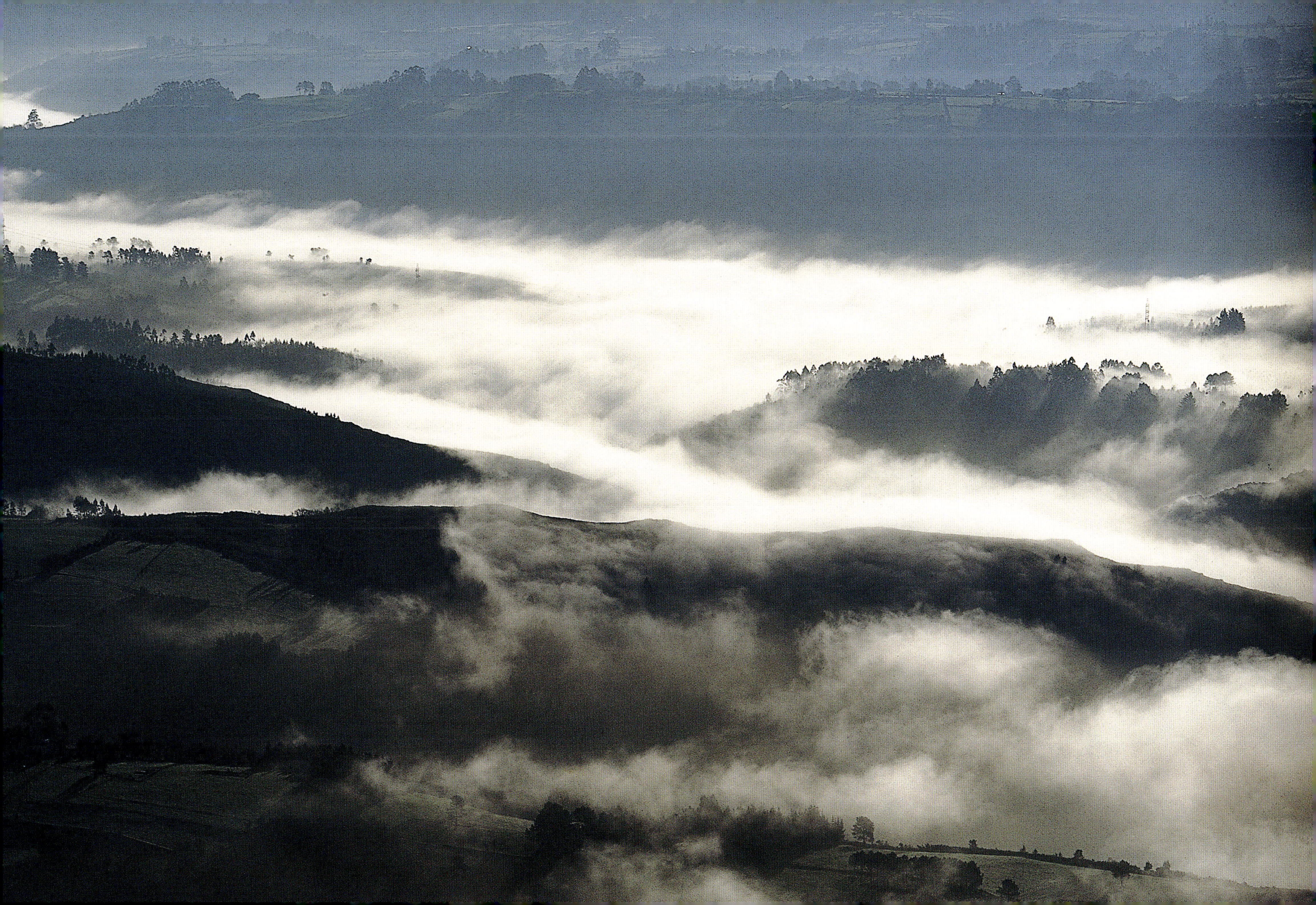

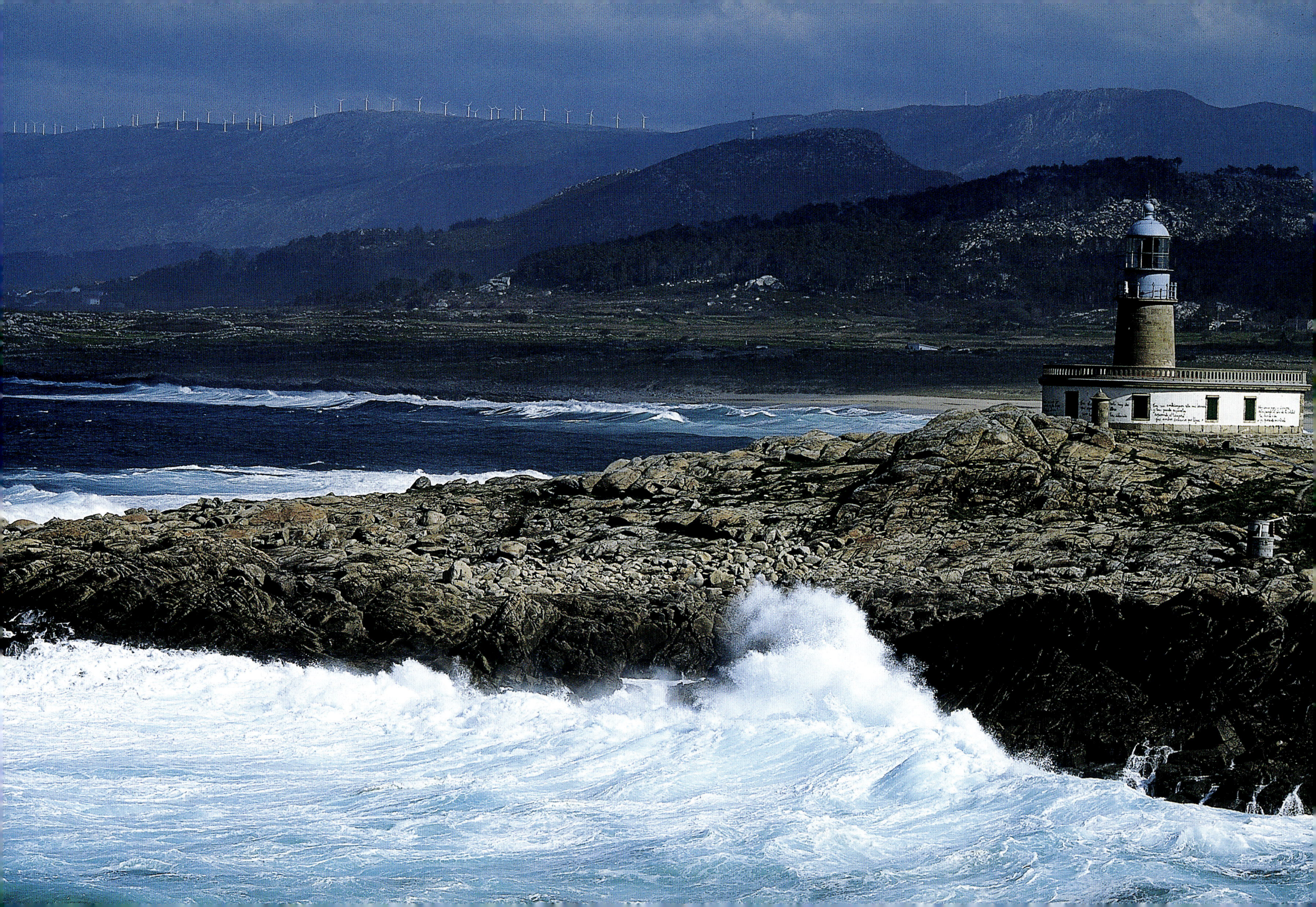

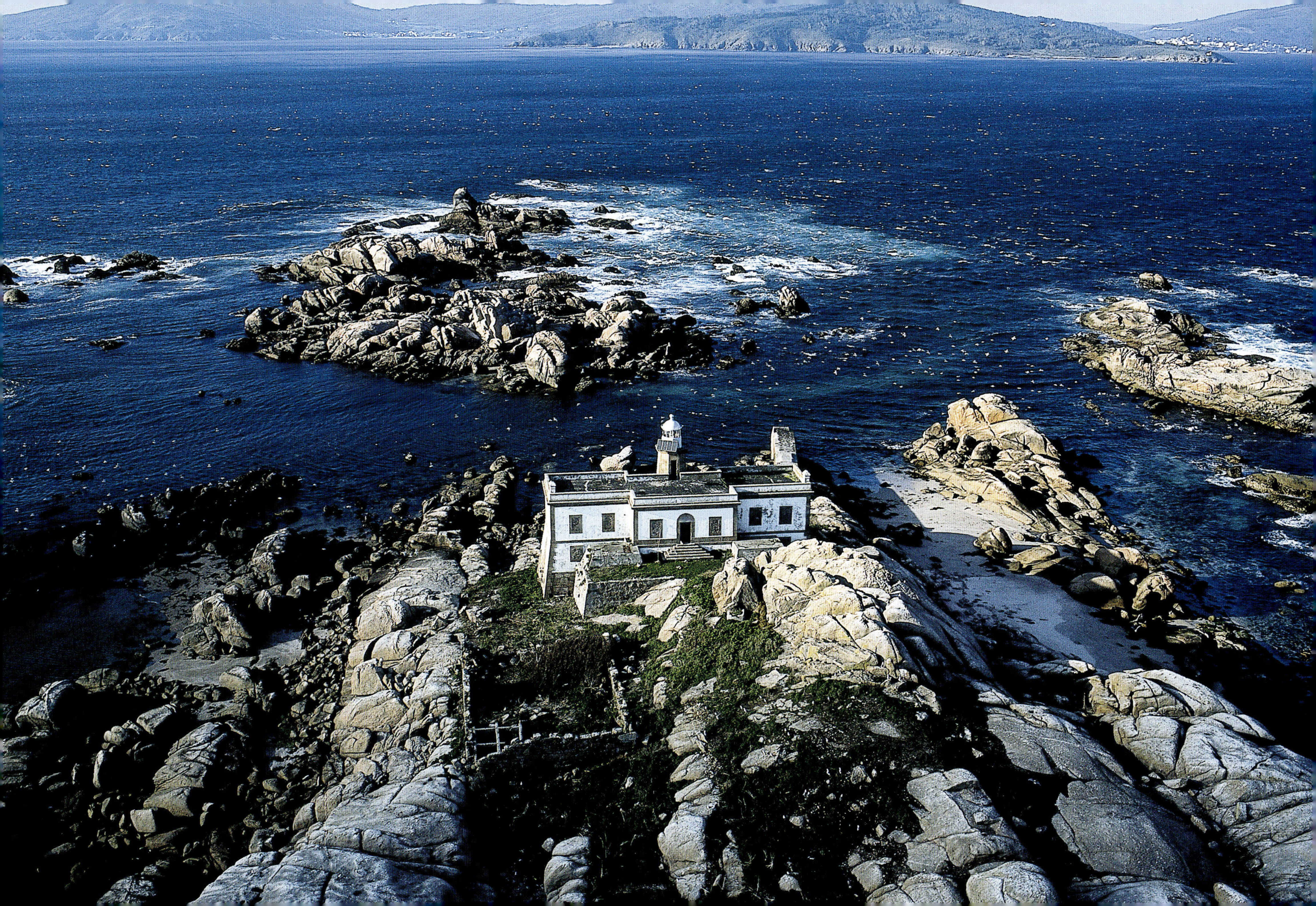

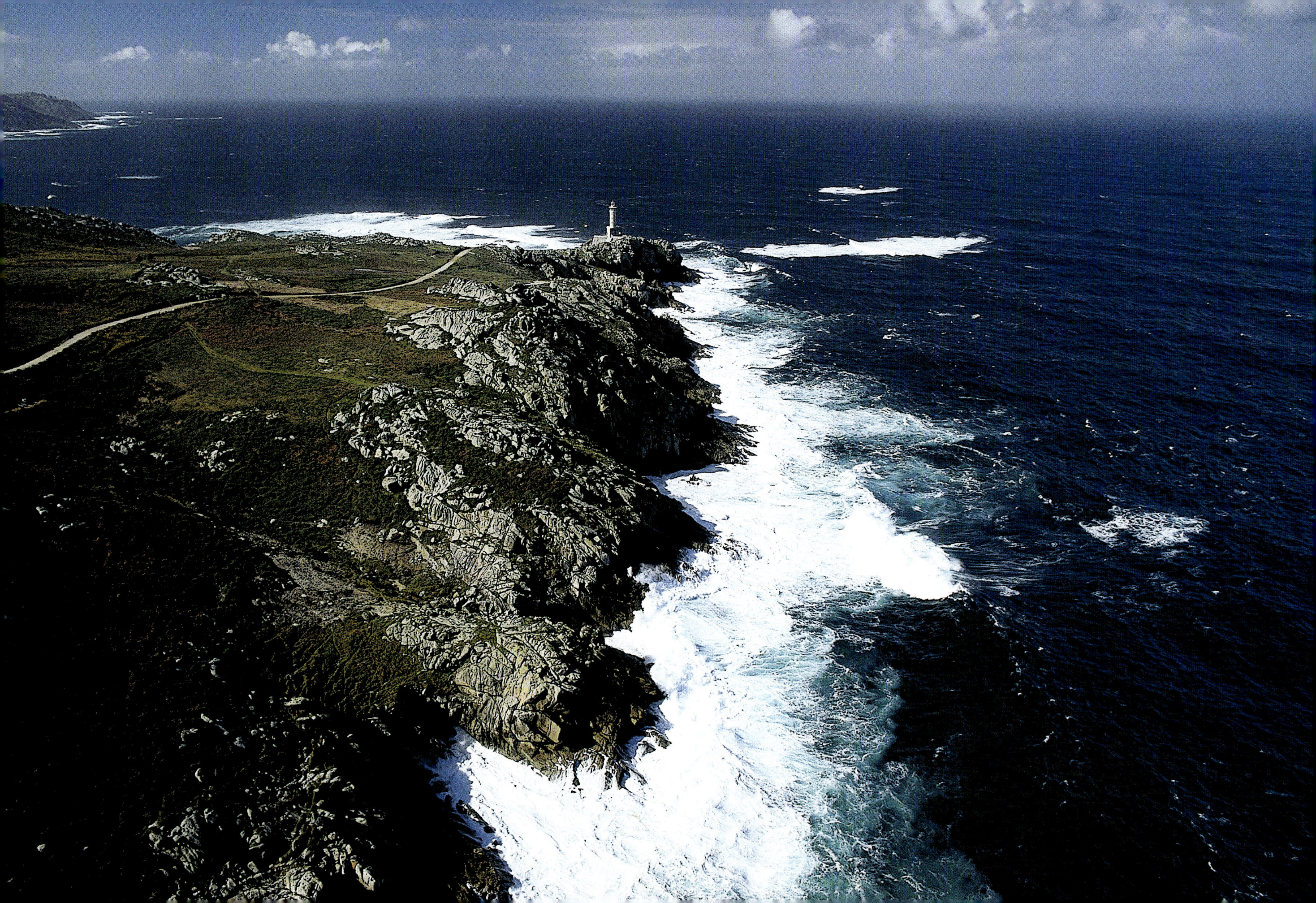

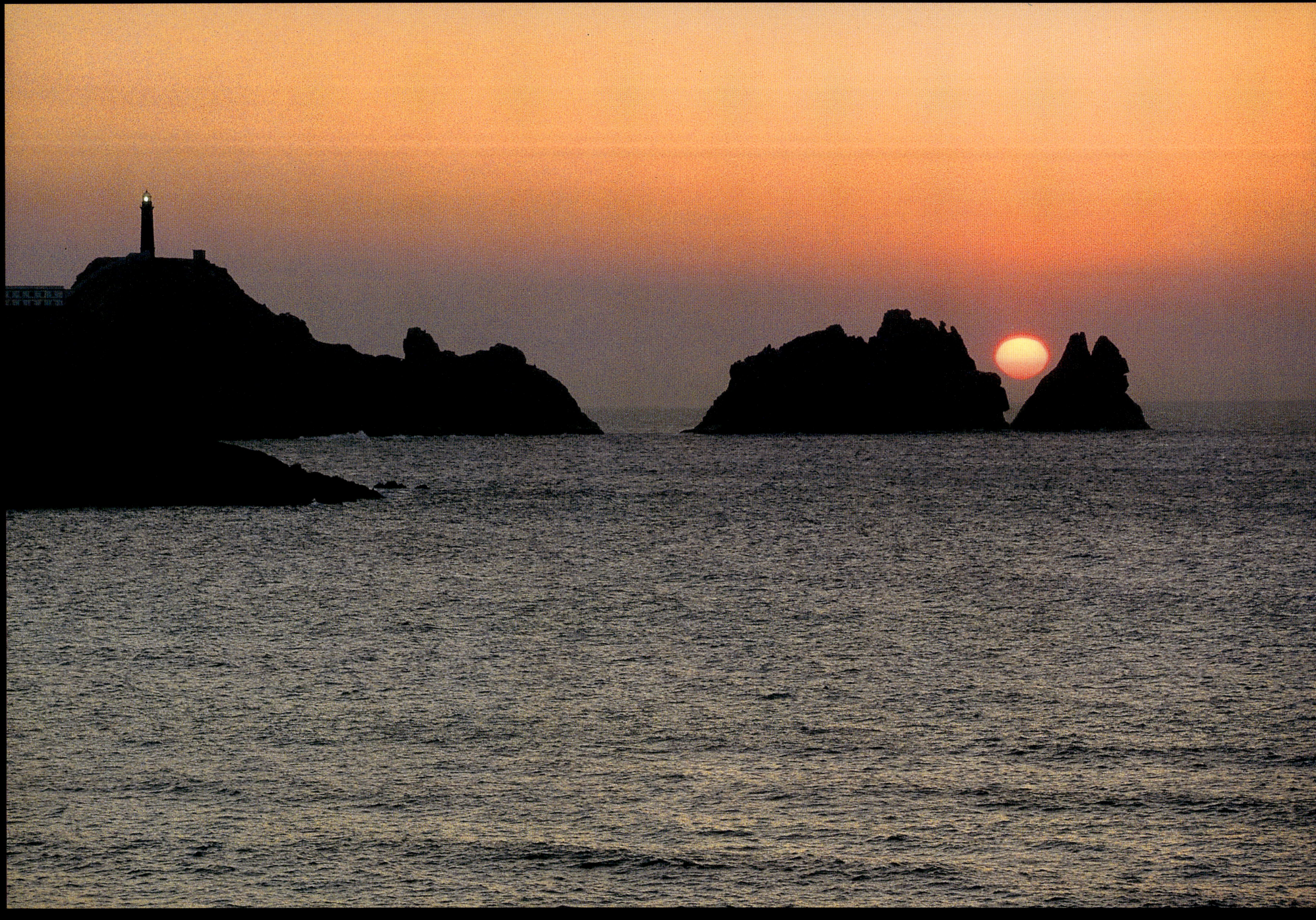

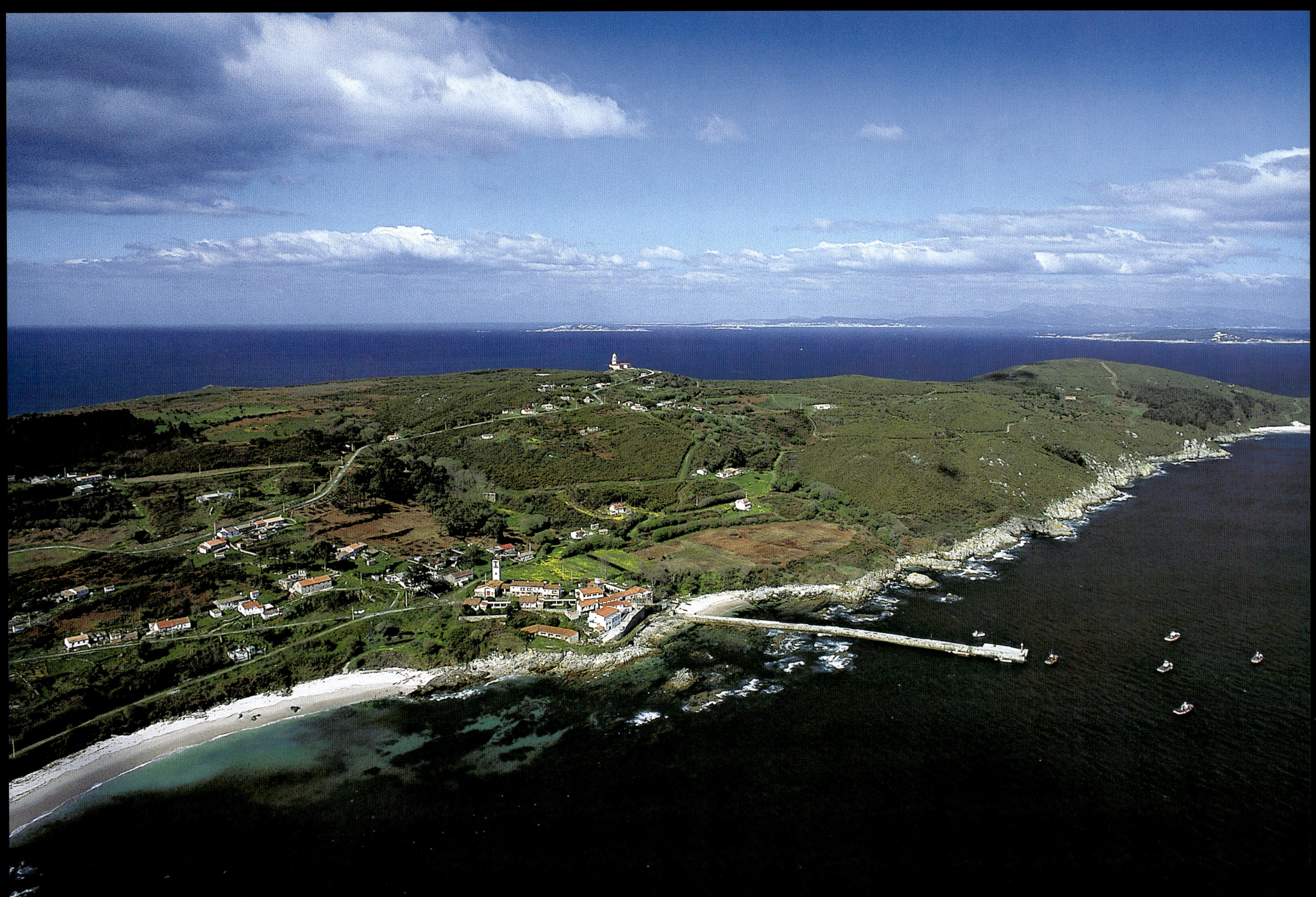

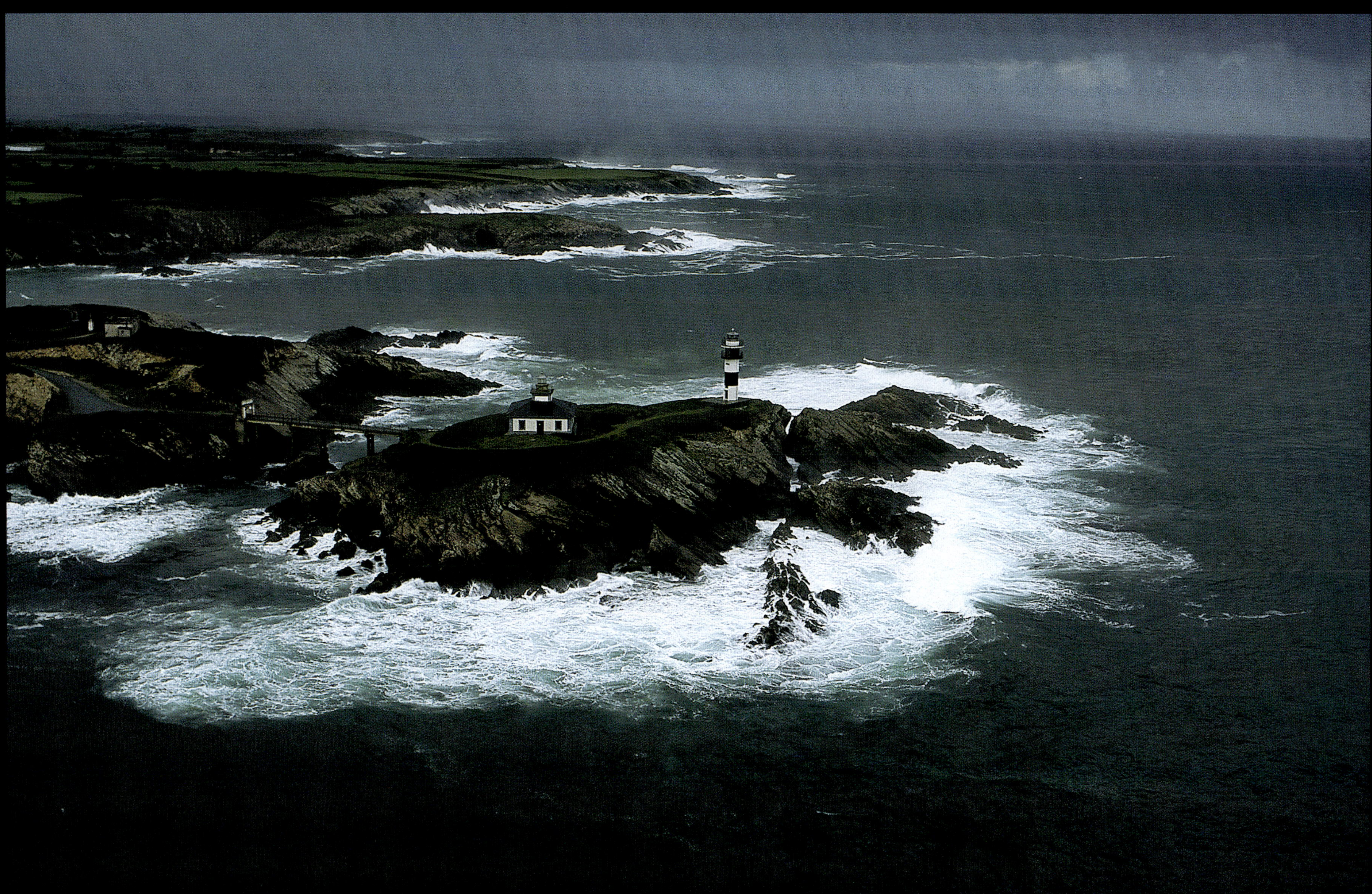

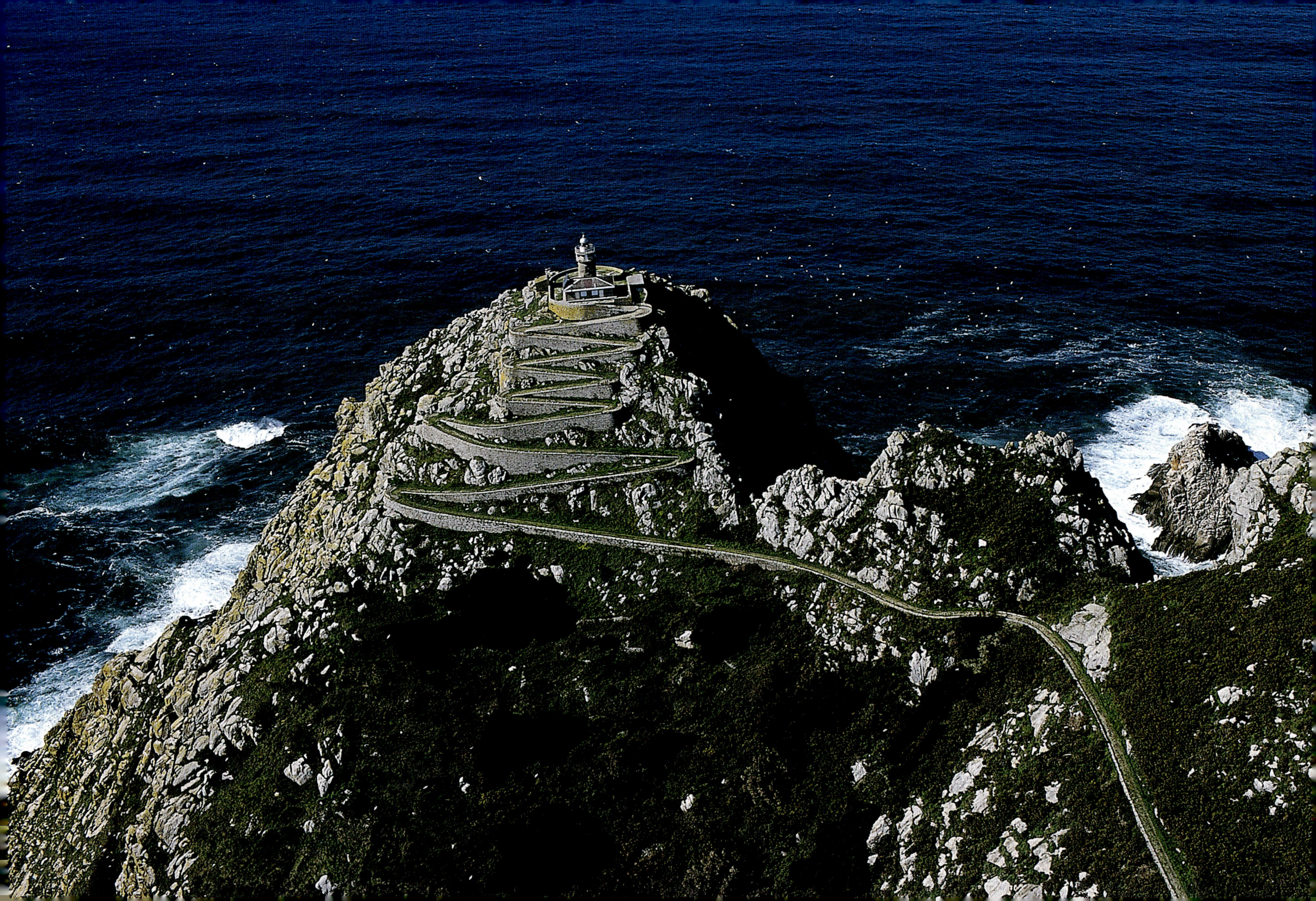

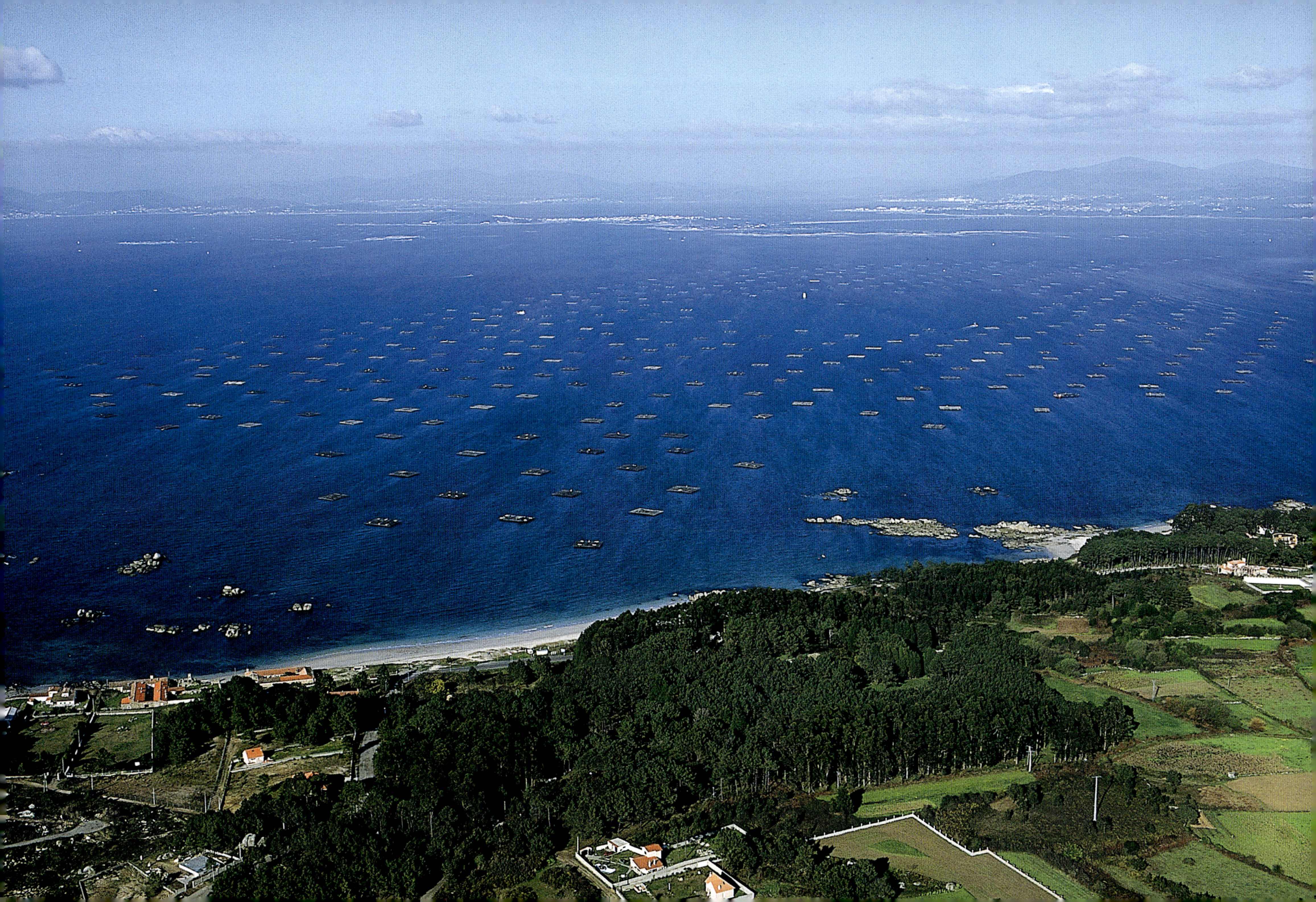

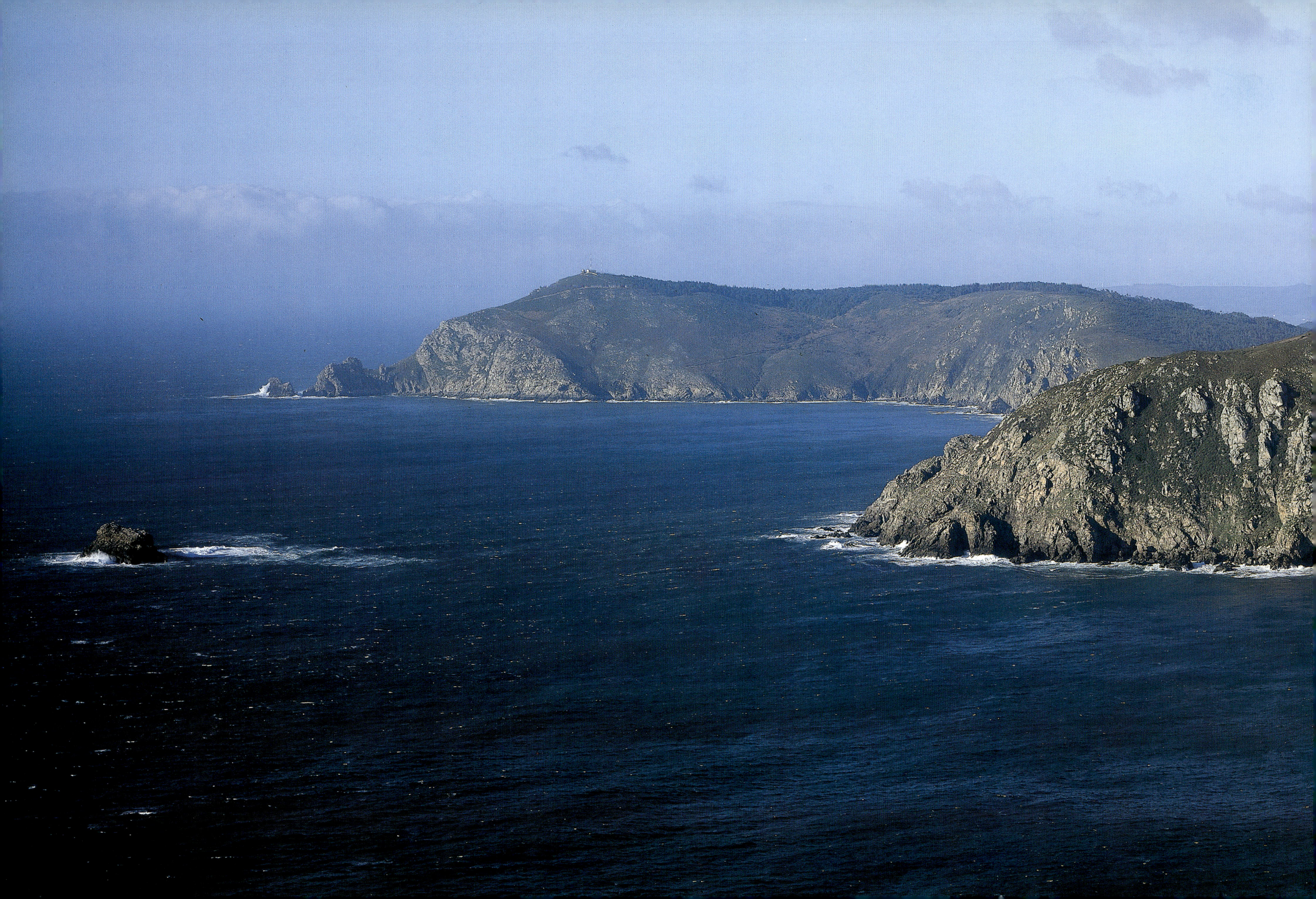

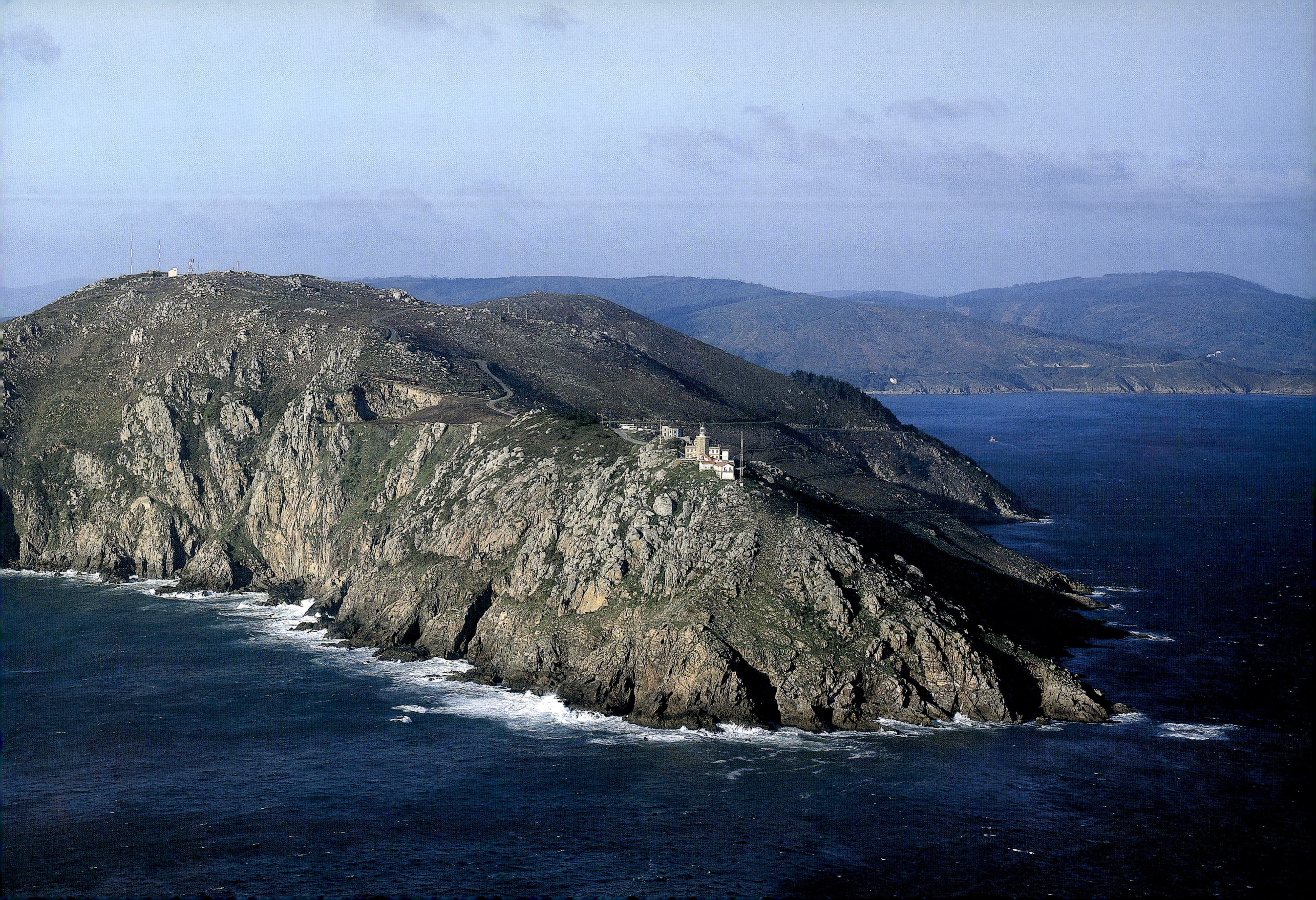

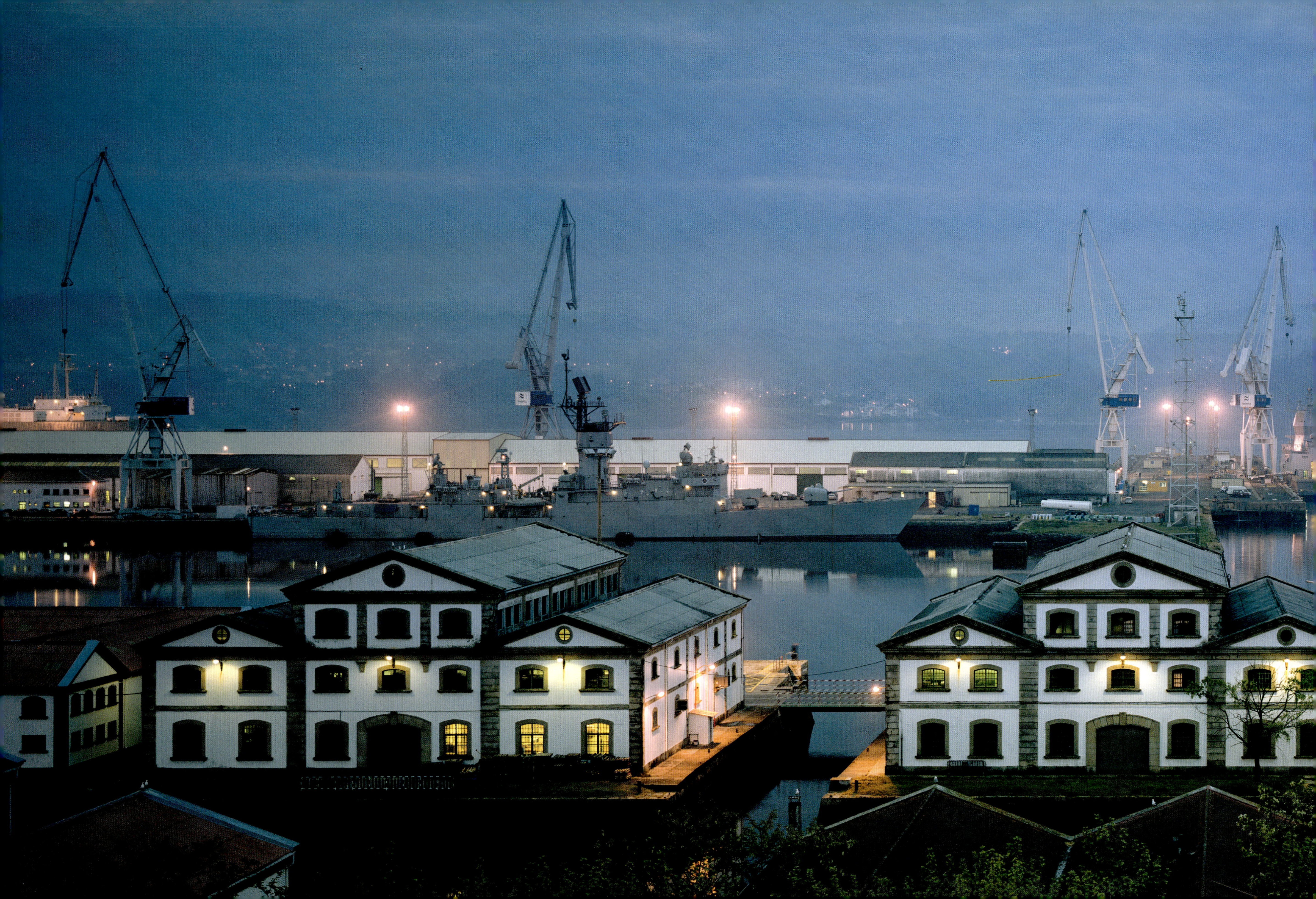

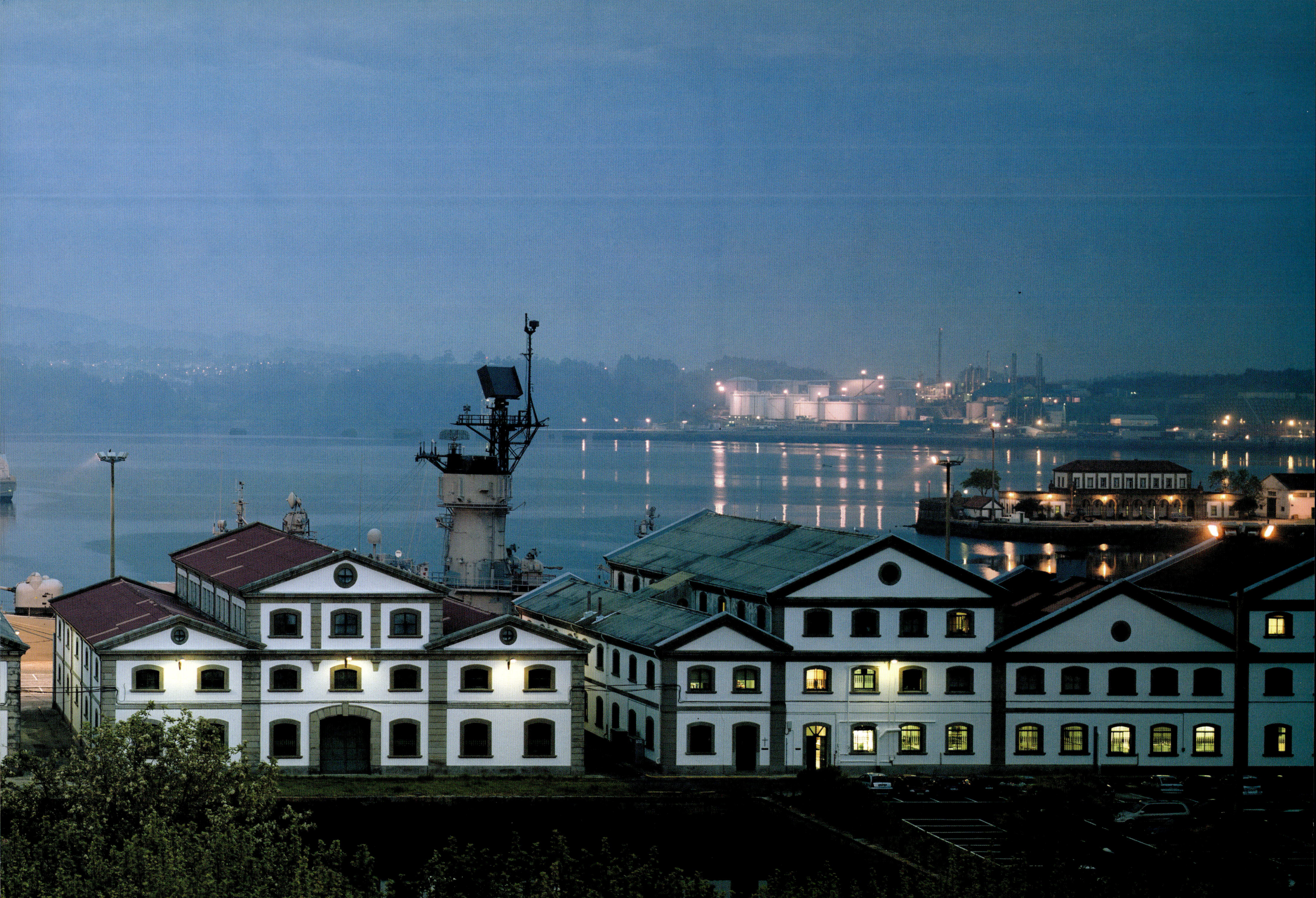

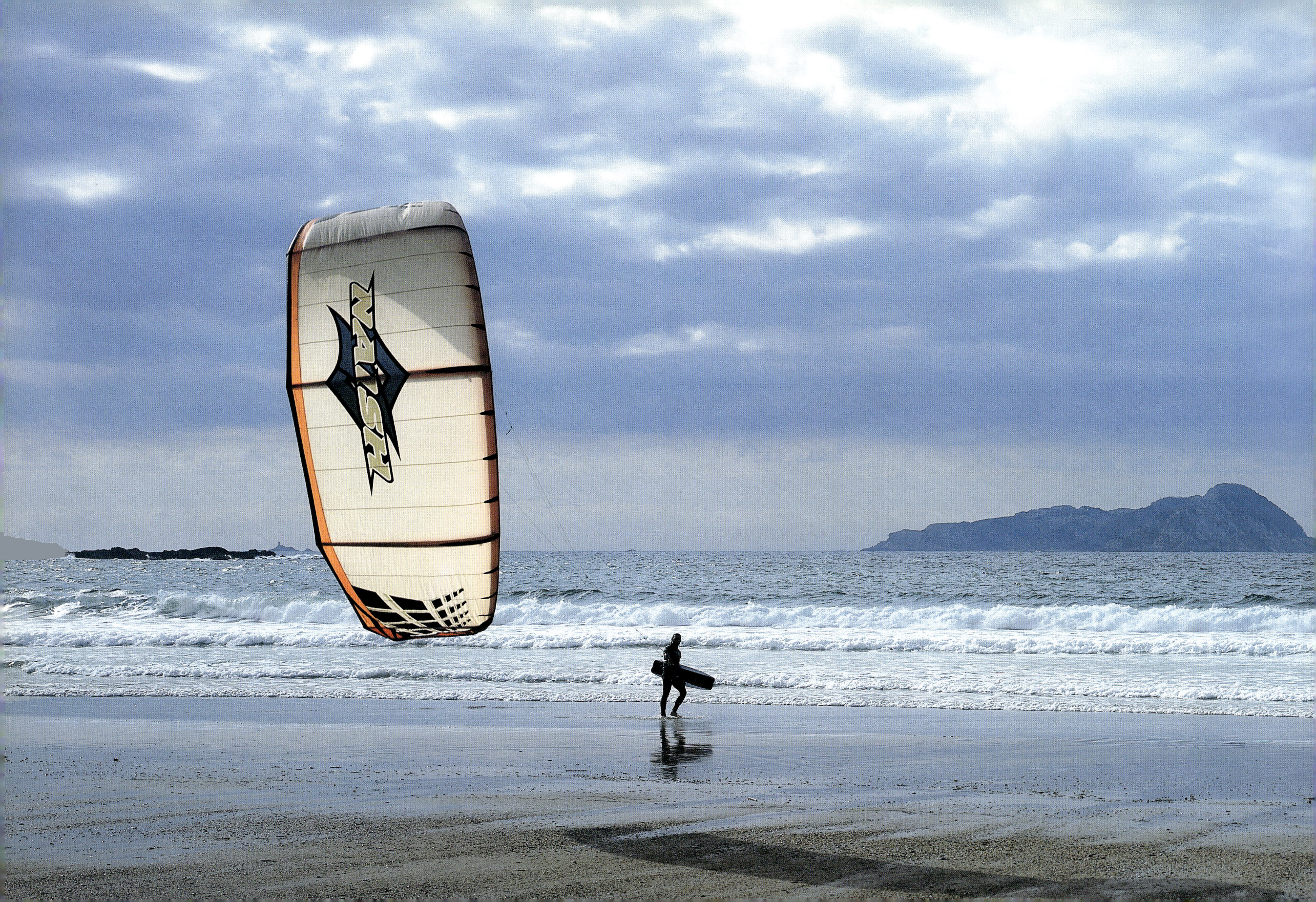

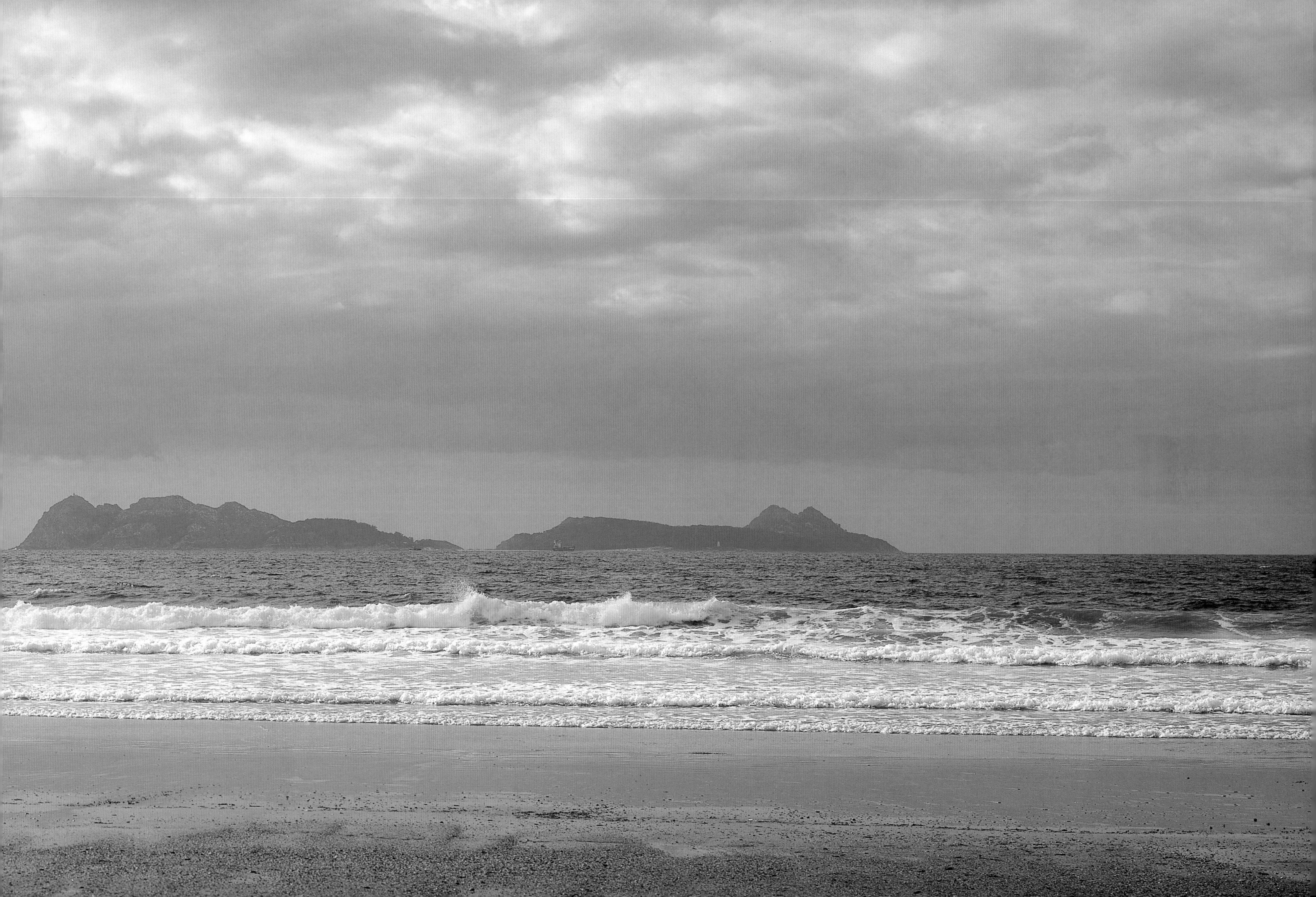

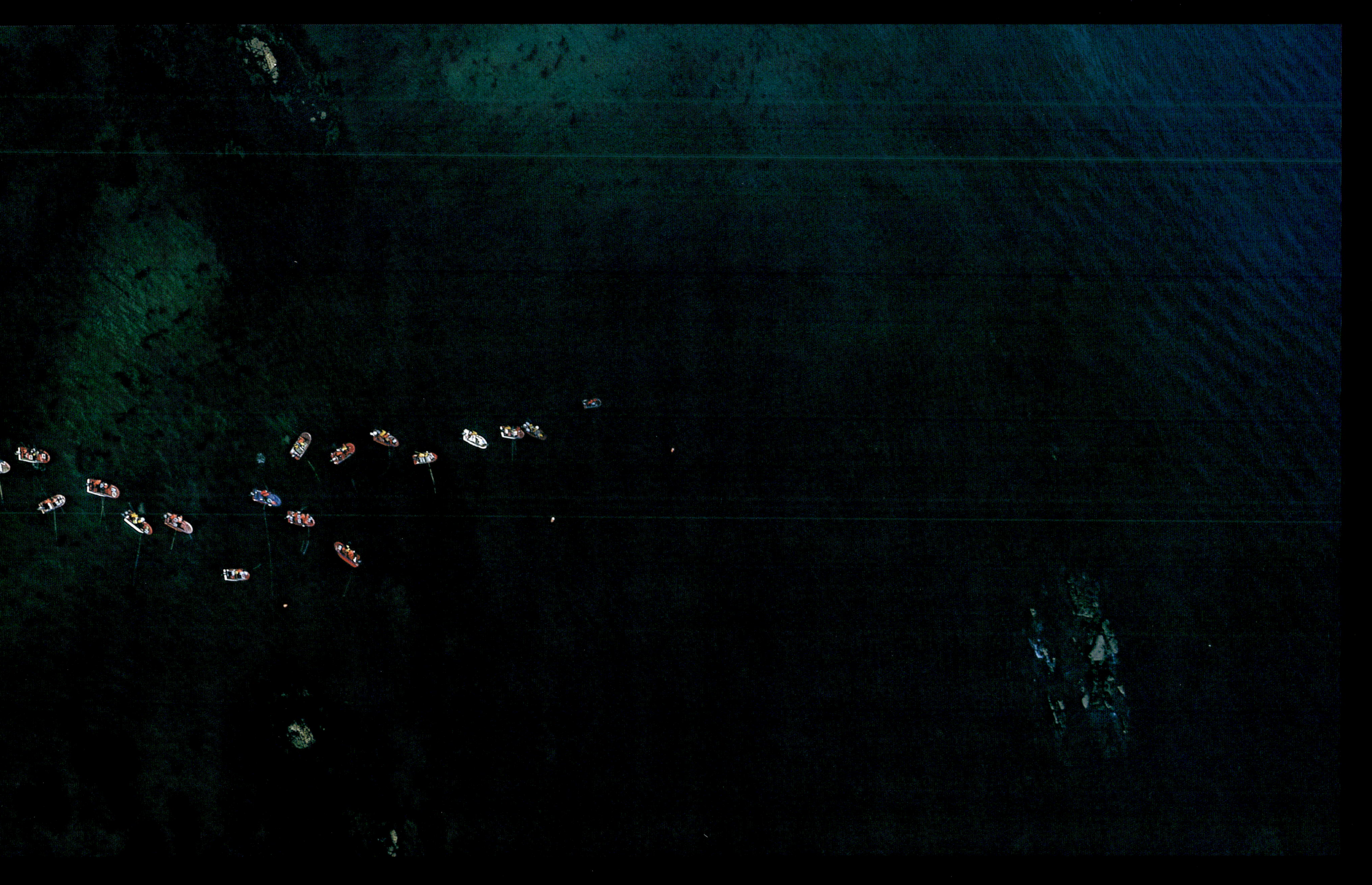

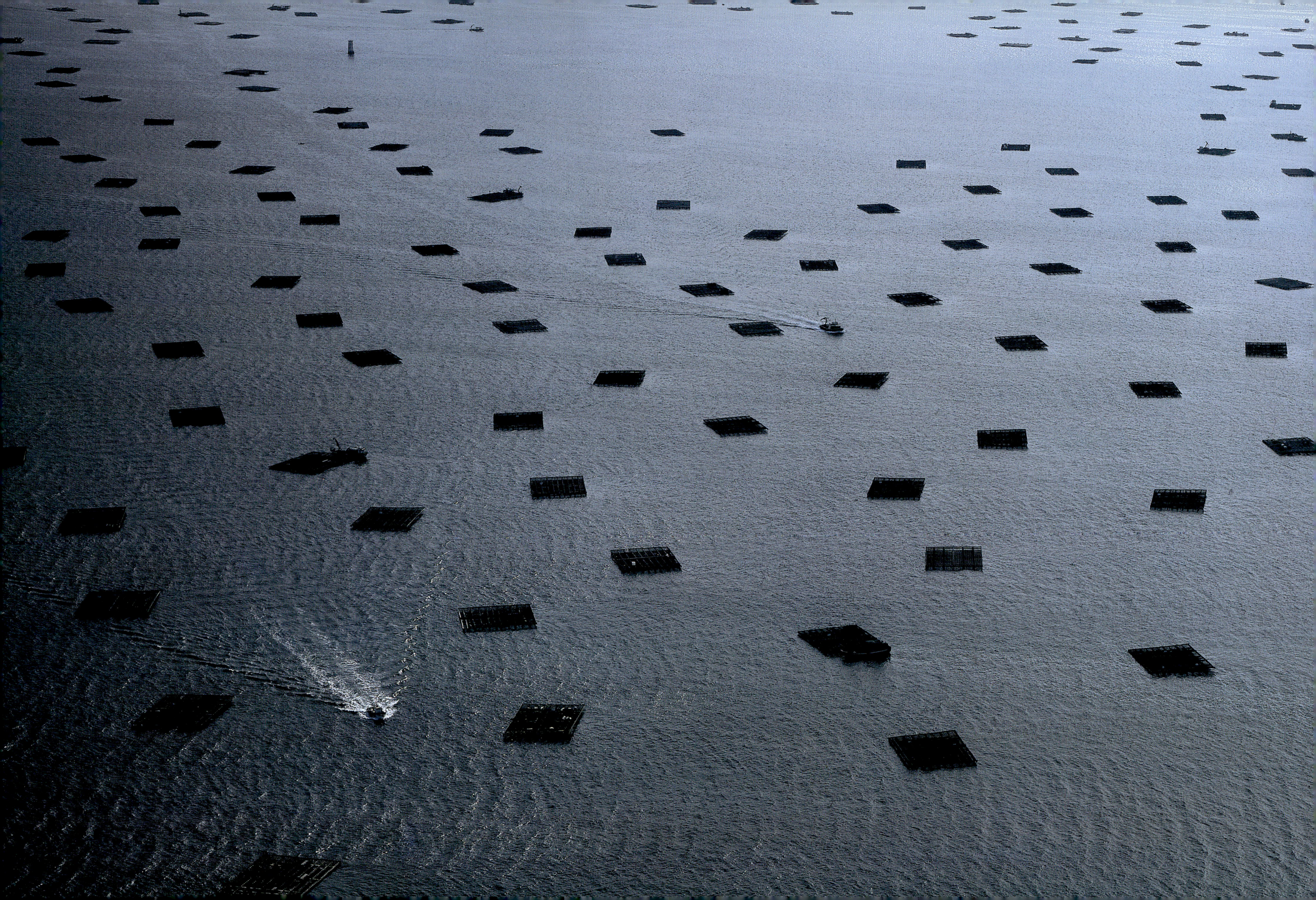

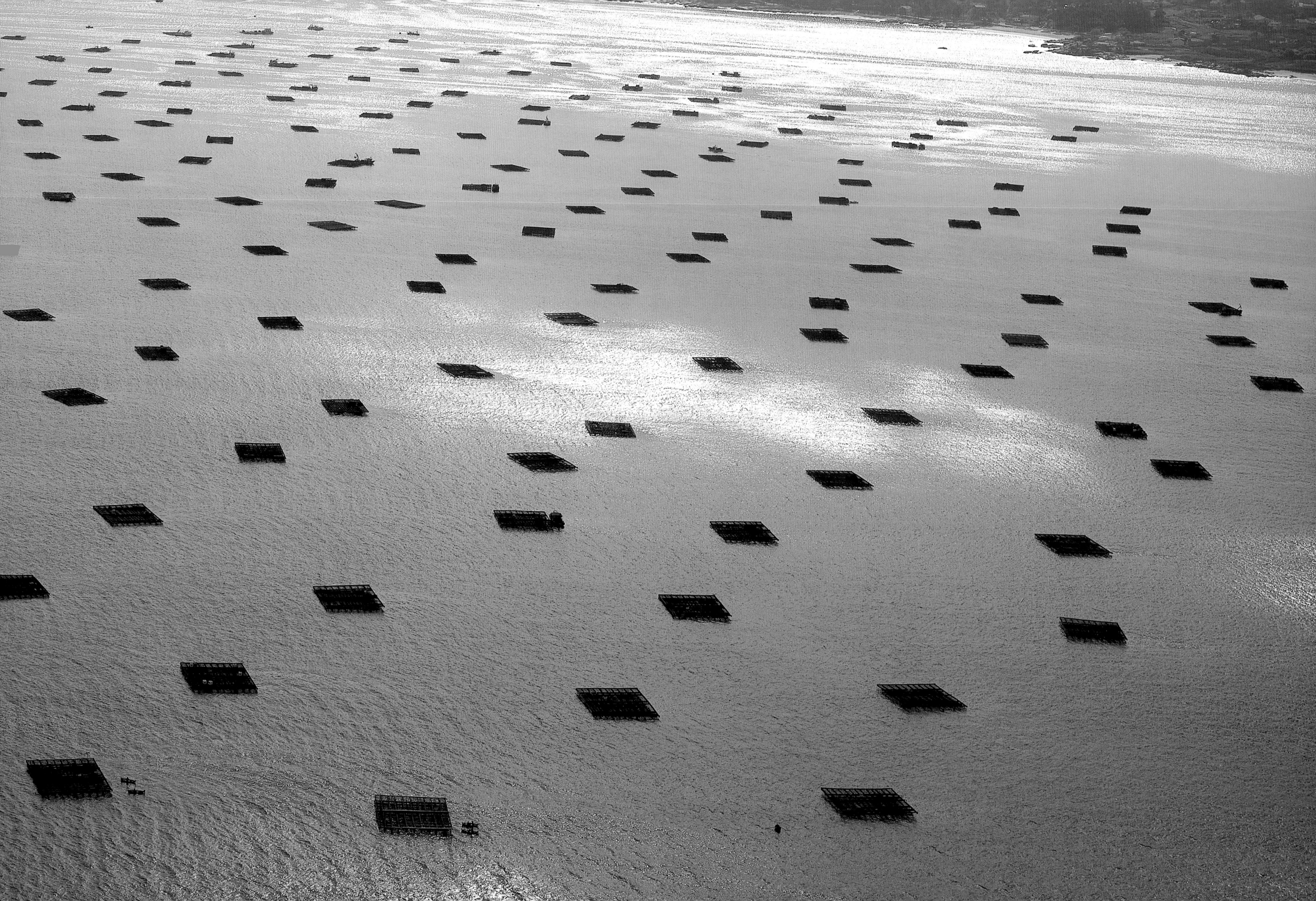

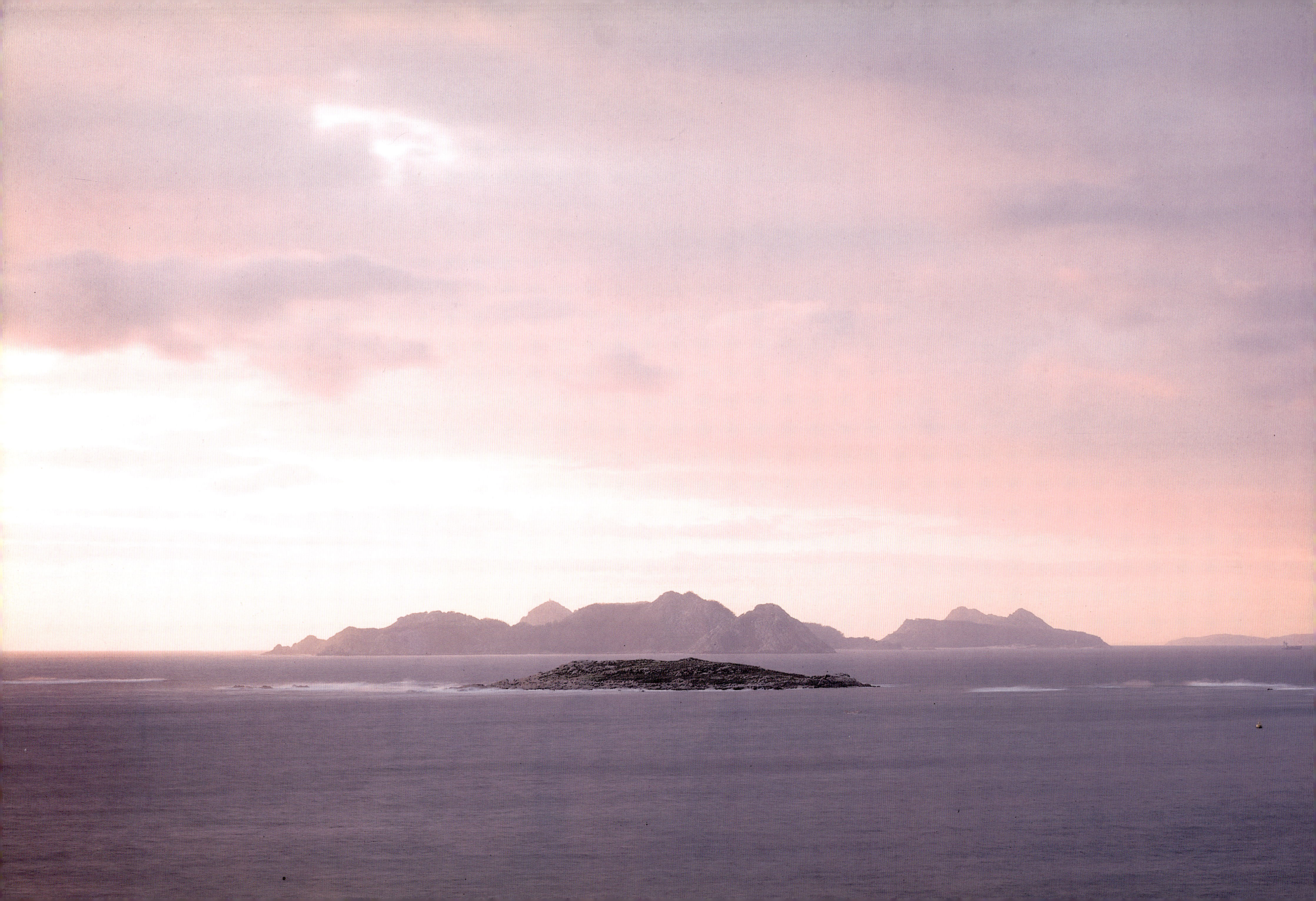

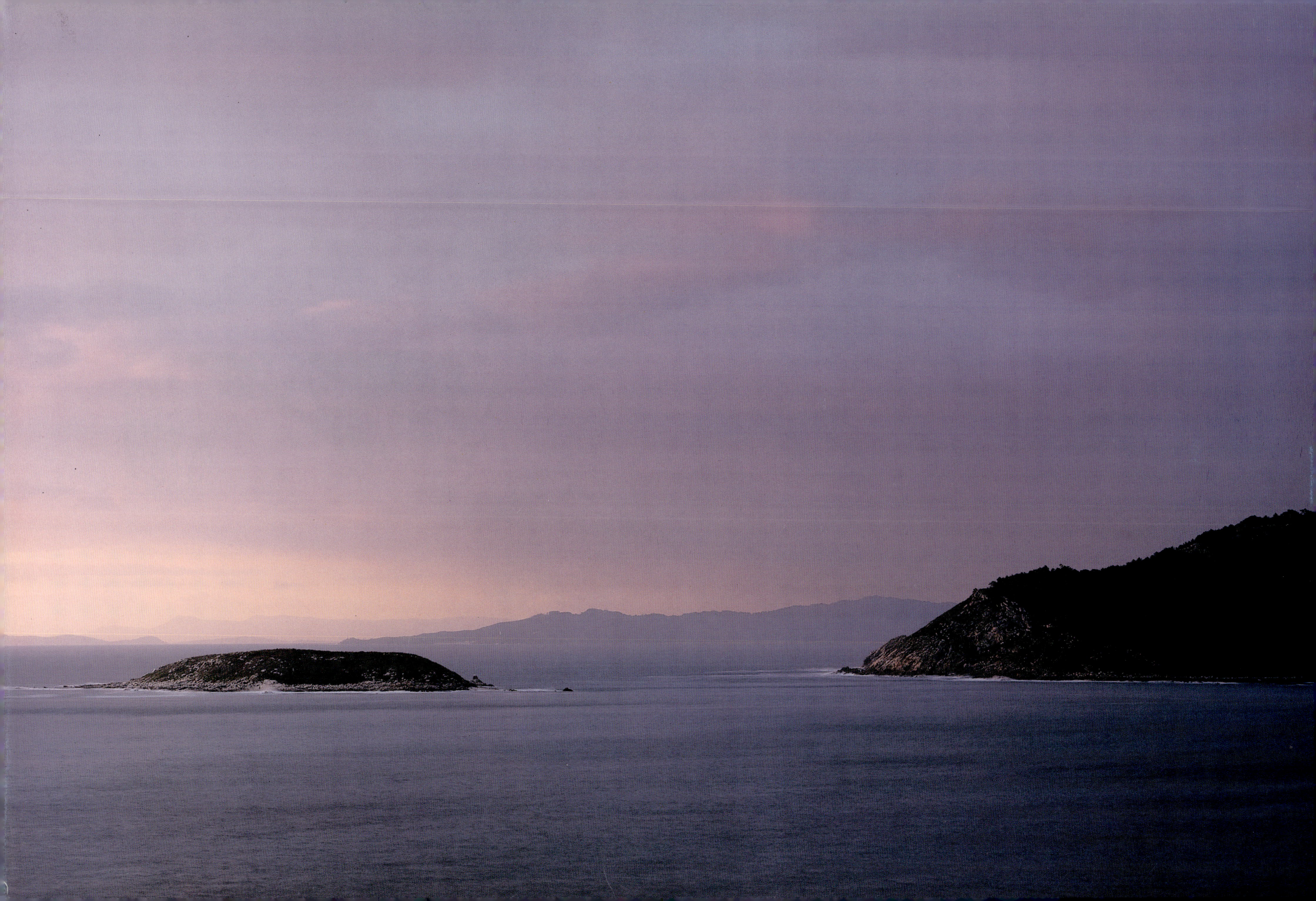

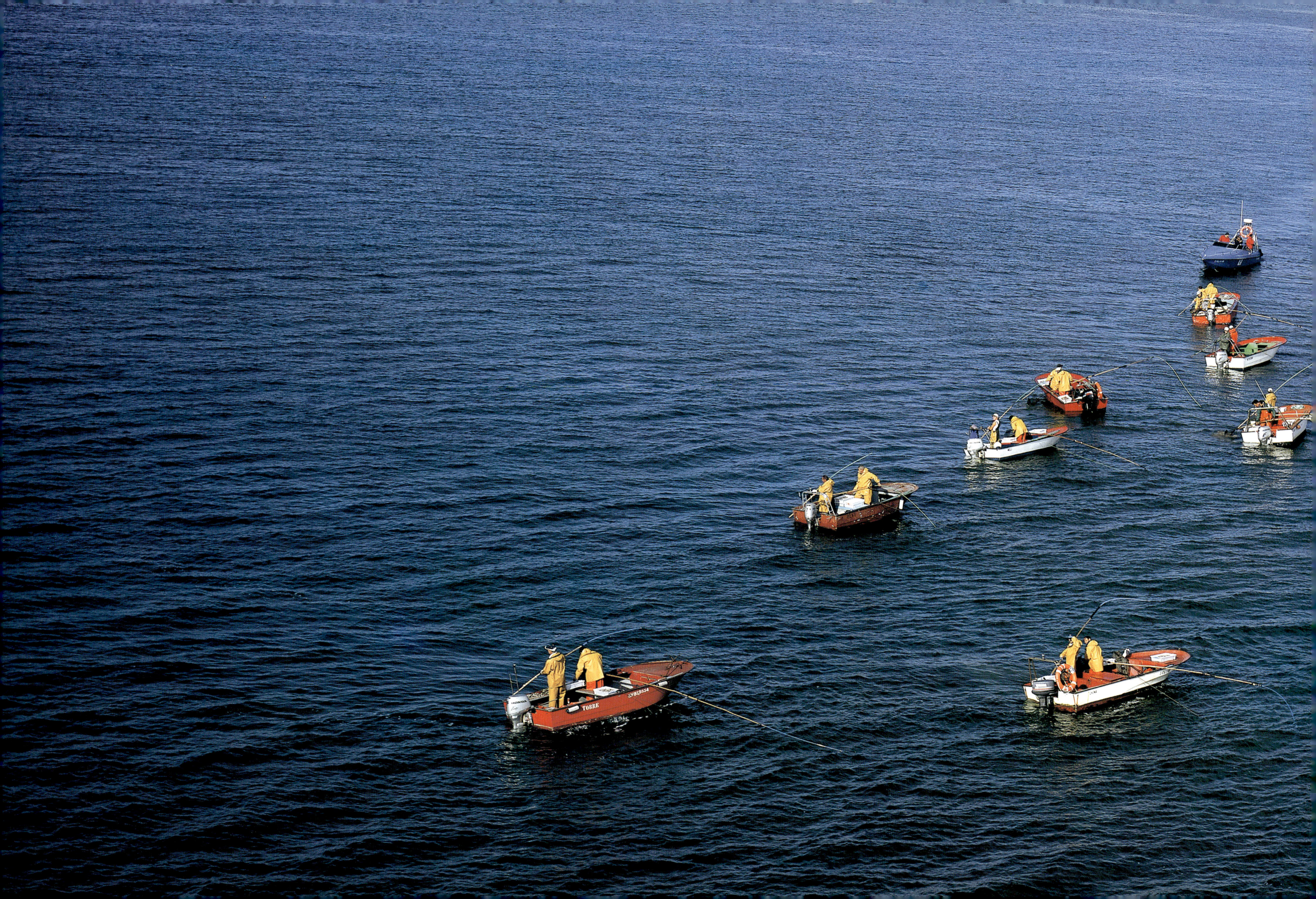

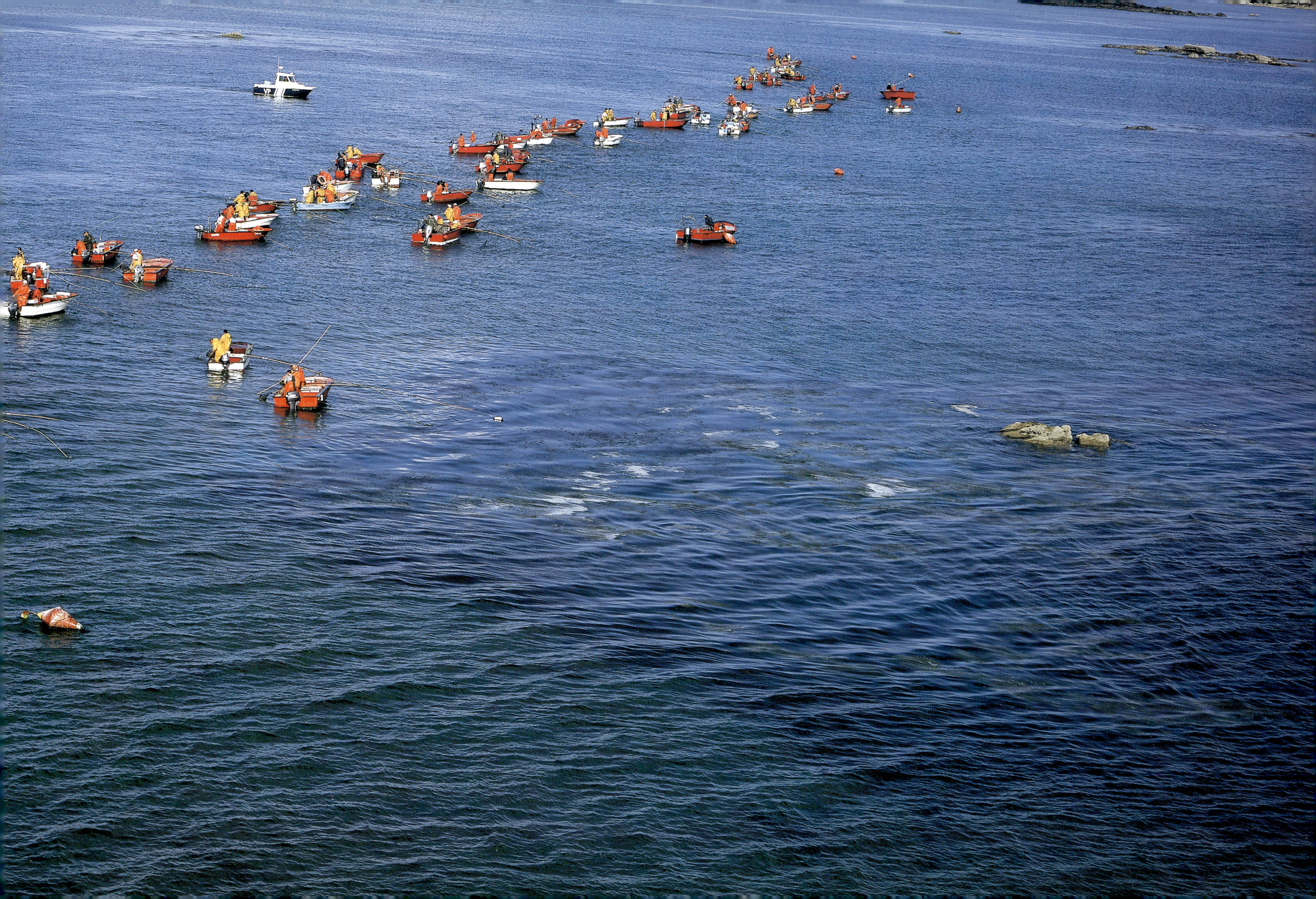

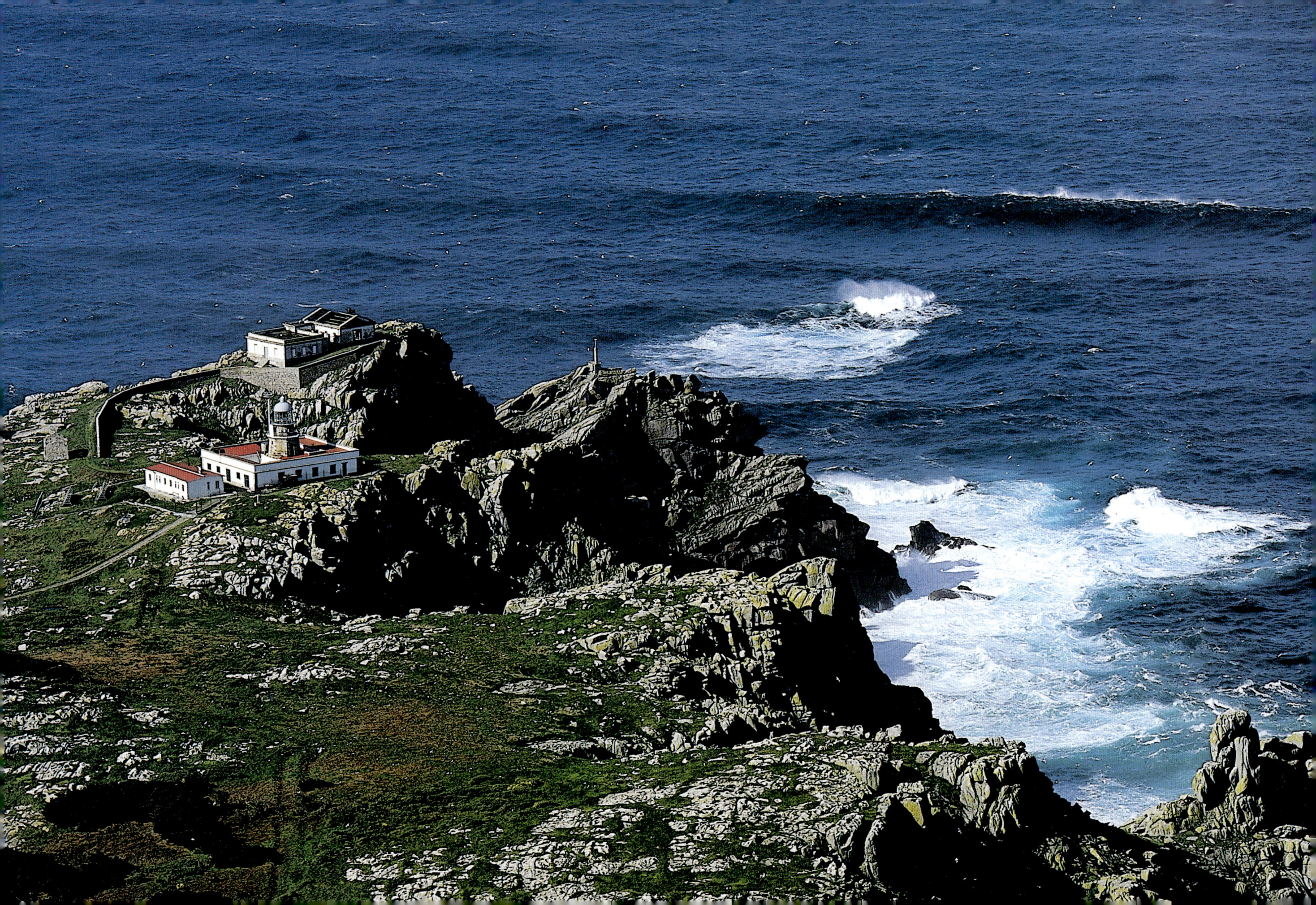

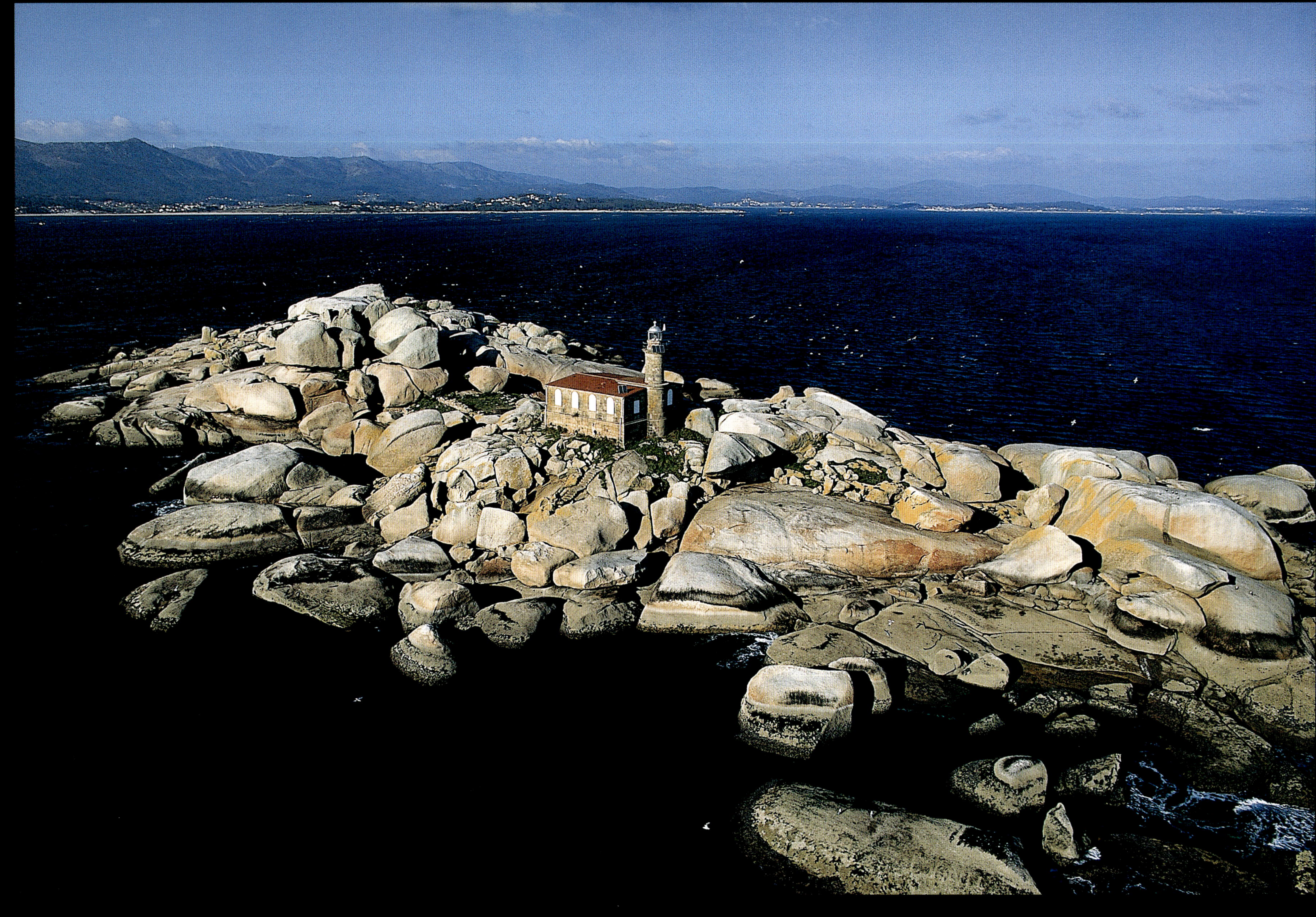

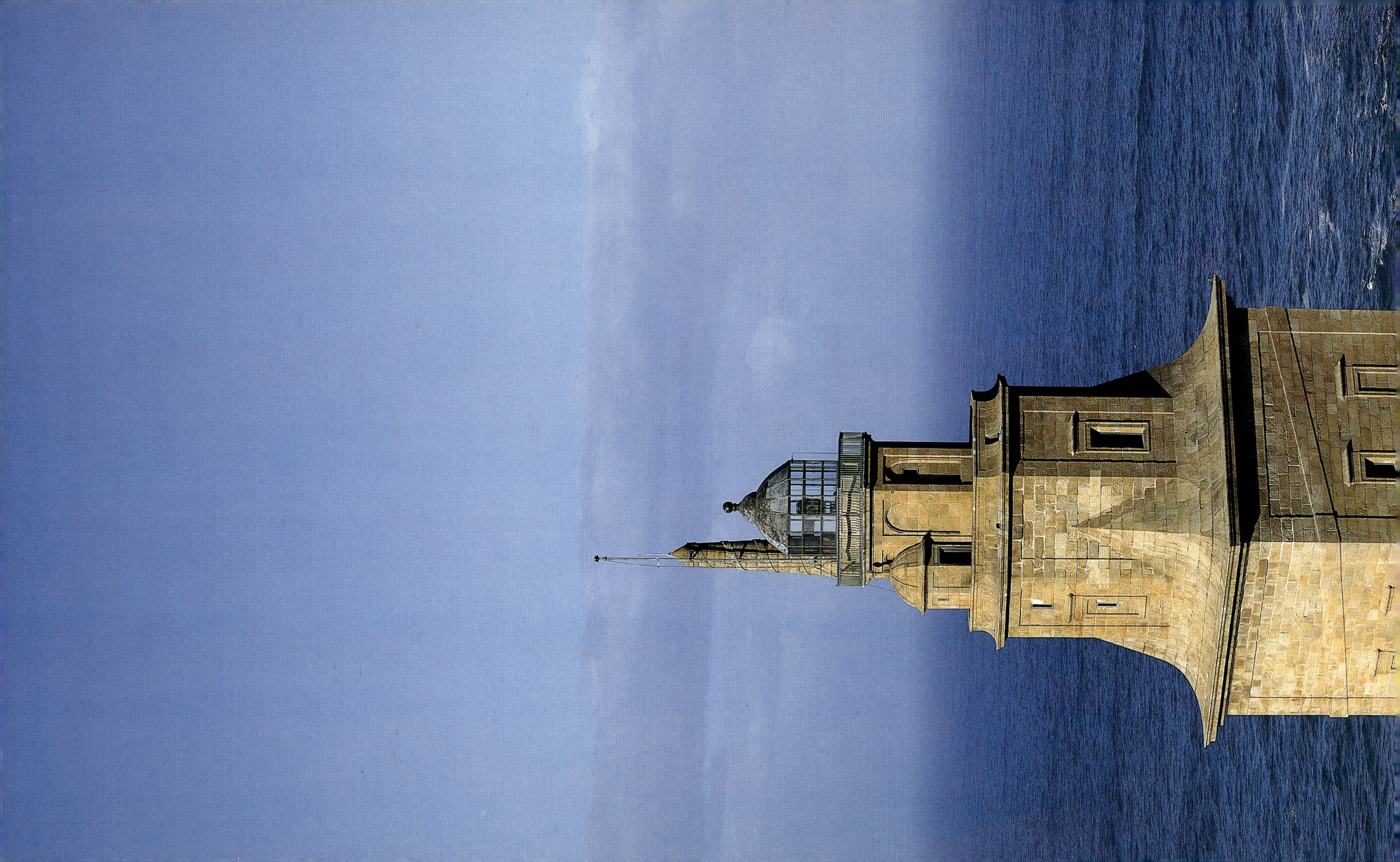

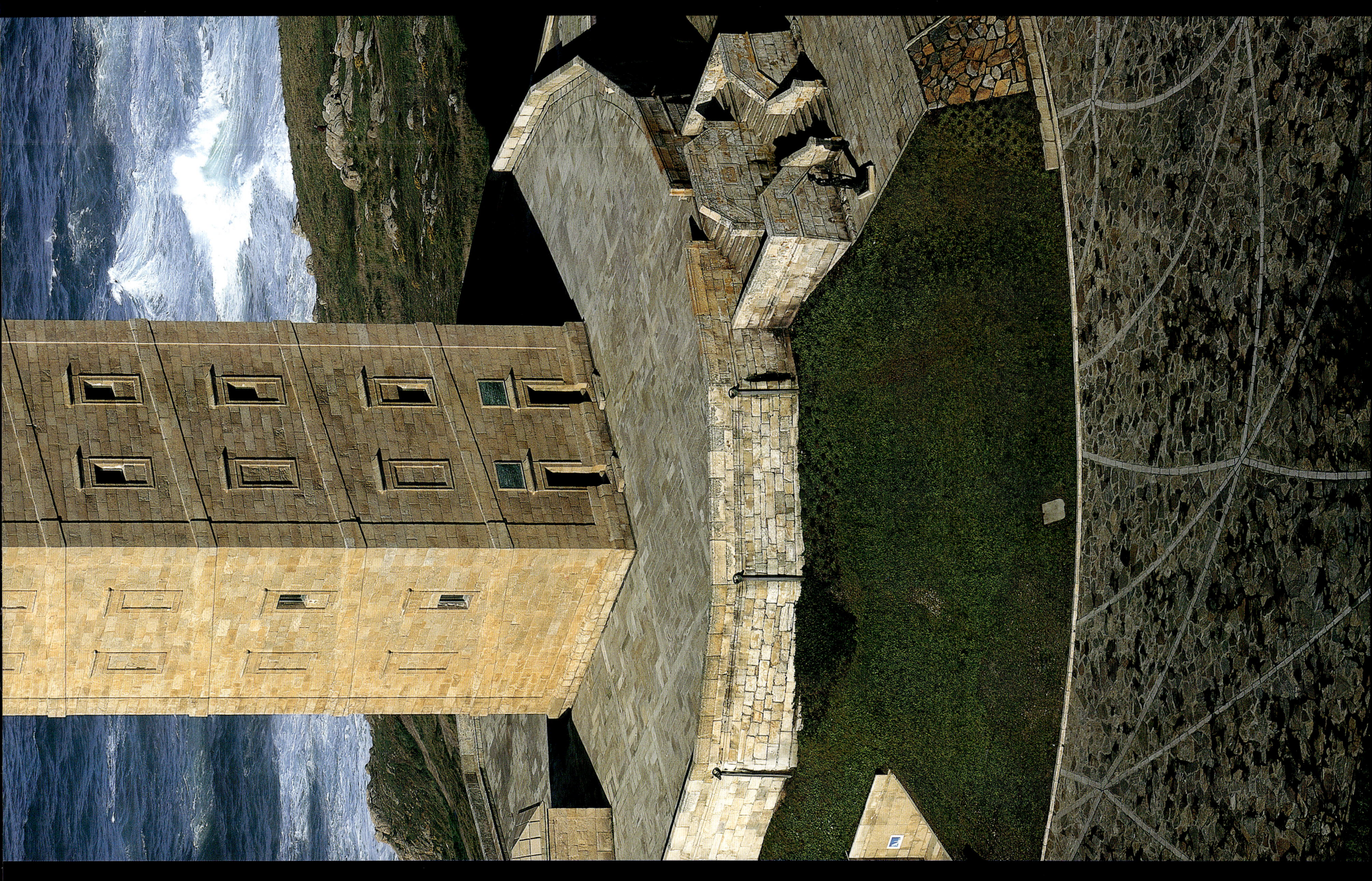

Philip Plisson, official artist to the French Navy
and master marine photographer, has published over 30 books.
Patrick Mahé has published over 20 books.
This is their fourth project together.

philip@plisson.com
Webite: www.plisson.com

Maps by interCarto: www.intercarto.com

Translated from the French *Mer Celtique / Mor Keltiek* by Catriona Cappleman

First published in the United Kingdom in 2007 by
Thames & Hudson Ltd, 181A High Holborn, London WC1V 7QX

www.thamesandhudson.com

First published in 2007 in hardcover in the United States of America by
Thames & Hudson Inc., 500 Fifth Avenue, New York, New York 10110

thamesandhudsonusa.com

British Library Cataloguing-in-Publication Data
A catalogue record for this book is available from the British Library

Library of Congress Catalog Card Number 2007901212

ISBN 978-0-500-54343-6

Printed in China